CIVIL SOCIETY
IN THE MIDDLE EAST

CIVIL SOCIETY
IN THE MIDDLE EAST

EDITED BY

AUGUSTUS RICHARD NORTON

VOLUME ONE

E.J. BRILL
LEIDEN · NEW YORK · KÖLN
1995

Also published in a hardback edition (cloth with dustjacket), ISBN 90 04 10037 7, in the series *Social, Economic and Political Studies of the Middle East*, volume 50.

The paper in this book meets the guidelines for permanence and durability of the Committee on Production Guidelines for Book Longevity of the Council on Library Resources.

Library of Congress Cataloging-in-Publication Data

Civil society in the Middle East / edited by Augustus Richard Norton.
    p.   cm. — (Social, economic and political studies of the
Middle East, ISSN 0085–6193 ; v. 50)
    Includes bibliographical references and index.
    ISBN 9004100377 (alk. paper). — ISBN 9004103538 (pbk.)
    1. Civil society—Middle East. 2. Middle East—Politics and
government. 3. Covenants—Political aspects—Middle East. 4. Islam
and politics—Middle East. I. Norton, Augustus R. II. Series.
JC336.C57   1994
320.958—dc20
                                  94-33780
                                  CIP

Die Deutsche Bibliothek - CIP-Einheitsaufnahme

Civil society in the Middle East / ed. by Augustus Richard
Norton. - Leiden ; New York ; Köln : Brill.
  (Social, economic and political studies of the Middle East ; Vol. 50)
NE: Norton, Augustus Richard [Hrsg.]; GT
Vol. 1 (1994)
  ISBN 90–04–10353–8 kart.
  ISBN 90–04–10037–7 Gewebe

ISBN 90 04 10353 8

PRINTED IN THE NETHERLANDS

CONTENTS

PREFACE

Two paradigmatic approaches to political reformation are in competition in the Middle East: one stresses the unity of the *ummah*, the singularity of the *shari'ah*, and seeks to make society dominant over the state; the other emphasizes the diversity of interests that mark society, the imperative for social tolerance and the role of government as law giver and protector of individual and group rights. Both paradigms respond to an environment of authoritarian rule, where economic failure or social iniquity is often marked. Although there is a tendency—justifiable in some cases—to consider the Islamist paradigm and the liberal paradigm as ineluctably on a collision course, increasingly activists within each paradigm are working toward accommodation. This volume, focusing on civil society in the Middle East and unapologetically inspired by the liberal paradigm, necessarily examines the prospects for such an accommodation in the context of political reform. The authors, often focusing on the cusp of state-society relations, provide a vivid portrait of Middle Eastern politics in the 1990s.

Launched in 1992, the Civil Society in the Middle East program has brought together dozens of leading scholars to analyze political life through an exploration of civil society within the states of the region. When I asked Jillian Schwedler, the program officer for the Civil Society in the Middle East program, to assemble a list of persons who deserved to be thanked for the intellectual energy, the calories or the patience that they invested in assisting the program, she came up with hundreds of names. One only needs to peruse that list to underline that this book, and the project that underpins it, is certainly not the work of any small group of people, or, needless to add, any one person. Were I to reproduce Jillian's list here, even without my own additions, one would see the names of deans, professors, foundation officers, program directors, accountants, editors, publishers, film-makers, students, secretaries, friends and relatives. The list would span three continents, and more than two dozen countries. I shall not, however, reproduce the comprehensive list here. Despite our most diligent efforts, someone deserving of thanks will doubtlessly be momentarily forgotten. Instead, I would like to single out those whose contributions, even in august and generous company, were especially crucial to whatever success this volume, and the overall project might enjoy.

The Civil Society in the Middle East program grew out of a project that I designed while senior research fellow at the International Peace Academy (IPA) in New York from 1990 to 1992. "Toward Enduring Peace in the Middle East," as the IPA program was known, was generously funded by the John D. and Catherine T. MacArthur Foundation. The president of the academy, Olara A. Otunnu, lent significant support to the project, as did Kathleen Cavenaugh, F.T. Liu, Abdeslam Maghraoui, and Peter Robinson. Each of these fine people were possessed of a vision that extended well beyond tomorrow's headline, and each shared an impatience with tired assumptions about the Middle East.

The inaugural meeting of the project, and the first cut at several of the chapters published here, was held at Princeton University in co-sponsorship with the Center of International Studies in February 1992. Two titans of academe, Henry Bienen and John Waterbury, were instrumental in making the meeting a fine one. Paulomi Shah worked very hard to arrange the meeting, with her customary aplomb. Later in the year, several authors presented drafts of their papers at a meeting in Giza, Egypt, co-sponsored by Saad al-Din Ibrahim's Ibn Khaldoun Center. Saad's gracious hospitality, his intense commitment to civility in public life and his intellectual vigor are well known to many students of the contemporary Middle East. His own project on civil society in the Arab world, in part inspired by the IPA exemplar, has helped to place civil society on the agenda of Arab intellectuals and political activists.

In the summer of 1992, the Civil Society program moved to New York University and its new home in the Department of Politics and the Hagop Kevorkian Center for Near Eastern Studies. Farhad Kazemi, one of the real gentlemen of academic life in New York City, and a fine scholar, agreed to become co-director of the program. NYU Deans C. Duncan Rice, Annette Weiner and Robert McChesney moved a myriad of obstacles to permit the program to set up shop in record time. Jill Claster, Director of the Kevorkian Center, never ceased her enthusiasm or her support for the program. Margaret Cordi and Richard Louth were expert navigators through sometimes tricky funding seas.

From the onset of the program's life at NYU to its conclusion in December 1994, the Ford Foundation provided consistent support. Salim Nasr, program officer in Cairo, and himself a distinguished sociologist renowned for his prescient work on civil society in Lebanon, never relented in his support. Salim, whose boundless energy is matched by his imagination, has arguably done as much as anyone around to lend impetus to indigenous scholarship in the Middle East.

In theory, good scholarship is its own reward, but one must admit that hosting a meeting in a spot like the Villa Serbelloni in Bellagio, Italy, generates excitement amongst participants that is not quite matched by meetings in the places where we work and live normally. Thankfully, the Rockefeller Foundation permitted us to hold an international meeting in Bellagio in the fall of 1993. A number of the chapters reproduced here and in volume two were presented at the 1993 meeting. Pasquale Pesce of the conference center and his peerless staff deserve considerable credit for fostering a truly memorable meeting.

A few of the papers appearing here (those by Alan Richards, Mustapha K. Al-Sayyid, Raymond A. Hinnebusch, Muhammad Muslih and Saad al-Din Ibrahim) were first published, in shorter, earlier forms in the *Middle East Journal* (volume 47, no. 2, Spring 1993). Two editors of the journal deserve credit for making this possible: Christopher Van Hollen who had the idea for a theme issue on civil society in the first place, and his successor, Eric Hooglund, whose deft editing and expertise gave decisive shape to the issue, have earned our gratitude and admiration.

The authors published here, and in other publications connected to the project, will earn whatever credit (or criticism) that their toils merit; however, each of the chapters has positively benefited from the extensive critiques of a number of leading scholars and public figures. Each of the papers was subjected, without exception, to a process of evaluation comparable to that used by leading refereed journals. Not all of the referees may be named according to the ground-rules that permit a referee to preserve his or her anonymity for whatever reason, so the following list is incomplete. Each person named, as well as those reviewers who are not listed by name, has bolstered the quality of this collection of studies: Ali Abdullah Abbas, Ziad Abu Amr, Lisa Anderson, Robert Bianchi, Laurie Brand, Louis Cantori, Ali Hillal Dessouki, Dale Eickelman, John Entelis, Shafeeq Ghabra, Nilüfer Göle, Jerrold D. Green, Mohamed Beshir Hamid, Steve Heydemann, Michael Hudson, Edy Kaufman, Gudrun Krämer, Ian Lustick, Ann Mayer, Ronald McLaurin, Fida Nasrallah, Mohammed Sahnoun, Shibley Telhami, and Jenny White.

Nine talented interns have worked with the project, some on special projects, like the data chart published here, and others have been immeasurably helpful in producing the *Bulletin* of the Civil Society in the Middle East project or in assisting with any of a plethora of tasks that come with an international program. The interns have been: Tehmina Aktar, Livia Alexander, Rima Askalan, Paul Carroll, Katherine Gallagher, Malene Kemp Jensen, Mark LeVine, Amy Sternberg, and Sandy Sufian.

The map used in this volume is used by permission of the Foreign Policy Association, which originally produced it for use in *Political Tides in the Arab World* that I wrote with Muhammad Muslih (New York: 1992). Nancy Hoepli kindly provided the map on short notice. The intrepid Robin Wright—dear friend and distinguished journalist—deserves credit for the Islamic Salvation Front poster, which she collected with some difficulty while on assignment in Algeria.

Projects that do not have a beginning, a middle and an end soon become flaccid and banal, leaving one to wonder about their raison d'être. Thus, this two volume set on Civil Society in the Middle East will live well beyond the project itself, which will be appropriately retired in December 1994. Although I shall not miss the countless small tasks that have buzzed about my head for the past three years, I shall certainly miss working with program officer Jillian Schwedler who, since January 1992, has contributed immeasurably to the Civil Society in the Middle East program. Readers of this volume will benefit from her deft recrafting of several chapters. Jillian is a first-rate colleague.

Others will judge the collective impact of this volume and the Civil Society in the Middle East program. If the framework for analyzing Middle Eastern politics has been jarred a bit by our efforts, if the terms of policy debate in the West has been nudged toward a constructive consideration of political reform and away from a tacit alliance with authoritarianism, and if the idea of civil society has become a subject of debate in the Middle East, then our efforts have been well invested.

Boston, May 1994   A.R.N.

Robert Mansfield

INTRODUCTION

Augustus Richard Norton

The global trend toward more open political systems is by no means immutable, and autocratic rule is certainly not obsolete, but "democracy" vibrantly resonates in all of the corners of the world. The simple ideas that people should have a voice in decisions that effect their lives, that government should respond to citizens' needs, that people have a right to not be mistreated by their rulers seems to provoke little controversy, except, that is, until we come to the Middle East and, particularly, the Arab world. There democracy is said to have little resonance.

Judging from recent articles in leading journals of opinion like *Foreign Affairs*, a new global bipolarity is emerging.[1] Unlike the Cold war, the yawning divide is not ideological but cultural. Yet, the stakes are every bit as high as during the Cold war when vast collections of people were ideologically summarized. Today, there is an alarming tendency for informed observers to argue passionately for basic freedoms in the West, while reacting with utter skepticism to the simple proposition that these same basic freedoms also have a home in the world beyond the familiar confines of "our" world. Any dichotomization of humanity is alarming, but this one also has a self-fulfilling quality to it, especially since leading statesmen and policymakers in the West now contemplate building policies on the presumption that the world is cleaved culturally between those with a yearning for freedom and those content to live in bondage.

The central arena for civilizational jousting between Muslim societies and the West is the Middle East. Not surprisingly, western arguments to the effect that the people of the Middle East are—in the main—ill-suited not to say hostile to democracy, have been music to the ears of autocrats who have repaired their frayed partnerships with the denizens of western policymaking circles, producing, at times, some unsavory alliances. The coins of the realm in these circles are stability and order. Thus, vocal advocates of elections and political participation are suddenly mute when they step into Middle Eastern realms. Often, the silence

---

[1] Samuel P. Huntington, "Clash of Civilizations?" *Foreign Affairs* 72, no. 3 (Summer 1993): 22-49.

is loud indeed, as in 1992 when the Algerian army nullified elections or in 1993 when successful elections in Yemen were met with studious diplomatic indifference in major western chanceries.

Nonetheless, the authoritarian rulers of the region confront burgeoning demands and continuing erosion of their legitimacy. The end of the Cold war has made the rulers' dilemmas even more severe, since they may no longer count on the automatic support of a world power, and since they have lost one rationale for maintenance of muscle-bound national security states.[2] As the end of the Arab-Israeli conflict appears increasingly plausible, if not over-determined, a related complication emerges for governments that have justified domestic shortages, the diversion of civilian resources to support the military, and the suspension of basic political rights by recourse to the Arab-Israeli conflict. Arguably, as the reality of an end to this central conflict sinks into public consciousness in the Arab countries and perhaps in Israel as well, demands for a share of the "peace dividend" will be heard. The Middle East after the Arab-Israeli conflict will likely experience an acceleration in domestic political crises, as well as a rejuvenation of domestic political opposition to the present governments.

Important experiments in opening up political space are underway in Jordan and Kuwait, and until civil war erupted in 1994, a fascinating experiment in democratization was unfolding in Yemen. Incipient political openings in Algeria and Tunisia have been harshly reversed—in the first instance quite abruptly, while in the second the clamps are being applied somewhat more gingerly. A loosening of the clamps, driven by the need to liberalize the stagnant economy, has started in Syria, although one would have to be an incorrigible optimist to foresee very quick positive results on the political liberalization front. In neighboring Lebanon, the restoration of free political life remains a prospect under the leadership of Prime Minister Rafiq Hariri, although the intimidating influence of Damascus is not reassuring, nor are Mr. Hariri's anti-liberal tendencies. In non-Arab Iran, the revolution has come to an end, associational life is reviving and elections are technically fair, if still ideologically constricted. Meanwhile, in the Arab Gulf states incipient democracy movements are trying to find their footing, and rulers have rejoined by bestowing consultative councils (sing., *majlis al-shura*) in Bahrain, Oman and, most notably, in Saudi Arabia. At best, these

---

[2] I owe the term "national security state" to Shibley Telhami, who used it at the inaugural meeting of the Civil Society in Middle East program, held at Princeton University, in February 1992.

appointive bodies are several steps away even from inchoate legislatures, but the direction of change is not in dispute. These are small increments of change obviously, hardly major experiments in liberalization or democratization.

If western observers express cynicism about democracy's short term prognosis in the Middle East, many of those who govern these societies are acutely aware that business as usual is not the answer. Indeed, although the Algerian attempt to foster a multiparty democracy was badly flawed, and ended disastrously, other, less discouraging experiments are underway in Jordan and Kuwait. These latter experiments are little known in the West, except among specialists, and this lacuna in public debate illustrates why informed discussion could stand some stimulation.

In each case, non-democratic regimes have calculated recently that political reform is a good survival strategy, and, as a result, have fostered reasonably fair elections (twice, in the case of Jordan). The resulting discernible, if subtle improvement in political life contrasts dramatically to the majority of Arab states where elections are acts of compliant approval and contestation is rare.

While there is wide disagreement about the outcome, there has long been little doubt that the regimes in the region are under increasing pressure from their citizens. In some instances, rulers—prisoners of their own promises to lead their people to glory—are under siege from citizens no longer willing to buy empty promises or tolerate self-serving and incompetent officials. Repression at the hands of the state has become a topic of public discussion, and human rights activists, though still relatively few in number, have become increasingly vocal. In short, the region's governments, especially the Arab ones, are facing persistent crises of governance. None of this is meant to imply that all Middle East governments will choose the path of political reform, even less democratization. In some cases, those at the helm will stubbornly resist reform and even strive to turn back the clock, but it is hard to imagine that these tactics will succeed. Other leaders will attempt reform, and not because they wish to relinquish power, but because they seek to keep it. Some two dozen states comprise the Middle East. General predications can hardly account for the vagaries of leadership, the play of chance, or the disparate roles that external powers will fulfill. Nonetheless, the pressures for change are general and growing, although they are obviously not equally intense in all states.

The Gulf war of 1990-91 did not create or unleash the discontent and the disdain that widely characterizes popular perspectives on government, but the war certainly accelerated the crisis by highlighting the inefficacy and the weakness of many of the regimes. Western pundits, particularly American ones, looked for eruptions in the street, and were reassured to find so few of them, but the impact of the war was more subtle than sound-bite profundities about the "Arab street" imply. In fact, pressures for change have been building steadily for almost three decades. The Gulf war provided a glimpse of the discontent and the routine repression of authoritarian governments that is usually masked from view. The war also exposed the divisive animosities that divide rich Arab states from poor ones, and put lie to the proposition that aid transfers, even generous ones, by the wealthier Arab states will sate popular discontent and anger.

Only in a handful of Middle East countries, notably Israel and less emphatically Turkey, is there a functioning, participant political system in which people vote regularly and meaningfully, where the freedom to speak freely is protected and where the rights of the individual enjoy significant respect. In many other instances, elections are shamelessly rigged, individual rights are pillaged and free association is prohibited. Time-honored remedies are still plied—co-opting critics, bribing recalcitrants with privileged access to power and to deals, locking up dissenters, and worse—but the scope of failure is so broad that few rulers have pockets deep enough or jails large enough to cope with the problem in the familiar ways. Even repression ceases to be effective at certain point, as Michael Hudson noted in 1988: "I would suggest that until recent years the costs of suppression have been lower than the costs of toleration, but that situation may be changing."[3]

The trends outlined here reflect global trends as well, especially the powerful demonstration effect of the momentous events in Europe since 1989. Middle Eastern autocrats have been no more successful in insulating their realms from the global revolution in communications, than autocrats in Africa and Asia. The Middle East is bombarded with information. Moreover, as Alan Richards succinctly argues here, the flow of information is part and parcel of the free market and to try to stifle that flow would be a fool's errand for any state pursuing economic liberalization. Even without the penetration of the electronic media or the fax machine, hundreds of thousands of labor migrants, moving back

---

[3] Michael C. Hudson, "Democratization and the Problem of Legitimacy in Middle East Politics," Presidential address of the Middle East Studies Association, 1987, *Middle East Studies Association Bulletin* 22 (1988): 157-171, quotation from p. 165.

and forth across the region, carry powerful images of change and dissent. The new language of politics in the Middle East talks about participation, cultural authenticity, freedom and even democracy. No doubt, the defining flavor of the 1990s is participation.[4] Like Coca Cola, "democracy" needs no translation to be understood virtually everywhere, yet the vocabulary of democracy is more succinct than the institutional variations that democracy may assume. There is no reason to presume, a priori, that one variant or another of western democracy is especially adaptable to the other locales. Instead, scholars must be alert to the possibility that the Middle East will evolve its own characteristic style of democracy, no doubt with an Islamic idiom in some instances.

Although skeptics abound, the last few years have seen a striking amount of speculation and discussion of the prospects for political liberalization in the Middle East, and particularly in the Arab world. Middle East rulers are talking, in cautious tones to be sure, about the need to renovate their political systems. Granted, their view of political change often amounts to little more than democracy by decree. Neither Thomas Paine nor Thomas Jefferson would be much impressed, but we need not belabor the arrogance of imposing an exogamous ideal-typical model of democracy. By now, it should be transparent that there is no single template for political reform in a region as diverse as the Middle East. A cynic might conclude that the goal, especially in those states in dire economic straits, is simply to spread the blame for failed economic policies, for spectacular rates of unemployment and underemployment, and for inadequate public services. Certainly, the discovery of a democratic vocabulary does not stem from idealistic conversion, but from pragmatic conclusions about the need to relieve pressure and vent political steam, as well as the shrewd recognition that democratization wins international favor. The result may look more like Singapore than New York, but that is not a choice to be made here.

Some political leaders have been willing to liberalize, but none has been willing to comprehensively democratize. Liberalization refers to reformist measures to open up outlets for the free expression of opinion, to place limits on the arbitrary exercise of power, and to permit political association. In contrast, democratization, namely, freely contested elections, popular participation in political life and—bluntly—the unchaining of the masses, has not occurred. Indeed, the electoral successes of the Islamic Salvation Front (FIS) in Algeria, and the disastrous spiral of

---

[4] As Albert Hourani noted in a letter to this writer in 1991.

events since the coup d'état of January 1992, have doubtlessly reinforced the anxiety that open elections inspire in the min   people
practiced in thwarting dissent and untutored in the cont
inely open elections.[5] At the same time, Arab intell
previously emphasized the imperative of democra
discernibly cooled on the project fearing that he
would replicate the electoral successes of FIS, and
the prospect of replacing one variety of authoritarian rul
The grounds for these fears needs to be addressed, of cou
basic issues are introduced in this chapter.

The Authoritarian Paradox

Why are authoritarian governments prevalent in the Middle East?
Culturalist explanations leave us with a very pessimistic picture of
societies condemned to despotism by virtue of deep-seated patterns of
endogamy, patriarchialism and patrimonialism, or by virtue of the
pervasive influence of Islam. Jill Crystal reminds us however, that the
question is not simply the absence of democracy, but the presence of
authoritarianism with its signature institutions of oppression and control, its ideology and its underlying political economy.[6]

Until recently, the comparative political history of Middle East
governments has been a story of attempts to mobilize support and instill
legitimacy around the notion of political unity and the imperative of
social solidarity.[7] Leading examples include Jamal 'Abd al-Nasir's
experimentation with mobilization politics in Egypt, particularly through
the Arab Socialist Party, and Shah Muhammad Reza Pahlavi's ventures
in political party creation, aptly described as pseudo-participation.[8]
These efforts failed.

Notwithstanding the ruler's emphasis on creating unity and solidarity, the paradox is that the result has been actually the opposite, namely
that such socially familiar and divisive forms of association, as family,
clan and sect, have become a refuge in times of peril and the only secure
base for structuring even modest political action. Thus, ancient hatreds

---

[5] Volume II of this set will contain John Entelis' study on Algeria.

[6] Jill Crystal has developed this theme in "Authoritarianism and Its Adversaries in the
Arab World," *World Politics* 46, no. 2 (January 1994): 262-289.

[7] See John Waterbury and Alan Richards, *A Political Economy of the Middle East*
(Boulder: Westview Press, 1990), esp. the chapter on "solidarism," pp. 330-52.

[8] For a well-crafted treatment of pseudo-participation see Jerrold D. Green, *Revolution
in Iran* (New York: Praeger, 1980).

and timeworn claims do not persist because people in these societies reject more inclusive, more participant forms of government, but because their present authoritarian governments breed exclusivity and thwart open participation. In short, authoritarianism and sectarianism, and other social particularisms, go hand in hand.[9] In his chapter on Syria, Raymond Hinnebusch generalizes about authoritarian-populist regimes: "While they exercise their power through the military and bureaucracy, they lack a stable social base in a dominant class (aristocracy or bourgeoisie) and, therefore, substitute the use of primordial (kinship, ethnic, regional) *'asabiyyah* and patronage to assure elite solidarity and the deployment of Leninist party organization and corporatist association to incorporate a popular constituency."[10]

Civil Society in the Middle East

The symbol of democracy is the contested election and the secret ballot. This is altogether understandable, since the right to cast a meaningful ballot free of coercion is a metaphor for a participant political system. But, democracy does not reside in elections. If democracy—as it is known in the West—has a home, it is in civil society, where a mélange of associations, clubs, guilds, syndicates, federations, unions, parties and groups come together to provide a buffer between state and citizen.[11] Although the concept of civil society is resistant to analytical precision, the functioning of civil society is literally and plainly at the heart of participant political systems.

In fact, the icon of the global trend of democratization is civil society. In the face of repression in Latin America, Eastern and Southern Europe, civil society is sometimes credited with thwarting authoritarian designs and challenging arbitrary rule. Nonetheless, civil society did not topple regimes, as much as the regimes crumbled from internal corruption and hollow claims for legitimacy. Civil society was more the beneficiary than the wrecking ball. Moreover, civil society is often idealized as an unmitigated good thing. Like any social phenomenon, civil society can, and, often, does have, a negative side. Self-interest, prejudice and hatred

---

[9] For a compelling polemical development of this argument see Samir al-Khalil [Kanaan Makiya], *The Republic of Fear* (Berkeley, CA: University of California Press, 1989).

[10] Raymond Hinnebusch, in this volume, p. 239.

[11] This definition of civil society, though developed independently, is similar to the one offered by Bryan S. Turner, "Orientalism and the Problem of Civil Society in Islam," Asaf Hussain, Robert Olson, and Jamil Qureishi, eds., *Orientalism, Islam, and Islamists* (Brattleboro, VT: Amana Books, 1984), p. 27.

cohabit with altruism, fairness and compassion, and the unrestrained free play of civil society is a chilling thought, not a warm and fuzzy one.

Civil society speaks in a myriad of voices. The vanguard of civil society has been human rights activists, religiously-inspired protest movements, artists, writers and professional groups of lawyers, doctors or engineers who insist on governmental accountability and thereby expose the excesses and the weaknesses of authoritarian rulers. There is no denying the awe-inspiring courage that must be summoned to speak out, to demonstrate, to stand one's ground in circumstances where the policing apparatus is both ubiquitous and untethered by legal restrictions, where the sovereignty of the individual is a gift rather than a right.

Civil society is also grounded in a free economic market and the quest of the bourgeoisie for political differentiation from the state. As Simon Bromley notes, the rallying cry of the bourgeoisie has been liberalism not democracy, but the formation of a civil society is enabling for democracy.

> [A] liberal civil society provides both the structural underpinning of representative democracy and the terrain on which an organized working class can develop. Historically, the latter have proved to be not capitalism's 'grave-diggers' but its democratizers. [12]

The fostering of civil society is a crucial step toward realizing a freer Middle East. One is hard pressed to design a participant political system which could survive very long in the absence of a vibrant civil society. In short, the existence of civil society is central to democracy.

However, civil society enthusiasts often contain their excitement when it comes to the Muslim world, and especially the Middle East. There, civil society is said to be deficient, corrupt, aggressive, hostile, infiltrated, co-opted, insignificant, or absent, depending on which observer one prefers to cite. For instance, in widely read essay, Ernest Gellner notes that Muslim societies "are suffused with faith, indeed they suffer from a plethora of it, but they manifest at most a feeble yearning for civil society."[13]

One way, an important way, of assessing the quality of political life in the Middle East is to inquire into the status of civil society there, to plumb their "yearning" for civil society. As Saad Eddin Ibrahim notes here, there has been impressive growth in associations since the mid-

---

[12] Simon Bromley, *Rethinking Middle East Politics* (Austin, TX: University of Texas Press, 1994), p. 167.

[13] Ernest Gellner, "Civil Society in Historical Context," *International Social Science Journal*, no. 129 (August 1991), p. 506.

1960s to the late 1980s. During this period the numbers grew from 20,000 to 70,000. Of course, only a minority are active and effective. Ibrahim cites a recent study in Egypt showing that 40% of registered associations are actually viable. Among the interesting blossomings of civil society is the emergence of political parties, including 46 in Algeria, 43 in Yemen, 23 in Jordan, 19 in Morocco, 13 in Egypt, 11 in Tunisia, and 6 in Mauritania. But, far more important are the professional syndicates (*niqabat*) which have sometimes given shape to politics. In Sudan, the professional associations effectively overthrew the government in both 1964 and 1985. Significantly, the present Islamist-cum-military government of Sudan rushed to regulate and stifle syndicates, apparently to preclude a reprise. In Egypt, Morocco and Tunisia, the syndicates have often been potent players, not least because of their linkage to international counterparts that enable them to enlist moral protection from abroad.

If, as we assume here, a vital and autonomous civil society is a necessary condition of democracy (though not a sufficient one), what does the present status of Middle East civil society portend? More fundamentally, does civil society exist in the Middle East?[14] Many observers are doubtful that civil society, particularly in the Arab world, is sufficiently diverse or mature to lend durability to open, participant systems.

Moreover, a number of respected scholars have expressed skepticism that vibrant, autonomous civil societies will soon emerge in the Arab countries, considering the statist economies that stifle free association and the intolerance of populist Islamist movements. In the Middle East, and particularly in the Arab states, democracy has been bestowed rather than won, and, as the Algerian example illustrates, the gift may be revoked. Gudrun Krämer's comment is to the point:

> The experiments in controlled liberalization that have occurred so far seem to be notable for the absence of what are commonly regarded as basic socioeconomic, political and cultural prerequisites of liberal democracy, such as involvement of broad sectors of "civil society," government dependence on internal mobilization of resources rather than oil or political rent, and a stable regional environment.[15]

Recent writings by leading scholars tends to endorse Krämer's skepticism.

---

[14] The absence of a civil society to counter-balance despotic power was taken to be a marker of Oriental society by Karl Wittfogel in *Oriental Despotism* (New Haven, CT: Yale University Press, 1957), and it is this lacuna that lies at the heart of the Orientalist analysis.

[15] Gudrun Krämer, "Liberalization and Democracy in the Arab World," *Middle East Report*, no. 174 (January-February 1992), pp. 22-25, 35; quotation at p. 22.

John Waterbury refers to the "non-nurturing environment" of the Middle East[16] and Michael Hudson reveals that he is more pessimistic than he was only a few years ago about the chances for democracy in the Middle East.[17]

Syria is a case in point. In his article here, Raymond Hinnebusch argues that economic liberalization in Syria is intended to broaden the regime's political base and to lift disabling economic controls stemming from Syria's failed statist experiment. Though the process is moving forward at a restrained pace, Hinnebusch notes that one result may be a more active civil society but not democracy. Syria's traditional merchants, until recently, were politically muffled and over-regulated. The merchants are benefiting from the economic reforms and are regaining influence in the process. In short, Hinnebusch is pointing to an increasing scope for civil society in Syria. These developments may have significant consequences for the stability of Syria when the inevitable moment of succession arrives. As Hinnebusch notes, it is unlikely that the reemergent civil society will give rise to pressures for democracy. The Syrian regime has grounded its legitimacy in the peasantry and the working class, and the promotion of democracy would, Hinnebusch surmises, enliven anti-capitalist populist forces. Although analysts prone to essentialist arguments posit a post-Hafiz al-Asad struggle along sectarian lines, Hinnebusch's argument points to a different logic of competition. The strata of the society that has benefited from Syria's state dominated economy will be at odds with the revived merchant class.

There is no disguising the western origins of the civil society concept, but the lineage of the concept should be largely irrelevant. The idea of civil society is potent analytically insofar as it exposes an important array of research questions. Applying the concept in the Middle East is not an exercise in imposing alien social values on the region, any more than exploring aspects of religiosity can be construed as proselytizing. For policymakers, activists, politicians and others committed to the buttressing or building of civil society, the study of civil society is unlikely to uncover a magic formula or reveal surefire prescriptions.

---

[16] John Waterbury, "Democracy without Democrats? The Potential for Political Liberalization in the Middle East," in Ghassan Salamé, ed., *Democracy without Democrats?* (London and New York: I.B. Taurus, 1944), pp. 23-47.

[17] Compare Hudson's "Democratization and the Problem of Legitimacy in Middle East Politics," *MESA Bulletin* 22, no. 2 (December 1988): 157-171, to his August 1992 testimony before the U.S. House of Representatives Subcommittee on Europe and the Middle East of the Committee on Foreign Affairs, August 1992.

Instead, the contribution is a more fundamental one, namely to provide an outline image of Middle East civil society without getting bogged down, unnecessarily, in post-modernist obfuscation or ideal-typical fixations.

One deft appreciation of civil society has stressed the historical specificity of the concept, while expressing doubt that the idea of civil society can travel much beyond western Europe and the United States, but this conclusion smacks of a familiar problem: a confusion of the ideal-typical and with the real world.[18] Certainly, the reality of civil society in the West, often contrasts sharply with ideal-typical civil society. Recent examples from eastern and central Europe, as well as from some quarters of the developing world, counsel that a categorical rejection of the idea of civil society in the Middle East is unwarranted, not least because the idea of civil society is fast becoming part of the indigenous intellectual and policy dialogues.

The existence of a civil society implies a shared sense of identity, by means of, at least, tacit agreement over the rough boundaries of the political unit. In a word, citizenship, with associated rights and responsibilities, is part and parcel of the concept. Citizenship underpins civil society. To be a part of the whole is a precondition for the whole to be the sum of its parts. Otherwise, society has no coherence, it is just a vessel filled with shards and fragments. Thus, the individual in civil society is granted rights by the state, but, in return, acquires duties to the state. All governments, but particularly autocracies, tend to trivialize citizenship, emphasizing displays of citizen support and patriotic ceremonies, while paying only lip service to the rights of citizenship.[19] Where the state, through its depredations and failures has lost the loyalty of its citizens, citizenship is an early casualty. As legitimacy crumbles, civil society threatens to fragment as well. It is meaningless to speak of civil society in the absence of the state.

Civil society is more than an admixture of various forms of association, it also refers to a quality, civility, without which the milieu consists of feuding factions, cliques, and cabals. Civility implies tolerance, the willingness of individuals to accept disparate political views and social

---

[18] Adam B. Seligman, *The Idea of Civil Society* (New York: The Free Press, 1992).

[19] This observation is borrowed from Guillermo O'Donnell and Phillippe C. Schmitter, *Transitions from Authoritarian Rule: Tentative Conclusions about Uncertain Democracies* (Baltimore: Johns Hopkins University Press, 1986), p. 48.

attitudes; to accept the profoundly important idea that there is no right answer.[20] I would like to emphasize that it is as relevant to look for civility within associations as it is to observe it between them. Ironically, groups which espouse democracy and other commendable values often do not exemplify these values internally.

Thus, a robust civil society is more than letterhead stationery, membership lists, public charters and manifestoes. Civil society is also a cast of mind, a willingness to live and let live. The antithesis of civility was grimly revealed by a gunman arrested in the June 1992 killing of Farag Fouda, the Egyptian secularist and critic of Muslim fundamentalism:"We had to kill him, because he attacked our beliefs."[21]

Unfortunately, civility is a quality which is missing in large parts of the Middle East. As Mustapha Kamil al-Sayyid observes in his cogent article, even in Egypt, widely revered for an active associational life, civil society is undermined by a deficit in political toleration and constricted by arbitrary government regulation. The absence of civility counsels skepticism about the short-term prospects for democracy in the region; however, if the art of association, as de Tocqueville called it, can be learned, then the promotion of civil society is no less than the creation of the underpinnings of democracy.

When groups and movements do emerge they often come in the form of human rights and women's movements. Both assert fundamental moral claims, namely the dignity of the person and the equality of the individual. Since the claims of such groups are truly basic ones, they are not easily assailed, at least explicitly, by the authorities of the state. Accordingly, they may enjoy more freedom of action than political opposition forces, or those groups which wish to affect the allocation of economic resources. These groups may also be less susceptible to co-optation, since their demands may not easily be assuaged by privilege, position or cash.

Though elements of civil society are likely to stand in opposition to the government, government must play the essential role of referee, rule-maker and regulator of civil society. Civil society, it needs to be emphasized, is no substitute for government. All too often, there is a

---

[20] See the timely essay by Edward Shils, "The Virtue of Civil Society," *Government and Opposition* 26, no. 1 (Winter 1991): 3-20.

[21] *The Economist*, June 13, 1992, p. 40.

tendency to commend civil society as a panacea, but the evidence is compelling that the state has a key role to play.

> Democratization is neither the outright enemy nor the unconditional friend of state power. It requires the state to govern civil society neither too much nor too little, while a more democratic order cannot be built through state power, it cannot be built *without* state power.[22]

Influenced by the events in Europe, some scholars have widely asserted that civil society is the natural enemy of autocracy, dictatorship and other forms of arbitrary rule. For instance, examining Eastern European cases, Giuseppe Di Palma argues that civil society is an organic part of democratic systems, but that it is in opposition to absolutist regimes by definition.[23]

Yet, it is naive to expect civil society to topple the state. The interface between government and civil society will often be defined by cooperation rather than conflict. As Michael Bratton emphasizes, we need to be alert to the "more subtle strategies" that may be adopted, especially in non-democratic settings.

> Just as we require a framework that enables us to account for citizen engagement as well as disengagement, we need to leave room for engagement between state and society that may be congruent as well as conflictual. And from a practical point of view, we cannot realistically expect fledgling civic associations to shoulder the onerous burden of opposition in a context where state elites are prone to equate opposition with disloyalty and treason. More subtle strategies than direct confrontation are required.[24]

Government remains crucial to the project of political reform in the Middle East, and political reform is vital to insure stability; not stability in any static sense, since it is obvious that the problems that plague governments—inefficacy, faltering legitimacy, and corruption—cannot be wished away. Instead, projects of reform must instill a dynamic stability and that means civil society must have room to breathe.

Given the integral central connection between civil society and democracy, the long-term prospects for successful democratization in Lebanon, Egypt and Iran may be better than is commonly assumed. Moreover, while the Palestinians lack a state, there are, as Muhammad Muslih notes, the stirrings of a vibrant civil society. Whatever political entity finally emerges on the West Bank and in Gaza, there is a sound

---

[22] John Keane, *Democracy and Civil Society* (London: Verso, 1988), p. 23.

[23] Giuseppe Di Palma, "Legitimation from the Top to Civil Society: Politico-Cultural Change in Eastern Europe," *World Politics* 44, no. 1 (October 1991): 49-80.

[24] Michael Bratton, "Beyond the State: Civil Society and Associational Life in Africa," *World Politics* 41, no. 3 (April 1989): 407-430, quotation at p. 418.

basis for attributing to the Palestinians a high potential for developing a participant political system. Elsewhere the prospects are more problematic, if not bleaker. In Iraq, civil society has been systematically decimated. Although in the Kurdish region associational life, if not civil society, has been rejuvenated, it is hard to imagine a durable participant system taking root in the entire country any time soon.

Ironically, the best opportunity to create a vibrant civil society may come in those states widely viewed as "traditional" or "backward." In cases where the state has not erected elaborate mechanisms for control and intimidation, nor fostered an enormous bureaucracy or a massive state elite, political development may follow different paths, though it is important not to underestimate the coercive power of even "weak" states. Yemen is an illustration. On the one hand, elements in proto-civil society—notably, some women's groups showed real vitality and assertiveness. Moreover, Yemen's strong tribal formations formulated quasi-liberal political demands upon government. In the run-up to the 1993 elections, when the government showed signs of attempting to shirk balloting, tribal "conventions"—sometimes involving 10,000 or more participants—assembled to insist that the electoral process go forward and also enumerated demands upon the government of the nascent unified Yemen. Until dashed in the spring of 1994, when heavy fighting erupted between the autonomous militaries of northern and southern Yemen, hopes rang high for the democratization experiment that began with the unification of the two Yemens in 1990. The elections were relatively fair and no party won a clear victory. As a result only a coalition government could successfully rule. Thus, the elections seemed to break the pattern of single party politics prevalent in the Arab world. The post-election period was marked by considerable violence, however, and despite the appearance of a fledgling civil society, clubs were once again trump. With the victory of the northern forces, and the preservation of a unified Yemen, authoritarian trends threaten to prevail.[25]

No doubt, political change will follow a variety of paths in the Middle East, and reformist programs will no doubt suffer further reverses. In some cases, people will be led in circles, only to find themselves where they began. In others, the rulers will adopt what the Arabs call "facade democracy" (dimuqratiyyah shikliyyah), employing the vocabulary of democracy while continuing business as usual. Muddling through is an option, but the pressures to open up the political systems of the Middle

---

[25] This is the subject of Sheila Carapico's study, to appear in volume II.

East may not abate, and, if civil society continues to gain its footing, issues of accountability and performance will grow in importance.

Though the region continues to be marked by regular encroachments upon the dignity of individuals, the trajectory of Middle East politics is clearly toward an increased emphasis on the right of the individual to be free from the arbitrary abuse of the state. The evidence is still mixed, but it is sufficient to suggest that the time has come to stop talking about Middle East exceptionalism when we discuss the global trends.

Although judging from the press in the West one would think that the Islamist groups are the only opposition groups in town, the Islamists are only one component in an array of groups that populate civil societies in the Middle East. In rich and poor states alike, incipient movements of men and women are demanding—in one form or another—a voice in politics. Women's movements are on the leading edge, especially in Algeria, Egypt, Iran, Israel, Kuwait, Turkey, Yemen and amongst the Palestinians. Businessmen's groups in Jordan and Egypt have assertively represented their own economic interests, while providing an organizational model adaptable to other purposes. In May 1992, organized labor toppled the government of Omar Karami in Lebanon and, later, an array of organizations boycotted and monitored parliamentary elections under Syrian tutelage.

Instructive vignettes illustrate the relevance of focusing on civil society. Admittedly, the state is not disappearing from view, and loyalties of kinship are not about to be eclipsed by secular organizations. Nonetheless, no understanding of the contemporary Middle East will be complete unless it takes into account the status of civil society in the region.

* In Lebanon, despite the accumulated destructive and financial power of the militias that reigned from 1975 to 1990, participants in civil society, such as the trade and professional unions, resisted the militia-populated war system and worked to thwart the fragmentation of Lebanon into sectarian enclaves. Large-scale public demonstrations for peace challenged the militias' claims to authentically represent the Lebanese.[26]

* In Kuwait, one finds the most impressive civil society in the Arab Gulf states. In addition to a reasonably lively press, an array of professional associations and a number of cultural clubs, Kuwait offers two relatively unique components of civil society. The *diwaniyyah* is an

---

[26] Antoine Messara, "Civil Society against the War System: The Lebanese Case" (in Arabic), a paper presented at an International Peace Academy sponsored conference in Giza, Egypt, May 28-30, 1992.

essential element in Kuwaiti civil society. The *diwaniyyah* is a gathering place in leading citizens' homes where men gather to socialize and share views on a range of topics from sports to politics. The *diwaniyyah* is traditionally a male gathering, but (in recent years) some women have started their own *diwaniyyat*. It is well understood that no candidate for office could win election if he did not visit most, if not all, of the *diwaniyyat* of his district. When the Law of Gatherings prevented the holding of any meeting without prior permission from the authorities, the *diwaniyyat* were excluded. As Ghanim al-Najjar notes, Kuwait's pro-democracy movement started in a *diwaniyyah*.[27] In the period following the suspension of parliament in 1986, the *diwaniyyat* became centers of opposition activity. In effect, the *diwaniyyat* function as proto-parties in a political system were political parties are proscribed. Since the institution of the *diwaniyyah* is culturally engrained, the government is hard-pressed to shut them down. At best, government agents can report on the discussions that take place there.

Less well known is the cooperative, which proved instrumental as a superstructure for lending support to the resistance during the Iraqi occupation of Kuwait. While the government quickly crumbled before the onslaught of the Iraqi invasion, the resistance found a firm footing in civil society. In 1990, as Neil Hicks and Ghanim al-Najjar report in their chapter here, there were over 170,000 subscribers in cooperatives, which were organized to meet a variety of consumer needs, especially purchases of food. In fact, the cooperative accounted for 80 percent of all food retailing. The structure of the cooperatives, with established financial systems, well-exercised roles and patterns of social interaction, lent itself to supporting the resistance, and since cooperatives pervaded Kuwaiti society, the Iraqis were hard-pressed to control them. Cooperatives, therefore, continued to function in the face of the Iraqi occupation. Moreover, serving on the board of a cooperative proved to be a good political apprenticeship—at least 19 members of the parliament elected in 1992 previously served on cooperative boards. It is also noteworthy that although women are denied the franchise to vote in national elections, they do vote in cooperative elections.

After the Iraqis were expelled, the democratic movement resonated even in Kuwaiti tribes where innovative primary elections produced anything but predictable results. In almost all cases, tribal chiefs lost the primary balloting to fellow tribesmen.

* Jordanian civil society truly found its voice during the Gulf crisis.

---

[27] Ghanim al-Najjar, "Civil Society in Kuwait," a paper presented at the International Peace Academy sponsored conference in Giza, Egypt, May 28-30, 1992, p. 12.

Professional associations in Jordan were very active in organizing congresses and demonstrations against the allies' actual goals of dominating the Arabian Gulf and of destroying Iraq, on the one hand, and in collecting donations to help Iraqis to face the blockade imposed over them on the other hand. In response to this, the Jordanian government had to respect the professional associations' stand over the Gulf crisis, even when their stand was, in some cases, against the official position of the government.[28]

The Jordanian case helps to illustrate that the development of civil society will not necessarily evoke applause for western policies. Moreover, as Laurie Brand notes in her chapter on Jordan, the process of opening up space for civil society also threatens to widen existing cleavages, as between Palestinians and East Bankers.

Of course, since 1989, King Hussein has been experimenting with democracy. As Laurie Brand notes in this volume, "What is currently unfolding in Jordan, however exciting, is a liberalization process managed from above, part of a strategy intended to ensure the continuation of the monarchy." Parties were only legalized in 1992, and few are more than cliquish formations. (The Islamic Action Party is a major exception. This is the force—derived from the Muslim Brotherhood—that won 22 seats in 1989.) As Brand notes, only 1.4 percent of respondents, in a recent survey, reported membership in a party and only 6 percent anticipated joining a party. Far more important are the professional associations (*niqabat*)—the groupings of doctors, engineers, lawyers, dentists, pharmacists, journalists, writers, geologists, agricultural engineers that often articulate political positions, though they seldom directly challenge the government.

* In Jordan, as in other authoritarian settings, government strives to manipulate and control civil society. A familiar pattern is the creation of competing groups to challenge assertive autonomous associations. For instance, in both Jordan and Tunisia, women's groups have been created by the government expressly to dampen support for autonomous groups. In Yemen, the League of Human Rights was countered with a government-created alternative, which, as Sheila Carapico notes, held its first meeting in a police headquarters.

* The associations that comprise civil society often provide an outlet for the free expression of political ideas. In Tunisia,

the absence of free space for social and political expression [in state-dominated corporatist structures] meant that dissenting voices sought substitute political arenas in the union, the university, and the mosques, [and even in]

---

[28] 'Atef Odhibat, "Civil Society in Jordan: A Preliminary Assessment," a paper presented at an International Peace Academy sponsored conference in Giza, Egypt, May 28-30, 1992, p. 18.

cultural associations such as the Association of Cine clubs which later led to the formation of the most leftist weekly ever to appear in the country, *le Phare*.[29]

The government clamp down on the usually vibrant labor unions, in the late 1970s and early 1980s, coincided with a dramatic rise of an assertive Islamic movement, illustrating, yet once more, that repressive government has helped to create the space in which the populist Islamist movements have thrived. The Islamist bogey man provides regimes an excuse not to move toward more open contestation, while simultaneously keeping a tight lid on civil society.

In fact, civil society in Tunisia is penetrated, co-opted and controlled. The combination of state surveillance and financing insures that no one steps too far out of line. Parties are controlled and precluded from meaningful representation. Yet, Tunisia is promising in some ways. There has been an impressive blossoming of NGOs since 1988 with the number growing from 3,300 to more than 5,100 in 1994. As Eva Bellin notes, the Tunisian military is weak, the middle class is unusually large, literacy is relatively high (74 percent for males and 56 percent for females, which is well above the comparable figures for Iran, Iraq, or Egypt), incomes are comparatively high, and Tunisia spurned Arab socialism and followed instead a quasi-liberal path of development. The regime self-consciously promotes civility, but it also prefers control. Moreover, the state's commitment to the development of civil society has one major exception, namely the Islamists. For many Tunisian intellectuals—like intellectuals across the Middle East—the Islamist alternative only poses a choice between laic and theocratic authoritarianism.

Islamists and Political Reform

Across the Arab world, the clarion call of pan-Arabism, in its several variants, now often falls on deaf ears. The prevailing ideology of opposition in the Arab countries, as in the broader Middle East, is signaled by the simple claim made more and more frequently across the region, "Islam is the solution." If those occupying the seat of power are sometimes indecisive and on the defensive, the Islamist groups are neither. Islam is viewed by an active minority as an emerging, durable and appealing political ideology, as well as a defense against the encroachments of "western decay." Islamist movements are as notewor-

---

[29] Abdelbaki Hermassi, "Notes on Civil Society in Tunisia," a paper presented at an International Peace Academy sponsored conference in Giza, Egypt, May 28-30, 1992, pp. 7-8.

This FIS poster was created in 1991 for the parliamentary elections. Atop the poster is the *basmala* (''In the name of God the merciful, the compassionate''), followed by ''the Islamic Salvation Front'' (*al-jabhah al-islamiyyah li-ingaadh*). The slogan arched over ''the Blessed Qur³an'' is ''for the sake of the Islamic solution.'' The front's name is repeated at the bottom.

(Courtesy of Robin Wright)

thy in the secular Republic of Turkey as in the Sudan, where a militantly
Islamic government challenges the cliché that Sunni Islam would be
inhospitable to governments bearing a family resemblance to the self-
styled Islamic Republic of Iran.

Yet, in contrast to the revolutionary example of Iran, many of the
region's Islamist movements are attempting to work within the existing
systems. Rather than toppling government, they push for reform from
within. This is a wise approach. Whatever their political and economic
failures, many Middle Eastern states are armed to the teeth and heavily
policed. Even after the stunning reversal—the coup d'état in January
1992—of the electoral victory by the Islamic Salvation Front (FIS) in
Algeria, many Islamists elsewhere continue to push for elections. In
Lebanon, Hizballah (Party of God), competed in the 1992 parliamentary
elections with great success.[30] In the West Bank and Gaza, HAMAS, the
Islamic Resistance Movement, has clearly signaled that it will compete
in elections as an organized opposition to the PLO. In the October 1992
elections to fill the 50 seats of the parliament in Kuwait, Islamists
captured about two-thirds of the seats won by the opposition in its
stunning victory.[31]

Although they certainly represent a region-wide phenomenon, the
Islamists are not a centrally-directed, monolithic force. This is true
despite the persistent tendency in some quarters to promote the "fundamentalist" trend as a product of Iranian manipulation and control, as in
the words of the journalist Charles Krauthammer: "Iran is the world's
new Comintern."[32] The legitimate concern of many thoughtful Middle
Easterners is that the Islamic solution will turn out to be a variant of
totalitarianism. One can hope that the realities of political life will tame
their excesses, even make pragmatists of them, but such social experiments can be very painful, even if the predicted results eventually occur.
Specialists are certainly right to emphasize Islamic concepts like *shura*

---

[30] Augustus Richard Norton and Jillian Schwedler, "Swiss Soldiers, Ta'if Clocks, and
Early Elections: Toward A Happy Ending in Lebanon?" Deirdre Collings, ed., *Peace for
Lebanon? From War to Reconstruction* (Boulder, CO: Lynne Rienner Publishers, Inc.,
1994), pp. 45-65.

[31] There is considerable disagreement about the number of opposition seats actually won,
because it is not altogether clear which members constitute the opposition and which are pro-
government. Contemporary press estimates claim that the opposition won as few as 19 seats
and as many as 37. The strong representation of Islamists is not at issue.

[32] Charles Krauthammer, "Iran to become new 'Evil Empire'?" *Democrat and Chronicle*, January 4, 1993 (Rochester, NY). Two days earlier, in a similar vein, Israeli Prime
Minister Yitzhak Rabin said: "We call on all nations, all peoples to devote their attention to
the great danger inherent in Islamic fundamentalism." Quoted by Michael Parks, "Israel Sees
Self Defending West Again," *Los Angeles Times*, January 2, 1993.

(consultation), *ijma'* (consensus), and *ba'ya* (affirmations of communal loyalty), but these concepts do not comprise a compelling theory of government. Moreover, there would be more comfort if *hurriyyah* (freedom), and *huquq al-insan* (human rights) received equal play in the discourse of Islamic populists.[33]

In fact, skepticism amongst some western observers runs so deep that even the logic of their own arguments is overshadowed by the danger presumed inherent in the emerging social forces of Islamic populism. One widely read argument runs along the following lines:

>The Arab regimes are inefficient, often corrupt, and persistently unresponsive to the needs of the majority of their citizens;

>simultaneously, the regimes' legitimacy is eroding under the strains of the shattering of Arab unity, the end of the Cold war, and the move toward a resolution of the Arab-Israeli conflict;

>the force of populist Islam has moved into the void, and is capturing the social base that the regimes are losing by offering a dynamic ethos of change and reform, while simultaneously providing a basis for erecting a network of social services that the government does not provide;

>however, these political movements are inherently anti-western, anti-Israeli, anti-women and anti-democratic. Therefore, there is no sensible alternative for western governments save to oppose these movements and lend support to the corrupt, ineffective and widely-hated regimes.[34]

This is a maliciously dangerous argument that could lead to precisely the sort of clashes of civilizations that leading conservative scholars like Samuel P. Huntington are predicting as the defining element of the post Cold-war world.

Therefore, it is imperative to examine the prospect that the Arab world is the asterisk, the exceptional case where societies are uncivil and where an emerging opposition force, namely the populist Islamist movements, is peculiarly inimitable to democracy. Should the global map of political change treat the Middle East as a land of fire-breathing anti-democrats? How can the prospects for tolerant and open political systems emerging there be assessed?

Consistently, the Islamists—skilled populists all—have dispensed promises more freely than programs, and there is certainly no evidence

---

[33] See John Esposito and James Piscatori, "Democratization and Islam," *Middle East Journal* 45, no. 3 (Summer 1991): 427-440.

[34] Judith Miller, "The Challenge of Radical Islam," *Foreign Affairs* 72, no. 2 (Spring 1993): 43-56.

that they hold the solutions to the vexing social and economic problems which plague many states in the region. Some—but not all, it is important to emphasize—of the Islamists are contemptuous, even hostile toward the idea of democracy, which is seen as socially divisive and endemically corrupt. Even more to the point, radical Islamist thinkers, such as the late Sayyid Qutb, argue that sovereignty belongs only to God and that any conception of popular sovereignty ascribes the power of God to others (*shirk*).[35] In point of fact, there is no question that democracy is rejected by *some* Islamists.

As Ahmad Moussalli argues in this volume, the rejection of democracy is not general to Islamists and he usefully distinguishes between the ideological perspectives of radicals and moderates. In fact, Moussalli establishes that there are categorical differences in the two perspectives, in particular around the construction of the institutions of consultation (*shura*). For the radicals, *shura* is an elite function of qualified *'ulama*. In contrast, the moderates entertain the idea that *shura* be construed more broadly as encompassing elections and parliamentary forms of representation. This dichotomy is a very important one that is often ignored even in scholarly writing on the Islamists, or, if not ignored then either dismissed as a ploy or minimized on the grounds that the radical perspective will necessarily prevail.[36]

In other respects, Islamist ideologies share a conception of state-society relations that contrasts with the familiar liberal view. For secular liberals, the state plays a crucial role in protecting the rights of citizens and in regulating the excesses of society. In contrast, while the Islamists do not advocate a vanishing state, they posit a state that is subordinate to society, and is effectively and appropriately the creature of society. This view of state-society relations has obviously negative ramifications for the protection of minority interests and the protection of some individual rights, particularly, the expression of political dissent as well as tolerance for religious diversity.

Gudrun Krämer's incisive summary of the moderate perspective, i.e., the Islamist mainstream, is to the point:

> The mainstream position is remarkably flexible with respect to modes of political organization, providing for institutionalized checks on the ruler in the form of a separation of powers, parliamentary rule, and in some cases even multipartyism. It is more advanced than is often acknowledged concerning the

---

[35] Sayyid Qutb, *Ma'alim fi al-Tariq* (Beirut: Dar al-Shuruq, 7th ed., 1980).

[36] The latter conclusion is developed by Emmanuel Sivan, *Radical Islam* (New Haven, CT: Yale University Press, 1985).

protection of human rights, which are generally founded on the duties towards God but nevertheless widely seen as part of the common heritage of all humankind. Indeed, the protection of individual rights and civil liberties from government supervision and interference, repression and torture figures highly on Islamist agendas. But mainstream attitudes remain highly restrictive with regard to the freedom of political, religious and artistic expression, if that involves the right to freely express one's religious feelings, doubts included, and even to give up Islam altogether.[37]

Politics is, by definition, contingent upon choices and opportunities. To assume otherwise is simply silly. Thus, it is imperative to consider empirical evidence to test the proposition that there actually is a categorical distinction between moderates and radicals.

To argue that popular political players are irremediably intransigent and therefore unmoved by events in the real world is simply foolish. But first, a word is also in order on the distinction between Islamist elites and followers. Because the work of influential writers working in the Orientalist tradition is textual, by definition, they expend little effort looking at the incentives of the Islamist rank and file.[38] Moreover, because they work out of culturally and historically essentialist concepts of Islam they miss the fungibility of popular participation in the Islamist movements. Those moved by the call are—it is true—responding to a culturally authentic and familiar ideology, but they are also making rational choices, for instance, for good health care. Without minimizing the revival of religiosity amongst Muslims, there is no question that the network of private voluntary organizations (PVOs) under the wings of Islamists have cemented and enlisted support among believers. Popular support for these movements is mobile. This means that reductions in Islamist social welfare and health activities will lead to a reduction in popular support especially if comparable or superior services are elsewhere available. Of course, for the foreseeable future, financially-strapped and bureaucratically-unwieldy governments, in Egypt for instance, are unlikely to be able to compete nose-to-nose with the Islamist PVOs.

A fundamentally important question is whether experiments in democracy (as are now underway in Jordan and Kuwait) will domesticate the populist Islamists movements. Put another way, does participation in the political process instill pragmatism and a political logic of give-and-take that will slake all but the most ardent true believer? The

---

[37] Gudrun Krämer, "Islamist Democracy," *Middle East Report*, no. 183 (July-August 1993), pp. 2-8, quotation from p. 8.

[38] Distinguished practitioners of this approach include Elie Kedourie and Bernard Lewis.

evidence is mixed, but instructive. In Jordan, Kuwait and Yemen, recent elections have brought Islamists into the political process, and in each of these cases leading Islamist politicians have proved willing to play by the rules. This points up that the very decision to participate in elections opens up the ideological cleavage between radicals and moderates, and thereby creates conditions for the formation of new alliances and coalitions. This dynamic process might aptly be called constructive divisiveness.

Of course skeptics marshal the case of Algeria, where the 1991 election—the rules of which were designed to magnify the victory of the ruling party—instead magnified the popularity of the Islamic Salvation Front (FIS). FIS was on the verge of seizing power until it was thwarted by a coup in January 1992. However FIS might have behaved once in power, and experts disagree profoundly, no quantity of *ex post facto ergo propter hoc* arguing will alter the simple fact that FIS won the election and that its victory was stolen from it. Invoking the post-coup anti-regime violence mounted by FIS is quite literally beside the point. Thus, the Algerian case tells us little about political behavior in reformist contexts, and much about how poorly designed elections can lead to unsettling results.

So long as the Islamist movements are given no voice in politics, there can be no surprise that their rhetoric will be shrill and their stance uncompromising. In contrast, well-designed strategies of political inclusion hold great promise for facilitating essential political change. The pace of change is obviously crucial. All too often, the great difference between governments wrought of revolution and those wrought of reform is neglected. This fact, even more than sectarian or ethnic differences, distinguishes the present regime in Iran from its counterparts in the Arab world. Revolutions bring with them a new class of rulers and a reconstruction of the political order, while reform is by definition incremental and familiar.

One promising example is provided by Jordan, where an important experiment in political reform is underway. King Hussein of Jordan argues that democratization is the only answer to ensuring political stability, and he chastises his fellow rulers for viewing democratic reform "as a luxury they cannot afford."[39] Notwithstanding the monarch's peroration, Arab rulers do have choices ranging from squashing dissent and co-opting potential opponents to political liberalization and

---

[39] Quoted by Associated Press, 29 April, 1993.

democratization. If some Middle Eastern states trod the path of democratization, others will remain mired in autocracy.

Meanwhile, essentialists, even highly readable ones like Ernest
Gellner, argue that civil society has no home in Muslim society where
din wa dawla (religion and state) purportedly know no separation and
where the very notion of secular society is anathema. (The presence of
liberal Islamist forces is pretty much downplayed if not ignored by
Gellner.) Not so long ago, the absence of democracy in the Middle East
was put down to the existence of the authoritarian states and weak
societies deficient in associational life and lacking a sense of public
space.[40] Now, with the emergence of the Islamist movements, as Yahya
Sadowksi notes critically, the explanation shifts to one emphasizing that
Middle East societies are so strong that they are in danger of the
overpowering the state.[41] Essentialists may, it seems, have it both ways.
Other writers, such as Şerif Mardin, have emphasized the historical
specificity of civil society, and its roots in the West. The empirical record
makes precisely the opposite point. Otherwise, how does one account for
the relatively rapid emergence of civil society in Turkey, where to
emerge democracy did not really begin until 1950?

Most important, though scholars of the Middle East may debate civil
society existentially, theoretically, conceptually, normatively, and
ontologically, the simple fact is that civil society is today part of the
political discourse in the Middle East. Scholastic debates notwithstanding, civil society is the locus for debate, discussion, and dialogue in the
contemporary Middle East.

---

[40] Fuad Khuri, "Invisible Meanings in Conflict Resolution: Some Macro-Ideological
Constructs in Arab-Islamic Culture," a paper presented at an American University of Beirut-
sponsored meeting in Larnaca, Cyprus, June 24-26, 1993; and Yahya Sadowski, "The New
Orientalism and the Democracy Debate," *Middle East Report*, no. 183 (July-August 1993),
pp. 14-21, and p. 40.

[41] Sadowski, "The New Orientalism."

Composite Information Chart on the Middle East, 1993

	Population in Millions, 1993	GNP per Capita: Annual growth rate (%), 1993	GNP per capita: US$, 1993	Real GDP per capita: PPP$ 1990	Oil Production: Million Barrels per Day, 1993	External Debt In Millions, 1993	Life Expect at Birth, 1993	Birth Rate per 1,000: 1965	Birth Rate per 1,000: 1993	Death Rate per 1,000: 1965	Death Rate per 1,000: 1993	Urban Pop (%) 1991	Urban Pop Annual Growth Rate (%), 1993	Literacy (%): Male, 1990	Literacy (%): Female, 1990	UNDP Human Development Index 1990	
Algeria	27.00	2.8	1,570	3,011	0.800	$25,500	67.35	50	30.38	18	6.41	52	2.37	70	46	0.528	Algeria
Bahrain	0.53	0.4	7,800	10,706	0.431	$2,568	73.12		26.89		3.87	83	3.01	82	69	0.790	Bahrain
Djibouti	0.50	-1.0	1,030	1,000	NA	$190	48.78		43.05		16.06	81	2.70	63	34	0.104	Djibouti
Egypt	57.00	0.5	730	1,988	0.888	$39,885	60.46	43	33.00	19	9.00	47	2.30	63	34	0.389	Egypt
Iran	60.70	6.0	1,500	3,253	3.440	$13,500	65.26	46	43.00	18	8.06	57	3.49	65	43	0.557	Iran
Iraq	18.70	10.0	1,940	3,508	3.000	$40,000	64.96	49	44.57	18	7.71	71	3.73	70	49	0.589	Iraq
Israel	5.30	3.5	12,100	10,840	NA	$25,300	77.77	26	20.72	6	6.45	92	3.08	96		0.938	Israel
Jordan	3.90	5.8	1,100	2,345	0.0006	$6,900	71.61	53	39.48	21	4.32	68	3.57	89	70	0.582	Jordan
Kuwait	1.33	35.0	11,100	15,178	1.890	$21,000	74.62	48	30.29	7	2.39	96	8.67	77	67	0.815	Kuwait
Lebanon	2.75	0.6	1,400	2,300	NA	$2,100	69.01	40	27.86		6.66	84	1.81	88	73	0.565	Lebanon
Libya	5.03	0.2	5,800	7,000	1.380	$2,901	63.47	49	45.66	17	8.37	70	3.73	75	50	0.658	Libya
Mauritania	2.10	3.0	555	1,057	NA	$2,227	47.59	47	47.97	26	16.54	47	3.14	47	21	0.140	Mauritania
Morocco	27.60	-1.0	1,060	2,348	NA	$23,524	67.5	49	29.23	18	6.56	48	2.16	61	38	0.433	Morocco
Oman	1.85	7.4	6,670	9,972	0.780	$3,050	67.32	50	40.56	24	5.94	11	3.46	47	12	0.598	Oman
Qatar	0.48	3.0	17,000	11,400	0.440	$1,480	72.25	74	19.61		3.53	89	2.84	77	72	0.802	Qatar
Saudi Arabia	17.70	0.8	6,500	10,989	8.210	$18,900	67.32	48	38.59	20	6.05	77	3.30	73	48	0.688	Saudi Arabia
Somalia	9.20	-1.5	120	836	NA	$2,447	32.91	50	41.95	26	28.41	36	1.35	36	14	0.087	Somalia
Sudan	27.47	-4.5	184	949	NA	$21,520	53.85	47	42.65	24	12.45	22	2.38	43	12	0.152	Sudan
Syria	13.40	5.0	2,300	4,756	0.530	$16,446	66.12	48	44.08	16	6.44	50	3.76	78	51	0.694	Syria
Tunisia	8.50	2.0	1,650	3,579	0.105	$9,100	72.54	44	24.24	16	5.04	54	1.84	74	56	0.600	Tunisia
Turkey	59.80	3.0	3,670	4,652	NA	$59,400	70.41	41	26.62	15	5.97	61	2.07	90	71	0.717	Turkey
UAE	2.09	1.0	13,800	16,753	2.220	$11,070	72	41	28.40	14	3.07	78	5.06	77	63	0.738	UAE
Yemen	13.41	3.1	775	1,562	0.320	$7,040	50.94	49	51.00	27	15.37	29	3.31	53	26	0.233	Yemen

This chart was compiled from the following sources:
Demographic Yearbook, United Nations, 1993
Economic Intelligence Unit, 1993-94 (various countries).
UNDP Human Development Report, United Nations 1993.
World Fact Book, US Government (CIA), 1992, 1993.
World Bank World Development Report, 1993

* Male and Female

NA Not Applicable: State may have reserves but production is insignificant
PPP$ Purchasing Power Parities: relative domestic purchasing power of currencies
Birth and Death Rates are per 1,000
Blank spaces indicate lack of information

Figures on this chart represent the most current information available. Where 1993 figures were unavailable, the most recent figures were used.

Updated May 1994 by Sandra Sufian, from earlier versions by Livia Alexander, Amy Sternberg, and Paul Carroll.

CHAPTER ONE

CIVIL SOCIETY AND PROSPECTS OF DEMOCRATIZATION IN THE ARAB WORLD

Saad Eddin Ibrahim

Much of the literature circulating in recent years on the prerequisites, requisites and modalities of transition from non-de mocratic to democratic rule[1] finds a fertile ground for testing in the Arab World. While belonging to one general political-cultural area, the twenty-one Arab countries display a wide variety of cases in terms of variables associated with such transition—e. g., nature and evolution of the state,[2] political regimes, class structure, political culture, levels of socio-economic development , and civil society.[3] Yet, despite its particularities, the Arab World is evolving along the same broad trends and processes that have been at work elsewhere in newly democratizing societies. Both internal and external dynamics, including regional and global demonstration effects, are salient in such an evolution. Put differently, four sets of variables have been interplaying to produce a mini-wave of democratization in the Arab World. They are socio-economic formations, the articulation of civil society, the state, and external factors. The interplay of these variable sets may vary from one Arab country to another; and it is such variance that accounts for the degree of democratization empirically observed in each Arab country at present.

A Theoretical Overture

The concept of civil society has especially emerged in the last decade as an overarching category linking democracy, development, and peaceful management of conflict domestically and regionally. While there are a

---

[1] See, for example, Larry Diamond and Marc Plattner, eds., *The Global Resurgence of Democracy* (Baltimore: The Johns' Hopkins Univer sity Press, 1993); Samuel Huntington, *The Third Wave: Democratization in the Late Twentieth Century* (Norman: Oklahoma University Press, 1991); Schmitz, G. and David Gillies, *The Challenge of Democratic Development: Sustaining Democratization in Developing Countries* (Ottawa: the North-South Institute, 1992).

[2] See Saad Eddin Ibrahim, et al., *Society and State in the Arab World* (Amman: The Arab Thought Forum, 1988); Giamco Luciani, ed., *The Arab State* (Berkeley, Los Angeles: University of California Press, 1990).

[3] Huntington, *The Third Wave.*

variety of ways of defining the concept, they all revolve around maximizing volitional organized collective participation in the public space between individuals and the state. In its institutional form, civil society is composed of non-state actors or non-governmental organizations (NGOs)—e.g., political parties, trade unions, professional associations, community development associations, and other interest groups.[4] Normatively, civil society implies values and behavioral codes of tolerating, if not accepting, the different "others" and a tacit or explicit commitment to the peaceful management of differences among individuals and collectivities sharing the same public space—i.e., the polity.[5]

Civil society, as defined above, emerged organically out of modern socio-economic formations—e.g., classes, occupational categories, and other interest groups. In the West, this process unfolded simultaneously with the processes of capitalization, industrialization, urbanization, citizenship and the nation-state. While the ultimate loyalty of citizens was supposedly held to the nation- state as the natural sovereign embodiment of all society; sub-loyalties were to follow interests—i.e., focused in class, occupation, and residential community. Volitional associations emerged and expanded around the saliency of the many interests of the citizens—e.g., political parties, trade unions, professional associations, clubs, and community organizations. Loyalty to the supreme sovereign of the state was an emotive, abstract, and only occasionally invoked; conversely, solidarities of volitional associations were interest-based, concrete and more frequently invoked. While loyalty to the state was supposedly universal and consensual among all citizens, solidarity to a volitional association was particularistic and variable in intensity and duration. That is to say while citizens hardly change their belonging to a nation-state, they frequently do so with regard to volitional associations, class, occupation, status, and residence, due to vertical and horizontal mobility. With competing, or even conflicting interests of various socio-economic formations in the same nation-state, governance would gradually evolve along participatory politics—e.g., democracy. Some socio-economic formations were more conscious of their interest and quicker than others in organizing their ranks to retain, seize, or share

---

[4] Saad Eddin Ibrahim, ed., *Civil Society and Democratic Transformation in the Arab World* (Arabic) (Cairo: Ibn Khaldoun Center, 1992), pp. 12-13.

[5] Augustus Richard Norton, Guest Editor's "Introduction" to a special issue on Civil Society in the Middle East, *Middle East Journal* 47, no. 2 (Spring 1993): 205-216.

political power within the state. The less conscious and less organized formations would, over time, learn by emulation the art of associational life. Thus, the organs of civil society in the West have multiplied in numbers and organizational sophistication.

The state apparatus is supposedly a neutral arena for all units of civil society. The competition among the latter is often over "government"— i.e., the decision-making nerve center of the state. The neutrality of the state may be debatable; and the boundaries between state, government and regime are often blurred in theory and practice, as well as in the mind of ordinary citizens. But because civil society has evolved simultaneously with the nation-state, both have been more concordant than discordant. Neither has been completely autonomous from the other, only relatively so. Hence, the positing of the relationship between state and society in "zero-sum" terms may be a misleading dichotomy. A strong state may not imply necessarily a weak civil society or vice-versa. In fact, most stable Western democracies represent cases of a strong civil society and a strong state. Similarly, as we will observe in the Arab World, a more common case is that of weak civil societies and weak states.

The linkage between civil society and democratization should be obvious. Democracy after all is a set of rules and institutions of governance through a peaceful management of competing groups and/or conflicting interests. Thus the normative component of "civil society" is essentially the same as that of "democracy". Aside from the "Athenian" or "town-hall" model of direct democracy, organs of civil society are believed to be the optimum channels of popular participation in governance. Couched in a different terminology, this is the essence of how the concept of civil society has been used by theoreticians of the "Social Contract", down to Hegel, Marx, de Tocqueville, and Gramsci.[6] The modern day users of the concept have merely refined or elaborated its manifestation in contemporary complex societies.

Of course, the relationship between civil society and democratization is neither simple, linear, nor operates in a vacuum. The relationship is often mediated and attenuated by the specific legacy of the "state," the collective memory and current norms and practices of individuals and

---

[6] See a review of how the concept of "civil society" was used in A. M. Orum, *Introduction to Political Sociology* (Englewood Cliffs, New Jersey: Prentice Hall, 1978), pp. 24-26; B. Redhead, ed., *Plato to Nato: Studies in Political Thought* (London: BBC Books, 1984).

groups—i.e., "political culture." Equally the regional and international factors could stunt or expedite the unfolding of the relationship between civil society and democratization. In his own terminology, Huntington elaborated those mediating and attenuating factors bearing on the relationship.[7]

Some Middle East area observers contend that the lagging democratization of the Arab World is due to the absence or stunting of its "civil society" and its corresponding "political culture". Some orientalists and mongers of ethno-centrism may go as far as to totally dismiss even the potential for the evolution of an Arab civil society, and hence any prospect of genuine democratization. Propagators of this point of view often forget the long arduous, and occasionally bloody, march of civil society and democratization in their own Western societies. It was more than seven centuries between the issuance of the Magna Carta (1215) and granting suffrage to women (1920) in Great Britain. What Huntington calls waves of democratization in the West during the last two centuries were followed by counter waves of authoritarianism in several European countries.[8] At any rate, the assertions made about the inhospitality of Arab society and culture to democratization will be examined in both pre-modern and contemporary Arab realities to argue a counter proposition—i.e., despite noted distortion and time lags, the Arab World is currently going through civil society building and democratization. The relationship between the two processes is essentially the same: as modern socio-economic formations sprout and take shape, they create their civil society organizations, which in turn strive for participatory governance.

Resilient Traditional Arab Civil Formations

Pre-modern society in what is now called the Arab world was fairly ordered around a political authority [9] whose legitimacy was derived from a combination of conquest and/or religious sources. But the public space was immediately shared by 'ulama, merchants, guilds, Sufi orders, and sects (millats).[10] Outside this first concentric zone, the public space was

---

[7] Huntington, The Third Wave, pp. 31-107.

[8] Huntington, The Third Wave, pp. 17-21.

[9] Y. L. Rizk, Civil Egypt (Arabic) (Cairo: Tiba, 1993); Manfred Halpern, The Politics of Social Change in the Middle East and the Arab World (Princeton, NJ: Princeton University Press, 1962).

populated by peasants and tribes. Political authority asserted itself most clearly in the first concentric zone of that public space. Outside the first zone, its assertion varied markedly. In most cases it was hardly felt. Other collectivities, especially the tribes, were quite autonomous from, if not outright defiant of the central authority.[11]

Even in the first concentric zone, often within city walls, various groups coexisted and interacted with a great deal of autonomy. Guilds, religious sects, and ethnic groups ran most of their own internal affairs through elected or appointed leaders. The latter were accountable to both the political authority and their own communities. Tension, no doubt, existed within each category but was of low intensity. Equally, tension may have existed between or among two or more of these communities, but was often resolved inter-communally; or occasionally warranted the direct intervention of the political authority. [12]

Leaders, elders, and notables of the above traditional formations performed several functions in the overall governance of pre-modern Arab society. Beside running intra-communal affairs and managing inter-communal conflicts, they acted as councilors and advisors to rulers. They were called those who "loosen and bind", *ahlu al-hall wa al-'aqd*, the important among them were the *'ulama*, learned men of religion. In this capacity, Solvers and Binders (SAB) reduced the absolutist nature of the pre-modern Arab Islamic state. They spoke for the people in general and for their respective constituencies in particular. SAB equally mediated and legitimated the ruler's decisions to such constituencies.

This traditional equilibrium of governance was maintained by a multitude of mechanisms-i.e., clear hierarchies, occupational and residential segregation, and autonomous resources (mostly from *Awqaf* or *hubus* religious endowments). Social solidarities existed along occupational, religious, and ethnic lines. Central authority collected taxes, administered justice through the *shari'ah*, maintained public order and defense; and occasionally patronized arts and sciences. Social services and direct economic functions were not expected obligations of the "state"; but mostly left to local communities. In this sense, traditional

---

[10] Iliya Harik, "The Origin of the Arab System", in G. Luciani, ed.,*The Arab State*, pp. 1-28; P. Crone and M. Hinds, *God's Caliph: Religious Authority in the First Century of Islam* (Cambridge: Cambridge University Press, 1980).

[11] For an elaboration on this traditional mode of governance, see the classic of Ibn Khaldoun, *Al-Muqaddimah* (Arabic) (Baghdad: Al -Muthanna, 1980); El-Baki Hermassi, *Society and State in the Arab Maghreb* (Beirut: Center for Arab Unity Studies, 1987).

[12] Rizk, *Civil Egypt*, pp. 40-48, pp. 90-91

Arab society not only knew the equivalent of civil formations but also survived through them. Individuals relied on these formations for their identity and much of their basic needs. They insulated them from direct dealing with political authority. [13] In the traditional equilibrium, the public space in which civil formations interacted coincided with the physical space in which they lived and worked.

This traditional equilibrium of governance was occasionally disrupted by seditions (*fitnat*) or calamities (*nakba*). The Arabic political vocabulary referred to *fitnah* as sharp internal strife, usually accompanied by armed conflict. While a *nakb* referred to an invasion by an alien (non-Muslim) power, often accompanied by mass looting, destruction, and population uprooting.[14] Both *fitnat* and *nakba* would lead to a disintegration of this traditional equilibrium for a shorter or longer time. Often, however, the equilibrium would be pieced together and reasserts itself. At least this seemed to be the case for much of the first twelve centuries of the Arab-Islamic history.

The last two centuries witnessed what seemed to be an irreversible disintegration of the traditional equilibrium of governance and of its accompanying socio-economic symbiosis. This was a direct function of Western penetration of Arab-Muslim societies, and their coercive integration in the budding world system. Most of the traditional civil formations were believed to be withering away; and new ones were being born through the hardest of labor. Among the latter was new Arab "state". But nearly a half century after the birth of such a state, we are discovering that some of the traditional formations are quite resilient; and several Arab ruling elites are willing or being forced to accommodate them. In five of the Arab Gulf countries, and modern version of SAB has been formally re-instituted under the label of *shura* (consultative) Council. Even in some of the countries which have their own elected parliaments, a similar consultative council has been added under the same name *shura* (e.g., Egypt) or something close to it such as "Notables Council" (e.g., Jordan). Despite their non-legislative and only advisory function, such councils are a definite accommodation of mainly traditional formations (e.g., ethnicity, sect, and tribe).

---

[13] Rizk, *Civil Egypt*, pp. 141-142.

[14] On the Arab political usage of the two terms (fitna, nakba) see Saad Eddin Ibrahim, *Exiting the Blind-Alley of History: The Arabs and the Gulf Crisis* (Arabic) (Cairo: Ibn Khaldoun - S. Al Sabah, 1992), p. 12.

The New Arab State: Expansion and Retreat

The birth of the new Arab states was midwifed by Western colonial powers.[15] They bore numerous deformities—ranging from the artificialities of their borders to the internal weakness of their institutions. Right from the start, they have faced severe problems and challenges from within and from without. Initially, the new states neither tapped the reservoir of traditional wisdom of pre-modern civil formations, nor adequately allowed enough public space for new ones to sprout and flourish autonomously. As a result, the new Arab state found itself embattled on many internal and external fronts, for the first four decades of independence.

The Arab World shared some, but not all, of the processes which had accompanied the emergence of the modern state and civil society in the West—e.g., the erosion of traditional equilibria, rapid population growth and urbanization. But the processes of capitalization and industrialization lagged far behind. Hence the new socio-economic formations which are the backbone of the modern state and civil society have not grown progressively or evenly.

a) Erratic State-Building and Development

The Arab World witnessed a phenomenal socio-economic growth in three decades following WWII, the birth period of most independent Arab states. But the growth was erratic or sluggish, resulting, among other things, in a distorted stratification. The bearing of this distortion on the development of Arab civil society will be obvious from the account sketched below.

In the decades of the 1950s and 1960s, many of the newly independent Arab states had embarked on ambitious educational and industrial expansions. As a result, two sprouting classes grew steadily: the new middle class (NMC) and the modern working class (MWC). Central planning and command socio-economic policies were the order of the day in most Arab countries.

But the two subsequent decades witnessed a mix of inconsistent, or outright confused, socio-economic policies. The initial oil boom of the 1970s tempted many of the poorer and sizeable countries to introduce what came to be known as liberal "open-door" policies, without successfully phasing out the command socio-economic policies of the previous

---

[15] Ibrahim, *Society and State*, pp. 45-78; Harik, "The Origin of the Arab System". pp. 19-24.

decades. Three formal sectors have been operating, or rather mis-
operating, simultaneously—a public, a private and a mixed one. In
addition, a growing informal or "underground" sector has appeared.
Multiple and extreme levels of efficiency, skill appropriation,
and salary scales prevailed in the same national economy, polity, and
society. Distorting effects were inevitable. Inflationary pressures, wors-
ening of equity, and mounting external debt became rampant in most
Arab countries.[16]

From a stratification point of view, two social formations grew
rapidly in the 1970s and 1980s—a "nouveau rich" class and a "lumpen
proletariat class". The first appropriated an increasing share of the
national GNP without adding much to the national wealth, engaged in
conspicuous consumption, and the flight of capital. The second, the
lumpen proletariat, has grown tremendously in size, added to open and
hidden unemployment, and has experienced anguishing relative depri-
vation. The poverty-belts around major cities represent ominous time-
bombs. Meanwhile, the new middle class and the modern working class,
on fixed salaries and wages, have been hard pressed by rampant inflation. These two classes would steadily be alienated from the ruling
regimes in their respective countries. The urban "lumpen proletariat", on
the other hand, would be easily manipulated by masters of street
politics.[17]

b) The State and Conflict Management

The predicaments of the state in the Arab World are further compounded
by old unresolved regional and internal conflicts, as well as by new ones.
Relevant to our main concern in this paper, civil society and democratization, is the dismal failure of post-independence ruling elites in
managing conflicts.

Among the old persistent problems are the protracted conflicts—e.g.,
the Arab-Israeli, the Iraqi-Iranian, the Libyan-Chadian, the Lebanese,
the Sudanese, the Somali and the Saharan conflicts. Some of these are
over forty years old (the Arab-Israeli); and the relatively shorter ones are
already several years old (the Iraqi-Iranian). Some of these have flared
up into armed conflicts on and off for four decades (the Arab-Israeli and
the Sudanese). All of them are nevertheless quite costly in material and

---

[16] Hazem Beblawi, "The Rentier State in the Arab World", in Luciani, ed., *The Arab State*, pp. 85-98; Jean Leca, "Social Structure and Political Stability: Comparative Evidence from Algeria, Syria, and Iraq," pp. 150-188.

[17] Ibrahim, *Society and State*, pp. 342-369.

human terms. The Middle East region is the first buyer and consumer of lethal arms in the Third World, at the average of $100.0 billion annually during the last two decades. Overall spending on defense is twice as high. Thus, some $4,000 billions have been spent, or rather wasted, on defense purposes without settling most of the above mentioned conflicts (including the $2,300 billions spent in the Arab armed costs as shown in Summary Table 1). The number of those killed, wounded, disabled, and displaced is estimated at 13.0 million during the same period (see Summary Table 1). With the rapid introduction and spread of arms of mass-destruction (e.g., nuclear and chemical), the human and material costs of these protracted conflicts, if unsettled, is bound to be astronomical in the 1990s.[18]

Summary Table (1)

The Cost of Armed Conflicts in the Middle East and North Africa (MENA) Region: 1948-1992

Type of Conflict	Period	No. of Casualties	Estimated Cost in Billions of U.S.$ (1990 Value)	Estimated Population Displacement
A)- Inter-State Conflict				
Arab-Israeli Conflict	1948-1990	160,000	300.0	3,000,000
Iraq-Iran	1980-1988	300,000	300.0	1,000,000
Gulf War	1990-1992	120,000	650.0	1,000,000
Other Inter-State conflicts	1945-1991	20,000	50.0	1,000,000
Sub-Total		**600,000**	**1,300.0**	**6,000,000**
B)- Intra State Conflicts				
Sudan	1956-1991	500,000	20.0	4,000,000
Iraq	1960-1991	300,000	20.0	1,000,000
Lebanon	1958-1990	150,000	50.0	1,000,000
N.Yemen	1962-1972	100,000	5.0	500,000
Syria	1975-1985	30,000	0.5	150,000
Morocco (Sahara)	1976-1991	20,000	3.0	100,000
S.Yemen	1986-1987	10,000	0.2	50,000
Somalia	1989-1992	110,000	0.3	500,000
Other Intra-State conflict	1945-1991	30,000	1.0	300,000
Sub-Total		**1,250,000**	**1,000.0**	**7,600,000**
Grand Total		**1,850,000**	**2,300.0**	**13,600,000**
(All Armed Conflicts)				

Source: Files of The Arab Data Unit (ADU), Ibn Khaldoun Center for Developmental Studies.

---

[18] See Saad Eddin Ibrahim, *The Question of Minorities in the Arab World* (Arabic) (Cairo: Ibn Khaldoun - Al Sabah, 1992), pp. 17-18; by the same author "Minorities and State-Building in the Arab World" a paper presented in the Annual American Sociological Meeting, Pittsburgh, August, 1992.

Equally relevant, intra-state armed conflicts outweigh inter-state ones in terms of human losses and population uprooting. Entire local communities were destroyed in part or in full. Many of these were ethnic and minority groups-based. The heavy losses, measured in economic terms alone as "opportunity cost", indicate what could have been achieved with these tremendous resources. Development has clearly been a major victim of such protracted conflicts. But more detrimental to the development of civil society have been the deep psycho-socio-political cleavages created by intra-state protracted armed conflicts. They have forced individuals and groups to re-intrench themselves behind primordial walls of solidarity. Traditional loyalties to ethnic, religious, sectarian, and tribal groups would take primacy over these to modern formations of civil society or to the state itself.[19]

The dismal failure of the new Arab states in managing internal and external conflict was a cause and an effect of the questioned legitimacy of many of them at birth by substantial sectors of their own new "citizens" (e.g., Lebanon, Iraq, Jordan, South Yemen). [20] More often, however, the failure was due to the questioned legitimacy of the authoritarian ruling regimes in the new Arab states. While the legitimacy question of the state seemed to be resolvable by passage of time, regime legitimacy worsened over time; hence the mounting pressure for more participatory politics, especially in the last decade. Much of the latter would either take the form of random outbursts of the lumpen proletariat through street politics, or the form of less sensational but more sustained pressure of civil society.[21]

New Civil Society: the Difficult Birth

Despite the authoritarian nature of governance in many Arab states for much of their history since independence, nuclei of modern civil society have sprouted in nearly all of them. Some of the new civil organizations, especially in the northern tier of the Arab World, date back to the second half of the 19th century; but they increased in number and thrived in the inter-war period (1918-1939). The embryonic new middle class was the backbone of these civil organizations. Under colonial rule, many of them took on an explicit political role of liberating their respective countries. And from the ranks of these organizations emerged the leaders of

---

[19] Ibrahim, *The Question of Minorities*, pp. 243-244.
[20] Ibrahim, *Society and State*.
[21] Ibrahim, *Society and State*.

independence. The modern civil organizations, however, were stunted under the populist Arab regimes in the 1950-1970 period. They regained their vitality gradually since the mid-1970s, as the populist regimes began to run out of steam.

a) Stunting of An Embryonic Civil Society (1950s-1960s)

A few years after independence, however, several Arab states witnessed a wave of radical politics, mostly through populist military coups d'etat—Syria, Egypt, Iraq, Sudan, Yemen, Algeria, Libya, Mauritania, and Somalia. These "radical" regimes ended the brief liberal experiments which some of their societies had engaged in briefly before and immediately after independence. One-party-rule or that of a junta became the dominant pattern of governance. The new populist regimes gave the state an expansionist socio-economic role. An explicit or implicit "social contract" was forged, by which the state was to effect development, ensure social justice, satisfy basic needs of its citizens, consolidate political independence, and achieve other national aspirations (e.g., Arab unity, liberation of Palestine). In return their peoples were to forego, at least for a while, their quest for liberal participatory politics. Pan Arab nationalist and socialist ideologies were used to popularize this social contract, and for political mobilization in support of the ruling regimes. The majority accepted or acquiesced. So attractive did this populist trade-off social contract seem at the beginning that even traditional Arab monarchies adopted it partially since the 1960s—i.e. Jordan, Saudi Arabia, the Gulf states, and Morocco).[22]

The populist social contract had, among other things, a detrimental impact, not only on existing political parties, but also on other organizations of civil society. The latter was either prohibited or severely restricted by an arsenal of laws and decrees, or were outright annexed to the single party in power.[23] In other words, under populist rule, organizations of civil society lost all or much of their autonomy. As a result, many of these organizations withered away due to aging membership and the disinterest of younger generations. Some became merely paper

---

[22] See an account of how Arab monarchies responded to radical ideologies, in Michael Hudson, *Arab Politics: The Search for Legitimacy* (New Haven: Yale University Press, 1980).

[23] For an elaborate account, see the proceedings of the Conference on Arab Civil Organizations, (Arabic), Cairo; October 31 - November 3, 1989; the papers of a seminar on Arab Civil Society, Beirut: January 21-24, 1993 and later published under the same title (Ar abic) (Beirut: Center for Arab Unity Studies, 1993).

organizations and only very few adapted to the new populist formula and struggled to remain active through political discretion.

The defeat of populist regimes at the hands of Israel in 1967 and successive reversals, culminating in the 1990-1991 Gulf crisis, led to the discrediting of the populist social contract and the steady erosion of the legitimacy of most Arab regimes. Clinging to power, many populist regimes escalated their oppression, others engaged in external adventures; and some did both. Some of them, as we elaborate later, would engage in token or serious revision of their systems of governance.

b) Mismanagement and Retreat of the State

The expansionist role of the Arab state seems to have reached its upper ceiling in the 1970s (in both rich and poor countries). Since then, the march of socio-political events internally, regionally, and internationally, has forced the state to retreat from several socio-economic functions. Most of that retreat has been disorderly, leaving in its aftermath structural and situational misery, which could have been avoided or reduced had their respective civil societies been in better shape. Instead, some of the public space vacated by the state has been filled either by extremist Islamic tendencies (e.g., Egypt and Algeria), or by separatist primordial tendencies (e.g., Sudan, Somalia, and Iraq).

Using a typology that pairs and crosses the variables bearing on the strength of state and civil society, as indicated in Summary Table (2), most Arab countries have oscillated between cells B,C, and D. None has ever been firmly established in cell A—strong state and strong civil society. Countries like Somalia, Sudan and Iraq are currently firmly located in conditions described by cell D—the worst possible combination of a weak state and a weak civil society.

While it does not explain why a given Arab country falls in a given cell at present, the above typology helps in systemizing comparative empirical data, and in monitoring the relative changes in respective Arab countries over time. Thus, while it was viewed as being a strong state and weak civil society until 1990 (cell C), Iraq has quickly drifted to cell D since and because of the Gulf crisis (1990-1991). Equally long believed to be strong states, Egypt and Algeria are sliding from cell A to either cell B (Egypt) or D (Algeria).

Summary Table (2)

Arab State

	Strong (+)	Weak (-)
	A	B
Strong (+) Civil Society	Conflict management through accepted participatory politics and democratic consensus	Governance imposed through interest groups manipulating the state at the expense of other groups (early years of independence)
	C	D
Weak (-)	Governance imposed by an autonomous state and an autocratic elite (Height of populism in the 1950s-1960s)	Disintegration or governance imposed by regional and international events or dictate. (The decades of the 70s, 80s and early 90s)

c) Revitalization of Civil Society in the Arab World

In the retreating years of the Arab state (the 1970s and 80s), some of the pre-populist civil formations revitalized themselves; and new ones have been created. Hundreds of private voluntary organizations (PVOs), community development associations (CDAs) have mushroomed in the last two decades. The number of Arab NGOs is estimated to have grown from less than 20,000 in the mid-1960s to about 70,000 in the late 1980s.[24] A case in point is human rights organizations. In the aftermath of the Israeli invasion of Lebanon (1982), one of the severest reversals since the 1967 defeat, such organizations sprang on the pan-Arab and country levels. [25]

Enhancing this phenomenal quantitative growth of Arab civil organizations in the last two decades are several factors; among them are the following:

1. Growing unmet needs of individuals and local communities by the Arab state. For the lower and lower middle classes these needs were mainly socio-economic services the state was no longer able or willing to provide—e.g., housing, health, more inc ome generation, better quality education, and food supplies, etc. For the middle and upper

---

[24] This estimate was aggregated from the country papers of the Conference on Arab Civil Organizations.

[25] On the birth of The Arab Human Rights Organization and similar civil formations in the 1980s, see Ibrahim, *Civil Society and Democratization*, pp. 9-12.

classes the growing needs were of an expressive, cultural, professional and political variety. Thousands of cooperatives, cultural, and professional associations have been created in response to such needs.

2. Expansion of educated Arab population. Whatever the faults of populist regimes, one of their undeniable achievements was free mass education. Much lacking in quality, this expansion of education has nevertheless created higher levels of consciousness, expectations, and rudimentary organizational skills. Such attributes have been instrumental in building formal associations.

Still lacking in internal democracy and managerial capabilities, these associations are steadily learning the promotion of both.

3. Growing individual financial resources. The 1970s and early 1980s were years of financial boom to many Arab individuals—due to skyrocketing oil revenues and the accompanying inter-state manpower movement on an unprecedented scale; and the beginnings of economic liberalization policies in previously state-command economies (socialist countries). Thus while governments mismanaged or wasted financial resources, many individuals earmarked some of their new fortunes to newly created associations. The Arab World witnessed for the first time the creation of American-style foundations (e.g., Ford, Rockfeller, Carnegie), such as H. Sabagh, A. Shuman, and R. al-Hariri foundations.

4. Growing margins of freedom. By defacto or default, margins of freedoms stretched gradually in many Arab countries. This was due partly to state fatigue or incompetence in controlling society. But it was also due to increasing repertoires of citizens' strategies to circumvent the state. The extensive travelling, Arab media abroad and Arab individual bankaccountsinforeign countries were expressions of such growing margins. In fact, many civil Arab organizations were conceived or established abroad before transferring their activities to their home countries.

d) Some Specificities of Arab Civil Society in the Arab World

1. Political parties in civil society. Political parties have been part of the rapid multiplication of Arab civil organizations in the last two decades. While some old parties, predating independence, have continued despite autocratic governance (e.g., *Istiklal* in Morocco, *Umma* and *Ittihadi* in Sudan), most other parties did not survive the populist phase in Arab politics. But with widening margins of freedom some old political parties resurfaced since the late 1970s (e.g., the *Wafd* and Young Egypt Socialist in Egypt). More important, however, is the mushrooming of

new parties, once it becomes legal to do so—e.g., 46 in Algeria, 43 in Yemen, 23 in Jordan, 19 in Morocco, 13 in Egypt, 11 in Tunisia, 6 in Mauritania, etc.[26]

The quantum jump of Arab civil organizations, however, should not imply that they are all effective. In fact the majority of them, including many of the new political parties, are too small to be significant in the public life of their respective countries. Egypt is a typical case in point. Claiming about one-third of the estimated 70,000 Arab civil associations, most of Egypt's 20,000 NGOs are inactive or only moderately so. According to a recent field study only about 40.0% of Egypt's NGOs were judged as active and effective.[27]

The same applies to Arab political parties. Recent parliamentary elections in Yemen (April, 1993) and Morocco (June 1993) revealed the political insignificance of most parties in building or attracting constituencies of any size. Only seven of Yemen's 43 political parties won seats; and only three captured more than 80.0% of those seats. In Morocco, out of the 19 parties only 9 appeared on the score-board; with four of them capturing 75.0% of the contested seats.[28]

2. Professional Syndicates. Professional associations are probably the most active civil organizations in the Arab World at present. Partly because they perform union-like benefits to their membership, partly because of the higher level of education and political consciousness, and partly because of their relatively independent financial resources, Arab professional associations or syndicates (niqabat, as they are termed in Arabic) have spearheaded the movement of civil society in their respective countries. In a country like the Sudan, they managed twice (in 1964 and 1985) to oust from power the ruling military regime. In Egypt, Morocco, and Tunisia they have been potent pressure groups during the 1970s and 1980s.

Enhancing the social and moral power of professional syndicates are two additional factors. First, they are further organized on the pan-Arab level as federations and are well-linked to their international counterparts. This has given them not only broader fora, but also added moral protection from outside their countries. Second, Arab professional syndicates are organically and strategically located at the heart of

---

[26] For a detailed account, see Ibrahim, *Civil Society*.

[27] *Grass-roots Participation and Development in Egypt*, a study by Ibn Khaldoun Center, commissioned by UNICEF, UNDP, and UNFPA (Cairo, 1993).

[28] See the *Civil Society and Democratic Transformation in the Arab World* (CSDT) Newsletter, an Ibn Khaldoun Center monthly publication (English and Arabic): May, June, July 1993.

production and service institutions, including those administered by the state. They can not easily be dissolved or dismissed by the ruling elites. Hence, when they all decide to go on strike, for example (as actually happened in the Sudan) in 1985, the entire society and state could be paralyzed. Among the most influential are the doctors, engineers, and teachers. More recently, businessmen's associations have joined the ranks of the influential.[29]

3. Politics by Proxy. In Arab countries where political parties are still prohibited or severely restricted, some civil associations have served many of their functions by proxy—e.g., articulation and debating public issues, formulating public policy alternatives, and exerting pressure on decision-makers. Kuwait's "University Graduates Society," Qatar's "Jassrah Cultural Club," and the UAE "Association of Social Professions" have been performing such functions.

Possibly for these reasons, some Arab civil associations (other than political parties per se), have recently become arenas of intensive political activities. Their elections, generally fair and honest, are very competitive, and are widely followed by the public at large. This has been observed in Egypt, Jordan, Kuwait, Tunisia, and Morocco during the 1980s and early 1990s. More recently in Egypt, for example, the Muslim Brothers, who are not allowed a political party of their own, have systematically taken over, through elections, the boards of the most important professional syndicates—the doctors, engineers, and lawyers.[30]

4. Traditional formations in modern garb. Without invoking the fruitless debate of modernism vs. traditionalism, we are using the terms (modern and traditional) in a strictly descriptive analytical sense—i.e., without any value-loaded "isms." A sizable number of Arab civil organizations still contain remnants of their society's traditional formations. The typical case would be the establishment of an appearingly modern civil association in an urban center, but whose membership is mostly or all belonging to the same tribe, village or religious sect. The trappings of modernity may be all there—e.g., formal registration, licensing, lofty by-laws, elections, boards, committees, etc. But in effect, the association is headed and run in nearly the same traditional man ners, briefly sketched in Part I above.

This observation should not take away from the importance of this type of civil associations. For the fact that its initiators have founded it

---

[29] Ibrahim, *Civil Society.*
[30] For facts, figures and analysis, see *CSDT Newsletter*, May, October 1992.

along modern lines to enhance "traditional" loyalties and/or serve traditional functions is still a testimony to a shrewed appreciation of the need to reconcile both traditions and modernity during a period of societal transition. When established in big urban centers, this associational type not only enhances traditional leaders but equally helps their kin and followers to land softly on their feet in an otherwise strange, alien, or impersonal environment.

In any case, this associational type has a latent protection function to both modern civil society and the state. Without it, the newcomers to the Arab cities from the hinterland are bound to be part of the amorphous urban lumpen proletariat (ULP), referred to in Part II, above. The ULP has been the fastest growing socio-economic formation in the Arab World during the last two decades. It represents the most flammable material of demagogic street politics. Urban riots manned by this formation were vividly displayed in Egypt (1977, 1986, 1992), Tunisia (1976, 1987), Morocco (1974, 1981, 1987), Jordan (1988), and Algeria (1988).

5. Civil society and crisis situations. Like many other dimensions of development in the Arab World, the advance of civil society has not been uniform or even in all Arab countries. But to the extent that civil formations existed and were relatively solid, rumblings for democratization were felt or heard, as we shall elaborate later. But more important, as it turned out recently, is the fact that in Arab countries which were subjected to severe crises, the presence or absence of civil formations would make a tremendous difference in how the country withstood a crisis.

Lebanon, Kuwait, and Somalia are cases in point. In all three, the "state" nearly vanished under catastrophic or overpowering circumstances—Lebanon and Somalia because of protracted internal strife compounded by regional and international factors; and Kuwait because of a swift Iraqi invasion. Different as they were in many ways, Lebanon and Kuwait had in common the presence of fairly well-developed civil formations—some 600 and 200 of them, respectively. While many such organizations were reduced to total impotence under the circumstances, scores of them remained active during the crisis. It was these active civil associations which provided material and moral support for survival to many Lebanese and Kuwaiti citizens both at home and abroad. Even sectarian-based Lebanese NGOs extended help across sectarian lines on many occasions. Also, many new neighborhood-based associations emerged in the height of the 16-year civil strife.

In Kuwait, it was, of all things, the consumers cooperatives which became focal points to perform many of the functions previously provided by the state—e.g., food ration, health, social welfare, education, mail and informal communication network. Other civil organizations which could not operate openly for fear of the occupation authorities used the less suspect food cooperatives an d mosques to give a hand.

In contrast, Somalia had no or very few civil organizations. For years of populist military rule, many Somalis who lived a way from their villages or tribes relied almost exclusively on the state for work and services. When the state machinery totally col lapsed in 1991, they found themselves without base or cover. As the ensuing internal conflict expanded and protracted, the very fabric of even primordial formations was severely ruptured and quickly disintegrated. The massive famine that struck all of Somalia in 1992 was not just because of the fighting, or even for lack of food-supplies (much was sent by foreign donors); but mainly because of difficulties of distribution. Had there been civil organizations, similar to those of Lebanon and Kuwait, much of the starvation, diseases, and death would have been avoided or markedly ameliorated. Somalia represents a tragic and extreme case, not only of disorderly retreat but of a total disintegration of the state without a civil society to provide a "safety net" or to pick up the pieces.

Regimes, Civil Society, and Democratization

No longer able to honor the terms of the old social contract, calm new socio-economic formations with the tired language of political discourse, or forge a new participatory social contract (for fear of being toppled from power), the Arab ruling elites resorted either to coercive repression at home or to riskier adventures abroad. Since 1980, Saddam Hussein's regime in Iraq has done both, reaching an all-time high on August 2, 1990, with the invasion of Kuwait, triggering what came to be known as the "Gulf crisis." During the crisis it was predicted that more participatory governance of the Arab world would be among its outcomes. This prediction was based on the proposition that the crisis was as much an internal Arab political crisis as it was a regional international crisis. In fact, predictions of participatory governance did materialize in a score of Arab countries. But the trend was already under way before the crisis. What the latter has done is to expedite it. That some countries are proceeding faster than others is due to many domestic and external factors. Among the domestic is the relative size and degree of maturation of civil society in each country. It was civil society organizations which staged the rumblings, followed by advances in democratization. In some, the march for democracy was set back; in others the rumblings are still there but have not yet led anywhere. What follows is a sketch of these three modal conditions of current Arab politics.[31] Their presentation below implicitly suggests the intricate interplay of domestic, regional, and international factors on the march (or retreat) of civil society and democratization in the Arab World.

a) Democratization: The Rumblings

In the few years immediately preceding the Gulf crisis, several Arab regimes were already sensing their mounting internal loss of legitimacy. It was expressed in increasingly frequent violent confrontations between regimes and one or more of the major socioeconomic formations. The upper rungs of the new middle class engaged regimes in nonviolent battles over basic freedoms, human rights, and democracy. On the pan-Arab level and within several Arab countries, this quest took the form of establishing human rights organizations and more autonomous professional associations, thus revitalizing stunted civil societies.

There were varying levels of popular demands vis-a-vis respective Arab regimes. On one level, the demands were for greater " liberalization," such as freedom of the press, associations, and the right to travel abroad. Nearly all regimes made some concessions in response to these demands. On a higher level, the demand was for serious and explicit democratization, such as legalized political parties, equal access to the mass media, and free and honest elections. None of the regimes has fully responded to these demands in the 1980s.

The lower rungs of the new middle class adopted Islamic political activism to challenge ruling elites. The modern working class opted more often for strikes or other forms of work slowdowns and industrial sabotage. The urban lumpen proletariat resorted to "street politics," such as demonstrations, rioting, and looting. Whatever formation started a confrontation and however its discontent was expressed, the other equally alienated socio-economic formations would join in to advance their own demands. During the 1980 s and into the 1990s, this phenomena occurred across the region: Algeria, 1988; Egypt, 1981, 1986;

---

[31] Much of these passages in Part V are adapted from an earlier paper, "Crises, Elites, and Democratization in the Arab World," *Middle East Journal* 47, no 2 (Spring 1993): 292-305.

Jordan, 1989; Kuwait, 1989, 1990; Mauritania, 1986, 1988; Morocco, 1984, 1988, 1990; Somalia, 1985-1990; South Yemen, 1986-1990; Sudan, 1985; and Tunisia, 1984, 1988. The ruling elites in these countries all responded to growing expressions of discontent with promises of economic and political reforms. In fact, some began to honor such promises before the outbreak of the Gulf crisis. Others took advantage of the crisis to renege on or to delay honoring them.

Algeria, Jordan, and Yemen had embarked on serious democratization processes before the Gulf crisis. All three had held national or municipal elections between 1987 and 1990 with few or no complaints regarding their integrity. The fact that anti-regime Islamist candidates performed well and captured more seats than expected added to the credibility of the process. The fact that democratically elected people in all three countries loudly supported Saddam Hussein during the Gulf crisis perplexed Western observers espousing democratization in the Third World.

Their support for Hussein is an irony to be pondered on its own. These newly elected members of the opposition were expressing discontent not only in regard to their own rulers, but also in regard to the overall Arab order, and, for that matter, the much-talked-about "new world order." Although no less despotic than some of the other Arab rulers on both sides of the crisis, Saddam Hussein tapped and manipulated that discontent outside Iraq. He was able to do this in part because Iraq's oil wealth had not been as flaunted in poorer Arab countries by Iraqi citizens as had that of their counterparts in the Gulf. The argument by the United States and other Western countries about international legitimacy seemed insincere to many Arabs and, in view of the Palestinian question, smacked of a double standard.

In 1987, a few years before the Gulf crisis, the Tunisian leadership changed peacefully— although via something of a constitutional coup —from Habib Bourguiba to Zaine al-Abdeen Ben 'Ali. The new leadership promised political reforms to secular opposition parties, but continued to deny legitimacy to the Islamist al-Nahda Party. A series of bloody confrontations took place between the regime and followers of al-Nahda in late 1989 and early 1990. The Gulf crisis, on which all Tunisian parties saw eye-to-eye, froze these confrontations for nearly a year, but they resumed subsequently. Other secular opposition parties remain disdainful of the ruling Rassemblement Constitutionnel Democratique, but their fear of the Islamist trend makes them view the status quo as the lesser of two evils.

Limited democratization in Egypt and Morocco several years prior to the Gulf crisis did not progress further in 1990-91. Although the Moroccan government sided with Kuwait and the US-led coalition during the crisis, the opposition condemned foreign intervention and mobilized Moroccan public opinion. Indeed, the biggest demonstration in support of Iraq was staged in Morocco. The crisis gave the opposition a chance to show its ability to mobilize, a fact that did not go unnoticed by the regime. The immediate response was to scale back Moroccan military involvement. A year after the crisis, King Hassan announced political reforms, which he would honor, as we see later.

In Egypt, there was less discordance between the ruling elite and the public over the crisis. In fact, the regime managed to call for a parliamentary election in October 1990, as if to show that life in Egypt was quite orderly despite the crisis. While two major opposition parties, the *Wafd* and the Labor-Islamic Alliance, boycotted the elections, their action was for reasons unrelated to the crisis, namely the government's refusal to guarantee fairness in the political competition. The Egyptian regime's self-assuredness was, however, shaken by two events: the October 1990 assassination of Rifaat al-Mahjub, the former speaker of the parliament, supposedly by Islamic militants, and the protests of thousands of Egyptian university students against what seemed to be the systematic destruction of Iraq. The students' clashes with the police left at least four dead, scores wounded, and hundreds arrested.

In Djibouti, Mauritania, and Somalia, mounting ethnic and tribal conflicts were kept under control during the Gulf crisis. I n the countries directly involved in or close to the heart of the crisis—Iraq, Syria, and the six states bordering the Persian Gulf and the Gulf of Oman—ruling elites claimed a "legitimate" excuse to put off action, if any had been intended at all, toward democratization. It was a full year after the crisis before Arab elites showed serious inclinations toward genuine participatory politics, although promises had been extracted from them in some instances—such as in Kuwait and Saudi Arabia. During 1991, it became obvious that something had to be done.

One positive among the many negative aspects of the Gulf crisis has been the unprecedented political mobilization of the Arab masses. Popular expressions of support for one or the other Arab side in the crisis were not always in accord with the official positions of regimes. This had the effect of breaking the wall of fear of many Arabs vis-a-vis ruling elites. Iraq is a dramatic case in point in that the Shi'a in the south and the Kurds in the north rose in arms against the regime of Saddam

Hussein, emboldened, it could be argued, by Iraq's crushing defeat and the prospect of aid from the victorious allies. Even the Gulf elites on the winning side faced mounting demands from their intelligentsia for more political participation.

b) Democratization: The Advances

In the last decade, at least two-thirds of the twenty-one Arab countries have engaged in varying forms of greater participatory politics. All but Iraq, Syria and Libya have opened up their political systems. Some have done so more than others. Nine Arab countries have reinstituted or instituted a multi-party system—Egypt, Morocco, Mauritania, Algeria, Tunisia, Jordan, Lebanon, Sudan and Yemen. During the same decade (1983-1993), ten Arab countries have held at least one parliamentary elections. Five out of the six countries of the Gulf Cooperation Council (GCC) have instituted *shura* (consultative) Councils. (See Part II, above.)

Still far short of what many Arab democrats aspire for, the above developments represent marked advances on the democratization road. In a sense, the Arab World is joining what Huntington calls the "Third Wave" of democratization. Should this claim be accepted, the question is how to account for it.

Huntington himself has formulated an elegant paradigm to explain the "third wave". He advances four causal patterns to explain the current world-wide trend of democratization: single cause, parallel development, snowballing, and prevailing nostrum.[32] At least two of these apply to Arab countries which expanded participatory politics. The "single cause" pattern is when one factor occurs apart from events in any of the countries involved in a given wave of democratization. Huntington gives the examples of the emergence of a new super power or some other major change in the international (or regional) distribution of power.[33] The single cause pattern clearly applies to the five GCC countries which have instituted *shura* councils—Saudi Arabia, Qatar, Bahrain, United Arab Emirates, and Oman. Kuwait has been far ahead—with a full parliamentary tradition, though still without a multi-party system. The single cause in their case was the traumatic Gulf crisis (1990-1991).

In at least eight Arab democratizing countries it has been the "parallel

---

[32] Huntington, *The Third Wave*, pp. 31-33.
[33] Huntington, *The Third Wave*, p. 32.

development" cause-pattern at work. As expounded by Huntington, this pattern is "caused by similar developments in the same independent variables."[34] In the eight countries—Egypt, Algeria, Morocco, Tunisia, Mauritania, Sudan, Jordan, and Yemen—the same structural forces seem to have been at work. These were namely the failure of ruling regimes to deliver the goods, services, and employment opportunities to aspiring and pressing social formations (see Part III, above). Facing widespread discontent and experiencing eroding legitimacy, regimes in these countries attempted or were forced to initiate "democratic reforms"—since the mid 1980s.

It may also be argued that some "snowballing" effect has accompanied the two causal-patterns, mentioned above. Thus, a country like Saudi Arabia had toyed with the idea of a *shura* council since the mid 1960s, but remained reluctant in implementing it until the Gulf crisis. And even then, the Saudi regime dragged its feet until all other GCC countries and two neighbors to the north (Jordan) and the south (Yemen) instituted such councils or outright parliamentary systems.

Regardless of the causal patterns, the above democratic advances are still embryonic. It is clear that they have been a product of structural forces, long socio-economic trends, and external factors. But it is not as yet clear whether the forces which helped their initiation are strong enough to sustain them.

c) Democratization: The Reversals

Despite marked advances of Arab democratization in the last decade (1983-1993), there were also major reversals. The most dramatic among these were in Sudan and Algeria. Tunisia and Egypt have also had some difficult moments in their democratization processes.

In 1985, Sudan's civil society formations, mainly professional and labor unions, managed to topple down the military autocratic regime of President Numeiry. A multi-party system was re-instituted; and parliamentary elections were held in 1986. The country looked ready for a democratic take-off. However, quibbling among major political parties in and out of governmental coalitions along with a continued protracted civil war in the south, caused widespread disappointment. A counter coalition of Islamists and a number of middle-rank officers toppled the democratically elected government of al-Sadiq al-Mahdi in mid-1989.

---

[34] Huntington, *The Third Wave*, p. 32.

Since then, a religious-military regime has been in power. It is a unique experience in the history of the new Arab states.

Like Sudan in 1985, Algeria at the end of 1988 seemed to be a promising contender for a transition from a populist autocratic to a pluralist autocratic to a pluralist democratic rule. Constitutional reforms and the institution of a multi-party system were effected for the first time since the country's independence (1962). Some 46 parties were established by 1990. By the first electoral contest for municipal elections, it became clear that religious-based parties, namely the Islamic Salvation Front (FIS) is the most potent political force in Algeria. It outmaneuvered and outperformed the long ruling National Liberation Front (FLN). In a semi-final show-down in December 1991, FIS swept Algeria's parliamentary elections.[35] Its victory sent shock waves at home and abroad. Apprehensions about an Islamic take-over with the possible alteration of the nature of the state and society led the Algerian Army to pre-empt the possibility by a take-over of its own in January 1992. Since then the country has been embroiled in a war of attrition between the security forces and the now outlawed FIS.[36]

Egypt and Tunisia have had to do battle with their respective Islamists in the early 1990s. Their situation has led to a different scenario than that of Sudan and Algeria. It has slowed down or frozen the democratization process which had been well under way in Egypt since 1981 and in Tunisia since 1988. Tunisia seemed to have overpowered its Islamists by a mix of legal and extra-legal means. The regime has lately indicated its willingness for some formula of "power-sharing" with secular opposition parties. Egypt has not been able to overpower its Islamic militants. But the regime has equally given signals of its willingness for a "national dialogue," if not outright power sharing.[37]

The dramatic reversals of democratization in Sudan and Algeria and its stunting in Egypt and Tunisia are not unique to the Arab World. Huntington has documented and analyzed similar reversals after the First and Second waves of democratization elsewhere in the world, including the developed western countries. Nor does he rule out similar reversals in the countries now involved in the Third Wave of democratization.[38]

---

[35] For facts, figures and analysis, see *CSDT* Newsletter, op.cit. January and February 1992.
[36] For a monthly account of such violence, consult *CSDT* Newsletters for the 1992 and 1993 issues.
[37] See *CSDT* Newsletter, op.cit. the November and December 1993 issues.
[38] Huntington, *The Third Wave*, pp. 17-26.

However, the Arab reversals do indicate at least two important facts bearing on the themes of this chapter. The first is the fragile nature of Arab democratization. The second is that Islamic militancy is a force to be contended with. The latter is clearly one of the factors behind, the two dramatic reversals in the Sudan and Algeria, though in a quite different manner. It has also been the real or claimed pretext for the Tunisian and Egyptian regimes to slow down or freeze the democratization process.

Conclusions

Civil society in the Arab World has revitalized itself in the last two decades. Underlying this development is a host of internal, regional, and international factors. Internally, there has been a steady growth of new socio-economic formations which the autocratic and/or populist regimes have no longer been able to accommodate or completely suppress. Regionally, protracted armed conflicts have weakened the state, exposed its impotence in managing such conflicts, and drained its resources. Meanwhile other regional developments have unwittingly empowered new and old constituencies within each Arab state. Internationally, the patron-client relationship between Arab regimes and the two super-powers has either ended or greatly altered. The global wave of democratization has also had its marked "demonstration effect" on a growing number of the Arab new middle classes.

The sprouting organizations of civil society in the Arab World have pressured for greater liberalization across the board—first to make-up for the failure of the state in meeting their socio-economic needs by tending for themselves; and later for its reluctance to respond to their political quest for participation. The sluggish performance of the state vis-a-vis these demands has led many disenfranchised youngsters of the lower middle class to espouse Islamic militancy as a mode of protest.

During the 1980s and early 1990s, the overall scene in the Arab World has appeared as a three-way race for maintaining or seizing power among autocratic regimes, Islamic activists, and democratically disposed forces of civil society. In some Arab countries one variant of the race has been the squeezing of civil society out of the public arena by autocratic regimes and Islamic activists. In another variant both the autocratic regimes and Islamic activists have attempted to win over or appropriate civil society organizations.

This second variant contains the greatest promise for civil society, and hence for the democratization process. For one thing, it has given an ample bargaining power to civil society vis-à-vis the state—to make concessions of a socio-political reformative nature. For another, it has had a moderating effect on several Islamic activist groups. In Jordan, Kuwait, Yemen, and Lebanon this promise has actually been unfolding. In all four, Islamists have accepted the principle of political pluralism, participated along other secular forces in national elections; and are at present all represented in these countries' parliaments. In three of them (Lebanon, Yemen, and Jordan), women have been elected for the first time; and the Islamists did not march out in protest.

The question of whether religious-based political parties could be part of civil society is as overly-academic as the same question with regard to primordially-based associations. In both cases, the ultimate answer is an empirical one. So long as such parties and associations accept the principle of pluralism and observe a modicum of civility in behavior toward the different "other," then they would be integral parts of civil society. In this respect, even the Islamists may evolve into something akin to the "Christian Democrats" in the West or the religious parties in Israel. There is nothing intrinsically Islamic which is in contradiction with the codes of civil society or the principles of democracy.

The variety of Arab regimes' responses to their civil society, regional and international environments in recent years provides ample food for thought. Among other things, such responses indicate that there is as much prospect for further democratization as against it. The modernizing monarchies, namely of Jordan and Morocco, have displayed impressive skills in engineering a smooth transition toward more democratic governance. Their example may tilt the balance in favor of a greater democratic prospect in the entire region. Such prospect would be enhanced by and would enhance peaceful settlements of some of the region's protracted conflicts.

Post Script: Beyond Gaza-Jericho

With the signing of the historic peace accord "Gaza-Jericho First" between Israel and the Palestinian Liberation Organization (September 13, 1993), it has become evident that this agreement transcends its basic purpose of attaining peace and stability in the region. One important element which the agreement will inevitably touch upon is the process of democratization and civil society building in the Arab world.

Primarily, the rudimentary nature of the agreement is inherently democratic. The Palestinian entity (whether manifested in autonomous self-rule or a state) will be created on democratic principles. The agreement stipulates that the Palestinian authority that will be designated to rule over this entity must be elected through a hopefully representative process. As such, Palestine would be the first Arab state to be born democratically.

Beyond the agreement itself, a close look at the Palestinian society reveals that in the absence of a state, the institution s of civil society have matured and are quite prominent. The PLO itself has been a federation of non-state actors. The *Fatah* group with its subsidiaries, the Islamic *Hamas* movement and its subdivisions, and numerous voluntary organs are examples of active organs of civil society. They have forcefully filled the public space between individual Palestinians and the alien authorities under which they have lived since 1948.

On a broader scale, the Gaza-Jericho accord would bring the Arab-Israeli armed struggle to a final phase. The implications of this would be a logical termination to the claims of most Arab regimes who have suspended democracy until a solution for the Palestinian question is reached, e.g., "no voice can be louder than that of the struggle." Substantial Arab resources were consumed in the protracted Arab-Israeli conflict. The end of the conflict is the end of pretexts to procrastinate the onset of democracy.

Palestine will join the ranks of those Arab countries that have already begun their democratization. The experiences of Yemen, Morocco, Kuwait, and Jordan will not only be fortified with that of the neighboring Palestine but they will also act as catalysts to more democratization in other Arab countries. A snowballing effect may very well get under way to include Syria, and even Iraq; in the ranks of democratizing Arab countries.

The Gaza-Jericho accord in its sum-and-substance has created a debate in the Palestinian society and the rest of the Arab world. The Islamist forces, represented in Palestine by *Hamas*, argue that the treaty with Israel is 'treason' to the cause and a capitulation to the Israeli aggressor. Yet most Palestinians, the majority of ruling regimes in the Arab world accept the agreement as a landmark towards peace. Even Syria which might not agree with the accord ideologically, has vowed not to stand in its way. This debate and pluralism of opinion has created an environment akin to that of democracy.

Finally, Gaza-Jericho and the secret negotiations that preceded it, has created a non-retractable mutual acceptance on behalf of both parties. The agreement in its entirety has broken the psychological barrier between both sides, entailing acceptance of past enemies and embracing alternative ideas. As a microcosm, the Arab-Israeli political clasp might be drawn upon from the individual illustration of each Arab state which will be influenced to implement the broad themes of the peace accord in its own civil society.

CHAPTER TWO

ECONOMIC PRESSURES FOR ACCOUNTABLE GOVERNANCE IN THE MIDDLE EAST AND NORTH AFRICA

Alan Richards

Introduction

Can democracy find a home in the Middle East? Many analysts find phrases like "Arab democracy" or "Islamic democracy" oxymoronic. Neo-orientalists assert that the absence of a tradition of civil society,the weakness of the middle classes, and Islamic conceptions of the state all doom any hope of the region's participating in the current world-wide upsurge of democratic politics.

Such arguments are hardly absurd. Only a very foolish analyst would predict a major thrust toward democracy in the lethal political environment of the late 20th century Middle East. And yet, the glimmerings of civil society undeniably glow rather more brightly in the region these days. Turkey has returned to parliamentary democracy, the Egyptian judiciary asserts its prerogatives mo re forcefully than at any time since Nasser's revolution, Jordan has held reasonably fair elections, and the Intifada has stimulated a flowering of Palestinian civil society, which now may get a chance to hold elections for self-government. Could these be harbingers of still better things to come?

The answer could be "Yes", simply because economic imperatives dictate heightened political participation in the region. Ever since independence, industrial technologies and development strategies have fundamentally favored centralization and autocracy. Today the opposite is true. Although the legacy of past decades will not be easily overcome, in the modern international economy of information technologies, discriminating consumers, and intense competition, only economies which are less centralized than those of the Arab world stand a chance of survival. The Turks recognized this over a decade ago, and have made important (though still inadequate) strides toward creating a modern economy. The Arab world is further behind, while the Iranians have hardly begun. Increasingly, however, national leaders recognize the necessity of change: structural adjustment and economic liberalization are on the agenda of nearly all regional states.

I argue here that successful economic liberalization will require increased political participation in some form. That is, I shall make an "instrumentalist" case for greater citizen political activity. Such an argument has the advantage of avoiding metaphysical questions such as the compatibility of "democracy" and "Islam". The argument here is far simpler: coping with the challenges of the food, jobs, and investment will require greater integration into the international economy; such economic changes imply enlarging the role of the private sector, widening the scope of the rule of law, and more generally restructuring the state's relations with its citizens. In short, expanded political participation will be a necessary tool in the struggle to forge a successful "Arab", "Turkish" or "Iranian" capitalism in the information age.

I am not arguing that economic forces make democratization inevitable. There are always choices in politics, but these choices are constrained by economic realities for the simple reason that if economic challenges are not met, socio-political problems accumulate and the range of choices narrows accordingly. In particular, old-style "Arab socialist" options are no longer viable. If rulers want to survive, they will be forced to make some concessions to economic logic. Such concessions can only be avoided if a regime has a dependable source of income whose acquisition generates few political demands. Although oil-rents provided such politically easy-money in the past, they shrunk markedly during the middle and late 1980s, and the prospects for future oil prices are uncertain. The choice has narrowed to the stark one between accommodation to economic reality (which, I shall argue, has political implications) or a descent into chaos.

Let us be clear: just because solving (or even ameliorating) mounting economic problems requires wider political participation does not mean that it will happen. Failure is possible, even likely for many countries. Economic suicide is a real alternative; challenges may not be met, and explosions are real dangers. Lebanon, Bosnia, and Somalia constitute all-too-vivid alternatives to economic progress, as do the continuing famines in Sudan.[1] Economic determinism will serve us poorly. But equally, ignoring economic forces will deceive us as to the consequences of policy choices. The negative model of repression, violence, and chaos

---

[1] These occur (for the Bashir regime) conveniently far from CNN cameras.

is feasible; the only positive alternative is broader participation and the rule of law.

Economic History on a Postage Stamp:
Centralizing and Decentralizing Eras

The economic history of the region since independence may be usefully divided into three eras:

1) the state-led, import-substitution era ("ISI" hereafter) (roughly, the 1930/1950-1973),

2) the era of the oil boom (mid 1970s to mid 1980s), and

3) the current era of structural adjustment (mid 1980s to date).[2]

The first two eras were fundamentally centralizing eras, in which the role of the state expanded. By contrast, our modern era is one of decentralization, for reasons of both market structure and technology. The political challenge is to build decentralized political economies atop the institutional sediment of earlier, centralizing times.

During the ISI period, regional states took very large responsibilities for economic management, extending their control to the micro level through state-owned enterprises and detailed price controls. Reasons for such actions ranged from the absence of a "majority ethnic" bourgeoisie (e.g., Turkey) to the accepted wisdom of economic development specialists, to more specific ideological commitments (e.g., the Ba'th in Syria and Iraq). In some cases, such as Egypt, the vagaries of international conflict also played a role in widespread nationalization of industry: British and French firms were nationalized because of the Suez War of 1956, Belgians during the Congo Crisis of 1960, and other incidents. Political and social factors pushed regional states to expand their control of the economy. State autonomy was reinforced by the "Social Contract" of the Nasserists: in exchange for expanded opportunities in housing, employment, and education, the mass of the population acquiesced in authoritarian rule. The ISI era was the age of centralization of power par excellence.

Industrial technologies of the time facilitated this trend. Although the centralization almost certainly went too far even by the standards of the day, industries with substantial economies of scale (e.g., heavy metals,

---

[2] Of course, the details of dates will vary from one country to another. In particular, Turkey pioneered both ISI and liberalizati on in the region. Space permits only the roughest sketch here. For more detail, see Alan Richards and John Waterbury, *A Political Economy of the Middle East* (Boulder, CO: Westview Press, 1990), chapters 7-9.

cement, canning) or with restricted domestic markets in relatively small, poor countries (e.g., consumer goods like textiles) could, at least initially, be centrally managed without economic collapse. Technological change was also somewhat less rapid than today, especially in the "mature" industries of consumer and intermediate goods upon which ISI drives focused. Slower technological change further concealed the inefficiencies of central planning. The example of Soviet industrialization and post-war recovery and the wider intellectual climate which it engendered also facilitated the centralization of the industrial economies of the region. In the short run, the deleterious implications of ISI for international competitiveness could be avoided, whether through foreign aid, or, for states blessed by geology, by oil exports.

The second period, the oil boom era, was, if anything, even more strongly centralizing. Everywhere outside of the United States, sub-soil mineral rights belong to the state. The massive infusion of revenues which accompanied the quadrupling (1974) and doubling (1979) of oil prices therefore flowed directly into the governments' coffers. Oil revenues were almost uniquely centralizing, because they constituted almost a pure economic and political asset for the government, generating no corresponding political liability, like miners to placate. Very few workers are needed to produce and market oil: contrast, for example, copper and its role in the political economy of Chile.[3] Oil revenues also obviated the need to tax the citizenry, thus avoiding the "Boston Tea Party Problem" of coping with the demands for political participation by those taxed. Even states which were closely allied with the Unite d States and ideologically committed to the private sector like Saudi Arabia found themselves creating state-owned enterprises; rath er despite themselves, the Saudis emulated their abhorred Arab Socialist cousins. Oil rents were a strong force for centralization in all oil-exporting countries.

The oil boom shaped all regional economies, including those without significant oil deposits, through the mechanism of labor migration. In sharp contrast to oil exports, however, labor emigration and remittances were decentralizing: scarce foreign exchange accrued to individuals, not states. Governments which hoped that such foreign exchange would enter the formal banking system were forced to offer realistic exchange rates. In a certain sense, structural adjustment in the region began here. At the same time, labor migration from Yemen, Jordan, Palestine, and

---

[3] See, e.g., Theodore Moran, *Multinational Corporations and the Politics of Dependence: Copper in Chile* (Princeton, NJ: Princeton University Press, 1974).

Egypt widened the horizons, in Egypt for the first time in history, of young poor rural and urban men.[4] No country in the region (possibly excepting Iran) now has a "peasantry" in the old, classical sense of rural people whose horizons extend no further than the next village. This phenomenon, combined with spreading education, bodes ill for rigidly authoritarian, isolationist political systems.

We are now fully into the structural adjustment era. In the wake of the mid-1980s collapse of oil prices, every state in the region, including Saudi Arabia, has had to practice budgetary stringency. But structural adjustment must go well beyond mere austerity; fundamental institutional reform is needed to overcome the pernicious problems inherited from the previous two eras. Fundamentally, the contradictions of over-centralization have strangled growth even as the numbers and wants of consumers continue to multiply: population growth remains very high in the region, and as noted in the preceding paragraph, the "boys down on the farm have seen Paree": expectations have risen dramatically. Adjusting economies to overcome the baleful legacy of the past while stimulating growth to satisfy the expanding wants of a growing population is, after the (related) problem of maintaining order, the challenge facing Middle Eastern economies and polities in the 1990s.

The catalogue of ills of ISI is all too familiar to students of development policy: biases against traded goods, especially exports; excessive capital intensity and therefore inadequate job creation; discrimination against agriculture; accumulating international debt. Such difficulties were exacerbated by the "Dutch Disease" of the oil-boom era.[5] These problems are the mid-wife of our age, the "structural adjustment era". Unfortunately, however, the centralizing legacy of the past, institutionalized throughout the political economy, is ill-suited to coping with the demands of the present.

The imperatives are evident: countries must be able to compete in today's information-based, highly competitive international economy.

---

[4] Between 1973 and 1985, roughly one-third of all rural adult Egyptian men worked at some point in one of the oil-exporting countries. Never before in that country's six thousand year history had anything remotely comparable to this taken place. See Alan Richards, "Agricultural Employment, Wages, and Government Policy During and After the Oil Boom," Handoussa and Potter, eds., *Employment and Structural Adjustment: Egypt in the 1990s* (Cairo, American University in Cairo Press for the International Labour Organization, 1991), pp. 57-94.

[5] The "Dutch Disease" afflicts countries with a fixed nominal exchange rate that experience a sudden influx of foreign exchange. Without very careful (and politically difficult) management, the real exchange rate quickly becomes overvalued, biasing price signals against traded goods production in industry and agriculture.

"Decoupling", always chimerical, is not a realistic option: Middle Eastern states must export, and must accelerate job creation. Only aggressive export-drives, with an expanded role for the private sector, has a chance of doing this. We have long known that private sector organizations can respond far more quickly than public sector ones, not only because of their superior incentives, but also because of their ability to focus on a single goal.

But not only the imperative of greater efficiency dictates decentralization. Modern technologies are inherently decentralizing: computers, faxes and other information technologies cannot be controlled centrally. The increasingly integrated world simply has too much information; international competition is so keen that only specialists can keep up with developments, and only those with information can respond successfully. Both the importance and logic of the acquisition of information and the (much older) greater and more rapid responsiveness of private economic actors suggest that there is a powerful economic imperative to decentralization of the political economy. There is no reason whatsoever why the Middle East is exempt from this trend. Indeed, as the next section shows, there are three specific regional economic problems which strongly suggest that the imperative is as great in this region as anywhere in the world.

The Core Challenges

Three core problems dominate the current structural adjustment era: jobs, food, and money.

a) Jobs

There is a demographic time-bomb ticking in the region: the growing supply of labor. During the past half-decade, the rate of growth of the labor force for the region as a whole was slightly above 3% per year (3.13% per year), the highest rate of growth of any major region in the world. [6] (See Table 1.) The labor force will be roughly 1/8 larger in 5 years, and more than 1/3 (36%) larger in ten years. More concretely,

---

[6] Corresponding figures for other parts of the developing world, 1985-2000 are: South Asia, 2.2%; Latin America and Caribbean, 2.6% ; sub-Saharan Africa, 2.6%; "High-performing Asian Economies" (i.e., Indonesia, Korea, Malaysia, Singapore, Thailand, and Taiwan), 1 .8%. The World Bank, *The East Asian Miracle: Economic Growth and Public Policy* (New York: Oxford University Press, 1993), p. 264.

Table 1: Labor Force Growth Rates, Selected Countries

Country	Period		
	1980-85	1985-91	1990-2000
Algeria	3.5%	3.7%	3.6%
Egypt	2.6%	2.5%	2.9%
Iran	3.2%	4.1%	4.2%
Iraq		3.1%	4.2%
Jordan	4.3%	4.3%	4.9%
Mauretania	2.7%	2.8%	
Lebanon		3.5%	2.4%
Morocco	3.2%	3.2%	3.3%
Syria		3.5%*	4.0%
Tunisia	3.1%	3.1%	3.0%
Turkey	2.3%	2.1%	
Yemen	2.7%	3.0%	4.5%
		*1985-90	

Sources: World Bank; I.L.O.

during the 1990s, the regional labor force will have grown by roughly 20 million; between now and the end of the decade, it will grow by roughly 18 million—which is about the combined size of the current labor forces of Egypt and Tunisia, or of the combined current labor force of the Maghreb (Morocco, Algeria, Tunisia). Notice that for some countries, the labor force is growing considerably faster than this regional average; notice also that for many Arab countries (Egypt, Iraq, Jordan, Syria, and Yemen), growth is accelerating. Although growth is roughly constant for others (Algeria, Morocco, Tunisia) only in Egypt and Lebanon are the rates less than 3% per year. As these stubbornly high rates are applied to larger bases, we have a phenomenon of demographic momentum, which ensures ever larger additions to the labor force.

These high rates are the result of two, somewhat contradictory forces: rapid past population growth, and currently increasing rates of female labor force participation. Fueled by poverty, and especially, low female literacy and autonomy, population growt h has been rapid in the region.[7] On the other hand, as many more younger women are now educated than was formerly the case, they have begun looking for jobs, a phenomenon which contributes to the high growth of the labor force. This phenomenon is in itself a source of much social tension in the region, as sociologists have long noted. Even if this were not so, finding jobs for all of these young people would be a daunting task.

---

[7] See Richards and Waterbury, chapter 4 for a detailed discussion of Middle Eastern population growth in international comparative perspective.

Table 2. A Compendium of Unemployment Rates for Selected MENA Countries

Country	Year	Age Group	Unemployment Rate	Source
Algeria	1990	16-65	19.7%	(1)
	1990	15-19	64%	(2)
	1990	20-24	46%	(2)
	1990	25-29	17%	(2)
Egypt	1986	6-65	14.7%	(3)
	1988	6-65	7.1%	(1)
Iraq	1987	10+	5.1%	(1)
Jordan	1991	15+	14.4%	(1)
	1991	—	23.4%	(4)
Kuwait	1985	15+	2.7%	(1)
Morocco	1986	15+	8.6%	(5)
	1990	15+	15.8%	(6)
	1991	15-24	31%	(6)
	1991	25-34	18%	(6)
O.P.T.*	1991	15+	7.9%	(1)
	1990	—	13-15%	(7)
	1990	—	30-40%	(8)
Sudan	1991	—	17%	(9)
Syria	1983	10+	3.3%	(1)
Tunisia	1986/7	18-59	14.1%	(1)
	1990	—	16%	(10)
	1992	—	15.8%	(11)
Yemen	1986	10+	6.2%	(1)
	1990	—	25%	(12)

Sources:
(1) Al-Qudsi, et. al. (1992)   (5) Morrisson (1991)   (9) UNDP (1991)
(2) UNDP (1992)   (6) E.I.U. (1992)   (10) Stevenson & Van Adams (1992)
(3) CAPMAS-1986 Census   (7) Israeli Govt (1992) (11) Tunis, Min. Planning (1992)
(4) UNESCWA (1991)   (8) P.R.I. (1992)   (12) World Bank (1992)

Job creation has failed to match the growth of job seekers. Given the noxious mixture of the anti-employment bias of ISI and the slowdown of growth due to the collapse of the oil boom, it is unsurprising that unemployment is rising while real wages are either stagnant or falling. The precise combination of wage versus quantity adjustments, of falling wages versus rising unemployment, remains opaque. We have very little reliable wage data for most countries, and unemployment statistics are equally spotty. (See Table 2.) Estimates of unemployment differ widely, for several reasons. First, definitions of "unemployment" vary. The International Labor Organization of the United Nations defines "employed" as anyone who worked, for remuneration (wage or self-employed) one hour of the sample survey reference week. That is, you are

*Ed: Occupied Palestinian Territories.

"unemployed" if you worked zero hours in same time period and were actively looking for work. This is clearly a very restrictive definition. When used in the West Bank and Gaza, for example, it gives an unemployment rate of 7.9%—this in the year when all males, and most females, were under a 24 hour curfew for the six weeks of the Gulf War! By contrast, Yussef Sayigh has been quoted in the press as saying that it is about 60% in Gaza—a number which is obviously using a very different definition. Few regional governments other than Israel use this definition. Some use the "self-definition" method, which asks people whether or not they "consider themselves to have been employed" during past week. By some accounts, this definition would roughly double unemployment rates.[8]

Such an approach also opens door to question of "what is a job"? For example, many of the educated young who work part-time in informal sector do not consider their work to be "real jobs". But by the economic definition of employment, they are employed.

Some Algerian government officials believe that reported unemployment rate is roughly doubled over what it "really is", because of the inclusion of those disgruntled individuals who are employed in the informal sector. The World Bank concurs. Within rural immigrant community of Istanbul, "poor women may spend up to fifty hours a week producing goods for export, yet deny that they actually "work".[9]

Governments sometimes use hybrid, ad hoc methods of defining unemployment, as when Jordan's Ministry of Labor counts those applying for jobs with government (in 1991, this yielded an "unemployment rate" of 23.4%), or in Egypt, where the unemployed are sometimes measured from list of those "waiting for a government job"—which requires you to be officially "unemployed" while you wait—even though the wait can be up to 8 years! This practice inflated the 1986 Census unemployment data. Differences in age groups (how old must you be before you are counted? 18? 16? 15? Surely not 6, as in the Egyptian Census of 1986. The timing of surveys also renders cross-country comparisons treacherous.

---

[8] e.g., Nader Fergany, "A Characterization of the Employment Problem in Egypt," Handoussa and Potter, eds., pp. 25-56; Al-Qudsi, Sulayman, Ragui Assaad and Radwan Shaban, "Labor Markets in the Arab Countries: A Survey." Paper presented at First Annual Conference on Development Economies, Initiative to Encourage Economic Research in the Middle East and North Africa, sponsored by the World Bank , Cairo, Egypt, June 4-6, 1993.

[9] Jenny B. White, *Money Makes Us Relatives: Women's Labor in Urban Turkey* (Austin, TX: University of Texas Press, 1994).

In short, all numbers on unemployment in the region must be taken with several truck-loads of salt. We should use our common sense, economic logic—and round numbers. But although the definitions may be in doubt, the frustrations are not. Unquestionably the greatest single social challenge facing regional leaders is providing jobs for the expanding, very young labor force. Take the case of Egypt, for example. There, some 6 million jobs must be created during the 1990s simply to provide jobs to new workers (that is, with no reduction in employment, increase in real wages, or expanded female labor force participation). In an economy whose total labor force in 1990 was perhaps 14 million, this is a daunting challenge.

The problem is complicated by the fact that so many job seekers are young. As Table 2 shows, unemployment is often related to youth. In Morocco, for example, nearly half (45.5%) of the unemployed are between ages of 15 and 24. A similar picture appears throughout the region (see Table 1). Of course, youth unemployment rates always exceed those of older workers. For example, in OECD countries, youth unemployment roughly 2-3 times higher than prime age unemployment.[10] The usual reasons given for this phenomenon are that the young can change jobs more easily than older workers, and can afford to spend more time unemployed while they look for a job. Part of the region's high unemployment rate, then, is what we may call demographic unemployment, in which the high proportion of young people in the labor market automatically raises the overall unemployment rate. In Egypt, between two census years of 1976 and 1986, the percentage of the labor force between 15-24 years old rose from 22% (1976) to 31% (1986). This fact alone would have raised the unemployment rate.

But this is only part of the picture. Many young job seekers, including those who are unemployed while they "wait" or "look for a job" have been poorly prepared by their education. Their schools provided few of the skills which are needed by the private, formal sector. Instead, they have the worst of both worlds: they have been educated enough to find manual labor demeaning (so they often refuse such jobs), but they do not have the skills to match their aspirations. In Jordan, for example, unemployment stands at perhaps 20%, while large numbers of Egyptians

---

[10] In the US in 1990, for example, when total unemployment was 5.5%, corresponding figures for those aged 16-19 were 16.2%; for 20-25, 9.6%, and for those older than 25, 4.4%. Compare Algeria, where, in 1990, total unemployment was (guessed at) 18.4%, while for 15-19 year olds it was 64%; for 20-24, 46%, and for 25-29, 17%.

clean the streets, harvest the tomatoes, and so on, because young, educated Jordanians find such work unacceptable. Such strictures recall Gunnar Myrdal's phrase, "unemployment is a bourgeois luxury".

During the first two eras of recent economic history, the public sector expanded to create jobs for the young. But this is no longer possible.[11] The public sector cannot provide these jobs. Government payrolls cannot continue to expand; indeed, the imperatives of structural adjustment are already shrinking them. Nor can the other safety valve of the past, emigration abroad, be counted upon any longer. Neither the EC nor the Gulf States are likely to generate employment opportunities for young Maghrebis, Egyptians, Turks and Yemenis as they did in past decades. If only by default, the sole hope of coping with the rising demographic tide is a flexible, rapidly growing private sector pursuing comparative-advantage-generated niches in the international economy. Entrepreneurs, if left alone, will find such niches (although governments can and must assist them with information and other logistical support). But above all, investors need to feel secure that their illiquid investments will not be confiscated. Only if governments can succeed in creating a suitable investment climate will Middle Eastern nations have a chance at solving the problem of job creation in the years ahead.

b) Food

Much nonsense is written about "food security" in the region. Food security is an insurance concept: ensuring food security means guaranteeing that consumers are reasonably certain of being able to eat properly. All too often, students of the region conflate food security with food self-sufficiency. Politicians, in particular, seem unable to resist the Siren Song of alimentary autarchy. Food self-sufficiency for most countries in the region is impossible, and this is no bad thing.

The "stylized facts" of the political economy of food during the oil boom decade may be sketched as follows. Rapidly increasing populations and swiftly growing per capita incomes quickly raised the demand for food. The increase in incomes was not limited to oil exporters, but was

---

[11] Ten years ago, John Waterbury pointed out that new public sector jobs were not being created in Egypt and that "Old Bureaucrats" with job security were "sitting on" (now not expanding) the number of places in public sector, blocking access by young people. *The Egypt of Nasser and Sadat: The Political Economy of Two Regimes* (Princeton, NJ: Princeton University Press, 1982). It is worth po ndering whether part of the conflict between Arab Nationalists (such as those in the Algerian FLN) and Islamists is a generational conflict of "fathers versus sons."

also enjoyed by the poorer countries, thanks to large-scale migration for work in the oil exporting countries. Domestic supply response was sluggish, thanks to the "Dutch Disease", to a continuation of ISI policies of taxing the agricultural sector, and to limited investment in the agricultural sector. Cereal production was especially weak, caught between rising labor costs, marginal rainfall, and government-imposed price disincentives. By contrast, the production of higher value crops like fruits, vegetables, and livestock did much better. There were also two countries whose agricultural performances stood out above the others: Syria and Sudan. But almost everywhere, the "food gap" could be plugged with imports: abundant foreign exchange and improving terms of trade permitted a dramatic increase in food (and especially cereal) imports.

The rise in the percentage of Arab consumers' food which came from abroad was disquieting to policy makers, who feared that reliance on foreign supplies was "too risky", whether economically or politically. Responses to these fears were already evident in the early 1980s. Subsidies of inputs usually either continued or increased, while taxation of output through price policies typically eased. Arab governments often began to allocate a higher share of investment to agriculture, and many urban entrepreneurs entered the production of horticultural crops, poultry, and livestock. Much hope was placed on the development of Sudan as the "bread basket" of the Arab World, and Arab bi-lateral and multilateral aid flowed into projects in Central Sudan (Darfur, Kordofan, Blue Nile). Visions of an Arab world self-sufficient in most food danced before the weary eyes of agricultural and strategic planners.

This doomed vision always rested upon a fundamental confusion: food self-sufficiency is neither necessary nor sufficient for food security. Food security recognizes that we all live in a risky world, and seeks to devise public policies to minimize the risk that consumption of food will fall below some minimally acceptable level. A country (or a household) can attain such security in three (not one) ways: by producing the food, by trading for it, or by having it given to them. Governments' relentless pursuit of food self-sufficiency has failed, on its own terms: Arab countries are, on balance, no better (or worse) off today with respect to food self-sufficiency than they were a decade ago. However, their food security positions are often more precarious.

During the 1980s, rate of growth of the demand for food decelerated, and was almost exclusively the result of population growth.[12] The rate

---

[12] The rate of growth of the demand for food in given by the formula: $D^* = n + ey^*$, where

of population growth for the Arab world as a whole during the 1980s was just under 3% (2.89%) per year, rising from roughly 155 million to some 208 million.[13] The Arab world "added an Egypt" during the 1980s (some 53 million new people, roughly the population of Egypt in 1990). There was no tendency for the overall rate to decelerate during the decade.[14] Such a rate of population growth implies a doubling of population by 2015, when there will be 415 million Arabs.

Although total fertility rates (approximately, "the number of children which an average woman will have") have fallen in nearly all countries, even under optimistic scenarios, Arab countries' populations will not stabilize for at least another generation. There will continue to be many more mouths to feed. On the other hand, in sharp contrast to the decade of the oil boom, per capita incomes stagnated in most of the region. Of Arab countries reporting the necessary information to the World Bank, only Egypt's per capita income grew faster than 2.0% per year (and there are reasons to think that this is an overestimate).

Two interrelated forces were responsible for this dreary performance: 1) the end of the oil boom, with its large increases in national income through the direct (oil exporters) or indirect (labor exporters) collections of oil rent, and 2) the need for structural adjustment, as the deficiencies of a former era of state-led, import substituting industrialization became increasingly evident. Of course, the Gulf Crisis and War had very serious negative consequences for incomes in the region. Labor exporters whose leaders were perceived to have backed the losers (Jordan, Yemen, Occupied Territories) were especially hard hit.

What of the supply response? Most Arab countries' agricultural sectors managed to keep up with population growth during the 1980s, but only in Egypt and Morocco did farm production outstrip population increases.[15] For most countries, there was little change in cereal self-sufficiency. Only Morocco and Saudi Arabia reduced their dependence on trade as a source of staple food consumption during the decade. Despite Egypt's impressive growth, cereal consumption expanded slightly more rapidly than population, a fact which is consistent with Egypt's positive rate of per capita income growth. For most Arab countries,

---

D^* = rate of growth of demand; n = population growth rate; e = income elasticity of demand for food; and y^* = rate of growth of per capita income.

[13] Unless otherwise specified, all data in this section were taken from the FAO *Production Yearbooks*. Unless otherwise stated, all growth rates are OLS growth rates.

[14] That is, augmenting the usual OLS growth equation with "time squared" (i.e., ln pop = a + b time + c time*exp 2), yielded an insignificant coefficient for "time squared."

[15] That is, the OLS growth rates are statistically insignificant.

population grew, cereal production stagnated, and cereal self-sufficiency remained unchanged. It follows that per capita consumption of cereals declined in most Arab countries. Cereal self-sufficiency of most Arab countries remained unchanged, while "cereal security" declined for many Arabs.

The increases in output were largely the results of additional inputs. The arable area continued to increase in those countries that experienced the strongest agricultural growth, and irrigated land expanded nearly everywhere. Fertilizer use increased at a diminishing rate. Mechaniation, especially tractorization, continued unabated throughout the region. The total number of tractors in the Arab world rose by over 55% during the 1980s, an increase of over 138,000 tractors. The farm labor force either continued to grow or resumed growing after an "oil-boom induced decline" in most countries. The oil boom of the 1970s drew labor out of agriculture: in Algeria, Iraq, Jordan, Syria, Yemen, Libya, and Egypt, the adult male farm labor force actually declined during the 1970s. However, the 1980s largely reversed this "Dutch Disease" phenomenon in all but Iraq, Jordan, and Libya. The numbers for Jordan might well look different today, in the wake of the return of migrants from the Gulf. In short, Arab agriculture used more land, more water, more fertilizer, more machines, and more labor—all just to keep up with population growth.

In a sense, Arab countries held the line on food self-sufficiency while permitting (or being unable to prevent) a deterioration in food security. The "relative success" on self-sufficiency was in an important sense the fruit of stagnation: only because per capita incomes stagnated was domestic supply able to keep pace with domestic demand, now reduced to population growth alone. Further, the decline in the apparent per capita consumption of cereals is disturbing. This, combined with continued rapid expansion of luxury foods like fruits and vegetables is consistent with a hypothesis of increasing inequality of income distribution in many countries. It is also very likely that poverty rose in most countries, simply because of the failure of growth. Such a development bodes ill for food security at the household level.

In any case, it is simply false to equate "food security" with "food self-sufficiency" in the Arab world: relying on "own production" is highly risky. The common conflation of food security with self-reliance tacitly assumes that own production is a less risky mode of satisfying domestic demand than is dependence upon international trade. Evidence suggests otherwise. Cereal production remained highly variable in the region, as weather shocks continued to plague staple food production. Only Egypt, with its entirely irrigated agriculture, escaped from repeated weather shocks. In Syria, for example, food production would fall below the avera ge by more than 5% every third year. Cereal production remains a very risky gamble on the rains. There is little evidence of either marked improvement or deterioration in variability over time for the region as a whole. Such variability has important implications for food security.

Fundamentally, the region cannot escape its geography: water is, and will become increasingly, scarce in the region. So long as water is needed for photosynthesis, there will be serious barriers to the achievement of "self-sufficiency" in food or agriculture anywhere outside of Turkey or (potentially) Sudan. Even in more geographically favored areas, attaining self-sufficiency extracts a heavy price in foregone incomes and wasted resources. The ecological dimension should also not be neglected: Saudi Arabia's vaunted self-sufficiency in wheat, achieved by heavy financial subsidies and unsustainable exploitation of ground water, has been aptly described as "paying money the Kingdom can no longer afford, to grow wheat surpluses it doesn't need, while consuming water it can't replace"[16] Food self-sufficiency is an expensive, wasteful, and ultimately doomed food security strategy.

This hardly means that attention to agricultural development is misplaced. Certainly more sophisticated production and marketing technologies must be developed and diffused throughout the region. As the water constraint binds more tightly in the years ahead, continued agricultural growth will require increasingly sophisticated irrigation technologies and management systems, which in turn will necessitate more effective collective action at the local level and heightened political participation. Fundamentally, irrigation systems must change from being "supply driven" (i.e., centrally planned) as they are at present, to being more "demand driven", that is, responsive to the needs of small groups of farmers. Water pricing can help, but for administrative reasons, prices will probably have to be charged to small groups of farmers rather than to individuals in most gravity-flow (e.g., river-based) irrigation systems. The formation and heightened effectiveness of "water users associations" is a necessary condition for promoting food security in the years ahead. Put bluntly, the expansion of political participation

---

[16] Douglas F. Graham, *Saudi Arabia Unveiled* (Dubugue, IA: Kendall/Hunt Publishing, 1991), p. 152.

is a necessary condition for more efficient allocation of the region's scarcest resource, water.

Even with the most sophisticated of irrigation systems, growing populations and (one hopes) rising per capita incomes will doom inefficient food self-sufficiency schemes. Fortunately, food security can be obtained in another way: through trade. Few would argue that Singapore or Korea fail to enjoy food security. Middle Eastern political economies will have to emulate other economically successful but agricultural resource poor nations to achieve food security in the 1990s and beyond. Increasingly, Middle Eastern nations must export in order to eat.

c) Money

This brings us to the final critical challenge facing the region, the shortage of capital. Given the vast financial resources of the Gulf, it may seem odd to posit such a shortage. However, the Gulf War has made it clear that the capital-rich states will invest their money only where it earns the highest return. Appeals to "Arab Unity", always hollow, have now been relegated to the history books. Calls by analysts to "share the oil wealth" are equally misplaced. Instead, the call should be to create a climate so that already existing savings can be properly allocated.

Many countries of the region do have a "debt problem". The combined debt of countries of the region is now just under $300 billion. (See Table 3). Egypt skillfully used its participation in the Gulf War Coalition to reduce its debt by roughly 50%, stanching some $2 billion of yearly debt-service outflows. But in Morocco and Jordan, for example, debt service payments consume nearly one-third of exports. All countries of the region compete with Eastern Europe and the countries of the former Soviet Union for capital investment. And the need for investment in more sophisticated technologies for production and distribution, for cities and farms, for communications and educational facilities, is extremely large. To take only one example, the World Bank estimates that the West Bank and Gaza will need something like $2.4 billion over 5 years. The government of Lebanon believes that it will need over $10 billion, merely to repair infrastructure. The needs in Egypt and the Maghreb are far larger.

But international indebtedness is not the root of regional capital scarcity. Neither can we blame deficient savings propensities: there is no evidence whatsoever that Middle Easterners do not save. Egypt offers a useful illustration: it has been estimated that the "off-shore" holdings of

Table 3. Debt and Trade, Selected Middle Eastern Countries

Country	External Debt (Million $, 1991)	Debt. GNP (Percent, 1991)	Debt Service Ratio (Percent, 1991)	Food Import Dependency Ratio (Percent 1986-88)	Growth of Exports (Percent per year) 1980-91	Growth of Imports (Percent per year) 1980-91	Net Remittances (Billion $, 1990)
Algeria	28.636	70.4%	73.7%	70.7%	2.4%	-5.6%	0.321
Egypt	40.571	113.4%	18.7%	45.2%	2.8%	-2.3%	3.744
Iran	11.511	11.5%	3.9%	n.a.	14.7%	7.9%	n.a.
Iraq	81.456	n.a.	235.4%	n.a.	7.8%	4.4%	
Jordan	8.641	226.9%	20.9%	85.2%	6.9%	-0.8%	0.5
Mauritania	2.299	214.7%	15.8%	57.2%	5.6%	3.1%	0.0
Morocco	21.219	80.0%	27.8%	28.1%	5.9%	3.8%	1.995
Sudan	15.907	n.a.	n.a.	14.5%	-1.2%	-4.0%	0.188
Syria	16.815	103.8%	n.a.	29.1%	20.6%	3.9%	0.375
Tunisia	8.296	68.2%	22.7%	59.3%	5.6%	1.5%	0.591
Turkey	50.242	48.1%	30.5%	5.2%	7.2%	7.4%	3.246
Yemen	6.471	88.1%	7.3%	62.1%	n.a.	n.a.	1.366

Source: Iraq: Petroleum Finance Corporation; all others: UNDP, World Bank

hard currency by Egyptians is some $40-50 billion, roughly equal to Egypt's pre-Gulf War international debt. In 1988, gross investment in Egypt was about LE 8.4 billion, or some $3 billion at 1988 official exchange rates. Middle Eastern savings are abundant.

The capital problem in the Middle East is fundamentally institutional. First, highly inefficient statist economies generate far less "bang for the buck" than do market economies. Algeria invested about 40% of its GDP for decades, one of the highest investment rates in the world. Although growth was respectable during the oil boom era, the country failed to create viable, competitive industries and farms which could compete internationally. As we have seen, it also failed dismally to create sufficient jobs. Second, savers and investors (with good reason) fear and distrust national governments. Specifically, they fear that their savings will be expropriated either directly by state decree, or by stealth via rampant inflation and overvalued exchange rates. Unsurprisingly, they hold their savings off-shore or in highly liquid form. Only if genuine political reform creates secure private property rights and an independent judicial system to enforce those rights will the savings of Middle Easterners be placed inside their own countries, and, still more difficult to induce, in the kind of illiquid, fixed capital investment (like factories) which the region needs to produce the goods to sell abroad to buy food and to create jobs.

From an instrumentalist, economic point of view, it makes little difference whether the legal system which protects property is based on common law, the Code Napoleon, or the *shari'ah*. Far more important than any of the details of the relative efficiencies of these different systems is the need for some predictable legal system to replace the arbitrary, confiscatory state power which has dominated regional political economies since the 1950s.

Do Dictators Do It Better?

In summary, the region must export in order to eat and in order to create jobs. The capital needed for such a massive push must largely come from its own citizens. They, and foreign investors, will only take the risks associated with tying up money in illiquid industrial investments if political systems cease to be arbitrary and capricious. At the same time, only the private sector can meet the challenge of increasingly sharp international competition in the age of information technologies. The conclusion is inescapable: only a more decentralized political economy with greater reliance on contract and the rule of law has even a chance of coping with the problems of the end of the twentieth century and beyond.

Some dispute the connection between solving the economic problems and more accountable governance. Many believe that only dictators can implement sweeping economic reforms. Adherents of this view assert that although there may be long-run connections between market economies and political democracy, only dictators can break the hammer-lock which the vested interests in state-owned enterprises, the bureaucracy, and their private-sector contracting cronies have placed on the policy process.[17] After smashing grid -lock, dictators with a strong commitment to economic growth can then allegedly pursue the necessary, albeit painful, stabilization and structural adjustment policies which alone can lead to prosperity. We are told that dictators (usually relying extensively on the military and the police) can ensure that their orders are carried out: they have solved the "principal-agent problem", through terror if need be. Partisans of this view illustrate their argument with countries like Pinochet's Chile and Park's Korea: strong-man governments which relentlessly, if ruthlessly, pursued economic growth with great success. These analysts conclude that liberalizing both economies and polities is like mixing oil and water.

The argument is simple, elegant, widely-held—and wrong. The argument fails both in general and in the specific regional context of the Near East. The errors of the "dictators do it better" school concern both the goals which dictators pursue and their implementation of even laudable goals. Quite apart from the (powerful, and for Americans, possibly determining) ethical argument that even "successful" dictators had no right to impose their policies without the consent of those affected, as a practical matter, the argument fails as an exercise in political economy for both conceptual and empirical reasons.

The argument fails as a general proposition. It is obvious that dictatorship is not a sufficient condition for economic growth. The reason is simple: dictators may have goals other than the pursuit of sound economic policies. They may be less concerned with "getting prices right" and more concerned with keeping their bank accounts full; the "kleptocracies" of much of sub-Saharan Africa are cases in point. Even if dictators are committed to economic growth, their very authoritarian-

---

[17] For example, Deepak Lal: "a courageous, ruthless and perhaps undemocratic government is required to ride roughshod over ... newly-created special interest groups." *The Poverty of "Development Economics"* (London: Institute of Economic Affairs, 1983), p. 33.

ism permits them to persist in egregious policy errors. Governments, like all the rest of us, make mistakes. The difference is that accountable governments are forced to take corrective action. No such strictures need bind the dictator. Such mistakes (often very costly) typically occur precisely because of the regime's single-mindedness: the dictator (really, his closest advisors) adhere to a vision or theory of development, whatever the cost. Examples range from the Pinochet government's relentless pursuit of laissez-faire macroeconomic policies even as unemployment soared toward one-third of the labor force in the early 1980s to the ghoulish disaster of the Chinese Great Leap Forward, in which perhaps 20 million souls perished. Economics is a highly imperfect science, and dogmatism, so often associated with the authoritarian mind, sooner or later leads to disaster.

Adherents of the "pro-dictator" argument overlook important elements of accountability in at least two of their favorite cases, Chile and Korea. In both of these countries, the regime faced vocal (sometimes vociferous) criticism from independent intellectuals, students, etc. The student movement in Korea helped to keep the government relatively honest and thus to minimize the damage which the growth of corruption, cronyism, and rent-seeking usually inflicts on authoritarian political economies.[18] A recent, thorough review of the political economy of poverty alleviation concluded that in the Chilean case, the long tradition of a critical civil society, although damaged and weakened by dictatorship, did not disappear. Fear of criticism contributed to the Pinochet government's successful formulation and implementation of targeted "safety-net" programs.[19] The evidence suggests that accountability is essential if only to keep dictators on the right track; without accountability, little restrains the corrupt, rent-seeking behavior which strangles growth.

In short, dictators often pursue non-economic goals, persist in costly mistakes, and, without accountability of some sort, permit the growth of a luxuriant and suffocating morass of corruption. These general considerations apply with special force in the Near East. Arab dictators are most unlikely to pursue economic growth single-mindedly; historically, they have always had another objective, which they felt was more important: confrontation with Israel. "The Quest", the semi- (and, with

---

[18] See Alice Amsden, *Asia's Next Giant: South Korea and Late Industrialization* (New York: Oxford University Press, 1989).

[19] Jacques Dreze and Amartya Sen, *Hunger and Public Action* (New York: Oxford University Press, 1989).

Islamic revivalists, explicitly) sacralized goal of fighting the Jewish state, has bedeviled Arab governments for a half-century: authoritarians of both the secular nationalist (Nasserists and Baathist) and the Islamic revivalist (al-Bashir of Sudan; Khomeini/Rafsanjani of Iran) variety placed fighting (and, they hoped, destroying) Israel at the top of their agenda. The same is true of would-be authoritarians like the Muslim Brotherhood.

The implications of The Quest for economic growth are straight-forward: any pursuit of sound economic policies will "trip on the Dome of the Rock", will falter because any Arab authoritarian regime will also pursue the unattainable: destroying the region's only nuclear power. The repeated defeats of Arab armies in battle by the Israeli Defense Forces and the massive diversion of all-too-scarce resources to military confrontation with a better organized, better armed, and better connected country have, of course, been fundamental to the failure of development in the Arab world. The diversion of capital has been massive; perhaps as bad has been the squandering of the scarcest resource, the time of talented people. Arab dictators pursue not economic growth, but a Quixotic and doomed regional political agenda.

Of course, we cannot blame the militarization of the region on the Arab-Israeli conflict alone. Intra-Arab conflict of the "Arab Cold War" variety and military confrontations with other non-Arab states (Iran, Turkey, Ethiopia) have either actually or potentially diverted scarce resources from development to military activity. One ruthless dictator spawns another: an Arab Pinochet in one country would engender an Arab Galtieri in its neighbor, further fueling the arms race. The grue-some spectacle of the Iran-Iraq war could be repeated by other authori-tarians. In short, the revival of economic growth in the Arab world requires the end of the regional arms race; and the end of the regional arms race necessitates ending unaccountable authoritarian rule.

Improved policy implementation in the region likewise requires a reduction in authoritarianism. The militarized societies of the Arab east have stifled the growth of an independent bourgeoisie and intelligentsia; unlike Chile and Korea, Arab countries have not benefited from inde-pendent, internal criticism. Unsurprisingly, the Arab world's dictator-ships present a spectacle of corruption and rent-seeking, often on a grand scale. This is not surprising; we now know that even under the ruthless terror of Joseph Stalin, corruption was common in the Soviet Union of the 1930s; modern would-be clones like Saddam Hussein's regime are also quite corrupt and incompetent. And in good Khaldunian fashion, the

longer the regimes are in power, the wider and deeper the rot spreads—
after a while, people with the proper connections find ways to mitigate
the terror and to get what they want.

Last but not least, modern information technology increasingly erodes
authoritarianism. These technologies are profoundly decentralizing;
they are essential for effective participation in today's fiercely competitive international economy. Since Middle Eastern states must expand
exports in order to create jobs and to buy food, they must rapidly diffuse
the use of these technologies. Economic imperatives necessitate decentralization and the end of authoritarianism.

In summary, dictators do not do it better: past history strongly
suggests that they only succeed in promoting economic growth if 1) they
are single-mindedly committed to economic growth; 2) they face sufficient criticism that their administrations are kept honest, and 3) they
avoid persisting in mistaken policies. This is a tall order for any dictator;
it is quite beyond the reach of any Near Eastern one. Reviving economic
growth in the Near East requires an end to the arms race, and much more
effective participation in the modern international economy, with its
decentralizing information technologies. Only accountable governments,
not dictators, have a chance of doing this.

Conclusion

The task will not be easy. The legacies of geography and history are
admittedly baleful. The natural resource base, with its mix of abundant
oil and scarce water, makes adjustment imperative, but also makes it
difficult. The habits of the past will die hard: entrenched interest groups,
engendered over nearly a half-century of state centralization, will not be
easily persuaded to abandon their privileges. With the exception of the
Mashreq, the level of human capital in the region, although far higher
than formerly, is very low in comparison with the competition in East
and Southeast Asia and in Eastern Europe. The road ahead will be very
difficult; but there are few alternatives to starting down it. The old
Nasserist Social Contract, the exchange of "welfare for political quies-
cence" is dead, because the state cannot fulfill its side of the bargain any
longer. There are really only two alternatives : repression or participation. Repression, with its violation of human rights which this author and
most people find repugnant, is likely to be ineffective, especially in the
long run. Middle Eastern rulers may conclude, with Lord Keynes, that
in the long-run (which may mean six months hence) they are well and

truly dead, and so clamp down. Apres moi le deluge seems to be the rallying cry of Algeria's FLN, and other senescent (not to say senile) regimes may emulate them. But the path of repression is very slippery, not least because of the maelstrom of violence into which it leads. Repression also impedes constructing the set of institutions which alone affords a chance of coping with the economic challenges of the immediate future.

The alternative is expanded participation. This need not mean "democracy" in the current western sense. We ourselves are unsure about the proper design of political systems, and we have plenty of problems of our own. Doubtless Middle Eastern nations will have to find their own, culturally authentic, paths to expanded participation. But whatever the precise forms, expanded participation will be essential for three reasons. First, the age of structural adjustment is the age of subsidy cuts. Economically, a subsidy cut is equivalent to a tax increase. Political participation is necessary to "share the pain"; if the cry in 1776 was "No Taxation Without Representation!", that of the era of structural adjustment may be "No Subsidy Cuts Without Participation!" Second, a stable legal environment is a necessary condition for a functioning market economy. Since we now know that there is no alternative to markets for many allocative purposes, the only alternative to the rule of law is economic stagnation, poverty, and ultimately, chaos. Third, modern information technology supports market functioning: properly functioning markets require widely available information as well as secure property rights. But the faxes which carry this morning's price data also may convey the latest statement of the exiled political opposition. A regime may outlaw faxes outside of its control (as does Syria). Such a regime cannot effectively compete in international markets. Accordingly, it cannot solve the problems of food, jobs, and money.

Middle Eastern governments have much adjusting to do if they hope to cope with the economic imperatives of the last decade of the 20th century. They will have to stop doing some things (e.g., privatize and acquiesce in the rule of law), start doing other things (e.g., assist their private exporters in foreign markets) and do some things much better (e.g., educate their young). Some countries may rise to the challenge. Some will likely fail. The costs of failure will be very high, and will affect not only their own peoples and their neighbors, but also the international community. The alternative road of repression, civil war, economic stagnation, food insecurity, poverty, and chaos is all too familiar to people of the region. The fact that there is an "economic imperative" does not mean that polities will rise to the occasion. But the stark choice needs to be place before policy makers, both within and without the region. All should recall the dictum of Sir Winston Churchill: "Democracy is the worst form of government, except for all the others".

CHAPTER THREE

MODERN ISLAMIC FUNDAMENTALIST DISCOURSES ON CIVIL SOCIETY, PLURALISM AND DEMOCRACY

Ahmad S. Moussalli

Introduction

Is there a civil society in Islam? Are Islam and democracy compatible? Or, are there liberal traditions in Islam? Such questions usually bring astonishment, or at least skepticism. Even a cursory look at the Arab world, however, will show how much the Arab people, including the majority of fundamentalists, are interested in democratization and the construction of civil societies in their political life. Indeed, the absence of political and social freedom and the tyranny of political systems are now believed to be the main causes of Arab defeats and underdevelopment in the region.

Since the collapse of the Soviet Empire, the issues of civil society, human rights and democracy—whose practical and theoretical absence in the Arab world is portrayed as both un-Islamic and the source of current miserable conditions—have become more urgent. The need to revitalize the institutions of civil society, loosen the grip of governments on their peoples, and democratize political processes has been newly emphasized in the media and at universities and other institutions. Many conferences have been organized around these issues, beginning with a 1981 meeting in Morocco on "Democratic Experience in the Arab World," and a later conference on "The Crisis of Democracy in the Arab World." Ironically, the latter was held in Cyprus because no Arab state would welcome a conference on that theme. In 1989 a conference in Amman addressed the issue of "Political Pluralism and Democracy in the Arab World," a theme further discussed in 1990 when Beirut's Center for the Studies of Arab Unity held a conference in Cairo. At that meeting, conferees agreed that Arab citizens lacked citizenship and political rights, as well as civil society. In August 1993, the widely read Arabic newspaper, *Al-Hayat*, serialized a long debate for five days around the idea of "Civil Society in Egypt and the Arab World" as seen by different political trends in the Arab world.[1]

These conferences took place at a time when most of the West had projected uncalled-for sensationalism about Islamic fundamentalist dangers, disregarding the plight of the peoples of the area and the dialogues and debates that have been going on among diverse political trends about political theories and rights of people. Themes such as "The Clash of Civilizations," "The Arab World Where Troubles for the US Never End," or "Will Democracy Survive in Egypt?" have become familiar in Western media. With the exception of the work of a few academics, the true issues discussed in the Middle East have been almost totally neglected.[2]

Recent events in Egypt, Algeria, Tunisia, Sudan and elsewhere—especially with the successful rise of Islamic fundamentalism—have brought about questions concerning the compatibility of Islam, with its fundamentalist interpretations and the quest for an Islamic state, with democracy, human rights, civil society and the emerging world order. In light of these concerns, this paper aims to articulate one of the important debates that has been going on in modern Islamic fundamentalist discourses about the role of civil society vis-à-vis the state. Although it might seem that the concept of civil society is Western and imposed on the non-Westerners in order to keep local systems in subjection to the West, this is not entirely true, at least in terms of the functions of civil society. Since the Prophet's death, many thinkers have postulated the problematic relationship between political authority and society as represented by its different segments: religious, professional and tribal. Nonetheless, the vast majority of Muslim thinkers, jurists, theologians, and (to a lesser extent) philosophers have given the upper hand over the

---

[1] Concerning debate on civil society and democracy in the Arab world, and the resistance of the region's governments to such a society, see *Al-Hayat,* 4 August 1993, p. 19, and 25 September 1993, pp. 14 & 17. The series ran 2-6 August. See also *Qadayah al-isbu',* no. 15, 10-17 September 1993, pp. 1-2, where the development of civil society is considered necessary for any future development. For a journalistic critique of current scholarly literature on civil society, see Hazim Saghiyyah, "Ma'zufat al-mujtama' al-madani," *Al-Hayat,* Tayyarat Section, 18 September 1993, p. 4. Fundamentalist theoreticians are no less interested in the same issues. See Rashid al-Ghannushi, *Al-Hurriyyat al-'amah fi al-islam* (Beirut: Center for the Studies of Arab Unity, 1993) and Fahmi al-Huwaidi, *Al-Islam wa al-Dimuqratiyyah* (Cairo: Markaz al-'Ahram li al-Tarjama wa al- Nashr, 1993).

[2] "Will Democracy Survive in Egypt?" *Reader's Digest* (Canadian Edition), vol. 131, no. 788 (December 1987), p. 149; "The Arab World Where Troubles for the US Never End," *US News and World Report* 96, 6 February 1984, p. 24; Samuel Huntington, "The Clash of Civilizations," *Foreign Affairs* 72, no. 3 (Summer 1993): 22-49. Academics that have dealt more objectively with the Arab world are cited below in footnotes 4, 5, 47, 73 & 76.

government to the variety of institutions that made up society, however informal they may be at times. While this was the case in theory, practice has shown more despotism on the side of the rulers.

The first section of this paper will present an historical introduction of the theoretical foundations of civil society as they developed under different Islamic regimes. The main body of the paper will focus on the general fundamentalist trends in thinking concerning the viability and necessity of the existence of civil society in Islam. Two main schools of thought emerge: the first, which represents the minority, looks negatively at the issue of strengthening civil society; the second, advocated by the vast majority of fundamentalist thinkers, calls for the establishment of civil society as the cornerstone of the new Islamic state. In fact, claim the latter group, civil society is precisely Islam's original and ideal form of society. Throughout this discussion, references will be made to major fundamentalist political underpinnings of government and politics, since the concept of civil society cannot be discussed outside the general theory of politics. Finally, this paper will conclude with a theoretical assessment of fundamentalists' positions on civil society and democracy, and an inquiry into both the possibility of grounding Islamic and Western political thought in a universal framework, and the potential for peaceful co-existence between Islamic and Western societies. Put more clearly, is a cultural clash between the East and West inevitable in the future?

Introduction to the Theoretical Foundations of Civil Society

A word on the concept of civil society is appropriate since it functions as the organizing principle employed below. The concept of civil society used herein signifies the part of society that is a distinct sphere from the state, and is composed of a network of political, economic, social, educational, professional, and religious institutions, that lobby governments for their own interests, rather than the interests of state. The "hallmark of civil society is the autonomy of private associations and institutions . . . Its pluralism comprises the partially autonomous spheres of economy, religion, culture, intellectual activities, etc., vis-a-vis each other. Civil society presupposes the existence of the state. It requires that the state be limited in the scope of its activity and execute the law that protects pluralism of civil society."[3] To put it more succinctly, and to use Augustus R. Norton's definition, it is a place "where a mélange of

---

[3] See Edward Shils, "The Virtue of Civil Society," *Government and Opposition* 26, no. 1 (1991), p. 9; and for an extended discussion of civil society, consult pp. 3-14.

groups, associations, clubs, guilds, syndicates, federations, unions, parties, and groups come together to provide a buffer between the state and citizen."[4]

Thus, civil society is employed to indicate those forces, organizations, parties, groups and political, educational, voluntary, and professional structures such as human rights organizations and women's liberation movements. But the most important feature of these organizations is their independence from the government. In the Arab world, emphasis should be directed at political parties, since many states and ideologies allow the formation of voluntary associations, but not of political parties. Once free political parties are allowed to function, then any other kind of association should be allowed, in principle at least, to function. For the Arab world, the basic problem right now is political.

John Voll has aptly summarized that "the evolution of Islamic social structures emphasized the ideal of a community that is integrated as a whole through personalized associations. Although there were rich and poor, leaders and followers, elites and masses, the social groupings did not create entities (like class or church...). That tradition of social order has helped to shape modern socio- political development in the Islamic world."[5]

The fact that the Prophet Muhammad did not appoint a political and religious successor was perceived as freeing the community to choose its social and political systems. Immediately after his death, social groups such as Muhammad's early supporters from the Medina and the immigrants from Mecca struggled over his political succession. Each tribal group represented an important segment of the population, but did not have any specific program to be applied. At that time, the tribal structure was perceived as the part of civil society that would cushion the relation between individuals and the government. In fact, that very same structure was responsible for electing the political leader whose legitimacy was considered of contractual nature. The social non-political structure drew up a contract with a leader to make him the ruler.[6]

---

[4] Augustus Richard Norton, "The Future of Civil Society in the Middle East," *Middle East Journal* 47, no. 2 (Spring 1993), p. 206.

[5] John O. Voll, *Islam: Continuity and Change in the Modern World* (Boulder, CO: 1982), p. 17.

[6] Muhammad S. 'Awwa, *Fi al-nizam al-siyasi li al-dawlah al-islamiyyah* (Cairo: Dar al-Shuruq, 1989), pp. 69-74; Voll, *Continuity and Change*, p. 15-17; and P. Crone and Martin Hinds, *God's Caliph* (Cambridge: Cambridge University Press, 1986), pp. 116-56. For the concept of community, see Abdo A. El-Kholy, "The Concept of Community in Islam," *Islamic Perspective: Studies in the Honor of Mawlana Abul' A'la Mawdudi*, Khurshid Ahmad and Zafar Ansari, eds. (United Kingdom: Islamic Foundation, 1979), pp. 171-181.

It is interesting to note that the first Islamic community was referred to as *al-mujtama' al-madani* (civil society), with 'civil' here indicating the establishment of the city that was composed of Muslim segments allied on tribal and geographic lines, as well as Jews and others who were allied on similar lines. The social structure reflected the diverse powers of the society that were accepted by the Prophet. The power of the social structure was reflected in the first Islamic constitution (*sahifat al-madinah*) where pluralism in terms of religions and ways of life was accepted. Thus each tribal or religious segment was constitutionally given the right to conduct its affairs without, of course, endangering the state. Furthermore, each group was represented by its leaders, who acted as facilitators between the authorities and individuals whenever necessary.[7]

During the reign of the third rightly guided caliph, 'Uthman Ibn 'Affan, other kinds of political blocs emerged aiming at forcing the caliph's practices to conform with the political doctrines of *shari'ah*. 'Uthman yielded to many of the demands, such as removing his governor in al-Kufah. But when asked to abdicate power, a demand voiced in many places, he refused by claiming that he had a right to rule since he had not committed any acts that could be considered contrary to Islam. Many trends in political theory, specifically around the issues of the proper ways of selecting and deposing a caliph and his accountability to his people, began taking shape. Quite a few well-established figures and their followers even contested the caliph's power to distribute financial rewards from state funds, impose his version of the Qur'an, and appoint his relatives to key posts in his administration.

Eventually, 'Uthman was killed for refusing to accept popular demands and 'Ali was selected as the fourth caliph. Around these two issues—and the events that surrounded them such as the battles of *al-jamal* and *siffin* and in particular the arbitration that took place therein—many political parties, or then groups, developed along lines that later became the main divisions among the Muslims: the Sunnis, the Shi'ites and the Kharijites.[8] The right of the people to form political movements

---

[7] On the city and its composition, see Akram al 'Umari, *Al-Mujtama' ul-maduni fi ahd al-nubuwah, khasa'isuhu wa-tanzimatuhu al-'ula* (Medina: Al-Majlis al-'Ilmi li-Ihya' al-Turath al-Islami,1983), pp. 57-70 & 72-80; and see Radwan al-Sayyid, *Mafahim al-Jama'at fi al-Islam*, (Beirut: Dar al-Tanwir, 1984), pp. 14-18 & 32, and al-Sayyid, *Al-Ummah wa al-jama'ah wa al-sultah* (Beirut: Dar Iqra', 1986), pp. 30-32. On the religious, tribal and geographic structures as reflected in the constitution, see al-'Umari, *Al-mujtama'*, pp. 199-122; and on the analysis of the constitution, see pp. 123-136.

[8] 'Awwa, *Fi al-nizam al-siyasi*, pp. 85-113; and see Al- Sayyid, *Mafahim*, p. 21 and *Al-*

along diverse ideological and political lines has never been seriously contested; however, what has been contested is the use of violence, by the Kharijites, for instance, to obtain political ends and the use by arbitrary power whether in legislation or politics.

Another example of the historical legitimacy of civil society is the role played by the *'ulama* (scholars). As one of the distinguished groups that formed part of civil society, the *'ulama* must control the state, at least in theory. Although there was no clergy, the *'ulama*'s real goal was not to preserve governments as such, but to provide law and order that might allow people to exercise their rights and duties as postulated by *shari'ah*. As mentioned, the Prophet Mohammed left his followers without any specific theory relating to politics and society. Legislation was not a governmental function, but one performed by one of the bodies of civil society, i.e., the *'ulama*.

Producing legal opinions to resolve new or controversial issues was not the prerogative of the state, but that of the private scholars who themselves were forming a tremendously powerful body in civil society and were organized into legal schools and doctrinal trends. Because their legitimacy was grounded in civil society and not in formal governmental institutions, the influence of the *'ulama* was moral and therefore beyond the coercive power of the state. They expressed only scholarly opinions, and depended primarily on the acceptance of other segments of society and not on governmental approval per se (although at times the government adopted one legal school or another). However, the survival of any school of thought depended on its followers. The state did not have any authority over the opinion that was given, but could debate unaccepted opinions in the scholarly circles. Supposedly, a ruler had opinions on certain legal matters only in his capacity as a scholar, and not as a ruler. When the caliph al-Ma'mun attempted, for instance, to force the opinions of the Mu'tazilites, specifically the notion of the createdness of the Qur'an, on the other schools, he was solidly opposed by the majority of the scholars. Although Muslim societies have given themselves the theoretical right to legislate, governments have succeeded in enforcing political wills that did not accord with the objectives of their peoples.[9]

Ummah, pp. 158-166. For a detailed study on the rise of parties in Islam see Muhammad 'Amarah, *Al-Kilafah wa nash' at al-ahzab al-siyasiyyah* (Beirut: Al-Mu'assasah al-'Arabiyyah li al-Dirasat al-Nashr, 1977), specifically, p. 6.

[9] On this issue, see Tariq al-Bishri, "'An mu'assasat al-dawlah fi al-nuzum al-islamiyyah wa al-'arabiyyah," *Minbar al-Hiwar*, no. 19 (Summer 1989), pp. 74-79 & 89; and on the

The development of jurisprudence was therefore the consequence of social interaction between the scholars and other segments of society. It was civil in nature and removed from the authority of the state, although it has extensively dealt with political matters, from the doctrine of good government to the defense of the community. Such scholarship was—and is still—freely taught at the mosques. If a scholar received many followers attending his lessons, he became a prestigious social personality whose authority sprang from social acceptance rather than political appointment. In fact, most political doctrines and religious issues were settled in such places, away from the intervention of governments. When a legal opinion of a scholar became widely accepted in society, it became a part of the legislative compendium of the community that the government had to honor and fulfill.[10] This is why, in my opinion, the Muslims did not formalize legislative processes separate from political authority until the 19th century, when Europe imposed its own views and mechanisms of legislation. At that time, legislation became part of the state itself and justified its tyranny in the Muslim world.

Nonetheless, the Ottomans could not completely incorporate the institution of the 'ulama in the structure of government, or force people to follow the state's declared legal school (the Hanafi). Instead, the community accepted various schools as equally valid. Until the collapse of the Ottoman Empire, the 'ulama proved resistant to absorption or disintegration, although some of them became functionaries of the state, such as the shaykh al-Islam in the Ottoman Empire and shaykh al-Azhar in Egypt. But the historical role of the scholars' institution has always been as intermediaries between the state and segments of civil society. In addition, a majority of the 'ulama were part of the crafts and worked in commerce, and thus exerted economic power.[11]

The moral and political duty of hisbah, to enjoin good and forbid evil (al-'amr bi-al-ma'ruf wa al-nahy 'an al- munkar), was shouldered by

---

concept of community, see Al-Sayyid, Mafahim, pp. 35- 40 and Al-Ummah, pp.164-166. For a historical narration on free opinion in Islam, see Mohammad H. Kamali, "The Approved and Disapproved Varieties of Ra'y (Personal Opinion) in Islam," The American Journal of Islamic Social Sciences 7, no. 1 (March 1990): 39-65.

[10] This topic will be discussed more extensively later in this paper. On the development of legislation in Islam, see Bishri, "'An Mu'assasat," pp. 79-82; and Al-Sayyid, Mafahim, pp. 41-42. See also, Al-Ijtihad, 5, no. 19 (Spring 1993): 23-55. For an earlier version, see Al-Mawwardi, Al-'Ahkam al-sultaniyyah (Cairo: 3rd ed, 1973), p. 3.

[11] See Mahmud Isma'il, Susiulujia al-fikr al-islami (Cairo: Maktabat Madbuli, 1988), pp. 154-156, Wajih Kawtharani, Al-Sultah wa al-mujtama' wa al-'amal al-siyasi (Beirut: Center for the Studies of Arab Unity, 1988), pp. 35- 38 & 43, and al-Bushri, "An Muassasat," pp. 83-90

civil groups and not by the state. The community's neglect of this duty was considered one of the social ills that befell civil society. This duty meant the right of society to participate in public debates, give its opinions, and criticize public actions and governmental policies. It went further than the abstract notion of citizenship and demanded the active involvement of diverse segments of society in running the affairs of society and the state. Those who participate deserve divine reward, but those who do not participate (and are capable) incur impiety.[12]

Another group that shows the deep-rootedness of civil society in the history of Islam is the role of the notables (*al-ashraf*), an informal civil section of society that cushioned the relationship between individuals and the state. Its members were historically connected to the descent of the Prophet, which gave them tremendous respect among other segments of society. Their leader (*naqib al-ashraf*) commanded a wide civil influence in the society and interfered on its behalf with the state.[13]

The professional organizations and Sufi orders were yet another powerful civil force, given that the notable's authority depended locally on economic and social structures forming the different segments of society. The complex web of interrelationships between the notables and the craftsmen and their activities in the marketplaces unified the two groups. Some of the notables occupied leading positions in the crafts such as the *shaykh* (leader) of the craft. All this unified the overall local social and political structures and rules that local authorities depended on to facilitate their exercise of power and relationships with society. In addition to blood ties and tribal organizations, these structures and rules played a central role in protecting individuals and social segments from the state's arbitrary exercise of power. The authority of the leader of a craft or a professional group involved the administration of the affairs of the members of that craft, solving their problems, and supervising the implementation of contracts and agreements. He usually had direct access to judges to register contracts and bring the complaints against other crafts. Furthermore, the leader was the avenue through which the local governor contacted the members of the craft.

On the technical level, the organization of the craft followed a very strict hierarchy, from initiation to the craft through various stages until craftsmanship was attained. An awesome ceremony was held in order to bestow the craftsmanship on an individual who would swear allegiance

---

[12]. Bishri, "'An mu'assasat," pp. 86-90; and Al-Sayyid, *Mafahim*, pp. 41-42.

[13] For more details see Wajih Kawtharani, *Al-Sultah wa al-mujtama'*, p. 46; Isma'il, *Susiulujia*, pp. 140-143; and Al-Sayyid, *Mafahim*, pp. 77-91 & 94-96.

to his master and to the rules of the craft, such as perfection of the work, honesty, fair prices and, above all, solidarity with fellow craftsmen. In many senses, it was more a fraternity than a business club.[14]

These groups illustrate how the exercise of social authority in civil society was conducted away from the political authority. The Sufi orders, connected with the crafts and the notables, reflect the right of civil segments to conduct worship in the manner deemed appropriate. Thus, Sufi, notable and professional intermediaries had created a multi-layered framework through which individuals belonged to each local community, and they connected this framework to the more general ideal of the Islamic community (the *ummah*). While the relation with local and national authority revolved around taxation and law and order, the crafts and religious institutions were connected with each other and played a very important role in social stability.

The civil role of the crafts and the religious movements began deteriorating by the late part of the nineteenth century, and was demolished completely by the 1920s with the emergence of modern states and unions. As Islamic markets increasingly became part of international markets, the traditional markets and crafts were lost, along with the civil society that they had created. Gradually, the Islamic city lost its authentic civil institutions, and the governmental associations that replaced them have been unable to either create a true civil society or replicate the independent role played by the crafts, Sufis, *ulama*, and notables.[15]

Many other civil groups existed in Muslim societies, and civil society may be said to have existed in the flourishing of minorities and their adherence to their own laws and scriptures. The leaders of these religious minorities played for their own people the very same role that Muslim scholars did, and were accorded considerable latitude to run their internal affairs. Even when the Ottoman Empire codified the *shari'ah* according to the recognized four schools of law, local authorities were permitted to decide which school was to be followed, given the Empire's diverse ethnic and religious ties. Because the *Hanafi* school of law, followed mostly by the Ottomans, considers the people of the Book a genuine part of the community,[16] Christian and Jewish minorities were

---

[14] Kawtharani, *Al-Sultah wa al-mujtama'*, pp. 47-49; and Al-Sayyid, *Mafahim*, pp. 100-101. On the limitations on political rule as developed historically, see Muhammad H. Kamali, "Siyasah shar'iyah or the Policies of Islamic Government," *The American Journal of Islamic Social Sciences* 6, no. 4 (Fall 1991): 225-237.

[15] Al-Sayyid, *Mafahim*, pp. 110-111.

[16] Kawtharani, *Al-Sultah wa al-mujtama'*, pp. 35-38 & 67-72; and Al-Sayyid, *Mafahim*, pp. 119-126.

permitted to conduct their religious practices, personal laws and religious endowments in accordance with their religions. Consequently, minority religious leaders held privileged positions vis-à-vis governments, acting as intermediaries between the government and the minorities.

Fundamentalist Discourses

a) The Radical Fundamentalist Trend

Although Islamic fundamentalism is not a theoretically and politically unified movement, the discussion enjoys common terminological underpinnings on a superstructural level: the supremacy of *tawhid* as the pivotal doctrinal and political foundation, the superiority of the *shari'ah*, the necessity of establishing an Islamic state and other important issues.

As these doctrines are translated into a political philosophy, however, they are, in fact, processed by extremely opposed methodological and intellectual formulas. One formula is grounded in a few exclusivist concepts: authenticity, one-sidedness of truth, purity, superiority and above all salvational knowledge. The adherents of these concepts tend to be self-righteous and undemocratic. Claiming exclusive, authentic, scriptural, salvational and superior knowledge, they push anyone who adheres to similar concepts to join them in essentially excluding the *other* from their philosophy of life, as well as in politics and society. In this chapter, such beliefs and practices will be termed radical fundamentalism.

The political and social philosophy of radical fundamentalism is more exclusive than its general philosophy. While adherents believe in the contractility between the ruler and the ruled, they hold that a properly conducted *shura* creates a social or public will that is more important than the individual who must submit to it. In an Islamic system, this public will represents the divine will, and therefore the individual or groups as such cannot legitimately stand against it. For these radicals, the freedom of the individual is not important, since the individual must always be watched. The well-being of the individual is secondary to that of the community, in which a political contract creates a public will for the whole of society. No splits (parties, associations and the like) are allowed to destroy social unity. The communal spirit sublimates individual rights that are in fact given up to the state, which becomes the controlling agency of the harmony between the individual and society.

Of course, the former is always sacrificed, since it is conditioned by a controlled educational and social system whose violation becomes a violation of religion itself.

The institutional structure developed out of *shura* and *ijma'*, which are based on the *shari'ah*, is embodied in a state that expresses the general will and has the right to set the course for people's life. Although the state is accountable to people, its legitimacy hinges on abstract notions of obeying the *shari'ah*. Insofar as the government is obeying the divine law it cannot be legitimately toppled, and by this the normative role of the original contract based on *shura* and *ijma'* is lost. In order to apply the general will, the state becomes tyrannical. It imposes controlled institutions because, according to the radicals, it is its business to make sure that people adhere to the moral and ethical teachings of Islam. This again strips the community of its right to supervise the government and, conversely, gives the government the right to control the people.

If political parties and associations cannot represent the people's choice and contend for power, the popular *shura*—direct democracy!— on which they rely is subsumed to be true only if it accords with the majority or communal views. The individual can only be represented communally, and parties, associations and other civil institutions cannot operate as possessing representation of the general will. Consequently, the individual is either with or against the whole of society, and minorities, special interest groups, private organizations and the like are subjected to the communal social interest. Finally, the communal interest is reified to represent the divine will.

Argued this way, any deviation is a crime punishable by death or imprisonment. The state is responsible for the development of moral order, and although enjoining good and forbidding evil was originally conceived as an individual act, the existence of the state turns that right into a communal duty enforced by the state on the individual. Radicals begin with the right of the individual; they end by negating individuality itself. Mutual social responsibility forces the individual not only to accommodate but to subject the individual interest to the communal interests, until the regulator of interests becomes the society at large. And since the state is the institution that implements this, it is transformed into the embodiment of that interest. Thus, the society that legitimately exists is religiously Islamic. Such an environment is of course not conducive to the establishment of pluralistic civil societies or the flourishing of freedom.

The Discourse of Sayyid Qutb

The views of radical Islamic fundamentalism is best represented by Sayyid Qutb. Insofar as the political consequence of *tawhid,* the govern-ance (*hakimiyyah*) of God and the formation of a virtuous and just society, is maintained, Qutb argues that the people are free to choose the social and political systems conducive to good life. The state's main objective is to develop a moral society on Qur'anic bases. By concluding that legislative matters are divine matters, Qutb denies the individual, society and the state any right to change or challenge Islamic normative principles. Both society and the individual must follow an inherent moral order based on universal divine laws as prescribed in the Qur'an. Because Qutb denies the social phenomenological aspect of alterable divine laws, he denies legislative rights to any institution or individual. Instead, institutions and individuals may only codify legal articles to meet the changing needs of social and individual life from the legislative substance of the Qur'an.[17]

Nevertheless, this perspective places the community before the state. While the state and society must yield to unequivocal Qur'anic injunc-tions, obedience to government is neither absolute nor timeless. For instance, if the government goes against a Qur'anic injunction, the people can, according to Qutb, declare civil disobedience and even revolution. While ultimate sovereignty is that of God, its exercise is delegated not to the state or government, but to the people. Therefore, the authority of the state is only a matter of delegation from the people, and is not self-acquired or divinely ordained. The willful consent of the people legitimizes social, political and intellectual institutions. Al-though the government must adhere to Islamic law, it must do so from a popular point of view, and not by the state's interpretation of what Islamic law is all about. To Qutb, the free choice of the people is the only vehicle that must be used in order to achieve divine will.[18]

Further, Qutb argues that jurisprudence is not a theoretical study, and therefore should not be linked to past explanations and developments, but to the needs of contemporary societies. Because political theory in

---

[17] Qutb, *Hadha al-din* (Cairo: Maktabat Wahbah, 4th ed., n.d.), pp. 32 & 123; and Qutb, *Ma'rakat al-islam wa al-ra' simaliyyah* (Beirut: Dar al-Shuruq, 4th ed., 1980), pp. 49 & 60.

[18] On the necessity of the choice of people, see Qutb, *Ma'alim fi al-tariq* (Beirut: Dar al-Shuruq, 7th ed., 1980), pp. 50 & 71-77; and Qutb, *Al-'Adalah al-ijtima'iyyah fi al-islam* (Cairo: Dar al-Shuruq, 7th ed., 1980), pp. 73, 107- 108 & 206-207; Qutb, *Ma'rakat al-islam,* pp. 67, 85 & 75; Qutb, *Fiqh al-da'wah* (Beirut: Mu'assasat al-Risalah, 1970), p. 61.

Islam is the outcome of juridical developments, people can develop new political theories and institutions without guilt. Rejecting the historical normative authority of the jurists' institution, Qutb extends authority to the majority of the people, enabling them to restructure their systems and life without obstacles from the past. People are then bound by "the spirit of Islam" and not by the conclusions of legal, political, social or intellectual circles.[19]

From this argument, Qutb moves to deny the unique legitimacy of any political system, since any system or form of government is acceptable on the condition that it is developed by the people and does not contradict the *shari'ah* (the eternal principles of religion). Thus a republican form of government is just as good as any other insofar as it is based on social consensual agreement and does not negate the people's authority. But by no means can an Islamic state be a theocracy, because no group may claim divine representation on earth. In fact, an Islamic state is a constitutional state and the government of the community because every one is bound by the law and the community chooses its leaders. Even judicial and legislative decisions stem from power delegated by the people. Qutb again points to the doctrine of *shura* as the central political theoretical and practical doctrine in the affairs of the government and society. Any form of government or society that is the outcome of social agreement is acceptable as Islamically developed; conversely, any elitist form, whether religious, political, social or intellectual, must be rejected.[20]

So far, one could say that Qutb is not far from the moderately liberal trend. This is true to a point, it is not quite so in terms of pluralist civil society, particularly party formation. Qutb argues that while enjoining good and forbidding evil forms the basis for individual and social freedom, this freedom must be bound by the interest of society at large. Special interests, whether political or social or individual, can be maintained only insofar as they do not infringe on others. Monopoly is cited by Qutb as an instance of special interest; military elitism is another. To avoid conflict and disunity, the private interests of groups and individuals must always consider the public interest. Islam unites all segments of society and communal interests and limits personal freedoms.

---

[19] Qutb, *Al-Adalah*, pp. 102-105 & 167; Qutb, *Fiqh*, p. 84; Qutb, *Ma'rakat al-islam*, p. 60; and Qutb, *Nahwa mujtama' islami* (Beirut: Dar al-Shuruq, 6th ed., 1983), pp. 46-52.

[20] Qutb, *Al-'Adalah*, pp. 37, 107-108, 111 & 157-169; Qutb, *Fi zilal*, vol. 1, part 3, p. 329; Qutb, *Ma'alim*, pp. 58-96, 72 & 132; Qutb, *Ma'rakat al-islam*, pp. 66-70; Qutb, *Tafsir 'Ayat al-riba* (Beirut: Dar al-Shuruq, 1970), p. 84; and Qutb *Nahwa mujtama'*, pp. 46-69.

In uniting a community into one creed as the source of social peace, Islam frees people from their petty interests and unleashes their energies to serve the individual, society and the world.

Finally, Qutb argues that a properly-construed society must not rise on conflictual differences and motivations, but on good feeling, solidarity, security and peace. Freedom for Qutb must be always tempered by equality, and rights counterbalanced by duties.[21] Emphasizing self-interest leads to a weakening of communal solidarity; focusing on mutual responsibility (takaful) leads to strong solidarity. The well-being of all is a religious duty on all members of society. However, this responsibility must be shouldered by society itself, and not the state. The state interferes only when neither society nor individuals can perform its social duty—for example, providing education, health, proper jobs, etc. In theory, the state has no business interfering in social life; however, if society fails to take care of its own affairs, it is the state's moral responsibility to correct that failure. In general, Qutb emphasizes the importance of voluntary civil institutions and makes the state's actions of supplementary nature. The stress here is on the communal nature of civil institutions and whether they serve more than the interest of segments. But if the focus of these institutions is narrow, it is problematic to accept them as legitimate. For instance, Qutb would find it very difficult to accept women's liberation movements as they exist in the West. Women's place is at home, and by leaving the house, they destroy the family structure, the most important fabric of civil society. Further, his belief that Western systems of government are based on false principles and deception leads to his prohibition of group formation along Western lines, and to his portrayal of the individual and society as the two basic levels of public action. Proper society is not composed of groups that have distinct interests, perceptions of life, or diverse political orientations.[22]

Although Qutb does not reject outright the legitimacy of multi-party systems, he believes in the necessity of the existence of a religious vanguard that will transform people from the darkness of paganism (jahiliyyah) to Islam. Any ideological group or system whose ideology

---

[21] Qutb, Al-'Adalah, pp. 66-68 & 111; and Qutb, Al-Salam al-'alami wa al-islam (Beirut: Dar al-Shuruq, 7th ed., 1983), pp. 102-118.

[22] Qutb, Fi al-tarikh, fikrah wa minhaj (Cairo: Dar al-Shuruq, 1974), pp. 23-36 & 76; Qutb, Al-'Adalah, pp. 35, 59, 73-80, 86 113 & 119; and, Qutb, Fi zilal, vol. 2, p. 689. On his view of women and family structure, see Qutb, Fi Zilal, vol. 1, part 1, p. 235, part 2, p. 234, and part 4, p. 587; Qutb, Al-'Adalah, pp. 60-65.

is not based on Islam must not be permitted to operate. Although minorities can keep their faiths, they cannot form political parties. Qutb ties the freedom of every individual to voice his opinion to the parameters of his ideological understanding of Islam, leading him to the conclusion that all existing societies of the world are *jahili* (paganist) societies.[23] Since a political party (the vanguard or *tali'ah*) can only embody properly an Islamic ideology, a multi-party system based on diverse ideologies is unworkable. His book *Ma'alim fi al-tariq* (Signposts on the Road) is his program to this vanguard that must be characterized by following the "true essence of Islam" and an uncompromising attitude toward other ideologies, societies, and ways of life. The Muslim society and by necessity the vanguard should be aloof philosophically, politically, socially and individually. The vanguard's duty is to struggle against division and individual gains, interests, ambitions and lusts. Only after an Islamic system is set up can Muslims conduct their affairs by applying *shura* as the organizing principle of politics and society. Direct or representative councils, unions, federations, and other means of revealing the public will are welcomed by Qutb, but only within the framework of an Islamic ideology. Ideologies motivated by principles other than Islam, or by a view of Islam that does not accord with his interpretation, must be forbidden. However, Muslims may benefit from Western technological methods and mechanisms to conduct *shura* and know the views of people.[24]

In his description of the characteristics that distinguished historical Islamic societies from Western societies, Qutb cites the example of the professional unions or *al-niqabat* that the West has adopted from Islam into its political system. Although Muslim unions are essentially based on brotherhood and solidarity, Western unions are selfish, their objectives twisted to focus on very narrow capitalist interests. The institution of the *fuqaha* also differs from its counterpart in the West. Because there is no clergy in Islam, only scholars, their role may only be of an interpretative nature that must not involve differences about the general principles of religion. Unlike in the West, they have no representation

---

[23] Qutb, *Hadha al din*, pp. 11 & 91; Qutb, *Ma'alim*, pp. 64-67 & 162-163; Qutb, *Al-'Adalah*, pp. 107, 198; Qutb, *Nahwa mujtama'*, pp. 62, 92-99, 102-120, 123 & 134; and Qutb, *Al-Salam*, pp. 161-165.

[24] Qutb, *Ma'alim*, pp. 11-15 & 22; Qutb, *Al-'Adalah*, pp. 197; Qutb, *Hadha al-din*, pp. 11, 29-30 & 65-57; Qutb, *Fiqh*, pp. 15-32 & 88-89. See also, Qutb, *Al-Salam*, pp. 118-120; and Qutb, *Nahwa mujtama'*, pp. 137-143; and Qutb, *Al-Islam wa mushkilat al-hadarah* (Beirut: Dar al-Shuruq, 8th ed., 1983), pp. 189-193. On the proper political system according to Qutb, see *Al-Salam*, pp. 122-143.

of God. In fact, Qutb sees no way of harmonizing Western philosophies and Islam, or even Western societies with Islamic ones; the first are *jahili* and belong to *hizb al-Shaytan* (the party of Satan), the other are Islamic and belong to *hizb Allah* (the party of God).[25]

Throughout his life, Qutb did not shy from practicing what he preached, which led to his execution by hanging in 1966. During a period out of jail in 1964, he formed a "party" that adhered to his rationalizations, including the following principles.

1- All human societies are far removed from Islamic ethics, system, and *shari'ah*. Hence, they need to be re-educated in the true essence of Islam.

2- Those who respond to this education are to undertake a study of the Islamic movements throughout history in order to set a course of action against Zionism and colonialism.

3- No organization is to be set up except after this highly ideological training has been applied.[26]

Followers of Sayyid Qutb

During a stay in the prison of *Liman Tarah* with Sayyid Qutb, Mustafa Shukri began to follow Qutb and established *Jama'at al-muslimin* (the community of the Muslims), known as *Al-Takfir wa al-hijra* and a fulfillment of the Qutbian vanguard. In his trial before the martial court in Egypt, Shukri declared that imitation in religion is not allowed, and every Muslim should try to understand the textual authorities without intermediaries. He refuses to accept the validity of systematic differences embodied in different schools of thought, let alone political parties. Instead, the relation between man and God should be direct, and cannot even be represented in groups. Any jurisprudence—let alone theories and philosophies—that is not textually derived is un-Islamic. Nothing can add or subtract from the Qur'an and the *sunnah*, and any

---

[25] Qutb, *Al-Islam wa mushkilat al-hadarah*, pp. 7-9 & 96-107, and Qutb, *Nahwa mujtama'*, pp. 150-152 & passim. On the characteristics of the two parties and the West, see Qutb, *Hadha al-din*, pp. 84-87; Qutb, *Al-Rasimaliyyah*, p. 58; and Qutb, *Ma'alim*, pp. 59 & 89.

[26] On these issues and his life, see Muhammad T. Barakat, *Sayyid Qutb: Khulasat hayatuh, minhajuhuh fi al-harakah wa al-naqd al-Muwajah ilayh* (Beirut: Dar al-Da'wah, 197?), p. 19; Salah A. Khalidi, *Sayyid Qutb, al-Shahid al-hayy* ('Amman: Dar al-Firqan, 1983), pp. 147-149; Qutb, "Limadha 'A'damuni?" *Al-Muslimun*, March 1985, no. 4, pp. 6-9; Ahmad Moussalli, *Radical Islamic Fundamentalism: The Ideological and Political Discourse of Sayyid Qutb* (Beirut: Amercian University of Beirut, 1992), chapter 1.

attempt to do this violates God's governance. Difference among the Muslims may only be resolved by referring to the Qur'an and the *sunnah*, and not by human rationalization. Shukri goes as far as rejecting *ijma'* or analogical deduction (*qiyas*) as a source of politics and conflict resolution. He accuses Muslims who do not follow his teachings and follow traditional schools of thought of unbelief (*kufr*), calling for their migration (*hijra*) from the Egyptian society a religious duty. All existing societies are *jahili* or pagan, while only his isolated community is a true Muslim society.[27]

Salih Sirriyyah, originally associated with *Hizb al-tahrir*, was intellectually influenced by Sayyid Qutb and became the leader of *Tanzim al-fanniyyah al-ʿaskariyyah*, another radical and militant fundamentalist group. In his "Risalat al-iman" (Treatise on Belief), Sirriyyah argues that all individuals fall into one of three categories: Muslims, infidels and hypocrites. An individual who neglects an Islamic duty is an apostate and may be legitimately killed. Parties and legal schools were originally formed as a mental luxury, but developed under the influence of heretics who wanted to fight Islam. Eventually, the political trends of Shiism, Sunnism and the Kharijism introduced deep theological and philosophical differences into the Muslim world.[28]

Since today's problems are different, Sirriyyah argues that they require radically more comprehensive changes. While Shukri refuses to deal with the the *jahili* society, Sirriyyah urges people to use, for instance, a democratic system to establish an Islamic state on the condition that the platform of the party contending for power should clearly state its objectives. If the activists are persecuted, they may secretly infiltrate the political system and even become cabinet ministers. Such behavior is permitted because the struggle to topple un-Islamic governments, organizations or social structures is a religious duty until the day of judgment. Muslims who die defending un-Islamic governments are infidels, as only Islam is the measure of all things.

---

[27] On the prison experience, see Rif'at al-Saʿid's article in *Qadayah fikriyyah: Al-Islam al-siyasi: Al-usus al-fikriyyah wa al-ahdaf al-ʿamalliyyah* (Cairo: Dar al-Thaqafah al-Jadidah, 1989) p. 15 and passim. See also, Moussalli, *Radical Islamic Fundamentalism*, pp. 34-36. On a first hand and sympathetic account of the torture to which Shukri, Qutb and others were subjected, plus more on the movement itself, see, Muhammad Mahfuz, *Alladhina zulimu* (London: Riad al-Rayyis Books Ltd., 1988), pp. 7-141. On Shukri's thought as put forward in his trial, see Rif'at Sayyid Ahmad, Second Document in *Al-Nabiyy al-muslah:Al-rafidun* (London: Riad al-Rayyis Books Ltd., 1991), pp. 53- 57. This book contains the basic documents, testimonies, trials, etc., written or said by radical fundamentalists.

[28] Salih Sirriyyah, Second Document, "Risalat al-iman," *Al-Rafidun*, pp. 31-32.

Individuals who participate in un-Islamic ideological parties, such as socialist or nationalist parties, are also infidels, whether or not the individual knows that such parties are contrary to Islam. Similar treatment is accorded to all kinds of institutions, philosophies, and ideologies, such as democracy, capitalism, nationalism and patriotism.

Since Islam's organizing principle is that sovereignty belongs to God, humans must therefore obey. For Sirriyyah, therefore, there are only two parties: *hizb al-Shaytan* and *hizb Allah*. The first consists of all who are loyal to un- Islamic governments, parties, associations or other organizations or practices; the latter consists of those who struggle to establish the Islamic state. One who supports un-Islamic parties in elections and opposes the true Islamic movement is an infidel, even if he has voted for a nationalist candidate who has liberated his land. Sirriyyah goes beyond the idea that supporting any law contrary to Islam is an act of infidelity: he considers any skepticism about the Islamic way of life infidelity. Acting on the logic that Islam aims to eradicate the *jahiliyyah* of the world, Sirriyyah attempted a coup d'état against Anwar al- Sadat, for which he was executed in 1974 (as happened latter to Shukri, in 1977).[29]

'Abud al-Zumar, an army intelligence officer, military leader of *Tanzim al-jihad*, and leader and one of the founders of *Jama'at al-jihad al-islami*, also followed Qutb's discussion of an Islamic system of government. He declares that Islam has not specified an unchangeable way of selecting the ruler, but established *shura* as a doctrine and a practice. Any political development must be ruled by the following bases: the Qur'an, the *sunnah, ijma', al-Salaf al-salih*, and the legal opinions of contemporary trustworthy *'ulama*. Like Qutb, he stresses the importance of method of action, and delineates the following as its central point: a clear and applicable Islamic vision that helps in uniting Islamic movements in one framework and leads to eradicating differences and individuality. This united Islamic movement must draw *ma'alim al-tariq* (signposts of the road)—a Qutbian political term—to insure that the movement does not go astray. While previous Islamic movements failed because they lacked such a method, the unification of Islamic movements would enable the establishment of the caliphate. Furthermore, al-Zumar rejects all of the *jahili* systems and societies— that is those that are un-Islamically based—including all aspects of life, from ethics and legislation to ideologies and thought. Such a move is

---

[29] Sirriyyah, "Risalat al-iman," pp. 42-44 & 48; and, Mahfuz, *Alladhina zulimu*, pp. 83, 120-123, 222 & 233 & 242.

necessary because Islam is comprehensive and cannot be divided without altering its meaning. A radical transformation is required because of God's command to enjoin good and forbid evil in order to bring about the governance of God. This transformation includes rejecting all of these Western invented concepts such as secularism, nationalism, parliamentary life and personal freedom, which have led, according to al-Zumar, to the destruction of the Islamic way of life. However, this cannot be accomplished without the true Muslims' freeing themselves from the rulers who do not rule by what God has revealed and change His *shari'ah*. Al- Zumar acted on his beliefs, and tried unsuccessfully to assassinate Egyptian President Anwar al-Sadat. Later, he helped members of *Tanzim al-Jihad* to successfully assassinate al-Sadat.[30]

A branch of *Tanzim al-Jihad* in upper Egypt known as *Al- Jama'ah al-islamiyyah al-jihadiyyah*, headed by 'Umar 'Abd al-Rahman, has formulated its views on party politics very clearly. A document titled "Mawqif al-harakat al-islamiyyah min al-'amal al-hizbi fi Misr" (The Islamic Movement's Stand on Party Politics in Egypt) articulates al-Jama'ah's positions on every party in Egypt. The Islamic movements are divided into two trends. The first trend accepts the legitimacy of the present political order and its institutions and therefore adopts election as the avenue for arriving at the establishment of the Islamic state. This trend is headed by the Muslim Brotherhood. The second trend, headed by *al-Jama'ah al-Islamiyyah*, rejects the totality of the political order and adopts a confrontation policy. *Al-Jama'ah* criticizes the moderate trend, especially the Brotherhood, for accepting the legitimacy of both the political order and alternative parties, including communist and nationalist parties. The Brotherhood has been complacent, working with Sadat and Mubarak, condemning the death of Sadat, rejecting violence and *jihad* against the rulers, visiting the Coptic Pope, forming alliances with the *Wafd, al-'Amal* and *al-Ahrar* parties, and the like. Meanwhile, the government has persecuted Brotherhood members and repeatedly denied the group the right to form a party.

The alternative trend, lead by *al-Jama'ah*, rejects integration into democratic institutions, arguing that differences are so deep that only radical confrontation will resolve contentious issues such as identity, ethics, value system and the like. As for existing civil institutions in Egypt, *al-Jama'ah* approves of only those with Islamic orientations, and

---

[30] 'Abud al-Zumar, Third Document, in *Al-Rafidun,* pp. 113-121; and Mahfuz, *Alladhina zulimu,* pp. 226, 254, 267-268, 271 & 273.

accuses the others of infiltration by the government and wrongly legitimizing the regime.[31]

In another document, *"Mithaq al-'amal al-islami"* (The Pact of
Islamic Action), *al-Jama'ah* declares that man should submit only to
God, an end to which the group aims to bring mankind. Secularism, as
Qutb rationalized, is a new religion that attempts to change the relationship between man and God, and therefore has corrupted people's
thinking about political and social systems, producing socialism, liberalism, and nationalism. Any system based on these notions belongs to
kufr and the *jahiliyyah*, and therefore must be overthrown. Following
Qutb's arguments further, *al-Jama'ah* denies the right of legislation to
any human being, party, community or parliament. Instead, people can
work to understand what God wants from them, and all disputes and
differences must be worked out from this point of view. Although *shura*
is accepted, it is of procedural nature only and cannot change any
substantive principle.[32]

These beliefs have led *al-Jama'ah* to declare a war against the
Egyptian Parliament and state. The Parliament must be seen as illegitimate because it has given itself (in Article 86 of the Constitution) the
right to legislate, resulting in a twisted kind of democracy. The Constitution declares its system to be democratic and allows for the formation
of parties, which means ideological multiplicity in society. According to
al-Jama'ah's interpretation of Islam, however, believers and non-be-
lievers cannot be treated equally.[33] In an Islamic society, there is only one
ideology, with Islam at the core of all political thinking.

The last document to be used here is the one written by the now
controversial *shaykh* 'Umar 'Abd al-Rahman, who states his views very
clearly and unequivocally. The 'democratic' system in Egypt aims to
incorporate Islamist movements into party politics so that Islam might
be viewed equally with other ideologies. Since Islamic movement are
distinctively superior, they need not respect the *jahili* positive law in this
secular swamp. 'Abd Al-Rahman further rejects the possibility of a
representative council as a way for reinterpreting and adjudicating the
Qur'an. Revelations obtain their legitimacy from their source, and as

---

[31] Fifth Document, *Al-Rafidun*, pp. 150 & 160-164; and 'Abd al-Khabir, "Qadiyyat al-
ta'addudiyah," pp. 118-120. See also Sa'id, *Qadayah fikkriyyah*, pp. 30-31.

[32] Sixth Document, *Al-Rafidun*, pp. 165, 169 & 173-174. On the organization itself, see
Rif'at Sayyid Ahmad, *Al-Nabiy al-musallah: Al-Tha'irun* (London: Riad al-Rayyid Books
Ltd., 1991), pp. 185-186.

[33] "Wathiqat I'lan al-harb 'ala majlis al-sha'b," *Al-Tha'irun*, pp. 187-189. For a description of how this organization views each political party and the political system in Egypt,
see pp. 193-197.

such do not need a council, which would itself be in need of legitimacy. Legislation is a divine matter, and not subject to discussion. A proper Muslim society, as well as the individual and state, must submit to revelations without attempting to philosophize the matter. Alternatively, secular societies have two Gods: the people and its legislature as one God; the heavenly God as another. A ruler who disregards divine injunction is a *kafir* and deserving of death. ʿAbd al-Rahman himself was implicated in Sadat's assassination, but was found innocent: his involvement was limited to offering legal opinions on the characteristics of legitimate and illegitimate rulers, and not on the legitimacy of assassinating Sadat.[34]

b) The Moderate Fundamentalist Trend

The Discourse of Hasan al-Banna
The views of the moderate fundamentalist trend on civil society develop the political discourse of the founder and the first supreme guide of the Muslim Brotherhood in Egypt, Hasan al-Banna, who was assassinated in 1949. Unlike thinkers such as Sayyid Qutb and Abu al-Aʿla al-Mawdudi, al-Banna does not extend the interpretation of the doctrine of *hakimiyyah* (governance) of God to the extremes of logical abstraction. His discourse is suitably pragmatic to provide a map through the realities of Egypt at his time and to his followers at other times. He sees no problem in infiltrating governmental apparatuses in order to induce the desired effects of his ideology. Although he accepts *hakimiyyah* as the necessary organizing principle of government—a move which has made the political discourses of other Islamic movements seem uncompromising—he nonetheless allows pluralistic interpretations of that doctrine, given that no human being can produce a final interpretative judgment. His insistence on the proper grounding of political and social doctrines does not preclude his view that Islamic law has provided leeway for Muslims to produce collective or individual reformulations of Islamic legislation appropriate to place and time. Legislative processes, therefore, must reflect a society's beliefs and interests.[35]

[34.] "Wathiqat muhakamat al-nizam al-misri," *Al-Thaʾirun*, pp. 273-275, and see pp. 290-291, where the diverse kinds of rulers are specified. On similar views, see "Wathiqat al-Ihyaʾ al-Islami" from *Jamaʿat al-jihad al-islami* by Kamal al-Saʿid Habib, pp. 199-229. On *Tanzim al-jihad* and its numerous offshoots see Mahfuz, *Alladhina zulimu*, pp. 213-283.

[35] Hasan al-Banna, *Din wa-siyasah* (Beirut: Maktabat Huttin, 1970), pp. 40-45; and al-Banna, *Majmuʿat rasaʾil al-shahid Hasan al-Banna* (Beirut: Al-Muʾassasah al-Islamiyyah,

Al-Banna concludes that Islamic law allows for multiple individual and collective adaptations of its stipulates because Islam is not the totality of its legislative matter. More than the issues of worship, it deals with practical issues of life; it is both religion and society, a mosque and a state, of this life and the hereafter. Muslims must harmonize religion and the world. To achieve this goal, one must allow for methodological and essential differences and conflicts, without endangering or negating the basic notions of religion. An act as this sort would constitute *jahiliyyah* or paganism.[36]

While *shari'ah* should be presented as a social law, its proper implementation, according to al-Banna, has no specific method, and depends instead on the following principles: it must maintain personal freedom and people's authority over the government, and must delineate the authorities of the executive, legislative and judiciary branches. Constitutional (Western) forms of governments are acceptable under two qualifying conditions: the grounding of constitutionality in Islamic law, and objectivity. Thus, al-Banna denounces Egypt's pre-Nasir parliamentary experience as a rejection of the Egyptian party life, and not a rejection of constitutional life and multi-party politics. Egypt's constitutional life has simply failed, and needs reorientation.[37]

Further, al-Banna accepts constitutional rule as equivalent to *shura* (consultation) by reinterpreting *shura* to suit modernity without contradicting the spirit or the text of the Qur'an. *Shura* is the basic principle of government and the exercise of power of society that must be employed to change government and to oversee political actions. The ultimate source of the legitimacy of *shura* is the community, since the exercise of power requires the continuous approval of the community. Governance is nothing more than a contract between the ruled and the

---

4th ed., 1984) (hereafter cited as *Majmu'at rasa'il*), pp. 161-165. On al-Banna's biography, see *Memoirs of Hasan al-Banna Shaheed*, translated by M. N. Shaikh (Karachi: International Islamic Publishers, 1981); and Rif'at al-Sa'id, *Hasan al-Banna, Mu'assis harakat al-ikhwan al-muslimin* (Beirut: Dar al-Tali'ah, 1981). For a study of Hasan al-Banna's views of constitutional rule, see Ahmad Moussalli, "Hasan al-Banna's Islamist Discourse on Constitutional Rule and Islamic State," *Journal of Islamic Studies* 4, no. 2 (1993): 161-174.

[36] Banna, *Majmu'at Rasa'il*, p. 165, Banna, *Majmu'at rasa'il al-Imam al-Shahid Hasan al-Banna* (Beirut: Dar al-Qalam, n.d.) (hereafter cited as *Majmu'ah*), pp. 304 & 343-47; and Banna, *Din wa-siyasah*, pp. 57-59.

[37] Banna, *Rasa'il al-imam al-shahid Hasan al-Banna* (Beirut: Dar al-Qur'an al-Karim, 1984) (hereafter cited as *Rasa'il al-Imam*), p. 48; Banna, *Majmu'ah*, pp. 14, 169, 309, 331-332 & 335-357; Banna, *Kalimat khalidah* (Beirut: n.p., 1972), p. 45; and, Banna, *Rasa'il al-imam*, pp. 56-60.

ruler; mere textual adherence without proper consciousness is incapable of causing an Islamic revival.[38]

By accepting the naturalness of political diversity and pluralistic interpretations, al-Banna lays down the basis for religious and, consequently, political pluralism. Although *tawhid* is interpreted politically to mean unity, it does not exclude many pluralist states insofar as the main underpinnings of Islam are maintained. Thus, al-Banna rejects party politics and systems founded on basic systematic differences, such as Marxism, but he accepts interpretative ideological differences and diversity in policies and programs. For instance, and to give an extreme case, a party that would call for atheism would not be sanctioned by al-Banna, but any other level of differences, even the doctrinal, would be allowed. In an Islamic state, all parties should believe in, or at least not contradict, the oneness of God. When condemning the Egyptian parties, al-Banna attacked their widespread corruption, not their view of religion. The collaboration of certain parties with the British had impeded the process of unity at a time when the society was in dire need of such to fight the colonialists.[39] This is a politically motivated act, with no specific and necessary Islamic connotation. Indeed, all people under occupation seek social unity and coordinated defense against the aggressor.

Prohibiting such infidel parties does not constitute for al-Banna any infringement on freedom of expression or association, insofar as the majority and the minority have adhered to and accepted religion as the truth. Such parties would be outside the consensus of the society and therefore threaten its unity. If the people have chosen Islam as the basis of their organizing principles of government and society, then to go against Islam is not a matter of freedom, but of anarchy. This does not, however, reject pluralism in Islam, in particular, or in religions or thought in general. Islam does not reject, al-Banna argues, foreign ideas and systems of thought; it absorbs them either through arabization or

---

[38] Banna, *Majmu'at rasa'il*, pp. 160-161 & 317-318; and Banna, *Al-Imam yatahadath ila shabab al-'alam al-islami* (Beirut: Dar al-Qalam, 1974), p. 99; and, Banna, *Majmu'ah*, pp. 99 & 332-337. See also the verse he used from the Qur'an (V: 48) to support his view.

[39] Al-Banna, *Majmu'at rasa'il*, pp. 95-96,165-167, 317, 320-323, 325 th 328-330; al-Banna, *Minbar al-jum'ah* (Alexandria: Dar al-Da'wah,1978), pp. 78-79 & 136; al-Banna, *Al-Da'wah*, no. 7, 1979, p. 9. On centrality of this demand, the Islamic state, in fundamentalist thought, see Bruce Lawrence, *Defenders of God: The Revolt Against the Modern Age* (San Francisco: Harper and Row, 1989), pp. 187-226.

transformation into Islamic Civilization without considering these processes as endangering the political and social unity of the society.[40]

In this context, the state plays only a limited role as the arm of society in the execution of social agreement, the regulation of social conflicts and juridical mechanisms, which govern accepted notions of the social system, education, and law. To reiterate, mere religiosity on the side of society without active commitment to social and political doctrines leads nowhere. Thus, the legitimacy of the state stems, according to al-Banna, from adhering to notions held by society and to the execution of social will.[41]

The relationships between multiple segments of society, such as the people of the Book (specifically Christians and Jews), is based not on adherence to the same beliefs, but on social interest and human good. Religions are one in terms of their origin, and are centered around common ideas of belief, good deeds and unity. The holy books are God's revelations, the believers one community. Therefore, diverse segments of society should direct their conflicts away from divine matters. Conflicts must be resolved by good arguments that lead to a softening of hatred, disputes, sectarianism and disunity. The exploitation of Islam for political objectives is un-Islamic and ought to be shunned.[42]

Furthermore, all individuals and communities must be free to enjoy complete equality of rights and duties in religious, civil, political, social, individual and economic spheres. Public opinion must be politically and socially involved in public life to enjoin good and forbid evil. This principle of involvement is the origin of pluralism of civil society, whether in terms of setting up political parties or social voluntary organizations. Al-Banna himself ran twice for election with his party, the Brotherhood. Some of the Brotherhood's founding members were simultaneously members of other political parties; the same applies to contemporary Brothers. Since 1984, the branches of the Brotherhood in Egypt and elsewhere have participated in elections, and have been involved in setting up civil institutions since the foundation of the

---

[40] Al-Banna, *Majmu'at rasa'il*, pp. 96-97, 161-163 & 167-169; and al-Banna, *Rasa'il al-imam*, p. 53. For a historical review of sedition and freedom of expression, see Muhammad H. Kamali, "Freedom of Expression in Islam: An Analysis of *Fitnah*," *American Journal of Islamic Social Sciences* 10 (Summer 1993): 178-198.

[41] Al-Banna, *Nazarat fi islah al-nafs wa al-mujtama'* (Cairo: Maktabat al-'I'tisam, 1969), p. 194; al-Banna, *Minbar al-jum'ah*, pp. 24-25, 63, 72 & 347; al-Banna, *Majmu'at rasa'il*, pp. 317; al-Banna, *Majmu'ah*, pp. 63, 72, 101, 104 & 317; al-Banna, *Rasa'il al-Imam*, pp. 53-55; and al-Banna, *Al-Imam al-shahid yatahadath*, pp. 15-17.

[42] Al-Banna, *Al-Salam fi al-islam* (Beirut: Manshurat al-'Asr al-Hadith, 1971), pp. 27-29.

Brotherhood. In Jordan, the Brotherhood has functioned as a political party since the fifties, with some members well-placed in the government and the parliament.[43]

Taqiy al-Din al-Nabahani

Another fundamentalist thinker who argues in al-Banna's vein is the founder of *Hizb al-Tahrir* in Jordan and Palestine, Taqiy al-Din al-Nabahani. In his *Al-Takattul al- Hizbi* (Party Formation) he accepts multi-party politics as an expression of enjoining good and forbidding evil. He sees that the political movements that have been working in the public domain have missed many opportunities by not having the proper Awwareness of the role parties may play in the revival of the community. Proper party formation must be based on clear doctrinal principles that philosophically bond people together. If this party survives and its ideology becomes acceptable, it is then transformed from a sectional party to a doctrinal one that can work for a sound revival. Thus, popular support is deemed by al-Nabahani as essential in the formation of civil actors.[44]

Al-Nabahani postulates a three-stage program for party development: the first is the spread of party education; the second is interaction with society to publicize the ideology of the party and ingrain it in public Awwareness; and the third is the control of government through the approval of the community. However, the party should always be distinct from the government, since its role is ideological and the government's function is executive. The government cannot isolate itself from society, and the party acts as a social force that supervises governmental actions. Put differently, the civil institutions of society are above the government, which must yield to public demands and interests. Nonetheless, the situation must not contradict any Islamic principle.[45]

---

[43] On his acceptance of pluralism, see Abd al-Khabir Mahmud 'Ata, "Al-Harakah al-islamiyyah wa qadiyat al-ta'addudiyyah," *Al-Majallat al- 'arabiyyah li al- 'ulum al-siyasiyyah*, nos. 5 & 6, (April 1992), pp. 115-116; on al-Banna's own declaration of accepting equal rights and pluralism, see *Al-Islam aw al-salam*, p. 37 and passim. On the active involvement of al-Banna and his organization in civil society, and their cooperation with other civil segments, see Ishaq Musa al-Husseini, *Moslem Brethren* (Beirut: Khayat's College Book, 1956); Richard Mitchell, *The Society of Muslim Brothers* (London: Oxford University Press, 1964); and Charles Adams, *Islam and Modernism in Egypt* (New York: Russell and Russell, 1986). Also see the views of 'Umar al-Tilmisani in Rif'at Sayyid Ahmad, *Al-Nabiy al-musallah: Al-Rafidun*, pp. 199-200.

[44] Taqiy al-Din al-Nabahani, *Al-Takattul al-hizbi* (Jerusalem: n.p. 2nd ed., 1953), pp. 23-25.

[45] Al-Nabahani, *Al-Takattul al hizbi*, pp. 24-57.

Because al-Nabahani views authority as belonging to the community at large, the upper hand must belong to society and its institutions. If the government does not enact the will of the people and protect its interests, al-Nabahani reserves for them the right to withdraw legitimacy. Both the ruler and the representative council, or *majlis al-shura*, must assume their functions through free elections. Only the representative council has the right to legislate and the duty to protect the natural rights of people, such as education, association, and the right to form parties.[46]

Of course, al-Nabahani's vision has not been realized, and the party seems to have been stuck in the second stage for a long time. *Hizb al-Tahrir* functioned in the East and West Banks from the 1950s until 1976, when the Jordanian government felt that the activities of the party might endanger the regime. After some persecution, al-Nabahani left first for Damascus, and then Beirut; his party's demand for a license has never been approved. Although the party has always condemned the use of violence, the Jordanian government has repeatedly accused it of violent attempts to topple the government.[47]

Munir Shafiq

Munir Shafiq, a fundamentalist thinker associated with *Hizb al-Tahrir*, puts the party's view of the relationship between government and society very eloquently. The major problems facing Muslim societies relate, first, to the issues of social justice and human dignity beyond the ideas of human rights and the sovereignty of law, and second, to the idea of *shura*, that includes and goes beyond democracy. Another problem facing Muslim societies relates to the relationship between the ruler and the people. There can be no explanation for social injustice, class exploitation, political despotism, the violation of people's rights in the interest of the ruler and his entourage, and the crushing of public opinion and political participation. Instead, what is needed to induce a revival is the fulfillment of social justice, the uplift of human dignity, maintenance of basic rights and the sovereignty of law, and an extension of the

---

[46] Al-Nabahani, *Nizam al-hukm* (Jerusalem: Matbaʿat al-Thiryan, 1952), pp. 56-59.

[47] Iyad Barghouty, "Al-Islam bayna al-sultah wa al- muʿaradah," *Qadayah fikriyyah: Al-Islam al-siyasi, al-usus al-fikriyyah wa al-'ahdaf al-'amaliyyah*, pp. 237-238. On an update of the status of Islamic parties in Jordan, see "'Itijahat al-harakah al-islamiyyah fi al-'Urdun," *Al-Safir*, 20 August 1993, p. 13; and "Tanzimat al-harakat al-islamiyyah: harakat al-ikhwan al-muslimin fi al-'Urdun: Al-Nash'ah wa al-tatawwur," *Al-Hayat*, Tayyarat Section, 14 August, 1993, p. 3. On the importance of justice as a political doctrine in Islamic political thought, see Charles E. Butterworth, *Political Islam, The Annals of the American Political and Social Sciences*, 524 (November 1992), pp. 26- 37.

meaning of *shura* and popular political participation. This must be done through the existence of institutions and laws.[48]

Sa'id Hawwa

In Syria, the Muslim Brotherhood participated in elections and government until 1963. According to Sa'id Hawwa, an ideologist for the Brotherhood in Syria, the movement has adopted the following political principles. First, all citizens, without exception, are equal; second, citizens must be protected from despotism, enslavement, martial laws and police-like practices; third, their dignity must be maintained regardless of race and belief by banning psychological and physical torture; four, *shura* must be based on the people's choice; and fifth and most importantly, citizens must be free to form political parties without offending society's beliefs. Such charges must be settled in courts, not by the government, and parties must have the freedom to express their views and publish uncensored newspapers. Sixth, freedom of association—whether in terms of setting up unions, civil right organizations or minorities' institutions, as well as the racial, the religious and the personal—must be maintained. Finally, the seventh principle stipulates the non-viability of a one party-system—a situation which is, to a large extent, still a common feature of Arab governments.[49]

Al-Hawwa emphasizes that although minorities in Syria should possess the same rights as the majority, ultimate authority must not contradict Islam. Minorities have the right to hold posts in the cabinet or be elected to parliament, but their representation must be proportionate to their numbers. Minorities are also free to administer their internal affairs and set up educational institutions and religious courts.[50]

Muhammad S. al-'Awwa

Muhammad S. al-'Awwa, a prominent Egyptian member of the Brotherhood and a lawyer, directly addresses and develops al- Banna's views on civil society. In a recent essay, he defended Islam against accusations that it does not allow the flourishing of civil society. First, he defines the

---

[48] Munir Shafiq, "Awlawiyyat 'amam al-ijtihad wa al-tajdid," *Al-Ijtihad wa tajdid fi al-fikr al-islami al-mu'asir* (Malta: Center for the Studies of the Muslim World, 1991), pp. 64-65.

[49] Sa'id Hawwa, *Al-Madkhal ila da'wat al-ikhwan al- muslimin bi-munasabat khamsin 'aman 'ala ta'sisiha* (Amman: Dar al-Arqam, 2nd ed., 1979), pp. 13-18. On the Muslim Brotherhood's participation in elections in Syria, see al- Habib al-Janhani, "Al-Sahwah al-islamiyyah fi bilad al-sham: Mithal Suriyya," *Al-Harakat al-islamiyyah al-mu'asirah fi al-watan al-'arabi* (Beirut: Center for the Studies of Arab Unity, 2nd ed., 1989), pp. 105-120.

[50] Hawwa, *Al-Madkhal*, p. 282.

concept of civil society as the freedom of those institutions that lead to the development of political, social and professional life. Civil society does not specify the exact kinds of institutions that qualify as civil, since they differ with time and from place to place. In this sense, al-'Awwa believes that every society has such institutions, although their presence may not be immediately evident to the outside observer. While the West considers unions, clubs, federations and parties as the institutions of civil society, Muslim societies have looked to the mosque, the church, religious endowments, teaching circles, professions and crafts organizations and the neighborhood (al-harah). These Western and Islamic institutions are all instrumental means of social action. Therefore, civil society can be achieved by authentic cultural means, and need not imitate the West.[51]

Al-'Awwa takes issue with descriptions of the Arab-Islamic state as despotic by nature, a factor that prevents Islam from developing a civil society. Through a historical narration, he shows that despotism has been rejected since the establishment of the first Islamic state, but he does not deny the existence of despotism as a matter of fact. In practice, however, such despotism has never been able to eradicate the legitimacy of free thinking, whether in terms of jurisprudence, professional development or culture, even when the state adopted an ideological stand opposing that of society. Nevertheless, the identification of Islam with despotism continues today, particularly when certain governments are depicted as representing the Islamic concept of state. This is wrong in al-'Awwa's view because these governments do not represent Islamic orientations; instead, they reflect European orientations such as nationalism, the national state minus political freedom, and the democratization of social organizations. These governments justify their seizure of power for nationalist goals and rule by martial decrees without any representation of their people.[52]

Therefore, the restructuring of the state requires the restructuring of society through which the institutions of civil society are free to develop without interference. As things are now, the state prevents society from forming real civil institutions in accordance with social interests. In fact, it has imposed its own institutions—such as political parties and professional associations—on the people, forcing underground the real parties

---

[51] Muhammad S. al-'Awwa, Al-Hayat, 3 August 1993, p. 19. Also see 'Awwa, "Al-Ta'addudiyyah min Manzur islami," Minbar al-hiwar 6, no. 20 (Winter 1991): 134-136; and footnote 6, above.

[52] 'Awwa, Al-Hayat, p. 19.

that represent society, such as the Muslim Brotherhood and other voluntary associations. To escape this problem and revitalize society, social forces must be free to form representative parties and pursue their interests. [53]

Al-'Awwa defines pluralism as the acceptance of political, economic, religious, linguistic, and other differences as natural products of human nature, and as rights that cannot be denied. The Qur'an allows not only for pluralism, but for whatever means are necessary to achieve identity and belonging, though they may differ fundamentally.[54] Outlining the basic principles of politics in Islam as have been developed by Islamic writings, he mentions six notions. First, the non-specification of Islam, in both the Qur'an and the *sunnah*, of a particular social and political system—Islam only offers general notions that must be maintained; two, the choice of the ruler by the people through *shura*—a term equivalent to direct and free election; third, the necessary nature of political freedom as a consequence of freedom of worship, which is the origin of all freedoms; fourth, the equality of all people in terms of both rights and duties; fifth, to enjoin good and forbid evil is a religious duty that must be performed by the community; and six, the rulers are accountable to the people.[55] Thus, al-'Awwa establishes the legitimacy of pluralism and civil society in Islam, as long as they work for the interest of the people and are not contrary to Islam. Furthermore, people are free to establish many kinds of associations, whose existence, especially political parties, is necessary for the well-being of society and the prevention of despotism. Simply put, in an Islamic system, people are free to form parties and organizations, so longs as they do not violate the provisions of the Islamic constitution.[56]

---

[53] 'Awwa, *Al-Hayat* p. 19. On the Islamic movement in Egypt, see Muhammad A. Khalafallah's article in *Al-Harakah al-islamiyyah fi al-watan al-'arabi*, p. 37 and passim. See also Rislan Sharaf al-Din, "al-Din wa al-ahzab al-siyasiyyah al-diniyyah," *Al-Din fi al-mujtama' al-'arabi* (Beirut: Center for the Studies of Arab Unity, 1990), p. 180 and passim.

[54] 'Awwa, "Al-Ta'addudiyyah al-siyasiyyah min manzur islami," pp. 129-132 and passim. The Qur'anic verses he quotes are An'am: 98-99, Fatir: 27-28, al-Rum: 22, and al-Hujurat: 13.

[55] 'Awwa, "Al-Ta'addudiyyah, pp. 133-134. For a summary of the historical acceptance of pluralism by scholars such as Ibn Taymiyyah, and authoritative exegesis of the Quraean such as *Tafsir al-Jilalian*, see pp. 136-152. On an independent source for the views of the scholars who accepted the people's choice as the legitimate means of government, see *Abu Bakr al-Jassas, dirash fi fikratihi: Bab al-ijtihad*, edited and introduced by Zuhayr Kibi (Beirut: Dar al-Muntakhab, 1993), pp. 29-41; on those who rejected it, such as the generality of Shiites, see pp. 75-86. On the relationship between actual politics and the development of religion and *ijtihad*, see Ismai'l, *Susiulujia*, pp. 139-138.

[56] 'Awwa, *Fi al-nizam al-siyasi*, p. 77; and 'Awwa, "Al-Ta'addudiyyah al-siyasiyyah min manzur islami,": 136-137 & 152-153.

Hasan al-Turabi

Hasan al-Turabi, a Ph. D. in constitutional law from France, is a leading and influential fundamentalist thinker of today's Islamic movements. The former general guide of the Muslim Brotherhood and now the head of *al-Jabhah al-Qawmiyyah al-Islamiyyah* in the Sudan (and the supposed broker of power behind the Al-Bashir regime), al-Turabi extends his discussion of civil society and the state beyond the limits set forth on the kinds of institutions that are allowed to function under an Islamic constitution and in an Islamic state. Like al-Banna, he views the limitations imposed by Islam on the state as parallel to those of liberalism and Marxism in conceiving the state as a vanishing institution. The role of the state is limited to setting rules to allow the society to conduct its affairs; it must then withdraw to allow society, the primary institution in Islam, to freely pursue its interests. Like the previous thinkers, he believes that the *shari'ah* and the jurists limit the role of the state and give society a free hand to conduct its affairs. The reason for this is, again, that the command to enjoin good and forbid evil is directed to the community, not the state. Through an elaboration of this command, he identifies democracy with *shura* and *ijma'*.[57]

For al-Turabi as others, enjoining good and forbidding evil is the source of pluralism because it is a task that must be performed by society. Since any society has the right to exercise *shura* and *ijma'*, and since this requires producing opinions or *ijtihadat*, pluralism then becomes necessary for sifting the best opinion for society. The challenges facing Muslims today require a new understanding of religion by looking more at its ultimate objective and less at its historical jurisprudence. Beyond mere additions and subtractions of the specifics of jurisprudence, such a necessary change requires the radical development of organizing principles themselves.[58] Since the specific organizing principles of religion are no more than the products of socio-economic and political environments that no longer exist, their historicity denies them any enduring normative stand and therefore must be replaced with new principles suitable to modernity. Although this process is not extended to the Qur'an and the *sunnah*, they must nevertheless be reinterpreted

---

[57] Hasan al-Turabi, "Islam, Democracy, the State and the West: Summary of a Lecture and Roundtable Discussion with Hasan al-Turabi," prepared by Louis Cantouri and Arthur Lowrie, *Middle East Policy* 1, no. 3 (1992): 52-54.

[58] Hasan al-Turabi, *Tajdid 'usul al-fiqh* (Jedah: Al-Dar al-Su'udiyyah li al-Nashr wa al-Tawzi', 1984), pp. 10-16; and Turabi, *Qadayah al-hurriyyah wa al-wahdah, al-shura wa al-Dimuqratiyyah, al-din wa al-fann* (Jiddah: Al-Dar al-Su'udiyyah li al-Nashr wa al-Tawzi', 1987), pp. 17-18.

according to new *usul* or organizing principles that result from a new *ijmaʿ*. Such an *ijmaʿ* must be derived from the contemporary *shura* of the people who represent the divine will.[59]

Shura and democracy, once stripped of their historical development, become to al-Turabi identical in aim. Although ultimate sovereignty in Islam belongs to God, the practical and political sovereignty belongs to the people, especially when methodologically exercised. Therefore, an Islamic *shura* does not negate the freedom of society to choose its interests, rulers and representative bodies. Again, this should not contradict any of the basic norms of Islam.[60]

Whatever method the Muslim society follows, the ultimate authority—to contract a political leader who will administer political and social affairs and delegate whatever power it deems necessary for the society's well-being—must be retained by the community. Al-Turabi calls for a political and social structure that arises on contractual mutuality, where the ruler never trespasses the original freedom that is given by the Qur'an to people. Indeed, Islam speaks essentially to the individual and not to the state, and his freedom and the aggregate freedom of individuals cannot be violated. Since this freedom must be embodied in a constitution, the leeway that any political leader has in administering the society can be counterbalanced by setting up representative councils.[61]

If any revival is to take place, a society must be free, according to al-Turabi, to restructure political institutions. Reformation without true reformulation of the philosophy of Islam will not lead to the swift and total cultural revolution that Muslim societies need. Mere religiosity and traditional jurisprudence and sciences, without renewal, are insufficient. The revolution required must be based on religion that supersedes temporary interests and whims, functions as a regulator of behavior, and aims at achieving justice. To reiterate, any renewal must be underpinned by social consensus. When a society has consensual principles and unified interests, it provides a wider margin of freedom than one without

---

[59] Turabi, *Tajdid al-fikr al-islami* (Jiddah: Al-Dar al-Suʿudiyyah li al-Nashr wa al-Tawziʿ, 2nd ed., 1987), pp. 20, 73 & 132-133; Turabi, "Awlawiyyat al-tayyar al- islami," *Minbar al Sharq*, no. 1 (March 1992), pp. 21-26, 69- 72, 81-82, 136-138, 167-169 & 198-199.

[60] Turabi, *Qadayah*, pp. 25-27 & 31-33, Turabi, *Tajdid al-fikr*, pp. 68-80; and Turabi, "Awlawiyyat," p. 16. On the differences between *shura* and democracy, see Salih Hasan Sami', *'Azmat al-hurriyyah al-siyasiyyah fi al-watan al- 'arabi* (Cairo: Al-Zahra' li al-I'lam al-'Arabi, 1988), pp. 49-61.

[61] Turabi, *Qadayah*, pp. 51-57; and Turabi, *Tajdid al-fikr*, pp. 45, 66-68, 75, 93-97 & 162-163.

such principles. Ultimately, society is the place where individual freedom is exercised and where the five social connotations of religion—brotherhood, loyalty, equality, dignity and individual honor—are embodied.[62]

Furthermore, for al-Turabi social adherence to *shari'ah* does not prohibit that which is not Islamic, but that society should take into consideration the general goals of Islam. For instance, Islam's exhortation to justice does not negate people's individual interpretation of it. Insofar as a concept is not directly opposed to a Qur'anic text, both the individual and the society can reinterpret and add to old concepts, and even entertain new ones.[63] In his book on *Al-Ittijah al-islami*, al-Turabi believes that the true Islamic view on woman, for instance, is that she is completely independent. The Qur'anic discourse speaks to her independently without a mediator; even her faith is not true unless founded on real, personal conviction. If this is her original status in Islam, then her actions, whether social, political or religious, should be independent as well. Thus, she can participate in all kinds of public life. When women have been isolated, it is not due to Islam but to backwardness and misinterpretation of textual authorities. What is needed to restore women's original rights is to reinterpret that part of religion that has been exploited by men to isolate women, and to provide a social context where women can exercise their freedom and independence.[64]

The freedom of all segments of society, as well as that of individuals, must include the reworking of complex intellectual, religious, social and political substances and structures. People, individually and collectively, have the right—the duty, even—to reform and change those things that are not conducive to a positive life. The Muslims, al-Turabi goes on, are living now in a world very different from the one that Islamic jurisprudence has legislated. New dimensions of human existence, social life, and human experience, along with a tremendous increase in

---

[62] On Turabi's definition of religion and the need for revolution, *Tajdid al-fikr*, pp. 200-203 & 106-119; on the bonds—both general and Islamic—that make the establishment of society worthwhile, see Turabi, *Al-Iman wa 'atharuhu fi hayat al-insan* (Jedah: Al-Dar al-Su'udiyyah li al-Nashr wa al-Tawzi', 1984), pp. 181-261; on the social connotations and their fulfillment, see pp. 112-121; on the role of science in society, see pp. 269-301; and on the importance of the unity of society for general interests, see pp. 325-329.

[63] Turabi, *Usul al-fiqh*, pp. 27-29.

[64] Turabi, *Al-Ittijah al-islami yuqadim al-mar'ah bayna ta'alim al-din wa taqalid al-mujtama'* (Jedah: Al-Dar al-Su'udiyyah li al-Nashr wa al-Tawzi', 1984), pp. 13 & 42-44. On the essential conditions and requirements for the independence of women, see pp. 45-49.

knowledge, now require radical social and political accommodations in Muslim societies.[65]

But al-Turabi goes even further. The historical development of jurisprudence, based on Aristotelian logic, must be rejected entirely in favor of a process that depends on free thinking without the strict limitations imposed by the jurists. The role of the state in this process is to conduct *shura* in order to identify and codify people's views. The state must, as much as possible, try to establish a new circle of *'ulama* but derive its jurisprudence from the people's choice—the source of interpretation. Civil institutions are the rightful sources of *ijtihad* for politics, society, philosophy and religious thinking, and no official institution can take that right from the people.[66]

Thus, freedom on intellectual, social, political and religious levels is postulated by al-Turabi as a fundamental right and formative principle in the life of people. More importantly, he negates any right for the state to impose its views on the people, even if they had been recognized legal opinions. The society must therefore conduct its affairs without the interference of the state, and when it does it must hold on to *shura*. Since to enjoin good and forbid evil is the Qur'anic legitimization of social power, it is to the people, not to the state, that is addressed. In the end, the state must always yield to public opinion.[67] Public opinion, however, does not have to be unified, since the insistence on having one public opinion leads to "halting the progress of life" and to in-adaptability to changing circumstances. Public opinion, whether through the media or polling, is an unorganized form of *shura* that must be taken into consideration by the government since it represents people's trends. Also, the *ijma'* of the jurists on a specific issue should be considered by the government. But the people themselves cannot be subjected to any specific institution, whether it is a political party or a religious sect. Furthermore, al-Turabi considers that the democratic development in Islam must cover not only the relationship between the state and the individual, but must include all the institutions of society, such as the family. Each institution, or segment, must work to further democracy in both public and private life.[68]

---

[65] Turabi, *Tajdid al-fikr al-islami*, pp. 108-109, 164- 165, 133-139 & 160-163.

[66] Turabi, *Usul al-fiqh*, pp. 18-25 & 32-35.

[67] Turabi, *Usul al-fiqh*, pp. 36-37 & 42-45; Turabi, *Tajdid al-fikr al- islami*, pp. 26-31, 36-49, 54-63, 76-77, 148-149 & 172-143.

[68] Turabi, *Tajdid al-fikr al-islami*, pp. 68-71; for a discussion of the forms of *shura*, see Turabi, *Qadayah*, pp. 72-77 & 80-81.

Political freedom, al-Turabi argues, is an original part of creed and nature because freedom is what distinguishes man from animal. This includes the freedom to voice his views; man is persuaded, not forced, to worship God. Tyranny can never be justified, including at the political level. The *shari'ah* calls on people to voice their views, but the truth of the matter is that today's rulers have at their disposal the necessary instruments of suppression. Therefore, the individual should never be identified with the state. He must always remain free, and his freedom cannot be given to institutions or to society. Since any institutionalization of freedom leads ultimately to its destruction, the individual should normatively be bound by Islam.[69]

According to al-Turabi, Muslim society has two characteristics that distinguish it from other societies: first, it has kept to itself the authority to legislate; and, second, it has maintained the power of taxation as the prerogative of society, and not the state. In the West, these characteristics have been surrendered to the state; in a Muslim society, they are socially developed and defined. Socially developed legal schools had tremendous influence over the state, and the state had always yielded to this institution. Today, this institution finds its political equivalent in political parties, and its legal equivalent in political legal schools. Not only might political parties be a means toward cooperation between individuals, but they are a step in the direction of the freedom and unity of the whole. *Shura* is conducted by and channeled through a structure of unifying systems for free Muslims.[70]

Al-Turabi warns against misusing the freedom of political parties and other institutions of civil society to distill disunity among the community, as happened with the historical split of Islam into Shi'i and Sunni variants. Although pluralism is allowed, it should be conducted within a consensual context of a set of principles that lead to the enhancement of society, not to its demise. This balance must be stricken between freedom and unity.[71]

The mosque is another important civil institution on which al-Turabi focuses. It is not only a place of pure worship, but a site of socialization where people get acquainted and form ideological bonds that lead to their unification in social and political orientations and activism. The mosque is a form of communal unity, solidarity, unified organization, communication and leadership—simply, it expands on the characteristics of

---

[69] Turabi, *Qadayah*, pp. 10-19 & 22-28.
[70] Turabi, *Qadayah*, pp. 20-21 & 29-30.
[71] Turabi, *Qadayah*, pp. 34-37 & 44-47.

today's unions and federations! Leadership is selected by the people; equality is accorded to all members regardless of color, origin, wealth or languages. Finally, everyone must follow a comparable set of rules.[72]

In practice, Hasan al-Turabi is pragmatic. In a hearing at the US Congress, he sounded as if he was a liberal democrat in the guise of a Muslim reformer. Yet, he has always called for freedom of association and multi-party systems. His political front or *Al-Jabhah* includes multiple segments of the Sudanese society, including the sufi and the political movements of *al-Khatmiyyah* and *al-Ansar*. He believes that the Sudanese system has been unable to set a viable party system and is in need of reformation. Although the main parties are traditionally based on a combination of sufis and dynastic affiliations, a proper party system should not be based on individuals. Instead, it should be based on supporting or opposing platforms and watching governmental policies. Al-Turabi has organized his own party along civil lines, including unions and professional federations such as the lawyers. Furthermore, he has been one of the powers behind the inclusion in 1985 constitution of its Seventh Article, which stipulates the necessity of basing the political system on the freedom to form parties, and its Thirty-Third Article, which stipulates the inalienability of individual rights and freedom except by a legislation from the representative council in order to maintain law and order, public health, or the well-being of the national economy. Following this line of thought, he calls for resolving the issue of Sudanese minority by giving them autonomy and freedom, much like the Prophet's practice with the Jews in the first Islamic state.[73]

In practice, however, the current Sudanese government seems to contradict al-Turabi's theory, highlighting the difficult political predicaments in which the people of the area find themselves, and the pressures of regional and international involvement. Nevertheless, one can use the theory propagated by al-Turabi himself to evaluate the practices of the Sudanese government.

---

[72] Turabi, *Al-Salat 'imad al-din* (Beirut: Dar al-Qalam, 1971), pp. 124-133, 138-147 & 156-158.

[73] On his political life, see *Al-Hayat,* Tayyarat Section, 14 August 1993, p. 1; on the hearing, see *House Foreign Affairs Africa Subcommittee Hearing, Witness: The Implication for U.S. Policy of Islamic Fundamentalism in Africa*, May 1992; on his view of current affairs of Sudanese party system, see Turabi, "Islam, Democracy, the State," Louis Cantouri, ed., p. 54; and on minorities' status, see p. 53. For a discussion of the *Jabhat al-qawmiyyah al-islamiyyah*, see Idris Salim al-Hasan, "Al-Din wa al-idiulujia," *Al-Din fi al-mujtama'*, pp. 249-266. On constitutional discussions, see Ahmad Shawqi Mahmud, *Al-Tajribah al-dimuqratiyyah fi al-Sudan* (Cairo: 'Alam al-Kutub, 1986), pp. 33-37, and Sami', *'Azmat al-huriryyah*, pp. 242-247.

Rashid al-Ghannushi

Following al-Turabi's line of thinking is Rashid al-Ghannushi, the leader of *Al-Nahdah* in Tunisia. Al-Ghannushi postulates the necessity of respecting all public and private freedoms and human rights as prescribed in the Qur'an and ratified by international covenants. These issues involve basically the furthering of the freedoms of expression, association, and political participation, and the condemnation of violence and the suppression of free opinion. In addition, he argues that these issues may provide a platform for peaceful co-existence and dialogue between rulers and the ruled, or between the state and society. [74]

Al-Ghannushi conditions his acceptance of any political order on whether the system provides for the peaceful competition of political parties and segments of society on social, political and ideological issues. By participating in social institutions and elections for all kinds of representative councils, people and parties will be able to contribute directly to the administration of state affairs. If this takes place, the Islamic movement is ready to recognize the system that would then carry popular support and, consequently, political legitimacy. Considering the people's authority as the highest authority in society—after acknowledging God's governance, of course—al-Ghannushi accepts people's right to form its civil institutions and parties, including setting up a communist party. In fact, a society even has the right to be atheistic. By accepting all forms of association, al-Ghannushi, as well as al-Turabi, drops any limitation that has been imposed on the freedom of society to organize in the manner it deems necessary. [75]

Concerning the relationship between democracy and religion, al-Ghannushi joins al-Turabi in emphasizing the non-contradictory nature of the two concepts, and the distinction between citizenship and religion. Citizenship is acquired without religious discrimination, while religion is a matter of conviction. Citizens may decide their interests are best served by forming parties and other institutions that are irreligious, or they may choose to change the political system entirely. This does not constitute a breach of religion since pluralism itself is sanctioned by

---

[74] Ghannushi, *Bayrut al-masa'*, 15 May 1993, p. 15; and Ghannushi, "Mustaqbal al-tayyar al-islami, *Minbar al-sharq*, no. 1 (March 1992), pp. 3-32. For a general discussion of Ghannushi and *Harakat al-itijah al-islami*, see Abd al-Khabir Mahmud 'Ata, "Qadiyat al-ta'addudiyyah," pp. 116-117.

[75] Ghannushi and Turabi, *Al-Harakah al-islamiyyah wa al-tahdith* (n.d.: n.p., 1981), pp. 34-35. See also on this matter and on the infiltration of the Islamic movement into civil society, Muhammad 'Abd al-Baqi al-Hirmasi, "Al-Islam al-ihtijaji fi Tunis," *Al-Harakat al-islamiyyah al-mu'asirah*, pp. 273 & 179-286.

religion. The sacred text represents a source for, a reference to, and an absorption of the truth; its human interpretations, on the other hand, represent diverse methods of understanding changes in complex social, economic, political and intellectual issues. This allows, according to al-Ghannushi, for unfettered possibilities of systematic development.[76]

Muhammad al-Hashim al-Hamidi

Perhaps the views of the fundamentalist trend that legitimizes pluralistic civil society may best be summarized by the circulated text of a pact (*mithaq*) that has been published by Muhammad al-Hashim al-Hamidi and distributed to other fundamentalists. He states that after the Islamic movement gets hold of government, success hinges on the establishment of a just and democratic system in the Arab world. "Removing the community from the tyrannical swamp [into which it has been plunged] necessitates that it puts down limits and a program for justice, *shura*, and human rights." The program must include the right to life, equality, justice, fair trial, minorities and political participation, as well as freedom of thought, belief, expression, religion and women. Al-Hamidi suggests some basic principles for governing the formation of parties and associations, including the following:

1- The freedom to form parties and political associations for all citizens without exception should be guaranteed by any constitution.

2- Parties do not need to be licensed by the government.

3- Internal party life must be governed by democracy. The call for dictatorship and totalitarian rule is prohibited under any circumstance, slogan or political propaganda.

4- Secular citizens, including communists, have the right to form parties, propagate their ideology and compete for power.

5- Financing of parties should be from its members.

6- Prohibited political propaganda revolve around racial, tribal, sectarian or foreign affiliations.[77]

---

[76] Ghannushi, "Hiwar," *Qira'at siyasiyyah* 1, no. 4 (Fall 1991): 14-15 & 35-37; and, Ghannushi, "Al-Islam wa al-Gharb," *Al-Ghadir*, nos. 10 & 11 (1990), pp. 36-37. On his and other fundamentalists' acceptance of democracy, see John Esposito and James Piscatori, "Democratization and Islam," *Middle East Journal* 45, no. 3 (Summer 1991): 426- 434 & 437-438. On his political life, see Ghannushi, "Hiwar," p. 5; and Abd al-Qadir al-Zugul, "Al-Istratijia al-jadidah li harakat al-itijah al-islami," in *Al-Din fi al-mujtama'*, pp. 346-348. On the possibilities of liberalization, see Gudrun Krämer, "Liberalization and democracy in the Arab World," *Middle East Report*, no. 174 (January-February 1992), pp. 22-25.

[77] Muhammad al-Hashimi al-Hamidi, "Awlawiyyat muhimah fi daftar al-harakat al-islamiyyah: Nahwa mithaq islami li al-'adl wa al-shura wa huquq al-insan," *Al-Mustaqbal al-islami*, no. 2 (November 1991), pp. 19-21; the quotation is from pp. 14-15.

Similarly, *Jabhat al-Inqadh* (Salvation Front) in Algeria has announced in its political program its adherence to *shura* to avoid tyranny and eradicate all forms of monopoly, whether political, economic, or social. In addition to political pluralism, it has argued for the use of elections and other democratic processes in politics and social life.[78]

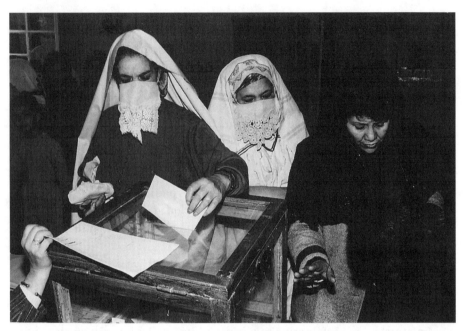

Algeria, December 26, 1991—Algerian women cast their ballots in downtown Algiers in the first round of parliamentary elections, which were won decisively by FIS. The elections were annulled when the Army seized power the following month. (AP/WIDE WORLD PHOTOS)

Conclusion

Radical fundamentalist movements do not represent the majority of Muslims or Islamic movements; they comprise but a few groups spread all over the Arab world. However, equally uncompromising thought has flourished in the tyrannical policies of many Arab states that are no more democratic—except, of course, in slogans and propaganda—than

---

[78] See: *The Political Program of the Islamic Salvation Front* [Al- Barnamaj al-siyasi li jabhat al-inqadh al-islamiyyah], *Minbar al-sharq*, no. 1, March 1992; on the Front and democracy, see Esposito and Piscatori, "Democratization," pp. 437-438; and on the possibilities of civil society in Islam, see "Bahth 'an mujtama' madani manshud," *Mustaqbal al-'alam al-islami* 1, no. 4 (Fall 1991): 225-237.

these radical groups. If one studies the thought of Sayyid Qutb, the founder of radicalism in the Arab world, one can understand—though not necessarily approve of—why these groups have become radical and uncompromising. Under Gamal 'Abd al-Nasir's regime, Qutb was transformed from one of the most liberal writers of Egypt to its most radical thinker. His imprisonment and ferocious torture have been reified into a radical political theology of violence and isolation. Maybe, this was his psychological compensation for the violence of the regime. 'Abud al-Zumar, now serving a forty-year term in an Egyptian prison, articulates the radical groups' views about current affairs very clearly. He says that Islamic violence is nothing more than a reaction against the violence of the governing authority, and the viability of the measures taken to suppress the fundamentalists, such as hanging, is highly questionable. Finally, he adds that fundamentalists are only involved in assassinating those individuals who have physically liquidated the fundamentalists.[79]

The moderate trend attributes this kind of violence to the absence of democratic institutions and a pluralistic civil society. Its highly-involved members emphasize pluralism and democracy in the context of civil society as the means of salvation of both the community and individuals. Civil society has not been absent from moderate Islamic thought, despite the tyranny of the regimes and empires that have ruled the Islamic world. More importantly, the moderates see no contradiction between, or obstacle to the integration of, Islam and Western philosophies and institutions. In fact, by insisting that these systems and institutions, when properly grounded, are truly Islamic, the moderates not only bridge the cultural gap between the East and West, but consequently deny the exclusivity of Islamic thought and attribute the East-West conflict to historical political factors, such as colonialism and imperialism. Since the East and West have common religious and philosophical roots, there is ample room for multi-cultural and religious cooperation and co-existence.

One of these roots is along the lines of Lockean liberal democracy, but grounded in Islamic law (as opposed to Rousseau's controlled popular democracy, which fits the radical concepts of *shura* and *ijma'*). Under no circumstance would the moderate trend allow the cannibalization of society by the state, as does the radical trend. By insisting that the individual is autonomous from society, itself autonomous from the state,

---

[79] *Al-Safir*, 25 September 1993, p. 10; and *Al-Diyar*, 25 September 1993, p. 14.

both the individual and society have the means necessary to protect themselves from totalitarianism and despotism—two more or less common features in the Arab world.

Moderate fundamentalist thinkers are not, of course, Western liberal democrats in the strict sense; however, they are indeed liberal and democratic enough in a context like the Middle East, which is plagued with nationalist totalitarian rules and traditional despotic kings. Moderates believe, along Lockean lines, that the government enjoys executive power as delegated willfully by the people—a characteristic of civil society. They postulate the division of power into the three well-known institutions: the executive, the legislative and the judiciary. Taxation is the people's prerogative and cannot be imposed by authorities, and basic human rights, such as those of association, expression and belief, are mostly accepted by moderates as both natural and religious rights. There is no inherent contradiction between or hierarchy of rights, as they all emanate from God.

It is interesting to stress that pluralism in the context of civil society replaces the radical trend's call for social justice in a religious society. Here Islam becomes the constitutional reference only if the people have chosen it as such, whereas the radical fundamentalists insist on the viability and constitutionality of Islam even in the non-Islamic *jahili* society, and as such requires no consent or approval.

While radical fundamentalism proves resistant to dialogue and cooperation with the Arab regimes and the West in general, moderate fundamentalism—which is often lumped with the radical trend for reasons of political expediency, ease in targeting Islam as the new 'green threat', and the interests of certain circles in the East and West and most governments in the Middle East—is open to dialogue, compromise and, more importantly, to universal rights, freedom, pluralism, and civil society. If this openness does not form the bases of cultural and political platforms for dialogue, what does? Are the moderate fundamentalists—the majority of whom are denied the right to form political parties, even when they represent substantial segments of society—in any way responsible for the tyranny and lack of democratic civil institutions in the Arab World?

In light of these questions, it is sobering to recall Rashid al-Ghannushi's description of our world. He says:

> The world has been transformed, through scientific advancement, into a small village that can no longer tolerate war. This matter poses the necessity of seriously rethinking the future of this village, since it shares a common fate.

This is true if the inhabitants of this village are serious enough to have a common fate. This presupposes, among other things, an end to the abstract geographic and cultural division of the world into East and West, and to the notion that one of them is rational and democratic while the other is perverse and despotic. Such a division is nothing but a recipe for war. Any objective analysis testifies to the fact that the negative and positive values and the forces of goodness exist both here and there. The forces of goodness are invited to enter into a dialogue and search for avenues of intercourse.[80]

---

[80] Rashid al-Ghannushi, "Al-Islam wa al-gharb," *Al-Ghadir*, p. 37.

CHAPTER FOUR

CIVIL SOCIETY IN FORMATION: TUNISIA

Eva Bellin

"Civil society" is an exquisitely ambiguous term. Ever since its introduction into Western political parlance more than three centuries ago, the
term has been used to vastly different ends by different social theorists.
Among its usages, civil society has been employed to signify: the
peaceable society human beings may enjoy thanks to the protection of
a Leviathan state (Hobbes); the stratum of social organizations (corporations, clubs, churches) that exist between family and state (Hegel); the
assortment of private associations that school citizens in civic virtue and
provide a hedge against tyranny (Tocqueville, Montesquieu); a simple
synonym for bourgeois society (Marx); and, the constellation of cultural
institutions (churches, schools, voluntary associations) that guarantee
ideological hegemony for the ruling class (Gramsci).[1] More recently, the
term has become a normative football in contemporary political debate.
For champions of the fall of communism, civil society represents a
venerable bulwark of freedom and democracy, those islands of autonomous social power (churches, labor unions) that countervail the state and
undermine totalitarian regimes.[2] For guardians of the traditional left,
civil society represents an arrant post modern project to disaggregate
society along the lines of personal identity (gender, ethnicity, sexual
preference), minimizing the salience of class and downplaying capitalism's priority as the premier source of human exploitation and oppression.[3] For defenders against Western imperialism, civil society repre-

---

[1] For excellent summaries of the historical uses of the term civil society see John Keane,
Democracy and Civil Society (New York: Verso, 1988); Michael Bratton, "Beyond the State:
Civil Society and Associational Life in Africa," *World Politics* 41, no. 3 (1989): 407-430;
Abdelkadir Zghal, "Le concept de Societé Civile et la Transition Vers Le Multipartisme,"
Annuaire de l'Afrique du Nord 28 (1989): 207-228; Mohamed Kerrou, "Howla muqawalat
al-mujtamaʿ al-madani if Tunis," *Al-Mustaqbal al-ʿArabi* 10, no. 104 (1989): 46-60; and
Muhammad Mahfoudh, "Usus al-mujtamaʿ al-madani" in *Al-Mujtamaʿ al-madani wa al-
Mashruaʿ al-salafi* (Tunis: UGTT Publications,1991).
[2] Andrew Arato, "Civil Society Against the State: Poland 1980-81," *Telos*, no. 1-2, pp.
23-47; Janina Frentzel-Zagorska, "Civil Society in Poland and Hungary," *Soviet Studies* 42,
no. 4 (1990): 759-777.
[3] Ellen Meiksins Wood, "The Uses and Abuses of Civil Society," *Socialist Register*
(1990): 60-84.

sents a spearhead for the West's newest imperialist project—"democratization"—a project of dubious value and questionable appropriateness to political and economic conditions in developing countries.[4]

Given the ambiguity and politically-loaded nature of this term, one might wonder why social scientists interested in analyzing the dynamics of politics in the Arab world persist in using "civil society" as a tool of analysis. Why not opt for more precise, more neutral terms, say, associational life, or democratic institutions, or civil liberties, if these are indeed the processes or institutions we are interested in tracking?

The simplest answer is that this is the term that Arab intellectuals and activists have themselves chosen to use. "Civil society" (that is, *al-mujtama' al-madani*) has entered the discourse of the Arab world and become a central concept in current Arab debate over the direction of politics in the region. State officials use it to promote their projects of mobilization and "modernization"; Islamists use it to angle for a legal share of public space; and independent activists and intellectuals use it to expand the boundaries of individual liberty.

The reason "civil society" has found so many champions of such varied political intent has much to do with the ambiguity of the term—elastic enough to accommodate a wide variety of political ambitions but historically weighty enough to imbue each with deep moral resonance. But despite the term's ambiguity, contemporary proponents of civil society are united in one way: they share a common desire to combat despotism. Of course, their conceptions of despotism—its sources and remedies—vary tremendously. For some, despotism lies in coercive rule, exemplified by military or theocratic regimes that do not tolerate dissent. Its remedy lies simply in championing civilian (i.e., non-military, secular) regimes. For others, despotism resides in the failure to empower men and women to determine their own destinies collectively. The remedy lies in championing the institutions of citizenship, the parties and parliaments, universal suffrage and majority rule that can transform passive subjects into active citizens. More skeptical democrats argue that formal democratic institutions alone cannot preserve citizens from despotism since passivity and ignorance may prevent the "man in the street" from using these institutions effectively. The remedy then lies in inculcating citizens with *civisme*, the participant culture of civics textbooks that trains citizens in activism, reason, and engagement

---

[4] al-Hannachi, 'Abd al-Latif, "Niqash," in *Al-Mujtama' al-madani wa al-mashrua' al-salafi* (Tunis: UGTT Publications, 1991), p. 54.

and thus makes them competent to shape their own political lives.[5] But even active engagement of the citizenry in political life cannot prevent the emergence of yet another form of despotism: the tyranny of the majority. For some the remedy for such tyranny lies in cultivating a culture of civility—one that tolerates difference and respects the rules of the game no matter the diversity in citizens' conception of the good.[6] For others, the remedy rests in the inviolate defense of civil liberties, the guarantee of the individual's most basic freedoms, no matter his/her political persuasion.

Civilian rule, citizenship, *civisme*, civility, civil liberties—all are remedies to different forms of despotism and all are evoked by the term "civil society". The term is useful then in that it focuses attention on these different sources of despotism and suggests a menu of remedies to address them. Of course, not all these remedies "go together" and none of them are easily achieved. To the extent that civilian rule, the rights of citizenship, and civil liberties have been attained anywhere in the world they are the sum of centuries of struggle, still in process. And even the most venerable democracies experience an inherent tension between the goals of liberty and community, the desire to guarantee citizens individual freedom and the will to impose upon them a certain conformity of values (as is necessary to sustain a political system founded on compromise rather than coercion). As Almond and Verba[7] pointed out thirty years ago (and as Robert Putnam[8] has rediscovered more recently in the case of Italy), democracies (and civic culture) thrive only when citizens share an underlying culture of trust, that is, when they share a sense of common political identity and (at least minimal) community of shared values and beliefs.[9] The protection of individual liberty, however, proscribes imposing conformity of values or identity upon the citizenry and hence contributes little to nurturing the solidarity democracies require. Civil liberties and civic spirit may then be modestly conflicting goals.

These two lessons (that the battle against despotism is everywhere a process—often prolonged—and that democracies everywhere experi-

---

[5] Gabriel Almond and Sidney Verba, *The Civic Culture* (Boston: Little Brown and Company, 1965), pp. 7-30.

[6] Edward Shils, "The Virtue of Civil Society," *Dissent*, no. 38 (Spring 1991), pp. 3-20.

[7] Almond and Verba, *The Civic Culture*, pp. 368-372.

[8] Robert Putnam, *Making Democracy Work: Civic Traditions in Modern Italy* (Princeton: Princeton University Press, 1993).

[9] According to Almond and Verba, such "trust" is the irreducible core component of a "civic culture".

ence conflict between the goals of liberty and community) should offer some comfort to the observers of Arab politics. In the Arab world there is a tendency to be pessimistic about the prospects for democratic politics because the boundaries of civil society (the rights of citizenship, the protection of civil liberties) are nearly everywhere constrained and the conflict between community and liberty is very often gravely charged (especially where Islamists seek to use the state to impose their notions of community upon society at the expense of individual liberties). But what is important to recognize (and what is most exciting about politics in the Arab world today) is that the current Arab debate over the nature of civil society represents an important departure for politics in the region—it marks the unprecedented engagement of ordinary citizens in political life. Urban poor mobilized by Islamist movements, women organized by women's movements, intellectuals speaking from the universities and through the press have all been drawn into the debate over the boundaries of civil society and the sources and remedies of despotism in the Arab world.[10] And even if that debate has not yet been concluded to the satisfaction of Western proponents of liberal democracy (has it yet been concluded satisfactorily in the United States, where citizens continue to battle over the boundaries of free speech and the right of religious fundamentalists to limit federal funding of abortion), atleast the process of self-determining politics has begun to gather steam.

Still, it is premature to be optimistic about the near-term prospects for beating back despotism in the Arab world. Many factors conspire to prolong its survival. Ethnic and sectarian fragmentation undermine a sense of national community in many Arab states and sabotage efforts to build the trust and solidarity necessary for the development of a "civic culture". Deeply entrenched military regimes prevail in many Arab countries and resist the introduction of democratic institutuions that might limit their privilege and power. Poverty and illiteracy deprive democratic institutions of their true force and prevent citizens from developing the civisme necessary to combat state tyranny. A tradition of economic statism in many countries insufficiently disperses economic (and political) power, making it more difficult to impose limits on state prerogative . . . The list is long.

It is for this reason that the Tunisian case is actually so interesting. Among the countries of the Arab world, Tunisia is uniquely well positioned to expand the boundaries of civil society and beat back the

---

[10] Mohamed al-Kilani, "Al-Mujtamaʿ al-madani" in Tahir Labib, et al., *Al-Mujtamaʿ al-madani* (Tunis: UGTT Publications, 1991), p. 45 .

domain of despotism. First, Tunisian citizens share that overarching sense of political community so essential to the development of a "civic culture" but so rare in the Arab world. Tunisian society is relative unfragmented by ethnic or religious cleavage (more than 98 percent of Tunisians are Sunni Muslims and the Arab/Berber cleavage has diminished to near political insignificance over the past 100 years). Moreover, the country has enjoyed a protracted experience of political identity long predating the era of colonial map-making. Second, the country has had a long history of civilian rule during which past president Bourguiba purposely contracted the size of the military and subordinated it firmly to civilian control. There is no powerful military competing with (or doubling as) the ruling party in Tunisia as is the case in many other countries in the region. Third, the state's long-held policy to promote education and spread widely the benefits of economic development has endowed the country with a large and relatively well-educated middle class. This generates precisely the sort of citizens that might possess the skills and leisure necessary to develop *civisme* and use democratic institutions effectively. Fourth, Tunisia was among the first Arab countries to break with "Arab socialism" and embark on a "quasi-liberal" strategy of development (at least in the sense of consciously promoting the development of private sector commerce and industry). Hence the state created space for the development of autonomous sources of economic power that might imaginably countervail it one day. Fifth, and perhaps most important, the state has publicly committed itself to the development of civil society in Tunisia. Thus, even if public policy has not always kept pace with official discourse, the state's public prizing of a Montesquieuian model of polity provides a legitimating ideological wedge for citizen lobbying on civil society's behalf.

Still, there is no reason to be complacent about the development of civil society in Tunisia. For while the country has made notabl e progress in combatting some common sources of despotism (nurturing a culture of *civisme* and civility, dispersing the loci of economic power in society, expanding the reach of some democratic institutions), it has still failed to achieve one important goal—the institutionalization of contestation sufficient to impose accountability upon a despotically-tempted state. The responsibililty for this failure lies squarely with the state, driven as it is by contradictory impulses to foster the development of civil society on the one hand, but also contain the latter's development so as not to cede political control. These contradictory impulses are evident in the state's management of associational life, economic liberalization, and the extention of civil liberties, three important trajectories in the development of civil society in Tunisia. The following essay then will trace Tunisia's experience in each of these areas in an effort to illustrate the state's contradictory agenda and its role in shaping the strengths and weaknesses of civil society in Tunisia today.

Associational Life in Tunisia

To begin with definitions, (and following A.R. Norton), the term associational life here signifies the mélange of associations, guilds, unions, interest groups, social clubs, religious organizations, and political parties that exist in the social space between the individual and the state.[11] Such associational life is generally celebrated by democrats for one of three reasons. First, associations are seen as schools of *civisme*. By participating in associational life citizens become schooled in public spirit, political initiative, political activism, and collective self-determination. Second, (and related to the first), associations are seen as schools of civility. By participating in associational life citizens are trained in the skills of cooperation and compromise (in addition to learning respect for the rules of the game). Third, associations are seen as potential nodes for the aggregation of social power independent of the state. As autonomous nodes of social power they contain the potential to countervail the state and serve as a hedge upon excessive state power. In this way associations may potentially remedy three forms of despotism, that born of passivity, that born of intolerance, and that born of excessive state power.

Of course, these remedies may come in different mixes in different associations. A given association might enjoy sufficient autonomy from the state to countervail its power but be too authoritarian in its internal workings to school members much in the art of compromise. Conversely, an association might be subject to state control and hence incapable of hedging state power yet be sufficiently mobilizational to school citizens in public spirit and political participation. *Civisme*, civility, and autonomy are not conjoined; they are discrete goods that can be nourished to varying degrees simultaneously.

This is a lesson Tunisian leaders know well and it is one they have tried to exploit since independence. Since the days of Bourguiba the

---

[11] Augustus Richard Norton, "Studying Civil Society in the Middle East," unpublished paper, 1992.

Tunisian elite has recognized the political value of nourishing *civisme* and civility in one's citizenry—for the energy and talent it mobilizes, for the power it creates, for the control it affords. At the same time, Tunisian elites have been highly suspicious of the development of autonomous power blocs in society that might challenge their rule, undermine their "civilizational" project, and contest their privileges. As a consequence, Tunisian leaders have consistently encouraged the development of associational life in their country, but in an extremely controlled way. Following a strategy of what might be called "controlled *civisme*", they have actively mobilized their citizens in parties and associations[12] but have subjected these parties and associations to very strict state control in an effort to limit their autonomy and their contestatory capacities. The level of this control has varied over time, reaching a high during the middle period of the Bourguiba era and declining somewhat during the early years of Ben 'Ali but it has remained a constant in associational life throughout the independence era.

The Bourguiba Years

The strategy of controlled *civisme* can be tracked first at the level of party organization. From his earliest years Bourguiba recognized the political value of mobilizing the masses and tapping their political energy to further his own ends. In fact, Bourguiba's party, the Neo-Destour, distinguished itself from its predecessor the Destour by abandoning the salon politics of the old elite and engaging the Tunisian masses in the country's struggle for independence. By tapping into their nascent *civisme* through a mixture of populist and nationalist themes, Bourguiba was able to build his own power base and conduct an effective campaign against the French. A network of party cells crisscrossed the country, mobilizing Tunisian resources and organizing the demonstrations, strikes, and guerrilla warfare that helped drive the French out. After independence Bourguiba recognized the value of this network and worked to reinforce the party structure, now with the benefit of state resources. Party cells were established in every village, a massive machine was built for the purposes of mobilization, indoctrination, patronage, and recruitment. During its early years, then, the party was indeed a vibrant

---

[12] Contrast this to the state-nurtured passivity of citizens that is, according to Linz, the hallmark of authoritarian regimes. Juan Linz, "An Authoritarian Regime: Spain," in Erik Allardt, ed., *Mass Politics* (New York: The Free Press, 1971).

institution, effectively drawing Tunisian citizens into political life and engaging their energy in a project of national development.[13]

But just as Bourguiba's party building strategy reflected his enthusiasm for mobilizing *civisme* so did it evidence his desire for control. Bourguiba brooked no contestation, either inside or outside the party. Within the Neo-Destour, Bourguiba used force to put down the one and only severe threat to his control. Trade union thugs were enlisted to repress the "Youssefist challenge" at a party congress in 1955[14] and Salah Ben Youssef himself was later assassinated by Bourguiba's agents. Once elected president, Bourguiba contracted the space for internal party debate, isolating those who pressed for more internal democracy (e.g., Ahmed Tlilli) and using his control over vast state resources to manipulate and divide his elite and thus retain sultanistic prerogative. Outside the Neo-Destour, Bourguiba also silenced political contestation, evidenced most dramatically in the banning of all rival political parties in 1963. Like many leaders in the region at this time, Bourguiba dismissed the liberal ideal of political competition as partisan and divisive, unconscionably wasteful at a time when citizens should be united in a consolidated effort for national development. The content of citizenship was to be found in symbolic participation in the political sphere (voting in referendums, electing a populist president) but not in the capacity to contest the regime and force it to be accountable through the free play of political competition.[15]

Bourguiba's penchant for controlled civisme was also evident in the realm of non-party association (unions, interest groups, professional associations). Again, Bourguiba recognized the benefits of mobilization but again wished that this mobilization be controlled. A corporatist strategy of interest group organization was the preferred tactic. Bourguiba organized the country's major social forces (workers, farmers, business-

---

[13] Clement Henry Moore, *Tunisia Since Independence: Dynamics of a One Party State* (Berkeley and Los Angeles: University of California Press, 1965).

[14] Salah Ben Youssef represented a conservative coalition of *'ulama*, Djerbans, and landlords that advocated a less conciliatory approach toward the French during the negotiation of independence. It was also identified with traditional Arab cultural symbols whereas Bourguiba was identified with more European ways. For more on the Youssefist challenge see Mohamad Abdelbakı Hermassl, "Islam, Democracy, and the Challenge of Political Change," in Yehuda Mirsky and Matt Abrens, eds., *Democracy in the Middle East: Defining the Challenge* (Washington, DC: The Washington Institute,1993), p. 153-156; Moore, pp. 61-69.

[15] This binary vision of the dimensions of citizenship (participation and contestation) is taken from Robert Dahl, "Governments and Political Opposition," in Fred Greenstein and Nelson Polsby, eds., *Handbook of Political Science*, vol. 3 (Massachusetts: Addison-Wesley, 1975), pp. 115-122.

men, and women) in monolithic, monopolistic, state-controlled organizations, geared to rally citizens in support of the president's programs as
well as provide the means for social control. At the same time an
associations law was decreed, significantly limiting freedom of association in Tunisia by requiring all associations to obtain visas from the
Ministry of In terior before they could operate legally. A network of
associations did develop in Tunisia, some organized in corporatist
fashion (the UGTT, UNAT, UNFT, and UTICA), some more pluralistic
(sports clubs, charitable groups). But most relied on the state for
financial support, most drew their leadership from the Destourian party
faithful, and all were subject to extensive state scrutiny. Few associations had the autonomous wherewithal to contest the state (and truth-
fully, few saw contestation as their mission in the early years of
independence). In those rare instances where the will and capacity for
contestation existed, the state moved quickly to quash it.

The best evidence for this can be found in Bourguiba's handling of
the UGTT. At independence the UGTT was a strong organization
equipped with a broad popular base (membership tallied at 180,000 in
1956),[16] a solid organizational structure, a cadre of dynamic and imaginative leaders (Ahmed Ben Salah, Ahmed Tlilli) and unquestionable
national legitimacy (given the central role the union had played in the
independence struggle). As such the UGTT rivaled the Neo-Destour's
mobilizational capacity and was in a strong position to contest Bourguiba's
leadership. When such a point of contestation did arise (specifically over
an imaginative social and economic reform program proposed by the
union leadership in 1956) Bourguiba took steps that would become his
paradigmatic response to political challenge in the years to come.
Bourguiba manipulated internal rivalries within the UGTT leadership,
played upon his own popularity among the rank and file, pressured the
Destourian faithful within the UGTT, even created a second trade union
(temporarily) to rival the UGTT, in short spared no effort to force the
union to cast off its dynamic leaders and renounce its independent
program . Political docility and subordination were Bourguiba's goals
vis-à-vis the country's associations and for the first decade and a half of
independence Bourguiba was able to impose this even upon the relatively strong national trade union confederation.[17]

---

[16] Hermassi, "Islam ...," p. 155.
[17] Eva Bellin, "Civil Society Emergent? State and Social Classes in Tunisia," unpublished Ph.D. dissertation, Princeton University, 1992, pp. 245-278.

In the realm of religious associations, Bourguiba's penchant for control was also evident. His civilizational project for Tunisia was unabashedly secular—traditional religious practice was to be sacrificed wherever it conflicted with the goal of development (hence the famous incident of Bourguiba drinking orange juice in public during Ramadan). As for traditional religious institutions, these were to be subordinated to, or incorporated into, the modern state, if not abolished altogether. Following in the footsteps of Atatürk, Bourguiba brought schools and courts under state control (including the ancient Islamic university Zeitouna) and nationalized religious *habus*.[18] Organized religion thus lost much of its institutional and financial autonomy. As for its popular base, although most Tunisian citizens could be counted among the faithful, the age of mass mobilization under the banner of Islam had not yet begun in Tunisia. Bourguiba would not be forced to face Islam as a contestatory force , until his last decade of rule.

During the 1970s Bourguiba's policy of controlled civisme lapsed briefly. The failure of the regime's collectivist strategy of economic development (associated with Ahmed Ben Salah) emboldened the Destour's liberal wing to press for further liberalization of the political system. At first Bourguiba seemed responsive to this initiative, mouthing pieties about the need to discuss the future of democratization in the country. But in fact his "conversion" to liberalization was short lived. Soon after some promising debate at the Destour Congress of 1971, Bourguiba expelled the leaders of the liberal wing from the party.[19] Over the next three years the President worked to reassert his monopoly over political life and by 1974 his success was clear—the Destour party congress declared him President for Life, formally precluding any possibility of alternance. For the remainder of the decade political competition was banned outside the party and debate was silenced within. The political system was indeed blocked, affording citizens little more than symbolic opportunities for participation but no effective means to impose regime accountability.

Blockage at the level of party life unexpectedly breathed life into non-party associations, specifically invigorating the trade union movement. Disaffected political activists of all stripes were drawn to the UGTT (its historic legitimacy and broad base of popular support afforded it some

---

[18] Lisa Anderson, *The State and Social Transformation in Tunisia and Libya* (Princeton: Princeton University Press, 1986).

[19] One of them, Ahmed Mestiri, was accused of "megalomania" for reflecting on the future of liberalization in the country.

protection from state repression, at least for a time, and made it one of the few spaces where the Bourguibist regime could be safely contested).[20] Riding a wave of rank and file frustration over decade-long wage blockage, the union movement developed new militance, expressed in rising strike levels and an increasingly strident tone adapted in its dialogue with the state. Bourguiba's response to this show of independence was predictable. After tried and true methods to disarm the UGTT threat failed,[21] the president resorted to bloody repression. On "Jeudi Noir" in January 1978 Bourguiba called in the army to take control of UGTT headquarters, killing and wounding hundreds in the process. This day of intervention constituted the single most bloody confrontation in the country's history since independence and demonstrated the lengths to which the regime would go to suppress autonomous contestation at the level of associational life.[22]

Coincident with the regime's repression of the trade union movement another equally significant contestatory force was emerging in Tunisia—this time in the domain of religious association. The Islamist movement in Tunisia began to take form in the early 1970s when a number of Islamic activists (led by Rashid al-Ghannushi) began organizing Islamic study circles in urban mosques around the country.[23] The movement started small but gathered speed in the wake of the Iranian revolution. An increasing number of female students donned the veil at the university; journals like *al-Ma'arifah* (founded 1972) gave voice to the Islamist point of view; in 1979 the fledgling Islamic Tendency Movement (MTI) organized its constituent congress to integrate Islamic study circles into a rigorous network of cells covering the whole country.[24]

The regime's response to this new development was characteristically harsh. Suspected "fundamentalists" were chased out of officially sanctioned religious associations (e.g., the Association for the Conser-

---

[20] Abdeljelil Bedaoui, et al., "Al-Mu'asasat al-niqabiyah al-'ummaliyyah fi Tunis: Hususatiha, Dawriha, 'Uzmatiha," in *Utruhat*, no. 10 (1986).

[21] Moral suasion, manipulation of elite politicians, appeal to Destourian members of the UGTT.

[22] In "Al-Muthafafun al al-Mujtama' al-Madani fi Tunis," *Al-Mustaqbal al-'Arabi* 10, no. 104 (1987): 45-60, Mohamed Kerrou points out that a number of professional associations (Journalists, lawyers) also became more politically active and outspoken during the mid and late 1970s. But without a mass base like that of the UGTT, these associations were clearly more vulnerable to silencing by the regime.

[23] Mohamed Abdelbaki Hermassi, "La Societé Tunisienne au Miroir Islamists," *Maghrib-Mashriq*, no. 103 (1984), p. 41.

[24] François Burgat, *L'Islamisme au Maghreb: La Voix du Sud* (Paris: Editions Karthala, 1988), p. 210.

vation of the Qur'an);[25] Islamist journals were suspended for questionably provocative acts (e.g., publishing a picture of Khomeini on the front cover);[26] Islamic leaders like Rashid al-Ghannushi and 'Abd al Fatah Mourou were arrested for subversion, defamation, and spreading false news.[27] The regime was consistent in its recourse to repression to eliminate a movement that threatened to contest not only regime power but its entire civilizational project for Tunisia.

The 1980s saw a narrow opening at the level of party life in Tunisia, but not much elsewhere. By the late 1970s and early 1980s discontent with the blocked political system manifested itself everywhere—in the growing appeal of the Islamist movement, in the Gafsa affair of 1980,[28] in the withdrawal of the Destour's liberal wing to form an (as yet unrecognized and hence illegal) independent political party, the MDS (Democratic Socialist Movement). Bourguiba recognized the need to accommodate this discontent and bolster at least the secular liberal forces in the country behind his regime. At the Destour Congress of 1980 he publicly sanctioned the principle of pluralism and soon after permitted a limited experiment in multi-partyism. Three opposition parties were given legal status: the Communist party in 1981 and the MDS and PUP in 1983.

Still, this sortie in the direction of political competition was hedged by many constraints. The regime retained an electoral system that required opposition parties to obtain 5% of the national vote to win representation in the chambers. (This threshold prevented the fledgling opposition parties from obtaining office, at least in the near term). Access to the media was highly restricted. The official media (radio, television, and most print journalism) typically ignored the activities of the opposition and the independent party press (al-Mustaqbal, al-Tariq al-Jadid) was subjected to routine censorship, suspension, and irregular supplies of (state-controlled) newsprint. Opposition party leaders were subjected to harassment by the state and their followers' freedom to associate was significantly limited.[29] Opposition leaders protested these

---

[25] Hermassi, "La Societé ...," p. 47.

[26] Burgat, L'Islamisme, p. 209-210.

[27] Burgat, L'Islamisme, p. 210.

[28] The Gafsa affair involved the attack of army barracks, police stations and National Guard posts in Tunisia's southern town in Gafsa by a 60 man unit of guerrillas trained in Libya and entering from Algeria in January 1980. The unit, composed of Tunisian nationals hoped to ignite popular insurrection in the South. In fact, the attack elicited no popular response and the commandos were efficiently suppressed by the Tunisian army. However the raid suggested the regime's vulnerability to attack, vulnerability enhanced by the regime's waning popular legitimacy in regions like the underprivileged South.

[29] Party-state officials would deny opposition parties permission to use public building

measures by boycotting elections (e.g., the municipal elections of 1985), but this only further voided the multi-party experiment. Thus although some limited opportunities for contestation were created, the experience of true political competition was still far from realized in Tunisia at this time.

At the level of non-party organizations, associational life continued to be constrained by the state's requirement of obtaining visas from the Ministry of Interior. Some relaxation of the state's grip on associational life was evident in the legalization of the Tunisian Human Rights League (LDTH)—the first human rights league organized in the Arab world.[30] But overall, Bourguiba remained hostile to the development of autonomous contestatory associations in Tunisia.

Again, this was most evident from his relations with the UGTT. Between 1979-83 the president attempted to mend fences with the trade union movement, overseeing its reconstitution in 1980 and inviting it to join a national alliance (the National Front) in parliamentary elections in 1981. But as soon as the union began to show signs of powerful contestation (evidenced in rising strike rates and strident demands for wage gains) Bourguiba moved to repress it again. At first his strategy focussed on legalistic maneuvers—changing the rules of trade union financing and assembly to compromise the UGTT's financial status and organizing capabilities.[31] But eventually it progressed to the abusive dismissal of trade union activists from their jobs, the seizure of trade union bank accounts and enterprises, the arrest of trade union leaders, the occupation of trade union headquarters, and ultimately the appointment of Destourian loyalists to head the trade union executive.[32]

But if repression was Bourguiba's preferred tactic vis-à-vis the trade unions, it was even more so with regard to his handling of the Islamists. The regime rejected the MTI's request to constitute itself as a legal opposition party in 1981 and it banned the major share of Islamic publications (al-Habib, al-Ma'arifah, al-Mujtama'). The Prime Minister issued circulars forbidding the donning of religious dress in the Administration and the schools and the Ministry of Interior made

---

for party events. Given the fact that most large buildings in Tunisia were the property of the party-state, this effectively denied opposition parties the possibility of organizing inside gatherings.

[30] The league was founded in 1977.

[31] That is, the right to automatic check-off was abolished in 1984 as was the right to hold trade union meetings at the workplace.

[32] Bellin, "Civil Society Emergent?", pp. 313-340.

membership in the MTI a legal offense.[33] Attempts to achieve some sort of rapprochément between the Islamists and the state were thwarted by a cycle of violence set off by Islamic extremists but sustained by the state which answered every act of violence in kind. Attacks on Club Med in 1981 led to the arrest of 200 Islamist activists; attacks on two public buildings in 1986 led to the execution of three members of Islamic Jihad; bombings of tourist hotels and the splashing of acid on political opponents led to massive arrests of Islamists in 1987.[34]

The Islamist threat became an obsession for the anti-clerical Bourguiba who vowed that "to eradicate the integriste poison...will be the last service I render Tunisia."[35] This obsession, however, was ultimately to be the aging President's undoing. When the courts returned sentences more lenient that he might have wished for the Islamists arrested in 1987, Bourguiba sought to intervene in the legal process and impose sentences of execution. The Prime Minister (and former Minister of Interior) Zine 'Abdine Ben 'Ali realized that the execution of pious Muslims not implicated in violence would inflame an important segment of the Tunisian population and might provoke riots, if not civil war. It was this danger which ultimately compelled Ben 'Ali to act and depose the old Combatant Supreme in a non-violent and technically-legal coup.

The Ben 'Ali Era

From his first day in office Ben 'Ali vowed to make a bold departure from the preceding regime, most notably in the area of political freedoms. In his opening speech Ben 'Ali proclaimed that the Tunisian people were mature enough to govern themselves in true Republican fashion. Consequently, he promised to rejuvenate political life, advance the progress of democratization, and guarantee civil liberties. Thus, the "new era" inaugurated by Ben 'Ali looked auspicious for the development of civil society. An assessment of his performance six years into his regime, however, gives him a mixed review.

First with regard to party life: Ben 'Ali's reform did indeed bolster multi-party competition in Tunisia. A new Party Code was announced shortly after Bourguiba's ouster which encouraged Tunisians to organ-

---

[33] In 1981, 107 members of the MTI were arrested for belonging to a non-recognized association, defaming the President, and spreading false information. Ghannoushi was among them and was condemned to 11 years in prison. See Burgat, *L'Islamisme*, 1988.

[34] Burgat, *L'Islamisme*.

[35] Cited in Hermassi, "L'État Tunisien et le Mouvement Islamiste," *Annuaire de l'Afrique du Nord* 28 (1989), p. 300.

ize new opposition parties (so long as they were not organized around the issues of language, religion, race, ethnicity, or religion). Tunisian citizens responded with enthusiasm and three new political parties were created, bringing the total number of legal opposition parties to six: the Democratic Socialist Movement (MDS), the Tunisian Communist Party (PCT), the Party of Populist Unity (PUP), the Social Party for Progress (PSP), the Progressive Socialist Assemblage (RSP) and the Unitary Democratic Union (UDU). Together with a new Electoral Code (which gave opposition parties a role in the distribution and counting of electoral ballots) and the provision of financial subsidies to help legal opposition parties cover the cost of campaigns (and eventually publications), the framework for real political competition seemed in place.

But in fact, Tunisia's foray into multi-partyism has not introduced sufficient competitiveness to force accountability upon regime elites. This is true for three reasons.

First, the regime continues to bias the political game by subjecting opposition figures to petty harassment and controls. The absence of secure civil liberties prevents opposition leaders from subjecting the regime to the fullest critical scrutiny. It also undermines the opposition's organizational capacities. Both constraints mute the competitive character of the political game.

Second, the electoral system is organized in a way that prevents the possibility of true alternance. Until now, legislative elections have been conducted on a winner-take-all (majority) basis, which effectively denies representation to all parties, save the dominant RCD. (In 1989, the RCD took all seats in the Chamber of Deputies although it won only 80 percent of the popular vote; Independents and the MDS saw no representation in parliament although they won 17 percent and 3 percent of the vote respectively). More recently, the president has proposed a reform in the election code that will reserve a certain portion of chamber seats for election on a proportional basis. This reform should give the opposition some representation in parliament though it will not provide for credible alternance in the near future.

Third, the failure of muscular, mass-based opposition parties to emerge in the country has constituted an extremely important barrier to the development of truly competitive politics. Tunisians complain that they do not have an opposition worthy of them and the responsibility for this failure rests with both the regime and independent political elites. First, as mentioned above, the regime's routine violation of civil liberties undermines the vitality of the opposition and impedes the organization of alternative mass-based parties. Second, the regime's ban on the engagement of religion for political purposes eliminates one of the most effective devices for mass mobilization in Arab politics today. Third, the regime's inclination to absorb rather than compete with its opposition has sapped the strength of opposition parties. This is most notable in the case of the MDS. Under Ben 'Ali the regime has appropriated the slogans of the MDS (pluralism, democracy, liberalism), has coopted some of the MDS' most dynamic leaders (with the offer of choice posts in the administration), and has exerted enormous moral, financial, and electoral pressure to persuade the party to work with the regime in a national alliance. Fourth, opposition figures themselves seem reluctant to organize the grass roots behind them. In Tunisia, as elsewhere in the Arab world, politics has long been an elite affair. The route to influence and advancement has traditionally lain in access to other elites, not in building a mass following. This is a culture that persists among politicians in Tunisia and it is likely to remain unchanged so long as the regime reinforces it with policies that actively discourage independent mass mobilization and that actively provide routes to individual advancement and influence through cozy relations with state elites.

The absence of real competition in the political system limits the meaningfulness of citizenship by denying the vote the power to express alternative preferences or impose accountability on regime elites. Nonetheless, the regime has made efforts to enhance the content of citizenship by undertaking reform within the ruling party itself. By democratizing the internal structure of the party and mobilizing higher rates of participation in it, citizens might conceivably obtain more meaningful opportunities for participation in the determination of their own political destinies.

In line with this reasoning, Ben 'Ali has launched some significant reforms. Within the party efforts were made to mobilize higher rates of participation. Party leaders undertook a mass membership drive in 1988 (which claimed to sign up 1.5 million members for the RCD) and extra effort was devoted to recruiting previously disaffected groups (e.g., intellectuals) under the rubric of the party's now all-embracing "rassemblement". Efforts were also made to make the party more responsive to the base. For the first time central committee members were assigned responsibility for specific regional districts (and encouraged to take field trips to learn the preferences of "their constituents"). Moreover, debate over party policy was significantly opened up to participation at the local, regional, and national levels.

Still, there have been clear limits to the party's democratization and increased accountability to the base. Six years into the new regime more than half of the party's central committee is still designated by the president from above, reflecting the leadership's continued penchant for top-down control. Moreover, the persistent failure to separate state and party finances has continued to make party functionaries more attuned to respecting the chain of command from above (i.e., from the state) rather than building sponsors from below.[36] Altogether, Ben 'Ali's reforms have gone far toward revitalizing a party that had become increasingly sclerotic and authoritarian under Bourguiba. Nevertheless, they have not radically altered the content of citizenship for most Tunisian citizens.

But if the regime's record with regard to launching meaningful party life has been less than spectacular, what about its performance regarding non-party associations? Here there might be more room for optimism given the official rhetoric of the regime. On repeated occasions (and most notably on *National Associations Day*), Ben 'Ali has enthusiastically embraced the development of associations in Tunisia for the "indispensable role [they assume] in modern civil society," for the contribution they make in "reinforc[ing] rela tions between the citizen and his community, between various communities and between society and state," for fostering the "principles of solidarity and altruism," and for contributing towards building "a modern and invincible Tunisian society."[37] Financially, Ben 'Ali has backed up word with deed, extending substantial subsidies to a wide spectrum of private associations to help defray the cost of housing, publications, conventions, and the like. Legally, the regime has taken steps to loosen constraints on freedom of association, retaining the visa system but encouraging the Ministry of Interior to be more liberal in visa distribution.[38]

In this context, associational life has indeed blossomed. Recent official counts put the number of associations in Tunisia at over 5,100, with 3,300 formed since 1988.[39] The number can only be taken as an

---

[36] Of course, the generous funding of the party by the state permits the sustenance of a truly vast, mass-mobilizing network of party cells throughout the country—a political good that would be lost should the party be forced into financial self-sufficiency.

[37] *Tunisian News*, April 24, 1993.

[38] There were also some symbolic changes made in the visa system. According to the new Law of Association announced in 1988, silence on the part of the Ministry of Interior would henceforth be interpreted to mean assent rather than rejection of visa requests. Interior however retained the right to reject visa requests without explanation and without appeal.

[39] In March 1992 the Minister of Interior, 'Abdallah Kallel gave the following breakdown of associational life in Tunisia: 3,171 cultural and artistic associations; 822 athletic

order of magnitude since it counts equally associations that have scores of cells across the country and associations that exist little more than in name. Attempts to get a complete list of associations by name (from which to compose a random sample for closer investigation) were met with stonewalling by the Ministry of Interior. Hence information on associational life in Tunisia can be anecdotal at best. Nonetheless, even anecdotal observation reveals some interesting lessons regarding the development of civisme, civility, and autonomous social power in Tunisia, the three goals we have linked to the development of associational life.

First, with regard to *civisme*: recall that the goal associated with *civisme* is the goal of imbuing citizens with public spirit, of training them in political engagement and initiative and so practicing them in the skills necessary to manage their own political destinies effectively. Participation in associational life is believed to foster *civisme* because it practices citizens in collective problem solving and nurtures in them the habit of public engagement.

In Tunisia there are certainly many associations that nurture these habits and skills in the citizenry. From environmental associations that monitor industrial pollution in the Mediterranean to associations for the handicapped that manage social centers for the deaf and blind, from a woman's organization that runs a battered women's shelter to a consumer advocacy group that monitors price and quality standards in every major domestic market, Tunisia boasts hundreds of associations that mobilize citizens' initiative and engage them in collective problem solving and self-help. The development of such associations is actively encouraged by the regime (which cites *civisme* as part of its political project) and consequently their number is likely to increase, as is the experience of civic engagement, under Ben 'Ali.

Second, with regard to civility, the aim is to inculcate citizens in a culture of tolerance that enjoins them to respect the rules of the game, no matter the diversity in their conceptions of the good. Associational life can conceivably foster this tolerance in one of two ways: (1) by bringing people of divergent world views together in common cause to solve common problems; (2) by developing associations that are expressly committed to the propagation of the values associated with civility.

---

associations; 509 charitable, relief and social associations; 400 friendship associations; 126 associations for development; 115 scientific associations; 41 associations of a general character; and 2 women's associations.

In Tunisia one finds associations fulfilling both these functions. In the absence of hard data on membership rolls it is hard to say just how many associations bring together citizens of diverse world views. But clearly many functional associations draw upon diverse populations (e.g., associations to serve the handicapped; regional development associations). And a variety of professional and "general" associations are devoted to the promotion of tolerance and legalism (e.g., the Tunisian League for Human Rights; the Association of Tunisian Lawyers).

The interesting question to consider, however, is the regime's attitude toward these associations. Theoretically, Ben 'Ali's government is committed to the development of civility in Tunisia. A culture of tolerance and legalism is intrinsic to the Western civilizational project that the regime seeks to realize. But civility is not the regime's only goal nor is it necessarily its most highly valued goal. This becomes apparent when civility collides with another regime objective: political control.

The clash between these two goals is evident in at least two cases, the first being the case of the Tunisian Human Rights League. The League constitutes the quintessential school for civility given the fact that it expressly recruits an extremely diverse membership and that it organizes these members around the defense of legalistic principles.[40] At the same time, the League represents a truly autonomous node of social power that routinely contests regime policy. During the early 1990s the League entered into a period of extremely contentious relations with the regime as it doled out harsh criticism of the regime's treatment of Islamist detainees . For Ben 'Ali's government, this mounting criticism grew increasingly intolerable and in March 1992 it amended the Law of Associations in a way that was intended to defang the League. In fact the amendment went further than the regime anticipated, ultimately provoking the League's dissolution.[41] It was only as a consequence of

---

[40] Hermassi, "Islam ...".

[41] The law was amended in two essential ways. All associations designated by the state to be of "general" character were forbidden to allow political party leader to hold positions of leadership on their boards. At the same time, associations of general character were forbidden to deny membership to any prospective member who embraced the association's goals and who was in full command of his civic and political rights. The regime justified this amendment on the grounds of wanting to "depoliticize" certain associations . The LTDH, for example, counted among its leaders many party activists and it rationed membership with an eye to maintaining a balance between different political forces in the organization. By amending the law the regime hoped to deny the League some of its most active leaders and to flood the organization with RCD loyalists who would push it in a more moderate and less critical direction. Members of the League voted to disband rather than comply with the terms of the new associations law and only after intense international and domestic pressure did the regime agree to (provisionally) reclassify the League as a non-general association and hence place it outside the jurisdiction of the new amendment.

intense international and domestic pressure that Ben 'Ali's government relented and permitted the League to resume operation (in semi-limbo status) a year later. Clearly then when the two goals of civility and control collided, the regime's inclination was to prize the latter even if that meant undermining one of the most vibrant associations in the country.

Further evidence for the priority of control over civility lies in the regime's handling of a cultural association proposed by a group of left-leaning intellectuals in 1989. Called *Nadi Ibn Rushd Li-Fikrah al-Takadum*, the club was to be devoted to reflection on progressive and rationalist traditions in Arab thought and hence was likely to promote an enlightenment-style message of tolerance and reason. (By the founders' own account, this reflection was to provide a nativist retort to growing religious fanaticism in the country). The Ministry of Interior, however, denied them a visa on the grounds that the association's objective was unclear (*ghayr wadih*). More likely, the regime was uneasy at sanctioning an organization that brought together a number of highly independent and charismatic political activists who might use the association as a forum for criticism of the regime.

The regime's penchant for control has important implications for the third goal linked to the development of associational life—the development of autonomous social power in Tunisia. Clearly, the regime is uneasy with the creation of countervailing nodes of power that might contest its authority. Hence, while it encourages the development of associational life for the civility and *civisme* associations foster, the regime hedges their development with numerous constraints. We have already mentioned the legal constraint imposed on associations, specifically the retention of a visa system administered by the Ministry of Interior.[42] Besides legal constraints, the regime also exercises significant financial controls on associational life. Ben 'Ali's government has proven quite generous in extending subsidies to budding associations (in fact, nearly every one of the dozen or so associations this author personally visited admitted to receiving some measure of financial support from the state, even those most jealous of their autonomy).[43]

---

[42] Interior continues to be extremely circumspect in the distribution of visas and much informal politicking is often necessary to obtain the ministry's approval. Members of one alumni association described the difficulties they encountered in getting their visa. Only after influential relatives and former professors intervened to vouch for the organizer's reliability would Interior grantt his apparently harmless association a visa.

[43] For example, the *Union des Femmes Démocrates*, renown for its independence, reported that they had received financial aid from the state in the form of key money for their

These subsidies, however, are distributed on a purely capricious basis, depending on the regime's judgement of the organization's utility and reliability. With subsidies so uninstitutionalized and politically contingent, the autonomy of the recipient associations is clearly constrained.

A third strategy adopted by the regime to contain associational autonomy is one borrowed from the Islamists. Mobilizational in intent, the regime rallies RCD loyalists to infiltrate civil society and control it from within. By flooding associations with RCD members (and encouraging RCD loyalists to found new associations of their own) the regime hopes to dominate associational life in the country and "guarantee...the interests of the nation...against any skids".[44]

A fourth strategy employed by the regime carries over from the Bourguiba era and involves the duplication of vibrant associations. When confronted by a dynamic association bent on contesting the regime (say, the Human Rights League), the regime creates a duplicate association under its own auspices to dilute and countervail the influence of the original. Fifth, and finally, when all else fails, the regime is not above using its coercive capabilities to contain a threat from an autonomous association. For example, the regime has used its control over the security apparatus to manipulate UGTT elections and nudge the organization in a direction it considers safe.[45]

Of course the best evidence of the regime's willingness to use force to contain the challenge of an autonomous social movement is found in the regime's handling of the country's Islamist challenge. Since 1989 the regime has opted for a strategy of repression rather than accommodation, denying the *Nahda* movement legal status, purging associations of Islamist members, arresting hundreds of Islamist activists, and even harassing individual citizens for wearing Islamic garb.[46] To some extent

---

headquarters. The president of the association saw no conflict of interest in taking state money and (citing French practice) asserted that such financial support was an association's right, not a reason for apology.

[44] Mohsen Marzouk, "Autonomie des Associations Tunisiennes: Les Enjeux Politiques," *L'Observateur*, no. 28 (August 4-10, 1993): 25-27. An example of this strategy can be found in the network of neighborhood associations (*Lijan al-Ahya*) created by the RCD in 1990-91, in large part to mobilize neighborhoods behind the RCD and contain the Islamist threat. By most accounts these associations are little more than RCD cells, working in league with the Ministry of Interior. (The latter has a department formally charged with re sponsibility to form, finance, and supervise the Committees de Quartiers).

[45] Specifically, during the course of UGTT local elections in 1992 the regime arrested several UGTT activists (reputed Islamist sympathizers) and held them in jail for the duration to preclude their availability for election to office. Once the elections were concluded, the "offenders" were released without charge.

[46] Note that the regime routinely denies visas to associations suspected of Islamist inspiration. Thus Tunisia is one of the few Islamic countries that lacks a network of Islamic

the regime's recourse to repression has been provoked by the use of violence by some extremist fringes of the Islamist movement (as well as by the cautionary tale of Islamist-led violence in neighboring Algeria). However, the regime's unwillingness to work with even the more moderate elements of the movement bespeaks its concern not simply with containing violence but with containing a credible threat to its hegemony. In the final analysis, Ben 'Ali's regime does not trust the development of autonomous social forces that might potentially contest its power. To the extent that the regime fosters associational life it is because the regime sees associations as "transmission belts" for its own policies.[47] Consequently, the autonomy of associations in Tunisia is made strictly conditional upon their dedication to serving "the national interest", with the "national interest" defined by the regime itself.[48]

Liberalism and Civil Society?

Associational life then can only go so far towards developing countervailing power to the state. So long as their autonomy and organization is hostage to state largesse, associations will play only a limited role in reigning in state power. But if associations a lone cannot beat back state despotism, might choice of economic policy engineer this end? Conventional wisdom (following Milton Friedman) tends to associate despotism with economies that are state-dominated since under such conditions an overwhelming share of power is centered in the state (Freedom is associated with power's dispersion). By contrast, where the economy is organized on a more liberal basis the possibilities for state despotism become more limited both because the state, by definition, relinquishes some of its power to the regulatory control of the market and because in a liberally organized economy the state cedes space for the development of private economic forces (forces that might conceivably contest or at least countervail the state in the determination of public policy).

In many ways Tunisia constitutes an excellent test case for this hypothesis given its relatively early conversion from a state-led strategy for economic development to one more "liberal" in character. After a decade of state-led growth in the 1960s, regime elites became persuaded

---

welfare associations (compare this to the situation in Egypt where Islamist run a vast network of clinics, schools, nurseries, etc.). Instead, the state channels the charitable urges of its citizens through its own institutions, specifically mobilizing funds through the Committees of Social Solidarity that exist at the neighborhood level.

[47] *Tunisia News*, 24 April 1993.
[48] Marzouk, "Autonomie ..."

that the state alone could no longer fuel Tunisian development; rather, private resources, both foreign and domestic, would have to be corralled to sustain the effort. To this end the regime initiated a number of reforms to encourage private sector investment. Among these was the provision of a battery of supports and shelters to sweeten the prospects of investment profitability, especially in industry. (These included formidable tariff barriers, guaranteed state contracts, guaranteed monopolies, subsidized credit and infrastructure, and cost-plus pricing).[49]

The response was not disappointing. Private investors answered the state's inducements with enthusiasm, trippling the number of private sector industrial ventures in little more than a decade, from a low of 865 in 1970 to a high of 2,866 by the mid 1980s. Private sector entrepreneurs tended to cluster in ventures that were technologically simple, least capital intensive, and most immediately profitable. However, their presence was felt in every sector and by the mid 1980s they were accounting for an ever larger share of the economy's value-added, export earnings, and employment creation.[50]

The question then is whether the development of this sizeable diversified class of private sector industrialists might really impose some limits on state power. Certainly the creation of this class meant some relinquishment of power by the state. Investment levels can no longer be determined by decree from the Ministry of Plan—the state henceforth was "condemned to seduce" investment on the part of private sector industrialists.[51] But did this turn toward "liberalization" really endow private sector industrialists with the power to countervail the state and contest it in matters of public policy?

The answer is clearly no. Three major obstacles prevent private sector industrialists from converting their economic power into true contestatory power in Tunisia.

The first obstacle derives from private sector industrialists' continued economic dependence upon the state. As mentioned above, this class emerged thanks to the provision of numerous supports and shelters from

---

[49] Clearly these "sweeteners" undermine the logic of the market hence one might validly question the use of the term "liberal" to describe Tunisia's new development strategy. Further casting doubt on the aptness of this term is the fact that throughout the 1970s and 1980s the state continued to play a persistently large role in investment and distribution in Tunisia. Nonetheless, the strategy was "liberal" in the sense that it marked a retreat of the state from its heretofore near monopolistic control of industrial investment in the country. It also reflected the state's desire to encourage the development of a private sector entrepreneurial class in the country.

[50] Bellin, "Civil Society Emergent?".

[51] Stoleru, cited in Steven Warneck and Ezra Suleiman, eds., *Industrial Polities in Western Europe* (New York: Praeger, 1975) p. 13.

the state, many of which were distributed on a discretionary basis by state elites. Consequently, the profitability of the private sector was long hostage to state largesse—a dependence likely to dampen any urge for contestation.

Since 1986 the regime has instituted a number of economic reforms within the framework of a structural adjustment program that have lessened the discretionary power of the state and have broadened the role of the market in determining industrial profitability. Nonetheless, private sector industrialists still rely on tariff barriers, tax concessions, and subsidized credit from the state; hence, structural adjustment has not entirely vitiated their dependence.

The autonomy of private sector industrialists is further compromised in another way as well. Tax evasion continues to be a rampant practice among Tunisian entrepreneurs (despite attempts at tax reform and tax simplification). Like state-sanctioned corruption elsewhere[52] this evasion is often ignored by the state but filed away for potential prosecutory use should a given industrialist prove politically "troublesome" to the state.

A second obstacle preventing private sector industrialists from converting their economic clout into true contestatory power derives from a common collective action problem. Although in aggregate these industrialists wield significant weight in the Tunisian economy, they find it difficult to harness that power in collective action vis-a-vis the state. Collective action is difficult to organize for all the usual reasons: Industrialists are a diverse group with potentially incompatible interests that vary depending on the size and sector of their ventures; the vast majority of industrial entrepreneurs in Tunisia preside over small scale, under financed, highly repetitive, hand-to-mouth operation, a context unlikely to foster collective solidarity; finally, Tunisia is a small country where the elite is small and well-known to each other. This leads to the personalization of problem solving by most powerful industrialists (i.e., those most able to support the transaction costs involved in organizing collective action). Rather than working through collective agencies, these industrialists tend to resolve their problems by appealing directly to the appropriate "responsable" in the state apparatus.

The third obstacle preventing private sector industrialists from translating economic clout into contestatory power is posed by the state's

---

[52] John Waterbury, "Corruption, Political Stability, and Development: Comparative Evidence from Egypt and Morocco," *Government and Opposition* 11, no. 4, (1976: 426-446).

explicit opposition to such translation. Most recently this was evidence in the state's handling of the "Moalla affair". Long a brilliant, if difficult, critic of the regime, this former minister and current bank president crossed the line of acceptable criticism when he complained to a *Le Monde* correspondent that Tunisia was a too dutiful student of the International Monetary Fund. Such public criticism deeply embarrassed the regime and so to punish Moalla, Ben 'Ali's government withdrew all state funds from Moalla's bank, jeopardizing the bank's viability and forcing Moalla to resign its presidency. The regime also threatened to investigate the bank's tax situation and loan programs for possible irregularities. In short, the regime was prepared to undermine an important financial institution simply for the sake of silencing contestation— a lesson not lost on other private sector entrepreneurs.

The regime, then, is not willing to permit the translation of economic clout into contestatory power. Yes, economic power does confer some political influence for private sector entrepreneurs, but only in the sense of winning them access to state elites. Successful entrepreneurs may consult with the regime, even criticize regime policies, but only "*doucement*" and "*entre amis*". The moment criticism is expressed as a public challenge the state perceives this as a test of force and brings all its strength to bear to quash it.

Thus, the adoption of a more "liberal" economic development strategy cannot guarantee the creation of contestatory forces in society, capable of reigning in the power of the state. As in the case of associations, the state continues to play a "gatekeeping" function, controlling the terms under which social power is mobilized and contestation is engaged. Thusfar, Ben 'Ali's regime has proven itself uneasy with the free play of contestation. The clearest evidence of this can be found in the regime's approach to the protection of civil liberties.

Civil Liberties—Guaranteed?

The guarantee of civil liberties constitutes the indispensable foundation of civil society. Without the inviolable protection of freedom of speech, press, and association, effective contestation is impossible. In Tunisia, however, the regime has refused to submit itself to the discipline of inviolable civil liberties. Certainly some steps have been taken to expand the boundaries of speech and association. The regime has permitted an ever larger number of associations to organize with legal status; it has encouraged the official press to give more coverage to the opposition; it has opened the air waves to foreign broadcasts; and, it has provided the opposition press with subsidies to keep it afloat. Nevertheless, the regime has permitted this expansion to take place only on it s own terms, hedged in by significant constraints. Freedom of speech and freedom of the press are limited by laws that prohibit "defamation" of both the president and the government as well as by codes that permit the seizure of publications (and the arrest of individuals) on the grounds that their views are subversive, likely to disturb public order, and/or are implicated in spreading false information. Freedom of association is checked by the regime's retention of the visa system which permits the Ministry of Interior to vitiate associations without explanation or appeal. Tunisian citizens, then, cannot be confident that their basic civil liberties will be protected—hence their capacity for contestation is significantly constrained.

But why is the regime so fearful of the free play of contestation? Two explanations are possible. First, the regime's fear of contestation might stem from the sheer play of interest. Ever since it won independence Tunisia has known only single party rule that has long endowed regime elites with uncontested privilege and prerogative. The free play of civil liberties and social forces would doubtlessly erode these privileges and hence some regime elites are bound to be disinclined to support political reform.

Aside from sheer interest, however, the regime's tradition of paternalism comes into play as well. Ever since independence the regime has been accustomed to playing a tutelary role with respect to Tunisian society, guiding the country's development in line with its own civilizational vision. During the Bourguiba era, regime elites considered Tunisian society too "immature" to determine its own destiny. With the rise of Ben 'Ali, the hope was that the new president would recognize the maturity of Tunisian citizens and share power with them. However, just at this time the Islamist challenge gathered steam (especially in neighboring Algeria). Regime elites believed the Islamists posed a mortal threat to their civilizational project. Moreover, they believed that any political opening might be used as a wedge for Islamist advancement. Consequently, regime elites fell back on old repressive habits to preserve their civilizational project.[53]

---

[53] The degree to which the Islamist movement in Tunisia actually threatens the regime's civilizational project is a matter of debate. As in other countries, Tunisia's Islamist movement is not monolithic; it comprises several different wings, some radical and violent (such as the PLI, Party for Islamic Liberation, which is responsible for some of the more

In the final analysis, both interest and paternalism play a role in the regime's hostility to open contestation (with each impulse weighing in to different degrees within different wings of the party and state). But clearly, the Islamist threat alone cannot explain the regime's position since state repression has not been limited to the Islamists but has extended toward left-wing activists and independents as well (Moalla, Nadi Ibn Rush, etc.).[54] Still, even if the Islamist threat is not wholly explanatory, it does provide the regime with an effective rationale for its policies. Moreover, this rationale has proven increasingly persuasive to the country's traditional advocates of political opening.

In the past secular intellectuals have been at the forefront of the campaign to expand the boundaries of civil society, pressing the state to guarantee civil liberties and tolerate greater autonomy in Tunisian associations. But faced with the vicious use of violence by Islamist extremists in neighboring Algeria (specifically the assassination of free-thinking intellectuals) and cognizant of the intolerance associated with many Islamist movements, Tunisian intellectuals have rallied behind Ben 'Ali's state in its authoritarian project. The choice, they argue, is not between authoritarianism and democracy but rather between laic authoritarianism and theocratic authoritarianism. Given this choice they

---

nefarious acts of bombing and acid-splashing) and some more moderate (such as the progressive Islamists associated with the journal *15/21*). The Islamist movement in Tunisia has been singled out by both Western and regional observers as containing some of the most progressive and intellectually flexible Islamist activists and intellectuals in the region. At times leaders from the progressive wing (as well as from the more mainstream MTI) have affirmed their fidelity to Bourguiba's liberal personal status code as well as asserting their adhesion to democratic principles, promising to recognize "any government that came out of a regular election...even a communist one" (Burgat, *L'Islamisme*, pp.195-6). The progressive Islamists call for a historicist (as opposed to literal) reading of Islamic texts and enthusiastically embrace the use of *ijtihad* to introduce innovative interpretations of Islamic law. Still the relative weight of the progressives in the Islamist movement nationwide is unclear. Specialists like François Burgat argue that the regime's recourse to repression tends to radicalize the movement and diminish the influence of the progressives. What is clear is that the regime has chosen a repressive course vis-à-vis all Islamists, ever since they made such a strong showing in the national elections in 1989. (Independents,who were primarily of Islamist stripe, won 17 percent of the national vote.) Recognizing that Islamists pose a true challenge to their hegemony, state elites denied the *Nahda* legal party status, closed down its journals , and began a massive campaign of harassment and arrests that persists to this day. (The campaign is routinely justified by exposure of violent plots and cabals linked to the radical Islamists.) This failure to distinguish between different Islamist wings prevents less radical elements from organizing and perhaps channeling popular sympathy for the movement in a less threatening direction. If the movement poses a civilizational threat to the regime then this is partly the work of the regime itself. For more see Mark Gasiorowski, "The Failure of Reform in Tunisia," *Journal of Democracy* 3, no. 4 (October 1992): 85-97, and Burgat, *L'Islamisme*.

[54] For example, the regime originally refused to grant a visa to the *Union des Femmes Démocrates* in 1989, in large part because the union was perceived as too independent and too daunting a competitor to its own state-sponsored women's organization, the UNFT. Ultimately the regime granted the union a visa, not out of respect for free contestation but rather because it realized the UFD could mobilize a significant force of feminists behind the regime's campaign to battle the Islamists.

prefer the laic authoritarianism, arguing (in a new twist on Jean Kirkpatrick) that at least under a secular regime (especially one that draws its ideological inspiration from Western models) there is hope that the battle for democracy might continue and democratic gains might be made in the future.[55] Given the Islamist threat, then, Tunisia' s traditional domestic constituency for civil society have retreated, vastly muting the pressure for civil society's expansion.

To conclude then, the prospects for civil society in Tunisia look mixed. On the one hand, Tunisia possesses the social conditions that are conducive to the development of a vibrant civil society—a large educated middle class, a society relatively unfragmented by ethnic cleavage, a vast network of associations that are training citizens in civisme and civility, an increasingly independent class of private sector entrepreneurs. The social basis for combatting despotism born of passivity, intolerance, distrust, and excessively concentrated state power is developing apace. On the other hand, state elites continue to resist sanctioning open, institutionalized contestation (denying civil liberties, undermining associational autonomy), for fear of losing their privilege and endangering their civilizational project. In this way the most important prophylactic against state despotism is denied. Clearly, the Islamist threat has provided the regime with a rationale to slow the pace of political opening (as well as dissuading domestic constituencies from campaigning on opening's behalf). Until this sense of threat diminishes (through the calming of the situation in neighboring Algeria, through the ascendence of moderate Islamists and the routinization of their participation in public life) the further evolution of civil society in Tunisia will likely be stalled.

---

[55] Salah Zghidi, "Une Question Democratique au Maghreb: Equivoques et Incomprehensions," *Esprit* (1992).

CHAPTER FIVE

"IN THE BEGINNING WAS THE STATE...":
THE QUEST FOR CIVIL SOCIETY IN JORDAN*

Laurie Brand

In November 1993 the Hashemite Kingdom of Jordan witnessed free parliamentary elections for the second time in four years, an unprecedented event in recent Arab history. Moreover, these were multi-party elections, with the full participation of groups from across the political spectrum, including the Islamists. Indeed, the success of the Jordanian political liberalization experiment to date owes in no small measure to King Hussein's strategy of including in the system all groups willing to accept the rules of the new game.

This round of elections was only the most recent step in a liberalization process that began in late spring 1989. By February 1989, the economic decline of the 1980s had forced Jordan to reschedule its external debt through the International Monetary Fund. Like other similar agreements, Jordan's deal with the IMF required serious deficit-reduction measures, and in keeping with budget-balancing goals, in mid-April the government lifted subsidies on a number of basic products. The announcement of the subsidy reductions triggered riots which rocked the kingdom and which convinced the king that the martial law regime could no longer ensure stability. A new governing formula was needed if the monarchy was to survive.

The new formula, the "survival strategy" as it were, chosen by the king and his advisors was political liberalization, a gradual relaxation or phasing out of the oppressive practices associated with the martial law regime and a concomitant opening of the system to allow for freer political expression. Less than three months after the riots, it was

* In addition to the specific sources cited, research that contributed directly and indirectly to the writing of this article was conducted during five research trips to the Hashemite Kingdom over the past 11 years: April-August 1984; July-August 1986; June-August 1990; September-December 1991; and June-July 1992. The author gratefully acknowledges support for these trips from the Center for International Exchange of Scholars, Fulbright Islamic Civilization Grants, and the School of International Relations, University of Southern California.

announced that parliamentary elections would be held, the first since 1966. Gradually, former politicos and party activists who had been in hiding or in hibernation for years began to emerge, testing the extent of the regime's commitment to liberalization. Harassment by the security services began to decline and greater freedom of speech began to be allowed. Consequently, the campaign period that preceded the 1989 elections was a virtual political festival of speeches, lectures, public meetings, and the like, all unknown in Jordan since the mid-1950s. The first round of free elections produced an Islamist plurality in the lower house (about 30 out of 80 seats), and raised for some the specter of an Islamist take-over of the country. Nevertheless, the long-standing relationship between the monarchy and the Islamists, combined with skillful maneuvering by the king, soon put such fears to rest, and Jordan continued along its liberalization path.

The centerpiece of the new state-society relationship underpinning the liberalization was to be a National Charter, which the king insisted be completed before even more extensive changes in governance could take place. In a move reminiscent of democratic transitions elsewhere in the world, the king assembled a team of professionals and politicos from across the political spectrum to draft this document, which was intended to serve as a supplement to the constitution in redefining the relationship between the state and its citizenry. The first prize of the charter writing process went to the king, since in agreeing to participate in the process the drafters made an implicit, but core concession: acceptance of the legitimacy of the Hashemite monarchy. They thereby acknowledged that while the expanded realm of political freedoms they expected to develop might target many things, the overthrow of the monarchy would not be among them. In exchange, the state in effect conceded certain additional space to civil society, and enshrined in the National Charter the principles of pluralism, tolerance, and civility as bases of interaction in Jordanian society and politics.[1]

Once the Charter was finalized and adopted in June 1991, more basic changes could be undertaken. Martial law had already effectively been abolished, and the parliament set about drafting new legislation on political parties and the press. In the meantime, exiles started returning home, political prisoners began to be released, and those who had been fired from their jobs for political activity were urged by the government

---

[1] See *Al-Mithaq al-watani* (The National Charter, January 1991); *Middle East International*, 2 February 1990.

to seek reinstatement. More and more public events—lectures, panel discussions, theater—dealt with political topics; and a lively "opposition" press was already challenging the lackluster semi-official dailies.

The November 1993 elections, then, appear as simply the most recent "triumph" in the liberalization process. In fact, however, the record is mixed and the issues involved are critical for a broader understanding the relationship between the Jordanian state and civil society, the topic of this paper. It is true that throughout the summer of 1993, the now-legal political parties from across the spectrum increasingly took part in public meetings, lectures, and debates. Such open political discussions, which often included stinging critiques of the government and state institutions, (although never the king or the royal family) are still relatively new for Jordan and are perhaps the clearest public indication that the liberalization initiated in 1989 has borne fruit.

However, debates about the peace talks or about the government's agreement with the IMF, which were expected to be leading issues in the campaign, were sidelined in mid-summer, as rumblings from the inner circles indicated that the government intended to change the electoral law before the November elections. The obvious target of the change (from a system of multiple votes per voter to one-person, one-vote) was the Islamic Action Front (IAF), the political party of the Muslim Brotherhood. The existing law had encouraged bloc-voting deals that had given Islamist influence a multiplier effect in 1989. The one-person, one-vote innovation promised to cut that influence, although analysts also expected it to give a boost to the already important tribal factor in Jordanian politics. Debate over the change was extensive and lively in the press and in public fora. Ultimately, however, it was introduced from above without benefit of parliamentary debate, since, in anticipation of elections (not to mention such discussions), the lower house had already been dissolved.

In another troubling move, as elections approached, the Ministry of the Interior attempted to prevent political parties from holding rallies on public property, with the main target again, apparently, the Islamists. In a victory for civil liberties, this attempt to restrict free speech was quickly overturned by the High Court of Justice, and political rallies resumed. Even more serious, however, was a challenge to the very holding of the elections, which came as a result of the signing of the PLO-Israel accord in mid-September. The accord's reference to the possible return to Palestine of those forced out of the West Bank in 1967 (the vast majority of whom reside on the East Bank) led East Bank nationalists to take the position that the Palestinians who might thereby return to Palestine should not be permitted to vote in the forthcoming elections. The king temporized for a while, but by late September reliable sources reported that Hussein had decided upon a postponement. Then, suddenly, in a stunning, apparent about-face, the king announced that the elections would take place on 8 November as originally scheduled.

What do the events leading up to the 1993 elections reveal about the process of liberalization in Jordan? In the first place, the broad discussion in the press and in public fora of such issues as the one-person, one-vote system as well as the High Court's decision on political rallies are positive signs that the right to freedom of expression (within the boundaries set by the National Charter) is being exercised by the public and respected by the state. The importance of such an atmosphere should not be underestimated. Moreover, the decision to proceed with elections on the originally scheduled date, rather than seeking a postponement because of the PLO-Israel accord is also positive from the point of view of the institutionalization of the political process in the kingdom. So is the fact that the elections were again, as they were in 1989, free and open.

At the same time, however, the process by which the electoral law was changed (as well as the reasons behind it) and the process by which the decision was made to hold elections on the originally scheduled date clearly show that the continuation of the process of liberalization and further development of civil society remain dependent upon the will of the monarch. What is currently unfolding in Jordan, however exciting, is a liberalization process managed from above, part of a strategy intended to ensure the continuation of the monarchy. Despite the proliferation of parties and other manifestations of an apparently blossoming civil society, in Jordan such institutions are still too weak to demand substantive concessions from the monarchy and the state. The civil society base that is currently developing may some day develop sufficient strength to challenge the state. For now, however, it remains largely beholden to it for whatever freedoms it does exercise.

The Concept of Civil Society

In traditional western writing, civil society has been treated as deriving from a particular stage of economic development, that after the breakdown of the extended family and the reduction of production units into nuclear families that sell their labor outside the home. In other words, civil society has been associated with the development of capitalism, with the right to private property and the need to protect other individual (initially, male) rights. In these writings, civil society, then appears in the public (and exclusively male) "space" between the extended family or clan (which is also seen as not providing for individual rights) and the state apparatus.

Civil society is defined by the parameters of this collection of works somewhat differently. Here it comprises three elements: associational life (including political parties that are outside the state and serve as a buffer between the state and the citizen), citizenship (meaning full rights and responsibilities), and civility in interaction. It is therefore most concerned with those associations and attitudes that may either have played a role in triggering a liberalization process and/or which may take advantage of the new space offered by liberalization to push back further the boundaries of the state and, by consequence, carve out an even larger realm for civil non-state, associational activity and for civil rights.

Because the story of the development or circumscription of civil society is generally told in terms of or in contradistinction to the state, it would seem reasonable to begin an exploration of civil society in Jordan, by examining that from which civil society seeks to wrest expressional and operational "territory"— the Jordanian state. The discussion below will show that the relationship between the state and civil society was largely shaped by external factors which gave early predominance to the state: Transjordan's early development as a "security state" to serve British imperial interests and its continuing preoccupation with security because of the ongoing Arab-Israeli conflict. The state-civil society relationship was then complicated in the case of Jordan by two additional factors: the traditional virtual identification of one communal group with the state and the problematic relationship between the state and the Palestine Liberation Organization on the one hand, and the state's Palestinian citizenry and the PLO on the other.

The presentation that follows will first examine the Jordanian state, particularly the factors relevant for understanding the nature of its relationship to civil society. It will then examine the issue of citizenship, particularly in light of the Arab-Israeli conflict—its impact on the composition of the Jordanian population and its implications for the relationship between the citizens and the state. Several civil society institutions will then be examined in some detail. The presentation will conclude with a consideration of the concept of civility and the role of the king.

The Jordanian State

While it is true that many countries of the third world are artificial entities, and that the bases of their modern state structures are largely the products of their colonial pasts, Jordan provides one of the more extreme cases. Transjordan was originally carved out of the territory assigned to the Palestine mandate, part of the Britain's World War I booty. In fulfillment of promises made to the Arabs during the war, and in order further to strengthen the line of imperial defenses from Iraq to Egypt, the British installed 'Abdallah, a son of their ally the Sharif Hussein, author of the 1916 Arab revolt, on the throne of the small amirate in 1921. From its inception, the country was poor in natural resources and commanded a population of only about 400,000, divided fairly evenly between urban merchants and settled agriculturalists on the one hand, and semi-nomadic tribespeople on the other.

Because of its underdeveloped economic base and because of the role Transjordan was to play in British imperial designs, the amirate's treasury depended upon an annual subsidy from England for survival.[2] The state, narrowly defined as the administrative and coercive apparatuses, was simple and rudimentary: the civil service was small, at least in part recruited from outside (Syrian exiles and Palestinians), and also trained by the British, while 'Abdallah ruled directly, much in the manner of a traditional tribal *shaykh*. Moreover, the British handled all matters related to defense, finance and foreign affairs. Perhaps the most significant development of the amirate period for later considerations of the role of the state was the establishment and funding by the British of a police force and a small mobile force including infantry, cavalry and artillery. In 1923 these two forces were combined to form the Arab Legion, which was commanded by British officers and which, by 1948, was the best organized and trained army found in the Arab states.[3] Recruitment for this force was not conducted through universal conscription. Instead, members of the southern Jordanian bedouin tribes, those with roots close to the Hijaz, the original home of their monarch, were sought for the Legion. The preferential recruitment of these groups not only provided what were otherwise very poor elements with employ-

---

[2] See Mary Wilson, *King Abdallah, Britain and the Making of Jordan* (New York: Cambridge University Press, 1987), chapters 4 and 5.

[3] For the classic study of the development of the Arab Legion see P.J. Vatikiotis, *Politics and the Military in Jordan: A Study of the Arab Legion, 1921-1967* (New York: Praeger, 1967).

ment; it also served to consolidate the legitimacy of the state among groups that lived in Jordan's southern border areas, and set a pattern of patron-client support that continued and further developed even after the departure of the British and the beginning of the Arabization of the Arab Legion in 1956. The traditional characterization of the bedouin and the army serving as the bedrock of regime support in Jordan refers precisely to this long-standing and carefully cultivated relationship.

Transjordan's foundation as part of a security defense line in large part set the stage for the importance of the army and police forces and their relationship to the state and the regime. However, subsequent historical developments further reinforced and expanded the security concerns of the state and of the various coercive apparatuses associated with it. The reference here, of course, is to the outbreak of the Palestine conflict into full-scale war. While there is no need here to rehearse the history of that period, it should be noted that whatever collusion may have taken place between the Zionist leadership and King 'Abdallah, the termination of the first phase of the conflict in only an armistice, not a full peace agreement, meant that thenceforth, Jordan was forced to live in the shadow of the potential of war from the West. Moreover, the swift extension by 'Abdallah of sovereignty over the rump of Eastern Palestine (the West Bank), his enfranchisement of its residents (as well as those Palestinians who had fled directly to the East Bank), along with the Jordanian state's suppression of Palestinian identity, meant that internal security would also be problematic. Even under the best of circumstances the annexation of territory and the enfranchisement of some 800,000 people (many of them destitute refugees) would have created a need to expand involvement to consolidate the state's hold on the new territory and people. However, by forcing the newcomers to identify themselves as "Jordanians," and denying them the right to a concomitant officially recognized Palestinian identity, the foundation was laid for dissatisfaction and future opposition to the regime, thus further reinforcing the domestic role of the security forces. This situation also led the regime to choose to continue to recruit its military and certainly its officer corps primarily from the loyal bedouin of the south, and not risk state security by implementing a policy of universal conscription which would have drawn larger numbers of Palestinians into the military.

Palestinian employment opportunities were somewhat better in the realm of the civilian bureaucracies. Indeed, coming from Palestine, where the bureaucratic diversification and the opportunities for education had been much greater than in Transjordan, skilled and educated newcomers were able to find work with the state, although they seldom rose to positions of great influence or sensitivity.[4] However, regional forces were to intervene again to further complicate the relationship. In May of 1964, the Palestine Liberation Organization was founded in Jerusalem. Enjoying the blessing of most Arab states, if only the grudging acceptance of King Hussein, the PLO posed the first, serious challenge to Jordan's claim to the allegiance of its Palestinian population, at that time a majority of the citizenry. To secure Hashemite acquiescence, PLO Chief Ahmad Shuqayri had to promise Hussein both that he would not recruit for his organization from among Jordanian citizens and that the territory he sought to liberate did not include the West Bank.[5]

The PLO's limited appeal in its early years posed little effective domestic threat, although the king did order its offices closed in 1966. Not until the 1967 war decimated the armies and the reputations of the so-called confrontation states, including Jordan, did the organization, or more precisely the various guerrilla organizations, begin to attract the Palestinians of Jordan in substantial numbers. The result, of course, was a swift and extensive expansion of a variety of Palestinian organizations in Jordan: health care, women's, student, teacher, and workers activity. The war had caused the temporary retreat of the Jordanian state and as a result these organizations, a nascent Palestinian civil society of sorts, some heirs to earlier Palestinian political and social activity, others more recent additions, blossomed.

Eventually, however, the Jordanian state and its security apparatuses recovered and struck against the spectrum of Palestinian institutions that had emerged in the post-1967 period. The bloody crackdown of September 1970, followed by a series of final blows in July 1971 drove out much of the leadership of the Palestinian resistance movement and destroyed its infrastructure. Just as important, the country then experienced a surge of "East Banker firstness," one of the most obvious results of which was the implementation of an unwritten policy of preferential recruitment of East Bankers into civil service jobs, while the armed forces retained their East Bank tint. Thus, the events of 1970 not only polarized the two communities, they also reinforced patterns of state employment recruit-

---

[4] See Pamela Ann Smith, *Palestine and the Palestinians, 1883-1983* (New York: St. Martin's, 1984), chapter 4.

[5] 'Isa al-Shu'aybi, *Al-Kiyaniyyah al-Filastiniyyah: Al-Wa'i al-dhati wa al-tatawwur al-mu'assasati, 1947-1977* [Palestinian Statism: Entity Consciousness and Institutional Development (Beirut: PLO Research Center, 1979), p. 104.

ment and of communal relations with the state, thus posing special problems for and influencing the future path of civil society development.

Closely related to the question of state development and potential realm for civil society is the nature of the Jordanian economy. Jordan is and has traditionally been a state that espoused a free market economic policy. However, the surface laissez-faire approach has masked a highly interventionist state. The state has traditionally been the largest employer, with nearly 50% of the active work force on its payroll. Moreover, because, as we have seen, Jordan developed as a security state largely dependent upon external grants and aid, the state developed a strong allocative as opposed to extractive role. That is, instead of being in a position of needing to tax its population to survive, the Jordanian state instead distributed the monies it collected from outside donors, through expanding the bureaucracy, developing the military and the security services, and building an extensive infrastructure, contracts for which were a major source of income for the small private sector. Such a situation would seem to have at least two key implications for the development of civil society. In the first place, by focusing on cultivating the tribes through state employment, the state in effect appropriated to itself one-half of the population, and in the process reinforced tribal ties as key lines to state influence and support. On the other hand, the (largely Palestinian) private sector from which civil society traditionally has sprung, has itself been an underdeveloped sector, subordinate to, if not parasitic upon, the state.

Communal Identity and Citizenship

The brief discussion of the East Bank/West Bank divide will not be new to most students of the region. Nor is the fact that Jordan, unlike any other Arab country, extended citizenship to the Palestinians that fled or were expelled to it or who were effectively annexed by it. However, citizenship should, in a full discussion of civil society, mean far more than simply possessing a passport or having the right to write "Jordanian" on the citizenship line in official documents. True citizenship implies shared rights and obligations and the provision of a climate in which a person feels him or herself to be a part of the whole. The argument made here is that for a number of the reasons touched on above, a majority of Jordan's Palestinian population has not over the years been or felt fully citizen of the kingdom.

Two key developments set the stage for the relationship between the Jordanian state and the majority of its Palestinian residents. The first concerned the 1948 war, the fate of Palestine, and Jordan's role in it. Long before Avi Shlaim published *Collusion Across the Jordan*,[6] rumors repeated with certainty reported secret dealings by King 'Abdallah with the leadership of the Yishuv, the Jewish community in Palestine. While there were variations, the basic belief was that 'Abdallah had struck a deal with the Zionists over the disposition of Palestine, that he had in effect agreed to a partition in which he would take control of what was not apportioned to the Jewish state in the UN partition resolution of 29 November 1947. People further believed that the British had been plotting all along to empty Palestine of its Arab inhabitants and that Transjordan's assigned role was that of population receptacle. One cannot have studied Palestinians during this period and not have heard stories of how the Jordanian army fought Palestinians, not Israelis, during the 1948 war. Jordan's subsequent close ties with the West and its repression of various Arab nationalist and assorted leftist parties only further strengthened the conviction that Jordan had in effect been "hired" by the West, first to absorb the Palestinians and then to suppress their identity as well as their national aspirations. Indeed, if one looks back through Arab discourse over the years, it would be difficult to find a leader who was labeled *'amil* (agent) more frequently than 'Abdallah. His assassination in 1951 was widely viewed as a proper reward for what was regarded by many as treasonous behavior.

The second element leading to Palestinian disaffection from Jordan was mentioned earlier; that is, the efforts by the Jordanian state after the incorporation of the West Bank to suppress or erase all references to Palestine. "Palestine" was no longer to be used in official documents; where applicable, the term "West Bank" was to replace it. Nor were civil society institutions that had operated under the mandate in Palestine allowed to continue functioning under a Palestinian name. Labor, women's, doctors', lawyers', and other organizations all were required to substitute "Jordanian" for "Palestinian" in their names and move their headquarters to the East Bank. Village associations could retain the name of their Palestinian place of origin (e.g., the Ramallah Charitable Society), but were also forbidden to use the word "Palestinian" in their

---

[6] Avi Shlaim, *Collusion Across the Jordan* (New York: Columbia University Press, 1988). Shlaim was the first scholar to bring together the relevant materials and narrate in written and university press form, the story of Hashmite-Zionist cooperation that many had long believed true.

official documents. While the state continued to proclaim that East and West Bank were simply two branches of the same family, Palestinians resented the suppression of these simple expressions of national identity, particularly at a time when the words Palestine and Palestinian had largely disappeared from discourse outside the region.

Hence, the Palestinians were excluded from or alienated by the major symbols of the state: the army, the upper levels of the bureaucracy, the monarchy, Hashemite hagiography, and so on. To add further insult, effort was made by the state to appropriate certain Palestinians symbols, such as the Dome of the Rock and traditional embroidery, and claim them as Jordanian. Moreover, the Municipal Elections Law restricted the franchise to those who had paid a land or municipal tax of at least one dinar in the year prior to elections.[7] This excluded those Palestinians who were poor refugees. Hence while many valued having a passport (unlike so many of their brethren who had taken refuge elsewhere in the Arab world and at best carried travel documents), the idea of a Palestinian's naturally or willingly identifying him or herself as Jordanian was rare.

Although most Palestinians, therefore, did not enjoy the equal rights and obligations that serve as a basis of citizenship, strong feelings of Palestinian nationalism did not emerge among a large sector of the population until the mid-1960s. Prior to that, many had been preoccupied simply with the struggle to survive. The founding of the PLO, however, provided an institutional and Arab League-sanctioned forum for the articulation of a national identity and a national program. Subsequently, in the wake of the 1967 defeat, the Palestinian guerrilla organizations began to attract large numbers of Palestinians. Thus, the eventual Jordanian assault against the commando organizations had an even greater impact than had certain earlier, and less obvious developments. The events of 1970 created a far more serious, explicit intercommunal divide than had existed before, as Palestinians became suspect in the eyes of much of the Transjordanian community as potential traitors. This perception reinforced the importance of the army and security forces' support for the regime and further institutionalized the communal division of labor by in effect closing off the public sector to Palestinian employment.

These feelings of mutual suspicion were further reinforced by the periodic ups and downs (1974, 1981, 1986, 1988) in the kingdom's

---

[7] Shaul Mishal, *West Bank/East Bank: The Palestinians in Jordan, 1949-1967* (New Haven, Conn: Yale University Press), p. 107.

relations with the PLO, such that when ties were strong, things were a bit easier for Palestinians and intercommunal tensions tended to subside. However, a deterioration in relations could once again exacerbate tensions. Indeed, the Arab League's recognition of the PLO as the sole legitimate representative of the Palestinians in 1974 was part of the reason behind the suspension of the Jordanian parliament, a move that left members of both communities without any direct voice in government. In 1976, the obligations of citizenship were extended as universal conscription was instituted: a move in part intended to extend the state's claim to the loyalty of its Palestinian citizenry in the face of competition from the PLO.

Not until July 1988 did this begin to change, the gradual transformation triggered by Hussein's announcement of his decision to disengage from the West Bank. The disengagement first sent shockwaves through the Palestinian communities on both banks (Jordanian citizenship was withdrawn not only from West Bank residents, but also from certain East Bank-resident Palestinians who were members of the Palestine National Council). However, after the dust had settled, many began to realize just what this act implied and offered. By relinquishing administrative and legal ties to the West Bank, the king was in part undoing what his grandfather had done in 1950. Furthermore, he was effectively opening the way for the eventual assertion of Palestinian sovereignty over the part of Palestine central to the establishment of a future state, the West Bank. Subsequent to the disengagement, the king's decision to liberalize politically, his position on the Gulf war (not siding with the Western coalition) and the joint PLO-Jordanian participation in the peace process all led to a reassessment by Palestinians of the king, the Jordanian state, and the role that they may play in it. While, as the discussion of associational life below will show, this does not mean all problems of equal rights and duties have been solved, nonetheless, a sea change of sorts has occurred, such that the younger generation of Palestinians is much more likely to express loyalty to Jordan, or at least Hussein, than ever before.

It is worth noting, however, that many Transjordanians remain skeptical and anxious. A certain segment has been most concerned, not just with questionable Palestinian loyalty to the regime, but with their numbers, and with their predominant position in the private sector. These Transjordanians are concerned that in the framework of a peace treaty (and possible confederation), and given the wealth of the Palestinian private sector, and the recent, gradual downgrading of the public sector, a more thorough Palestinization of the East Bank will be set in motion in which they, the native Transjordanians, will be the economic, political and social losers. The implications of such developments for the question of equality of citizenship as well as maintenance or further development of civility should be clear and troubling.

Much more could be said about intercommunal relations in Jordan, but that is not the central focus of this paper. What this discussion has attempted to demonstrate is that the historic development of the Jordanian state and its relationship to its Palestinian citizens has affected the degree to which Palestinians, now probably just over 50% of the East Bank population, may be viewed as full citizens. The discussion will now turn to the diverse associational life of the kingdom, the component most commonly associated with civil society.

Associational Life in the Kingdom

Despite the fact that during most of its pre-1990 history Jordan lived under martial law, which outlawed the free operation of political parties and severely circumscribed the activities of many other organizations, the kingdom has, nonetheless, seen the continued operation of a number of key civil society institutions. Professional organizations such as doctors', engineers', lawyers' and similar unions, which have drawn members from both the Palestinian and Transjordanian communities succeeded, despite regime pressure, in maintaining an independent and vibrant existence throughout the period of martial law. Other organizations such as labor unions, although they continued to function, were so intimidated and coopted by the state that their ability to serve their constituencies was severely compromised. In other instances, such as that of the women's union, the state actually froze activity and then established a "replacement" organization. The discussion that follows is not intended to be exhaustive, but rather, representative of the experiences of various institutions that have struggled to maintain a relatively autonomous existence in the face of what were often extreme regime pressures.

Political Parties

Although there was a burst of political activity in 1955 and 1956, the attempted coup in April 1957 led to the imposition of martial law and the outlawing of political parties.[8] Despite a period of somewhat greater political freedom between the 1967 war and Black September in 1970, parties remained illegal. This is not to say that political party activity ceased. In Jordan one found Palestinian and Transjordanian adherents of the entire range of Arab political parties: communists, Ba'thists of both Syrian and Iraqi stripes, Arab nationalists, as well as members of the entire range of PLO constituent factions, from *Fatah* to Ahmad Jibril. Political orientation was often determined by where one had studied and political bonds forged during university days often continued to serve people well, even after former comrades had joined the *mukhabarat* or the government. But this was the only way that a political party could serve to mediate between the citizen and the state. With the exception of the 1967-70 period, when the various political forces operated more openly and did take up a variety of their members' daily concerns, political parties in Jordan have served almost exclusively as a cause for imprisonment or persecution, nothing more. The only exception to this rule was the Muslim Brethren (*Ikhwan*), which will be discussed in more detail below.

It was not until the liberalization of April 1989 that parties began to emerge from their underground existence. While none was officially permitted to participate in the parliamentary elections of 1989, the king did suspend an article of the elections law which forbade the candidacy of those with "political pasts" and many well-known politicos entered the electoral fray. Not surprisingly, the only group that enjoyed anything like a mass base was most successful at the polls: the *Ikhwan* and other assorted Islamists. Thereafter, other parties began operating more openly, and tens announced their intention to register, awaiting only the finalization of the new political parties law, which itself had to await the finalization of the National Charter, which was ratified in June 1991.

An interesting question related to the issue of communal political equality raised in the previous section arose in the 1989 elections. At the time, the Israeli government was waving the "Jordan is Palestine" banner, and many Arabs feared the possibility of a "transfer" of Palestinian population out of the occupied territories to the East Bank. As a result, there was concern regarding how the candidacy and mass participation of East Bank Palestinians in the 1989 elections would be interpreted and used abroad: there was no desire to provide the Likud with

---

[8] For a detailed discussion of party activity during this period see Amnon Cohen, *Political Parties in the West Bank Under the Jordanian Regime, 1949-1967* (Ithaca: Cornell University Press, 1982).

additional ammunition. Palestinians had long had an unwritten agreement with East Bankers about not running for too many East Bank parliamentary (and municipal) seats and for certain seats in particular, but the issue had lain dormant during the long years in which there were no parliamentary elections. In 1989 it was rumored that PLO chief Yasir Arafat had ordered Palestinians not to participate in the Jordanian elections because of concern over the potential Israeli reaction.[9] Whatever the reasons, in the first truly free elections in Jordan's post-1956 history, observers agreed that the participation of Jordan's Palestinians citizens was far lower than their numbers would have suggested.

Further development on the electoral front awaited the promulgation of the new political parties law, finally passed in July 1992. There are a number of important, if controversial, elements in the new law, several of which concern parties' having extra-Jordanian connections. For example, founding members of political parties may not be members of any non-Jordanian party or of any other political or party organization. If interpreted literally this would include the PLO, although, given the cordial relations between Hussein and Arafat at this writing*, the government is likely to overlook a PLO connection to Jordanian parties, at least for the time being. Further, "the party must depend entirely for its financial resources on local, known Jordanian resources that are declared and specified."(Article 19) Parties are forbidden to be organizationally or financially associated with any non-Jordanian group, nor may party activity be directed by orders or directives from any foreign state or party.(Article 21)

Members of the armed forces, the security organs, and the civil defense do not qualify as founding members and parties are to refrain from recruitment or polarization in the ranks of the armed forces. (An earlier proposal to prohibit party membership among teachers was eventually dropped from the draft law.) Moreover, trade unions, welfare societies, and clubs are forbidden to use their organs and funds in the interest of any party, thus presumably preventing contributions to and endorsements of candidates. All of these provisions put a variety of restrictions on the organizational freedom of parties. A notable positive contribution to the quest for civility, however, is the requirement that parties abide by the principle of political pluralism in their programs.

Since the promulgation of the law, more than twenty parties have

---

[9] Such rumors were widely reported, but never substantiated.

* It should be noted that by late summer 1994, as this piece was going to press, PLO-Jordanian relations had deteriorated markedly.

been licensed. While a Ba'thist and communist party were initially denied their requests by the Ministry of the Interior, they appealed the decision and, after only minor changes in name and program, were granted licenses. Only one well-known political party remains underground: the *Tahrir* party, an Islamist group that believes the Jordanian state, like its Arab counterparts, is illegitimate. Its view of the state prevents the party from accepting the principles enshrined in the National Charter and thus makes its licensing impossible.

The Islamists

Most parties continue to be little more than gathe-rings around a particular individual or the remnants of an earlier era. The most prominent exception is the Islamic Action Front (IAF), com-posed overwhelmingly of the *Ikhwan*. It has the most extensive and effective organizational and mobilizational apparatus of any political group in the country. While there are other, independent Islamists, for the purposes of this discussion, the *Ikhwan* is the only organization of consequence.

The strength of the Brotherhood is in large part explained by its historical development; specifically, its relationship to the Jordanian state. Unlike its counterparts elsewhere in the Middle East, the *Ikhwan* was cultivated or coopted by the Jordanian state over the years to help counter the power of what were seen as more threatening leftist and Arab nationalist currents. Indeed, the state classified the Brotherhood, not as a political party, but as a social organization. Hence during the long years of martial law, the Brotherhood was able to receive substantial external financing (primarily from Saudi Arabia), and to operate openly and with impunity (if not outright support) in the kingdom.

For example, because of its special relationship with the state, despite the general prohibition against organizing on campuses, the *Ikhwan* has been allowed to recruit members at the universities and even at the secondary school level. On the secondary level, recruitment has often been accomplished through teachers involved with the *Ikhwan*. On university campuses *Ikhwan* student organizers have sponsored special classes in Qur'an, *Hadith*, Islamic history, and the like. They have also offered lectures on "Islamic external affairs," such as the conflict in Afghanistan in the 1980s, and have collected donations for "Islamic causes." Other activities have included holding special prayer sessions, establishing new mosques on campus, or sponsoring demonstrations (although, reportedly, never with the intent of precipitating confrontation with the authorities). All activities have been aimed at demonstrating a strong presence which, it was believed, was more likely to recruit additional members to the hierarchical and gender-segregated organization.[10]

In the social/charitable realm, the *Ikhwan*'s most important organization is the *Jam'iyyat al-Markaz al-Islami*. Founded in 1965, it runs two hospitals, one in the capital and one in Aqaba, four schools, a community college, clinics and health care centers, sewing centers, and orphanages, in addition to distributing money to the poor.[11] The strength of the *Markaz* and the support it receives even from within government circles have exempted it from many regulations to which all other such societies are subject. For example, by law all branches of charitable societies must be licensed, and the *Markaz* has four such branches. However, to expand further and avoid the licensing issue, the *Markaz* has, unchallenged, opened some 32 "committees." (As a point of comparison, the Ministry of Social Development has only 30 branches in the entire country). Moreover, although each charitable society is required by law to be audited every year, in practice the *Markaz* has been able to avoid this regulation, presumably because of pressure brought to bear from outside the ministry. Given the privileged position the *Ikhwan* has enjoyed since the 1950s, such a situation should not be surprising. The Brotherhood has been able to develop a large presence in a number of the country's institutions. It has virtual control over the ministries of education and *awqaf*. Indeed, if one examines the background of the executive committee of the Brotherhood one finds that a large number used to be or are still employed by the Ministry of Education.[12] Not surprisingly, most of the lijan al-zakat (alms committees) are also run by the *Ikhwan* as is the country's network of mosques, where one has recruiting access literally five times a day. A clear indication of the extension of the *Ikhwan*'s power may be seen in the actions of one of its members, Yusuf al-'Athm, who used his term as Minister of Social Affairs to register a large number of Islamic charitable societies, some of which did not meet the established legal requirements.[13]

---

[10] Interview with Rana 'Assaf, former *Ikhwan* student activist, 28 June 1993.

[11] In 1985 (the last year in which the Guide to Charitable Societies was published), this society's expenditures for 1985 were 1.85 million JDs (approximately $5.2 million). Center for Social Studies and Research of the Federation of Charitable Societies, *Dalil al-jama'iyyat al-khayriyyah* [Guide to Charitable Societies] (Amman, 1985), p. 200.

[12] Hani Hourani et al., *The Islamic Action Front Party* (Amman: Al-Urdun al-Jadid, 1993), pp. 12-13.

[13] Al-'Athm reportedly tried to register seven new societies on his last day in office alone. Interview with employee of the Ministry of Social Development who requested anonymity, 19 July 1993.

In light of its organization throughout the country and its presence in various ministries, the Brotherhood's performance in the 1989 elections (in which it won 22 seats and 8 others were won by independent Islamists) should not have taken anyone by surprise. Its less successful performance in the 1993 elections (winning only 16 seats with 2 seats going to independent Islamists) owes in part to the change in the voting law, but also in part to the fact that during the previous four years of serving in parliament and operating, since 1992, through the Islamic Action Front, its position has, in a sense, become regularized. As one analyst commented, "the *Ikhwan* is no longer viewed as the Party of God," as it was prior to serving in government.[14] The Brotherhood still enjoys a strong core of support in society, just under 20%,[15] but the aura that surrounded it in 1989 has been somewhat dispelled by its members' less than impressive performance in parliament, especially from January to June 1991, when they held several cabinet posts.

Other parties

Of the remaining twenty-odd parties operating in the kingdom, the only one that comes close to the IAF in terms of number of offices opened throughout the kingdom (although certainly not in terms of present mobilizing capability), is the conservative Transjordanian party *al-ʿAhd*, headed by the powerful former chief of security, ʿAbd al-Hadi al-Majali. However, overall public interest in political parties is quite low: a winter 1993 poll revealed that only 1.4% of respondents were affiliated with a political party and only 6.5% were inclined to join in the future.[16] In the short term, with the exception of the IAF, virtually all other party affiliation is either an expression of family or tribal ties—even *al-ʿAhd* is heavily reliant upon the Majali family name for attracting support— or the remains of groups that held sway during the heyday of Arab nationalism.

Professional Associations

The absence of functioning political parties after 1957 left a void in Jordanian political life, which eventually came to be filled in part by a range of professional associations: unions of doctors, engineers, law-

[14] Talk given by Dr. Mustafa Hamarneh of the Center for Strategic Studies, Jordan University, at the Council on Foreign Relations, 17 November 1993.

[15] Hamarneh talk, 17 November 1993.

[16] Center for Strategic Studies, Jordan University, "A Public Opinion Survey on 'Democracy in Jordan': Preliminary Findings," (Amman: Unpublished Study, spring 1993), p. 16.

yers, dentists, pharmacists, journalists, writers, geologists, and agricultural engineers. Like professional associations elsewhere, these organizations served to oversee standards, create a sense of community among members of the same profession, provide various services to members who might be in special need, sponsor professional development activities, and the like. Most of these organizations were founded in the 1950s by only a handful of professionals and, with the exception of the doctors' and lawyers' unions, maintained a low political profile. However, in the absence of legalized political parties it was elections for leadership posts in these organizations that citizens (well beyond the membership rosters) watched in order to gauge the shifting relative power of the illegal, but nonetheless operative, political parties in the country. The year 1967 marked a turning point, however, as the professional associations took the initiative in formulating a societal political response to the defeat in the war with Israel. In coordination with a number of well-known national figures, leaders of these unions held a meeting and proclaimed the formation of what was called the National Grouping (*al-Tajammu'* *al-Watani*). Even the king attended the organization's first meeting.[17]

However, in the wake of the war, the political spotlight was captured by the Palestinian guerrilla organizations. The National Grouping coordinated activities (meetings, displays, and the like) with the resistance, but eventually political differences arose which paralyzed the group. Another organization was formed to overcome this paralysis, the Professional Grouping. Comprising labor and professional union representatives it was in constant contact with the state regarding political matters. It continued to meet following the events of September 1970, until 1971, at which point the regime disbanded it on the grounds that its work was political, not professional.[18]

Although the unions continued to function after 1971, no coordinated professional or trade union activity was permitted. Not until Egyptian President Sadat made his November 1977 trip to Jerusalem were new efforts initiated by the professional association leaders. At this time a Council of Professional Unions was established, which then began limited political work. Following the Israeli invasion of Lebanon in March 1978, the council called for an enlarged framework, which led to the founding of the General Secretariat of Patriotic and Popular Forces in Jordan, with members from across the political spectrum. Again,

---

[17] Laurie A. Brand, *Palestinians in the Arab World: Institution Building and the Search for State* (New York: Columbia University Press, 1988), p. 178.

[18] Brand, *Palestinians in the Arab World*.

however, although it officially operated for four years, political infighting prevented it from devising a joint program for political action. In 1983, regional politics in the form of the split in the PLO led to the freezing of its activities. The Council of Professional Unions, however, did continue to function: its members made two visits to the prime minister's office after the violence at Yarmuk University in May 1986; it drafted a memo outlining its objections to the 1986 electoral law; and it requested (but was denied) permission to hold a march protesting the US raid on Libya.[19]

Hence, beyond the professional services rendered their members and occasional charitable functions carried out for society more broadly, these unions came to fill the gap in articulation of political concerns left by the absence of legal political parties and the suspension of the parliament. In the pre-liberalization period, the professional associations were the only bodies in Jordan that held democratic elections. They were also the only organizations that could attempt to put together broader, non-governmental councils to address the pressing political problems or crises of the day. While they were not immune to regime pressures, they were less vulnerable because of their membership composition: these were men and women who not only were generally not employees of the state, they were largely self-employed and many were quite successful. Their economic power (as well, often, as family connections) translated into a political power that Jordan's labor unions, as we shall see, did not enjoy.

In the wake of the liberalization, these associations have continued to function, but their political leadership role has been relatively eclipsed by the surfacing of the underground political parties and by the generally freer atmosphere for political expression. Nevertheless, their elections are still hotly contested and, between parliamentary elections, are a primary means of gauging the shifts in the relative power among the country's political forces.

Labor

Labor has traditionally been one of the most repressed sectors in Jordan. Trade union activity on the West Bank after 1948, a continuation of activity under the British mandate, was fairly swiftly reined in by the Jordanian state following the annexation in 1950. The fate of an attempt to establish an East Bank affiliate of the Palestine Arab Workers Society

---

[19] Brand, *Palestinians in the Arab World*, p. 179.

met the same fate, on the grounds that East Bank law did not permit the
establishment of labor unions. Nonetheless, labor activists continued
their work, if underground, and contacted the International Labor Organization to complain about the government's refusal to permit free trade
union activity. Finally, as a result of ILO pressures combined with a
somewhat more liberal policy of a new prime minister, Fawzi al-Mulqi,
Jordanian Labor Law Number 35 of 1953 legalized labor unions (although it outlawed their involvement in politics). Labor organizers then
wasted no time. In July 1954 the Federation of Trade Unions in Jordan
(FTUJ) was registered. By mid-1956 thirty-nine unions counted over
nine thousand members (although thereafter the growth was slow, due
in large part, no doubt, to the general atmosphere of repression that
attended the imposition of martial law in 1957). However, regime-labor
union differences were common, as for instance in 1956, when union
headquarters were used to plan demonstrations against the Baghdad
Pact. As a result, the state periodically intervened in union affairs, at
times preventing union leaders from attending meetings outside the
country.[20]

As was the case for other civil society institutions, the post-1967 war
period offered labor a needed respite from regime interference. However, the record of the period is mixed precisely because of the growing
role of the Palestinian resistance movement at the time. The various
commando organizations drew large numbers of workers to their ranks,
and as a result, during this period, workers often preferred to address
problems through their respective political organizations rather than
through their union. For example, instead of approaching the Union of
Phosphate Workers, a worker with a complaint would go to *Fatah* or the
Popular Front for assistance. All of this served to fragment the composition and power of organized labor in Jordan.

Moreover, during the 1970 civil war, the FTUJ called for reconciliation between the government and the Palestinian resistance movement.
As a result of this position, in the aftermath of the army-resistance
clashes, the government dissolved the federation's executive committee, appointed a new one, and introduced changes in its constitution to
give the state greater access and influence. In subsequent elections the
government pushed for and succeeded in having elected candidates who
were more sympathetic to regime concerns, primarily, but not exclusively, Transjordanians.[21] Thereafter, organized labor came increasingly

---

[20] Brand, *Palestinians in the Arab World*, pp. 189-90.
[21] Brand, *Palestinians in the Arab World*, p. 193.

under siege. A battle against the gradual introduction of foreign labor into the Jordanian market was fought, and lost by successive unions. The government then further reorganized the structure of the federation in such a way as to increase dramatically the numbers of those who would support the regime. A revision of the Labor Law further empowered the state to dissolve, redivide and reorganize unions. In 1974 a special bureau was opened by internal security (*mukhabarat*) to monitor labor and in 1975 a separate Ministry of Labor was established. As the number of strikes for improved wage and working conditions increased, the government was persuaded again to revise the Labor Law empowering the Minister of Labor to reorganize unions without requiring it to consult the FTUJ. When these measures did not accomplish their goal, more direct means were employed. The state would "persuade" potential candidates not to run, imprison activists, or dismiss them from their jobs. By the mid-1980s the government had gained control of most unions and intimidated most Jordanians into not joining or not becoming active.[22]

One might then have anticipated that with the advent of political liberalization in 1989 the labor movement would have witnessed a revival, much like that of the political parties. So far, however, for a variety of reasons, the record is mixed. One positive sign of change was the victory in the spring of 1990 of Walid al-Khayyat, an old-time labor activist, in the Electricity Workers Union, after years of being forbidden to run for office for so-called "security reasons." Another indication of gradual change came at a meeting of the Central Council of the FTUJ in late April 1990 for elections for the executive council and the president, when thirty-nine members signed a memorandum protesting the participation of several unions that had under earlier circumstances and with government blessing in fact violated membership and accounting rules. While one of the major forces within the pro-labor group, the communists, ultimately came to an agreement with the Ministry of Labor, in effect betraying the rest of the original group of thirty-nine, the very fact that the challenge had been posed and that the federation could no longer be run according the past principles of state-coopted business as usual, seemed to indicate that one of the goals of the pro-union forces had been achieved.[23]

Another issue that appeared promising for galvanizing workers was that of the fate of the employees of the failed Petra Bank, who were fully

---

[22] Brand, *Palestinians in the Arab World*, pp. 194-95.
[23] Brand, *Palestinians in the Arab World*, pp. 64-65.

backed in their demands for reemployment at the same wage and seniority levels by the Jordan Banking and Insurance Employees Association. However, Petra's former employees were confronting more than just the reorganized management of the bank. The story behind the bank's failure constituted a part of the web of corruption of the previous regime, with unsubstantiated charges that the scandal reached into the highest levels of the government, including the royal family. Hence, the workers were caught, not in a traditional labor dispute, but in a challenge to some of the most powerful men and networks in the country. While initially their case attracted a great deal of support and attention from other unions, professional associations, and others, [24] by the summer of 1990, this author attended a rally in which only two MPs were present and in which only a handful of other union activists participated along with the Petra employees.

In addition to the festering Petra Bank problem, the internal problems of the FTUJ continued, and the Union of Electrical Workers' threatened to strike against the Jordan Electric Power Company in late July 1990. However, all labor disputes were temporarily set aside once Saddam Hussein invaded Kuwait, and labor issues did not return to the agenda until after the end of the ground war in the spring of 1991. Thereafter, one issue of major concern to Jordanian workers, certainly since the late 1980s but particularly since the return of more than two hundred thousand of their compatriots from Kuwait, was that of unemployment and of the continued presence in the country of large numbers of foreign workers. While many such non-Jordanians fill manual labor jobs that Jordanians do not want, as noted above, the presence of these workers has made it easier over the years to dismiss Jordanian employees. In 1991, Labor Minister 'Abd al-Karim al-Dughmi began to press for broader and swifter dismissal of foreign laborers in an attempt to reduce unemployment. He encountered stiff resistance from the private sector and when he refused to back down, was ultimately forced to resign. In this one instance in which it appeared the state (through an individual minister) was attempting to defend organized labor, other powerful interests from within the state and from some of its allies in the private sector thwarted the attempt.[25]

In sum, the years of repression and cooptation of labor have led union work to be controlled largely by groups supported by the state—an

---

[24] *Jordan Times*, 21 February 1990.
[25] *Jordan Times*, 26 October 1991.

entrenched, semi-official trade union bureaucracy that is not easily dispatched. Moreover, with real democratic expression prohibited for years, the existing, weak Jordanian trade union tradition that had developed in the 1950s was further undermined. While in the 1970s participation rates in the unions were between 18 and 20%, more recently they have dropped to below 13%. As a result, although Jordanian labor was hardest hit by the cuts and retrenchment that accompanied the economic decline and the IMF-dictated austerity measures, neither the FTUJ nor the individual unions have attempted to intervene against arbitrary dismissal, reductions in social services, or wage cuts. It appears that there simply has not been enough time for the factionalized pro-labor forces to unite against the entrenched pro-government bureaucracy and push for changes. [26]

Also at work, however, is a broader factionalism that has characterized the post-liberalization Left in Jordan. Workers have lost their confidence in the unions, while the pro-union forces have demonstrated a less than lofty example of democratic behavior, tainting the climate for healthy coexistence, as they have engaged in virtual internecine political infighting. Thus the history of organized labor in Jordan demonstrates a continuing struggle against the power of the state or of interests closely aligned with the state. The traditionally weak nature of the working class in Jordan certainly made cooptation easier. But it is also clear that, unlike the situation of the professional associations, the inferior economic position of workers enabled the state to penetrate, and when necessary, intimidate the unions to accomplish its goals.

Women

Between 1951 and 1979 some 32 charitable societies were founded in the kingdom that had only women members and provided services such as kindergartens, nursery schools, feeding centers, care for the elderly, literacy classes, and the like. There were also numerous women's clubs. Although two other societies were founded with royal sponsorship in the 1940s, the Women's Social Society and the Society of the Jordan Women's Federation, the two merged and then were disbanded in the same year, 1949.[27]

---

[26] Yusuf Hawrani, "Al-Harakah al-niqabiyyah al-'ummaliyyah ila ayna?" [Where is the Labor Union Movement Going?] *Al-Jadid*, 1/2, 1991, pp. 63-64.

[27] Suhayr Salti al-Tall, *Muqaddimat hawla qadiyat al-mar'ah wa al-Harakah al-Nisa'iyyah fi al-Urdunn* [Introductions to the Women's Issue and to the Women's Movement in Jordan] (Beirut: Al-Mu'assasah al-'Arabiyyah il al-Dirasat wa al-Nashr, 1985), p. 122.

The most important organization in the early period that combined an external role (developing ties with other Arab women) with a domestic agenda (promoting literacy and greater economic independence) was the Federation of Arab Women, founded in June 1954 and presided over by Emily Bisharat, the first female lawyer in Jordan. Political conditions at the time were propitious both for the union's founding and for its activity. The advent of a more liberal or nationalist government in the kingdom combined with a groundswell of popular political activity around such issues as opposition to the Baghdad Pact and support for the nationalization of the Suez Canal Company in neighboring Egypt created an atmosphere that encouraged political activity and expression. In such a climate, the women fought for the franchise, engaged in solidarity work for Algeria and Egypt, attempted to change the personal status law's provisions regarding arbitrary divorce and polygamy, and worked to alter the Labor Law to benefit women and to expand the educational system in the rural areas. At the time of its closure in 1957 as part of the general political crackdown in the country, the union counted more than 3000 members in branches in Amman, Irbid, Zarqa, Salt, and Karak.[28]

On the other side of the river, following the annexation of the West Bank in 1950 the various chapters of the Arab Women's Society, a Palestinian organization founded in 1929, continued to operate, retreating from involvement in the national cause to work in the social and humanitarian realm. Most of this activity took place in the cities or large towns of the West Bank, not in rural areas and the refugee camps where it was most needed. However, in 1965, in Jerusalem, the General Union of Palestinian Women was founded, bringing together Palestinian women's groups from throughout the diaspora. An official chapter of the union was never opened in Jordan because of the sensitivities regarding ethnic loyalties noted earlier; however, unofficial chapters sprang up across the kingdom, from the refugee camps to the cities of Amman, Salt, Irbid, Aqaba and Karak. Like other institutions discussed above, women's union activity flowered in the period following the 1967 war, under the protective umbrella of the Palestinian resistance. Activities ranged from sewing and literacy classes to civil defense. Like other institutions, the Palestinian women's union was effectively destroyed by the events of September 1970.[29]

Not until 1974, in order to be represented in UN activities in honor of the Year of the Woman, did a group of Transjordanian and Palestinian

[28] Al-Tall, *Muqaddimat* ..., 125-130.
[29] See Brand, *Palestinians in the Arab World*, pp. 196-200.

women begin a campaign to obtain government approval for the establishment of a women's union. The first conference of the Women's Union in Jordan (WUJ) was held in November 1974. Branches were quickly founded in Salt, Madaba, Karak, Irbid, Ramtha, Ribbah and Zarqa. Activities included offering a variety of training classes, operating nurseries and child care centers, and providing a range of social services and cultural activities. Although composed of women representing most of the political spectrum, the membership was able to work together to improve women's economic, legal and social status. For a brief period it produced an irregular publication entitled *al-Ra'idah* (the leader or pioneer), but the state Publications Department eventually demanded that it cease publication. Despite numerous attempts to reinitiate publication, permission was not forthcoming, and the union had to content itself with internal publications and circulars. The union did, however, continue to make its views known through participation in various national and local events and by using the media whenever possible.[30]

Among the women's goals were securing the right to run for municipal elections (women finally officially received the franchise in 1973), to participate in discussions of revisions of the labor law, and to participate in regular symposia and seminars to raise women's issues. Like its 1950s predecessor, the WUJ also sent representatives to various women's and other international gatherings to discuss the situation of Jordanian women and to express solidarity with others, including activity on the Palestine question.[31]

It appears it was union activism on the Palestine question that the state found particularly problematic. At first it charged the union with "taking positions antagonistic to the country" at international conferences. It then moved to terminate a union-sponsored Karak area dairy and traditional handicraft center. In February 1981 the union received a letter from the Ministry of the Interior ordering its closure on the grounds that it had violated its constitution. At the same time, the Ministry of Social Development (under whose direct jurisdiction the union came) was attempting to establish an alternative women's union, the General Federation of Jordanian Women (GFJW). The WUJ fought the order, and the High Court even rescinded it. But the women's power to enforce the High Court's ruling was dwarfed by the power of the opposition, the

---

[30] Al-Tall, *Muqaddimat* ..., pp. 130-36.
[31] Al-Tall lists these activities year by year in *Muqaddimat* ..., pp. 146-153.

Ministry of the Interior, which succeeded in continuing to obstruct the union's work and finally froze its activity.[32]

The alternative federation was completely beholden to the government and as a result was not recognized by the General Arab Women's Union, which continued to accord legitimacy to the WUJ. The GFJW was essentially an umbrella organization for existing women's societies and assorted individuals, but had no real program of its own, just as it had no branches or activity outside the capital. In the most benign interpretation, it served a liaison function between the Ministry of Social Development (the state) and the constituent units. It also, however, made it unlikely if not impossible that another women's organization would be able to establish kingdom-wide branches and serve a mobilizing and representative function for women across Jordan. State intervention in women's affairs has continued even since the beginning of the liberalization. In the period preceding the 1990 elections, a new set of federation by-laws was drafted which, according to one interpretation, gave disproportionate representation to individual members over the constituent societies and federations. The problem was most pronounced in the Amman chapter, in which some 1200 individual women, apparently of an Islamist persuasion, registered in the spring preceding the elections. As the controversy over representation and voting rights unfolded against the background of charges that Islamists were attempting to take over the union, the Minister of Social Development dismissed the union's executive committee and appointed an ad hoc committee to oversee elections.[33] Representatives from the union met with the speaker of parliament to protest the move, and women from both the executive committee as well as the Irbid branch, took the ministry to court over its interference. While the Gulf crisis delayed action, eventually the case was resolved in favor of the non-Islamists, as a partial Islamist boycott led to the victory of a centrist election list in the fall of 1991.[34] In the meantime, the liberalization allowed the WUJ to become active again, and the country then faced the unprecedented situation of having two women's unions, each with its own leadership and political affiliations, vying for position.

In 1993, the government, in the form of the National Committee on Women (comprising, among others, a number of cabinet ministers ex

---

[32] See al-Tall, *Muqaddimat* ..., pp. 153-158; and Da'd Muradh, "Tajribat al-ittihad al-nisa'i", 1974-1981," *Al-Urdunn al-Jadid* (Spring 1986) 7: 61-64.

[33] *Jordan Times*, 10 July 1990.

[34] *Jordan Times*, 20 October 1991.

officio) and under the patronage of Princess Basma, became actively involved in crafting a "National Strategy for Women." The government sought the involvement of a wide range of women and women's groups in drafting position papers and discussing proposals. But participation in the process by the two official women's organizations was undertaken with some skepticism and caution, in part a function of each one's concern over turf, but also in part a concern over state encroachment. Given past history it would be difficult to argue that their fears were ungrounded, although it appears the greatest threat is that the document produced will go the way of many previous government studies, (sitting on a shelf unimplemented) rather than that it may serve as a basis for renewed attempts by the state to coopt the women's movement.

The 1993 elections were also of concern to women, and tens of public meetings, panel discussions, and lectures were held to consider the role Jordanian women might play in them, whether as voters or candidates. The question of a parliamentary quota for women was hotly debated, with women as divided on the issue as men. (Only the Islamists, men and women, opposed the idea as a group, although it also seemed clear that had such seats been set aside, principle was unlikely to have prevented the IAF from running candidates for them.) More interesting, the Professional and Business Women's Association, a group of some of Jordan's wealthiest and most powerful women, sponsored voter-awareness workshops throughout the kingdom during the registration period in late July and early August in very much a League of Women Voters style. And final statistics indicated that female voter registration increased significantly throughout the kingdom during this period. Perhaps more important, unaffiliated to political party or women's union, Toujan Faisal, whose campaign in 1989 had been severely damaged by charges of apostasy leveled by Islamists, was elected as the first woman to serve in the lower house of parliament.

Again, the discussions, workshops, and debate in the media are all positive signs of a nascent civil society attempting to carve out a greater role for itself. The fact that there is no unitary women's movement in Jordan, but rather a small collection of rather fractious and competing organizations says more about the history of civil society in Jordan than it does about the women's potential. And, as should now be clear, the difficulties faced by women's organizations in Jordan are not so different from those encountered by other civil society organizations, with perhaps one key exception. Women face not only the possible opposition of the state in their attempts to broaden and better serve their constituencies. They also encounter discriminatory and oppressive patriarchal structures and traditions of longstanding that pervade the existing male-dominated civil society institutions. Hence, women's quest for greater and more meaningful participation in civil society requires not only carving out a great realm vis-à-vis the state, but also efforts aimed at further legitimizing their activities outside the home, the family, or the tribe.

A more detailed exploration of the role that the Jordanian state is playing vis-à-vis women as part of the process of political liberalization is properly the topic of a separate paper. To conclude briefly, it is probably not a coincidence that certain women's activities have been allowed relatively unobstructed operation by the Jordanian state. Charitable societies in particular, those dealing with children, the aged, the handicapped, and the poor appear both non-threatening politically as well as "appropriate" for females. It is other aspects of women's activities that pose greater threats: pressing for changes in personal status laws and other legislation that would make them more fully citizen, seeking to open economic opportunities for women that offer them greater independence, creating solidarities or mobilizing across tribal or ethnic lines, pressing for state prosecution of those guilty of "honor crimes," and broader activity in national and regional politics— in other words, those efforts that would lead women to be treated as both more fully citizen, and more "civilly," by and in the state.

It appears it was efforts along these lines that led to the repression of all the three major women's movement experiments in Jordan discussed above. For women's activity of a non-charitable association nature may challenge not just state policy, but the patriarchal underpinnings of the state as well. Hence women's charitable organizations appear as benign as their mobilizing counterparts appear subversive. It is perhaps for this reason that in repressive societies one is more likely to see women's civil society activity permitted by the regime than other types, but only to a point. Once it transgresses the line between teaching embroidery to advocating an end to polygamy (and this is really a continuum not a dichotomy of activity), women's organizations are just as threatening as any political party, indeed, perhaps more so.

The Media

Given that Jordan has lived most of its life under martial law, it should not be surprising that its media have enjoyed very little freedom over the years. Heavy government censorship restricted the range of topics that could be discussed, prevented the emergence of new publications, and banned many books and periodicals, both Arab and foreign language, from abroad. The press was semi-official, while television and radio stations were officially government-run. The one bright spot was the functioning of the Jordanian Writers' Association, which served as a forum for public lectures on literary, cultural and political topics, despite the otherwise broad suppression of such discussion. However, as repression in the kingdom increased in 1987, the Association was closed, charged with being a front for radicals and subversives and a government-appointed alternative, the Union of Jordanian Writers, was established in its place. In a further move against press freedom, in August 1988 the boards of the three major dailies, al-Ra'i, al-Dustur, and al-Sha'b, were dissolved and reorganized to include members more sympathetic to the regime.

Following the beginning of the liberalization, the situation began to change. New publications emerged, most representative of particular political trends, and a range of publications from abroad that had formerly been on the censor's list started to make its way into the country. Television talk shows also began to host guests and raise issues that previously had been taboo and the Jordanian Writers Association was reopened in late 1989. The press also started publishing extensive segments of parliamentary debates. Nonetheless, the consensus seems to be that the print media has been less than daring in testing the extent of the new liberalization.[35] The three major dailies continue to be only marginally distinguishable. Now that the newspapers themselves are responsible for their own publication decisions (rather than relying on a censor), many feel they have become even more conservative. The opposition press has occasionally printed serious stories that the semi-official press will not,[36] but only the English-language *Jordan Times* carries regular, dependable political analysis.

The king himself was rumored to have been unhappy with the lack of development of the press since liberalization, but real changes seemed destined to await the issuance of a new Press and Publications law. Issued in late summer 1992, the new law is an improvement over the previous law to the extent that the state can no longer close a publication without explanation.[37] However, the extent of liberalization seems to end

---

[35] *Jordan Times*, 26-27 September 1991.

[36] Examples abound, but perhaps the most important recent example was that of *al-Ahali*, which broke the story in June 1993 about the al-Mu'ta University military cadets who had been arrested for an April 1993 assassination plot against the king.

[37] *Middle East International*, 7 August 1992.

there, indicating that the parliament, at least, was not particularly interested in encouraging greater fourth estate freedoms. One controversial element is that the new law continues to uphold the requirements that one be a member of the Jordan Press Association in order to be considered a journalist. The JPA admits only those who have trained with a local newspaper for a certain period of time, thus excluding a large number of those who are in fact working as journalists, but for publications outside the kingdom. This in effect reinforces the predominance of a circle of traditional, state-coopted journalists and largely prevents the input of others. In drafting this article, the parliament in effect acted on behalf of entrenched, conservative interests rather than with the intent of developing or protecting the profession at large.

Worse, certain elements of the new law contravene international standards of freedom of expression and information. In this respect, while the stipulation forbidding the publication of items that harm the royal family or reveal information about the armed forces is not particularly surprising, the further insistence that nothing be published which may hurt national unity, insult Arab or Muslim heads of state, or conflict with "public ethics," combined with the law's denial of a journalist's right to protect her sources has led the law to be described by observers as the epitome of tyranny.[38] While some publications, particularly the "opposition" Arabic press as well as the *Jordan Times* periodically challenge the limits of what is acceptable to print, the promulgation of the new law was hardly a signal of government support for the further development of independent journalism in the kingdom.

Other Organizations

The focus above on several key associations or sets of associations is not meant to obscure the fact that many other institutions that may be characterized as part of civil society also operate in the kingdom. Of long-standing are the Chambers of Commerce and Industry, both of which have diversified their infrastructures and become more vocal in the post-1989 period. New associations have also emerged, as in the case of university professors and students. Student unions had been particularly suspect over the years, forced to operate underground or outside the kingdom. When they were permitted to organize on campus their activities were very limited and very closely monitored.

---

[38] *Middle East International*, 18 December 1992.

One may also point to the development of a number of private educational institutions. Some have been in existence for a long time and serve elementary through high school students. In the 1980s, there was a proliferation of so-called community colleges, privately funded and run two-year institutions that teach a variety of skills and trades. More recently, in response to the increasing demand for places in Jordanian institutions because of the drop in the value of the dinar and because of the return of many Jordanians from the Gulf, several private universities have been established by groups of investors.

Jordan also has a range of sports clubs and youth organizations, some independent and some semi-state sponsored. The kingdom also hosts a large number of charitable institutions, some of which are completely private, while others, such as the Nur al-Hussein foundation, are clearly tied to the royal family. A number of other societies and clubs are associated with a particular ethnic (e.g., Circassian, Chichen) or religious (e.g., Greek Orthodox) community, along with family or village associations and welfare societies. Finally, as noted earlier, there is a range of Islamic educational and welfare societies and institutions that operate generally as an extension of the Muslim Brotherhood.

Family and Tribe

While neither family nor tribe is regarded as a civil society institution in traditional writings on civil society, both must be considered in any discussion of Jordan that seeks to understand those forces that serve as a buffer between the state and society, as well as those forces that may play a role in furthering the liberalization process. Jordan is a small country where it is not much of an exaggeration to say that everyone knows everyone else. Even if the individual him or herself is not known, the family name will speak volumes to a school teacher, a state bureaucrat, or an intelligence officer. In Jordan it is often obvious from one's name if one is Palestinian or Transjordanian, from what town, village, or tribe one hails, and one's religion. This type of information is crucial to carrying on business or more generally to effective interaction in society.

Having a particular family name, or having a relative in a particular position in business or the bureaucracy can mean improved chances for university admission, certain employment, the forgiveness of a traffic violation, or instant issuance of a passport. Being without such a name (particularly a problem for Palestinian peasants whose family affiliations carry little weight—Jordanian peasants have East Bank clan or tribal affiliations tied to the state apparatus that can protect them) one is more likely to spend hours in line to renew a driver's license, have greater trouble finding employment, and be more likely to be arrested if stopped by the authorities. Thus the family or clan can play an important role in protecting a member's interests against a sometimes sluggish, sometimes uncooperative, occasionally inefficient, but also periodically predatory state and its bureaucracy.

Hence, while a great deal has changed in the last seventy years, family and tribe remain two of the strongest institutions in Jordanian society. The key role that the tribal factor played in the 1993 elections simply underlines this point. In addition, however, if one is concerned with prospects for the continuing institutionalization of political liberalization in Jordan, it is quite significant that prior to the 1993 elections, some tribes actually held their own primaries: each of the major clans or branches made its own choice and then elections were held to determine the tribe as a whole's preferred candidate. While tribes have long been involved in interest articulation, the "primaries phenomenon" may suggest that the nature of their participation in the political system is gradually being transformed in ways that have important, positive implications for the continued development and institutionalization of the liberalization process.

The King as an Arbiter Above the State

While the king has largely succeeded over the years in creating the illusion of distance from domestic political issues, the period of liberalization has further reinforced his position or people's perception of his position as being above the political fray. Now not only is there a prime minister to take responsibility for policies gone awry, there is also a popularly elected parliament.

The king periodically does intervene almost as a deus ex machina, to right a wrong, address an injustice or simply to demonstrate monarchical benevolence that is (or seems to be) above politics. In this respect he plays a role of guardian or protector of the citizenry, preventing the excesses of the state from taking their toll, in his own way serving as a buffer between average citizens and the state. It is of course, a careful cultivation of a false image of the power and role of the king. It has, nonetheless, in numerous cases served the citizens and the monarchy quite well.

For example, in August 1992, some 500 Jordanians from the southern town of Tafila went to Amman to express their anger that their own Mahmud al-Hawamidah, Minister of Public Works under the pre-liberalization Rifaʿi government, had been indicted on corruption charges that other members of the previous cabinet (including Zayd al-Rifaʿi himself) had escaped. The protesters demanded to see King Hussein and asked for his protection against the injustice of the parliamentary deputies. "Down with Parliament. We want to see the King, the only fair leader who can protect us from the injustices of the deputies," was their cry.[39]

The king also annually pardons political prisoners on his birthday. However, in 1992, this move took on special significance. In addition to announcing a general amnesty for some 1000 people held for security-related offenses, the pardon included two MPs who had been sentenced to death only two days earlier for belonging to an organization that reportedly advocated the overthrow of the monarchy. The pardon of the popular Islamist Layth Shubaylat along with Islamist Yaʿqub Qarrash came as the Jordanian public had grown increasingly skeptical of the state's case. By intervening, not only did the king in effect overturn an excess of the government, he also sent a clear message to the Islamists about what kind of activity would or would not be allowed in the kingdom.[40] Such actions also contribute to the development of an atmosphere of tolerance or civility in Jordan that king seems keen on cultivating.

Civility

A number of the topics covered above have touched on the question of civility as used in this volume. While the martial law regime in Jordan was not as repressive as have been its counterparts in Damascus or Baghdad, nonetheless, an atmosphere in which free expression was so curbed and attempts at pushing back the boundaries of the state so staunchly resisted did not encourage the development of civility. While there is a general respect for the elderly (and, in some instances, for women) that protects them from many potential excesses by the state, the rest of society was generally fair game.

Since the beginning of the liberalization and the lifting of martial law, one finds evidence from which to be encouraged as well as disappointed. The improvement in the human rights record of the regime, the pardon-

---

[39] *Jordan Times*, 10 August 1992.
[40] *Middle East International*, 20 November 1992 and 8 January 1993.

Amman, Aug. 16(ap)pro-Saddam of Iraq demonstration—Banner carrying demonstrators march down a main street in downtown Amman this afternoon towards the United States ambassy to deliver a petition demanding that President Bush remove U.S. forces from the Middle East. They carry a poster of Iraqi President Saddam Hussain. (AP/WIDE WORLD PHOTOS)

ing and release of political prisoners, and the National Charter's emphasis on the principles of pluralism and tolerance are certainly encouraging signs. A particularly important development came in the summer of 1990 when the members of the various outlawed political parties agreed to keep their pro-Iraq, anti-American demonstrations peaceful so as not to require a use of force on the part of the government security forces.[41] Moreover, the king himself regularly speaks of tolerance and pluralism, and decries extremism. Given his apparent stance above politics, there is probably no more important symbol and model for the rest of society.

But state and society do not change overnight. In the fall of 1991, as the opening of the Madrid conference approached, a group of Islamist and leftist deputies organized an anti-peace conference rally at the headquarters of the professional unions. Before the rally could begin, young men in the middle of the room began chanting pro-government and pro-peace conference slogans, taunting the Islamists. After a few minutes chairs began to fly and a number of the several hundred people in attendance exited the hall via the windows.[42] There seemed little question in the minds of those who attended that the chanting had been organized by an arm of the state.

In August 1992, in elections for a Madaba parliamentary seat vacated by the death of an MP, the police were forced to use tear-gas to disperse rioters protesting the extension of balloting time by two hours because they felt it hurt the chances of their candidate. There were also charges of women's attempting to vote twice, using false identification cards. For their part, the accused, the Muslim Brotherhood supporters, denied the charges and contended that the police had harassed the women and delayed their entry into the polling center.[43]

Finally, and perhaps most disturbing, have been the alleged discoveries by the Jordanian security forces of caches of arms and munitions in the homes or in the possession of a number of Islamists, including Layth Shubaylat and Ya'qub Qarrash, mentioned earlier.[44] These events point either to the existence of a number of small but well-armed Islamic groups who may be preparing to use force against the regime, or to a well-coordinated effort by the regime to discredit the Islamists. In either case, the prognosis for civility should perhapsbe "guarded, but stable."

---

[41] This was reported to me by organizers of a huge demonstration on 12 August 1990.

[42] Observing from an adjacent terrace, I was forced to jump over a nearby wall so as not to be crushed by those pouring out of the hall.

[43] *Jordan Times*, 19 August 1992.

[44] See *Foreign Broadcasting Information Service, Near East and South Asia*, 8 September 1992; and 15 and 16 October 1992.

Conclusions

What do the processes of state consolidation, economic development and the record of the recent liberalization process tell us about civil society and its future in Jordan? In the first place, the historical development of the Jordanian state and economy has given the state a much larger "space" vis-à-vis civil society than has probably been the case in many other developing countries. Moreover, the alliance between the state and one of the two communal groups in the country (combined with the emergence of strong ethnic tensions between the Transjordanians and Palestinians) has meant that the state and its bureaucracy developed as the primary form of identification, support, and protection of about one-half of the kingdom's population. While there is no necessary reason for a state employee to be automatically excluded from the realm of civil society, in the case of Jordan, given the security situation, the antagonism toward Palestinians, and the role of the tribes, the incentive for a Transjordanian to seek expression outside state or tribe appears to have been minimal.

Against such a backdrop, the process of liberalization begun in 1989 has led to unprecedented gains for civil society and its institutions. Greater respect for human rights, far greater freedom of expression, the emergence of political parties, the development of political satire (particularly in the theater), and the multitude of conferences, lectures, panel discussions, and meetings on a variety of topics, both directly political and otherwise all indicate a growing vibrancy in the civic realm. Even skeptics believe there is little chance of return to the more repressive atmosphere of the pre-1989 period. Nonetheless, while the gains have been many, there is also no question that the king and his advisors are involved in a process of "managed liberalization," which at this point appears to have clear, if unspoken boundaries. While greater popular participation is certainly being encouraged, greater decentralization of authority (gradual relinquishment of power by the monarch) is not on the agenda. The "managed liberalization" is presented as ensuring stability and order, but the stability and order are to be preserved in the context of a continuingly powerful monarch. However wise and benevolent the king, this factor is the most basic obstacle to a full flowering of the liberalization process. Beyond this constraint, the Constitution and now the National Charter are the most obvious sources of the potential limits of the liberalization, as they contain the principles to which Jordanians must subscribe if they are to be fully citizen and participant. Most of these principles are above reproach, but the fact that the state has stipulated them and insists on enforcing them implies clear limits on the range of expression and activity to be permitted.

One potential challenge to these principles, and the one that is generally noted in discussions of threats to the continuation of the liberalization process, is the Islamists. The rise and appeal of Islamist parties demanding that certain elements of *shari'ah* become part of state law have raised the specter of an end to the pluralism called for in the National Charter. The discovery of armed cells of Islamists during the fall of 1992 certainly suggests that Jordan has not yet succeeded in convincing all groups to play by the new rules of the game. Moreover, as long as economic woes continue to grow and the Islamists are able to provide some material relief through their civil society institutions and their simple message, one should not expect their appeal to decline substantially.

However, this discussion has tried to underline another, less frequently mentioned challenge to the future development of civil society: the structure and bases of intercommunal relations. Political liberalization has effectively given the Palestinian community the opportunity to have a more effective and authentic voice in Jordanian politics; economic liberalization, on the other hand, attempts to cut back on the size and allocative nature of the state sector. Both processes, therefore, have medium-term negative implications for a good portion of the Transjordanian population. If such a process is, for whatever reason, allowed to run roughshod over their interests, it could be a prescription for intercommunal conflict. (There are already clear Palestinian and Transjordanian wings in the IAF.) The evidence of the continuation of such tensions was clear in the suggestions in early fall 1993 that the 1967 refugees who may be eligible to return to Palestine as part of a peace settlement be denied the right to participate in the 1993 elections.

Neither the Islamist nor the inter-communal challenge is likely to disappear in the near future. In the meantime, serious issues with potentially destabilizing effects continue to confront the kingdom: the ongoing Arab-Israeli negotiations and their political and economic implications for Jordan, continuing economic hardship for the majority of the population as a result of IMF-dictated policies, high levels of unemployment, and galloping population growth in the context of scarce resources. It is too early to make final pronouncements about the fate of the liberalization or about the future of civil society. This paper has argued that a clear, yet still civil, battle has been joined, but on a field that remains largely defined and controlled by the state.

CHAPTER SIX

THE UTILITY OF TRADITION: CIVIL SOCIETY IN KUWAIT

Neil Hicks and Ghanim al-Najjar

Since the beginning of major oil production in 1946, and the achievement of independence from Britain in 1961, Kuwaiti politics has been dominated by the ruling al-Sabah family. Prior to the discovery of oil, and despite the fact that the al-Sabah family had been rulers since Sabah I became Amir in 1752, the family was dependent on large merchant families which offered financial and political support to the monarchy in return for a say in state affairs. In contrast to other Gulf States[1] Kuwait had developed "a conscious and politically organized merchant élite before oil."[2]

The pre-eminence of the ruling family grew with the increase of oil revenues and the powers of patronage deriving from them. In 1938, merchants pressed for a share in the control of oil revenues among a series of demands made by a short-lived legislative assembly made up of representatives of merchant families. However, with British collusion, the Amir Ahmad was able to resist these demands. The assembly was dissolved and control of oil revenues remained in the hands of the al-Sabah family.[3] As oil revenues increased through the fifties, the ruling family became less dependent on the financial support of the merchants. However, by 1954 extravagant spending plans and widespread corruption obliged the family to turn again for support to the merchants.

It was at this point that the deal was struck that has essentially characterized the ruling family's political relations with Kuwait's preeminent political class, the large merchant families. In the ensuing decades, the family has attempted to strike similar deals with the other sectors of Kuwaiti society that emerged to play a political role. The elements of this deal are simple. In return for ceding to the ruling family effective control

---

[1] See the comparison between Kuwait and Qatar in Jill Crystal, *Oil and Politics in the Gulf: Rulers and Merchants in Kuwait and Qatar* (Cambridge University Press, Cambridge 1990), pp. 15 - 33.

[2] Crystal, *Oil and Politics*, p. 5.

[3] For an account of the 1938 *Majlis* movement see Crystal, *Oil and Politics*, pp. 47 - 57.

over key areas of state policy making, initially the merchants, and over time other Kuwaitis, received payment. The merchants were the beneficiaries of state spending on domestic development contracts, of laws which excluded foreign competition or obliged foreign contractors to take on Kuwaiti partners, and of an understanding which minimized the family's involvement in Kuwaiti business. All Kuwaiti citizens have benefitted from substantial state subsidies that provide free education and health care, employment for those that want it, and state assistance in purchasing a home.[4]

The state has thus taken on primarily distributive functions, leaving the executive branch of government free from accountability to taxpayers, and reliance on domestic sources of revenue, which is the lot of most governments. Such an economy, based on revenues paid directly to the state with minimal reliance by the rulers on local elites, creates what has been referred to as a rentier state. In a rentier state, participatory forms of government are less likely to emerge because the rulers, with their monopoly control over immense resources, have no incentive to accommodate demands for participation and representation from their subjects. Such governments do not need their citizens to sustain the trappings of state. While the government of a rentier state may be expected to have a good deal of latitude for independent action, it is not necessarily stable or secure because its rule is not firmly rooted in the consent of the people. The lack of organic ties between government and people lend an aura of fragility to the relationship. In fact, the Gulf monarchies have proved remarkably resilient. Their demise has been confidently predicted for decades. But they remain, constant reminders of the venal truth that political consent can be purchased.

A rentier state is also unlikely to be fertile ground for the development of the diverse array of private associations and institutions autonomous of the state, with a tendency to seek to hold state power in check, which we refer to as civil society. In this respect, Kuwait has been an odd kind of rentier state. In order to facilitate the articulation of competing political and religio-political trends within Kuwaiti society—the better to control them—the state has fostered the development of a broad range of semi-autonomous associations.[5] These voluntary, professional and

---

[4] See Crystal, *Oil and Politics*. pp.62 - 83.

[5] Shafeeq Ghabra states that there were more than 50 voluntary associations registered in Kuwait prior to the Iraqi invasion of August 2, 1990. Shafeeq Ghabra, "Voluntary Associations in Kuwait: The Foundations of a New System?," *Middle East Journal* 45, no. 2 (Spring 1991), p. 200.

mosque-based groups benefitted from state subsidies, and are regulated by legislation that ensures ultimate governmental control over their affairs.[6]

Civil and political liberties have waxed and waned, partly as a function of the government's perception of its need to garner support from different elements within Kuwaiti society. However, toleration of oppositional views and the creation of institutions with real powers to hold the government accountable have been a feature of Kuwait's history since independence, setting it apart neighboring Gulf states.

The government has at times shown itself unwilling to live within the constraints created largely by its own manipulations of groups within the society. Nevertheless, when the legitimacy of the Kuwaiti state was put to the sternest possible test with its invasion by Iraq in August 1990, and the claim that the Iraqi-Kuwaiti border was an anachronistic creation of the colonial powers of no further relevance, it was the non-governmental groups, and many of the government's critics, that held fast to the idea of Kuwaiti sovereignty and rule by the al-Sabah family, fighting and dying for it. Perhaps inadvertently, Kuwait's ruling family can be said to have demonstrated that decentralization of power, and the fostering of a competitive political environment, albeit within limits, can greatly enhance the legitimacy of a government.

The utter collapse of the Kuwaiti government in the wake of the Iraqi invasion removed paternalistic constraints from Kuwaiti civil society for the first time, albeit in the highly adverse circumstances of Iraqi military occupation. The immediate post-war period saw the emergence of a number of completely autonomous voluntary organizations with their roots in the network of self-help and resistance movements that had emerged under occupation. Established voluntary associations also developed new habits of independent action in the absence of official control and established leaders.

The Kuwaiti government restored at the end of February 1991 did not immediately challenge the position of Kuwait's newly-energized non-governmental sector. On August 6, 1993, however, the government announced the decision of the Council of Ministers to disband all "unlicensed popular committees," targeting in particular broad-based movements, cutting across tribal, confessional and class divisions which the government has traditionally sought to use to its own advantage.

---

[6] See Mary Ann Tétreault, "Civil Society in Kuwait: Protected Spaces and Women's Rights," *Middle East Journal* 47, no. 2 (Spring 1993), p. 276.

This has sparked a confrontation that echoes earlier attempts by non-governmental forces to free themselves of governmental control. It is this confrontation which will decide whether the unique experiences of the occupation will be translated into a lasting shift in the balance of power in Kuwait between the ruling elite, dominated by the al-Sabah family, and the diverse elements of Kuwaiti society calling for a more active role in shaping state policy. This confrontation will shape the future of civil society in Kuwait. Will it be constrained by state subsidy and control? Or will it manifest itself in lasting institutions independent of and ultimately challenging to the government's monopoly on power?

Democracy in Kuwait

Kuwait is unique among the Gulf monarchies in having established a parliamentary tradition. The Constitution of the State of Kuwait, promulgated in 1962, provides for many of the institutions considered essential to the existence of civil society; what Edward Shils refers to as "the institutions by which the state is kept within substantive and procedural confinement."[7] The Constitution provides for an independent judiciary, a free press and upholds basic freedoms of association, assembly and expression. It also provides for a National Assembly "composed of fifty members elected directly by universal suffrage and secret ballot."[8]

The Kuwaiti government has exhibited a marked disinclination to govern within the confines set down by the constitution. The independence of the judiciary has been undermined by the powers vested in the Minister of Justice by legislation. The minister appoints, and dismisses judges, and organizes the work of the courts. No fewer than 46 of the 68 articles of Decree Law 23 of 1990, governing the operation of the judiciary, provide for the minister to exercise executive influence over judicial matters.[9]

Press laws have historically made criticisms of the Amir or the ruling family a punishable offense, and stringent secrecy laws have placed restrictions on the reporting of government business, however innocu-

---

[7] Edward Shils, "The Virtue of Civil Society", *Government and Opposition*, 26, no. 1, (Winter 1991), p. 10.

[8] Constitution of the State of Kuwait, Article 80.

[9] See Kuwait, *Building the Rule of Law*, Lawyers Committee for Human Rights, (New York, January 1992), p. 24 - 26. For a description of the efforts of legislators to repeal this law, and to bring about a more independent judiciary see, *Laying the Foundations, Human Rights in Kuwait: Obstacles and Opportunities*, Lawyers Committee for Human Rights, April 1993, pp. 27 - 31.

ous. Pre-publication censorship, enforced between 1986 and 1992, was lifted prior to the October 1992 elections for the National Assembly. Nevertheless, some journalists and editors risked prosecution for infringing press laws.[10] The latitude of the press to report on controversial issues increased with the reconvening of the National Assembly, and the press was free to report fully on parliamentary debates in which previously taboo subjects were aired.

Public gatherings require prior government approval, which is sometimes refused. However, the Kuwaiti tradition of the *diwaniyya*, a form of public meeting based in the home and therefore beyond the scope of the law governing public assembly, has provided an alternative forum for the discussion of politics, or any other subject, relatively unimpeded by the state.[11]

Freedom of association has been qualified by laws providing for government control over the activities of voluntary groups. Non-governmental groups must seek registration from the Ministry of Social Affairs, and must accept the governmental oversight that goes along with this status. Kuwaiti law has never recognized the existence of fully independent voluntary organizations.

The National Assembly is elected on a very limited franchise of male Kuwaiti citizens over 21 who can demonstrate that they or their forbears were continuously resident in Kuwait between 1920 and 1960.[12] The electorate in the 1992 elections amounted to some 82,000 voters out of a Kuwaiti population in excess of 800,000. Yet despite its limited franchise, the Assembly has exhibited "an institutional inclination to represent"[13] and at times when it has been in operation there has been an attendant erosion of governmental prerogative.[14] Nevertheless, the National Assembly's inclination to encroach on the government's powers have been held in check.

The tactics employed by the government in responding to the challenge of the National Assembly exemplifies the complex process of give

---

[10] Interview with Muhammad Jasim al-Saqr, Editor-in-Chief, *Al-Qabas*, January 9, 1993. At the time of the interview, Mr. al-Saqr had already been prosecuted twice for alleged infringements of the Press Law since the lifting of pre-publication censorship.

[11] See Tétrault, "Civil Society," p. 279.

[12] The residency requirement is in fact largely theoretical since many registered voters are unable to demonstrate that they have fulfilled it. Nevertheless, an exclusive group of electors with an interest in protecting its privileged position in the political process has been created because of the restricted electoral roll.

[13] Crystal, *Oil and Politics in the Gulf*, p. 104.

[14] Ghabra, "Voluntary Associations," p. 205.

and take by which it has sought to contain threats to its authority. As Crystal observed, "Kuwait's amirs have usually chosen to make concessions to the opposition even as they tried to undermine it."[15]

While the ruling family has attempted to benefit from the National Assembly as "a forum for containing opposition, a way of letting off steam ..." and, as "an opportunity to take the country's pulse,"[16] the Assembly has also provided a forum for diverse interests within Kuwaiti society to find common cause in restricting the influence of the ruling family. At times the family has found the demands of the assembly intolerable. Between 1976 and 1981, and 1986 and 1992 the assembly was suspended and the Amir ruled by decree in consultation with his appointed council of ministers. An issue in the dissolution of parliament in 1976 was the parliament's insistence on the establishment of an independent judiciary.[17] In 1986 a contributory factor in parliament's dissolution was its attempt to hold the government responsible for financial scandals that took place in the early eighties, such as the 1982 *Suq al-Manakh* (stock market crash).[18]

Ghabra points out the irony of the fact that the constitutional power of the National Assembly to force the resignation on members of the government, as it did with the Minister of Justice in 1985, and even to bring down the government, as it is empowered to do under Article 102 of the Constitution, has contributed to a situation where in order to ensure its own survival, the government has had to dissolve the National Assembly.[19] Ghabra characterizes this conflict between the parliament and the government as a "zero sum game," and one in which the Kuwaiti people have been the perpetual losers.[20] Ghabra is referring to an overemphasis by both the government and the opposition on the question of who is in control, at the expense of necessary attention to issues demanding a policy response.

There were however benefits in the open adversarial relationship between government and opposition. Kuwait is a small wealthy country with a predatory neighbor in Iraq, and potential threats to its sovereignty

---

[15] Jill Crystal, *Kuwait: The Transformation of an Oil State* (Boulder, Westview Press, 1992), p.175.

[16] Crystal, *Oil and Politics,* p.85.

[17] Ghabra, "Voluntary Associations" p. 205

[18] Crystal, *Kuwait,* p. 108.

[19] Shafiq Ghabra, "Kuwait: Elections and Issues of Democratization in a Middle Eastern State," *Digest of Middle East Studies* 2, no. 1 (Winter 1993), p.3.

[20] Ghabra, "Kuwait," p.4.

from Iran and Saudi Arabia. Its survival has depended to some extent on its success in balancing these three major regional powers against each other. The various political currents that have emerged in Kuwait since independence have included elements broadly representing the interests and ideologies of these neighboring states, and indeed the competing ideological currents of the region as a whole. The relatively open debate of competing ideas that has been permitted throughout most of Kuwait's independent existence has enabled the government to gauge the support among Kuwaitis for these divergent political trends, a useful early warning system.

The controlled checks and balances of the political system have also provided a safety valve to the government. If contentious issues arose between it and a neighboring state, they could be referred to the National Assembly, where the eventual decision may be displeasing to a neighbor, but could be blamed on the influences of other regional powers expressed through the debate in the Kuwaiti press and parliament. Such an open system would also serve to alert regional powers of the designs and intentions of their counterparts, and to engage them in steps to counteract any threats perceived by the Kuwaiti government. While such an open system is by its nature difficult for a government to direct to serve its interest, Crystal notes that the Assembly has been used as "a foil" by the Amir to good effect in Kuwait's negotiations with the oil companies in the seventies, and with the Gulf Cooperation Council in the eighties.[21]

By this analysis, in 1986, once the government dissolved the National Assembly and added to that pre-publication censorship, it became uniquely responsible for its actions towards neighboring countries. At times this contributed to increased tension in Kuwait's relations with regional governments. For example, soon after the introduction of pre-publication censorship in 1986 King Hassan of Morocco met with Israeli Foreign Minister Shimon Peres. The censor neglected to issue any guidelines on how the Kuwaiti press was to report on this controversial meeting. The media followed standing instructions to print no criticism of a friendly state, such as Morocco, and reported on the meeting without comment. The following day, the Kuwaiti government came under Arab diplomatic pressure, led by Syria, asking whether the media's lack of comment on the meeting indicated Kuwaiti governmental approval or toleration of Morocco's breaking of Arab ranks by entering into dialogue with the Zionist enemy. The government then issued instructions to the

---

[21] Crystal, *Oil and Politics,* p. 85.

press to comment on the meeting and tens of articles critical of Morocco's position appeared in the press. The government was then faced with diplomatic protests from Morocco over hostile coverage in Kuwait's state-controlled media. Naturally, the Moroccan government held the Kuwaiti government responsible for these articles. Thus, one result of the dissolution of parliament and the imposition of pre-publication censorship was an erosion of Kuwait's traditional neutral role in regional politics.

In this way, the closure of the political system after 1986 contributed to the disaster which befell Kuwait in August 1990 with the Iraqi invasion. The absence of reliable indicators about the popularity of the government and the ruling family among Kuwaiti citizens enabled Saddam Hussein to form the tragic misperception that an Iraqi take-over in Kuwait would be welcomed by its populace. Additionally, the restrictions on open debate in Kuwait meant that the government's policies over oil production quotas, and the rate of Kuwait's exploitation of the Rumailia oil field, policies which Saddam Hussein found intensely provocative, and were, in his own words, a direct cause of the Iraqi invasion,[22] were not subjected to searching public debate in the press and the parliament.

There is evidence to suggest that Kuwait's rulers have understood the utility of the National Assembly, and of a vibrant civil society, in terms of enhancing the legitimacy of the government's rule among Kuwaitis, and in consolidating its position in the face of regional threats. The National Assembly was first convened after elections held in January 1963 at a time when Iraq, under President 'Abd al-Karim Qasim, was threatening to annex the newly-independent state. In 1981, the government responded to the surge in support for militant Islamic ideologies, inspired by Ayatollah Khomeini's accession to power in Iran in 1979, by holding elections and reconvening the Assembly. At the Jidda Conference of October 1991, during the Iraqi occupation, the government implicitly conceded that constitutional government would have been a better safeguard against the Iraqi invasion, and committed itself to holding elections and restoring the Assembly.

Support for the National Assembly, and the principles of constitutional government, has broadened in the decades since independence. In the sixties and seventies the Assembly's supporters were representative

---

[22] See, Walid Khalidi, "Iraq vs. Kuwait: Claims and Counterclaims," in *The Gulf War Reader*, Cifry and Serf eds. (New York: Random House, 1991), pp. 57 - 65.

of secular, leftist and Arab nationalist groups. A factor in the dissolution of parliament in 1976 was the early ascendancy of the Lebanese left and the Palestine Liberation Organization in the Lebanese Civil War.[23] The opposition to the dissolution was led by such groups as the General Federation of Kuwaiti Workers, the Lawyers Association, the Society of Kuwaiti Teachers, the National Union of Kuwaiti Students, and the *Istiqlal* Club, led by prominent parliamentary opposition member, Ahmed al-Khatib.[24] All of these groups were dominated by leftist and Arab Nationalist groups at that time. In contrast, the Islamic Social Reform Society, viewed as the seat of Muslim Brotherhood influence within Kuwait, did not oppose the 1976 dissolution.

In contrast, the 1986 dissolution of the National Assembly was met by concerted opposition from both Islamic and secular nationalist and leftist groups.[25] This common ground on the need for constitutional government between the two major competing ideological trends within Kuwaiti society is an important indicator of growing civility within the Kuwait political system. However, a cautionary note should be sounded over the persistent influence of the ruling family and its tribal allies, sustained by its control of oil revenues. It should be recalled that the broad alliance of political forces did not succeed in restoring the National Assembly prior to the rude intervention of external forces in the form of the Iraqi invasion. Furthermore, immediately prior to the Iraqi invasion, the government had announced the establishment of a National Council to supplant the National Assembly. The ruling family hoped to create a body over which it would exercise more control than it had over the National Assembly. Elections for the Council's 50 elected members, who were to serve together with 25 government-appointees, were held in June 1990. Although the opposition called for a boycott of the process, the Council had started to function by the time of the Iraqi invasion.[26]

It remains very much an open question whether the al-Sabah family is interested in presiding over the creation of institutions in Kuwait which will lead to a serious diminution of its power. While diverse groups within the society, beginning with the merchants, but including tribal and religious interests have been brought into the political process, the family has sought to orchestrate this process playing off competing groups against each other.

---

[23] Ghabra, "Voluntary Associations," p. 204.
[24] Fred Lawson, "Class and State in Kuwait," *Merip Reports*, May 1985, p. 19.
[25] Ghabra, "Voluntary Associations," pp. 211 - 212.
[26] Crystal, *Kuwait*, pp.119-120.

The ruling family has sought to control Kuwaiti democracy, but the family has not been able to prevent the National Assembly from becoming an independent voice for accountability and participatory government. While the Assembly has proved to be an effective forum in which the government could "strike a deal with the public,"[27] it is also the vessel in which broad based opposition to unrestrained family privilege has crystallized.

Associational Life

While Kuwaiti political life has been more participatory and more competitive than other polities among the Arab states of the Persian Gulf, the formation of political parties has not been permitted.[28] Consequently, political competition has tended to take place within and between the various social, professional and cultural associations and clubs that have developed in Kuwait. As noted above, the ruling family has sought to control the political debate within the country by seeking to create a restricted forum in the National Assembly, over which it would exercise control. In as much as Kuwaiti politics can be characterized as a competition between the al-Sabah family, the opposition united around the cause of constitutional government and an active National Assembly, the politically active groups within Kuwait have had an interest in building their constituencies among the public, through the creation of independent non-governmental associations. Such associations would be a counterweight to the centralized influence exerted by the family. Thus, the position of associations has tended to improve during periods of parliamentary rule. Whereas, while the National Assembly has been dissolved the government has also sought to suppress associational life, the natural repository of support for the return of parliament.

This commonality of interest between the National Assembly and the associations is apparent from an overview of the vicissitudes of the government's relations with the associations in post-independence Kuwait. With the convening of the Constituent Assembly charged with drafting the Constitution in early 1962, a ban on the activities of associations in force since 1959 was lifted. The law governing the operation of associations, Law 24 of 1962, envisaged associations

---

[27] Crystal, *Oil and Politics*, p.102.
[28] Some loose party organization was permitted prior to the October 1992 elections for the National Assembly.

which, in return for state subsidies, accepted the *de jure* control over their affairs of the Ministry of Social Affairs.

In 1965, the National Assembly approved amendments to the law of association restricting the right of associations to engage in politics. The definition of what constituted political, and therefore proscribed, activity was left to the discretion of the Minister of Social Affairs. Shafiq Ghabra observes that:

> The ability of the 50 elected members to pass such regulations was enhanced by the presence of 16 appointed government ministers who, in addition to their executive role, served as voting members of parliament, thus giving the government an advantage.[29]

This restriction of the freedom of action of associations brought about a major conflict between the government and the opposition which led to the resignation of eight out of the 50 elected members of the National Assembly.

The 1976 dissolution of the National Assembly, which was vigorously opposed by secular nationalist and leftist controlled associations was followed by repressive measures against the government's critics. Using the powers of the 1962 law, the elected boards of the teachers and workers' associations were dismissed and replaced by government appointees. The students' union board avoided dissolution because it was not licensed under the law.[30] The opposition stronghold, the *Nadi al-Istiqlal* was completely disbanded.

Further amendments to the 1962 law have had a restrictive emphasis. In 1985, shortly prior to the second dissolution of the National Assembly, the government announced a moratorium on the registration of new associations. In 1988, an Amiri Decree removed the right of judicial review of decisions to dissolve associations from the provisions of the law.

Professional associations, labor unions and student groups have traditionally been dominated by secular nationalist and leftist political movements. Kuwait, with its substantial population of migrant workers from different parts of the Arab world, and its relatively permissive atmosphere, built on the foundation of the 1962 Constitution, became a center of relatively free debate of issues in Arab politics. With the outbreak of the Lebanese Civil War in 1976, Lebanese and Palestinian

---

[29] Ghabra, "Voluntary Associations," p. 204.

[30] The legal status of the National Union of Kuwaiti Students has remained unresolved, although the Prime Minister has traditionally opened its annual conference, and arranged for the donation of state funds for its activities.

journalists and intellectuals were attracted to Kuwait's free press, and vibrant nationalist institutions. The criticisms of autocratic rule in Kuwait, and in the other Gulf monarchies, prevalent in Arab nationalist circles, found a ready audience among the increasing numbers of educated Kuwaitis who had taken advantage of generous government scholarships for study abroad, in other Arab countries, and in the west. Although these Kuwaiti graduates were guaranteed a job commensurate with their qualifications in a government controlled enterprise, or ministry, many remained disenfranchised and excluded from the closed circle of the Kuwaiti power elite.

The 1976 dissolution of the elected boards of the teachers' union and the banning of the *Nadi al-Istiqlal* was designed to limit the influence of secular and liberal groups within Kuwaiti society. Islamist political organizations grew in influence in an environment where other forms of political expression were discouraged. The most conservative Islamist group was the Heritage Society which supported the austere tenets of the *Salafi* movement. It was only in the early eighties that the Heritage Society began to be involved in formal politics, and its positions tended to be supportive of the government. However, by the end of the eighties the Heritage Society was united with all other groups in advocating the reconvening of the National Assembly. A second Sunni group, the Social Reform Society became more critical of political conditions in Kuwait in the late seventies and early eighties. The Social Reform Society joined with secular nationalist groups in condemning the 1986 dissolution of the National Assembly. The Shi'i Islamic Cultural and Social Society adopted an increasingly critical attitude towards the prevailing political conditions in Kuwait, in which Shi'ites were not represented in senior government posts in proportion to their numerical strength. The Iranian Revolution of 1979 politicized Kuwait's Shi'a community, and brought the Cultural and Social Society into an alliance with other to form a broad coalition in favor of placing constitutional checks on the rule of the al-Sabah family. It was this coalition, for example, which was the primary element of a joint petition for the return of the constitution, circulated in the Fall of 1988. Shafiq Ghabra wrote of these groups:

> It is likely that associational groups—which served in the past as platforms for unofficial political groups and parties—will play an essential role in developing a system of government based on greater popular participation.[31]

---

[31] Ghabra, "Voluntary Associations," p.199.

So, political opposition in Kuwait found expression in the major formal religious, professional and labor associations. However, it was not completely reliant on these formal structures, which were subject to legislative and administrative restrictions, and at times closure, at the hands of the government. As the movement for the return of the National Assembly, and for a return to constitutional government gathered momentum in the late eighties, the *diwaniyyah* took on increasing importance as the platform for political protests. In December 1989, a group of 32 parliamentarians from the dismissed 1986 National Assembly, with the support of the associations, began convening a regular Monday evening *diwaniyyah* at which political arguments for the reconvening of the Assembly were aired, and at which participation from diverse groups was made possible.[32]

The movement began with the preparation of a petition signed by more than 30,000 Kuwaiti citizens calling for the restoration of the assembly, and a return to constitutional rule. On July 1, 1989 a 45 - member committee, designed to be representative of "all sectors" of Kuwaiti society and drawn from the leadership of the major professional and cultural associations, as well as members of the dismissed assembly, presented the petition to the Amir. The Amir refused to accept it, and four months later the *diwaniyyah* protests began. After the first protest was held at the home of veteran nationalist opposition figure, Jasim al-Qataami on December 4, 1989 the government sought to prevent any repeat by taking the unprecedented measure of seeking to close down the *diwaniyyah* of parliamentarian Mishari al-Anjari,[33] where the December 11 protest was scheduled to be held. There was no basis in Kuwaiti law for this measure, and the protest movement was able to rally broad support by stating that the attempt to close down a *diwaniyyah* was a blow against a deeply cherished Kuwaiti tradition.[34]

The *diwaniyyah* protests led to escalating confrontation between the government and those advocating a return to constitutional rule. The December 11 meeting went ahead, with between 2,000 and 3,000 in

---

[32] For a detailed contemporaneous account of the campaign for the reconvening of the Assembly, based largely on interviews with participants in the movement see, Lawyers Committee for Human Rights, "Kuwait: Recent Human Rights Developments," New York, March 1990.

[33] Mishari al Anjari was appointed Minister of Justice in the government appointed after the October 1992 elections.

[34] Lawyers Committee for Human Rights, 1990, cites a telegram sent by 28 leaders of the protest movement to the Crown Prince on December 13, 1989 charging that the government decision was "incompatible with the meaning [of the diwaniyyah] that Kuwaitis hold in their hearts with their customs. Ghabra, "Kuwait," p. 4.

attendance, despite the government's deployment of riot police on roads leading to Mr. al-Anjari's house. According to eye-witness accounts, participants in the meeting pushed their way past police barricades, and were not met by force.[35] Two further *diwaniyyah* protests went ahead without serious clashes between the authorities and the participants. Then at a *diwaniyyah* convened in Al-Jahra, on January 8, 1990 riot police stormed the crowd, and arrested the host, parliamentarian Ahmad Ash-Sharii'an, who was released later the same day without charge after hundreds of protesters had surrounded the police station demanding his release. Confrontation occurred again at a meeting convened on January 22, 1990. Ten people attending the meeting were detained for two weeks before being released without charge.

The *diwaniyyah* protests were effective, and in February the government agreed to receive the petition, and to enter into negotiations for the reconvening of the Assembly. The protests had shown that the traditional gathering could be used by a coalition of groups with common objectives to overcome governmental constraints on freedom of assembly and expression in the context of a contemporary political dispute. Thus the institution of the *diwaniyyah* should be seen as an element of civil society, having a life of its own and acting as a counterweight to governmental autonomy. As an intrinsically non-governmental institutions beyond the reach of the Law on Associations, it provided a vehicle for professional, cultural and other more formal associations, to press their political demands for the return of the Assembly, in ways which were not open to them through their own government-controlled structures.

Another institution which has taken on political functions within the society is that of Cooperative Societies. These are very large bodies which in 1990 had over 170,000 subscribers. Cooperatives are based in all areas of the country. Their primary function is the purchase and distribution through retail outlets of foodstuffs and household goods. In 1990 there were 42 Cooperative Societies running 70 supermarkets and more than 700 small stores. The Cooperative Societies controlled more than 80% of the retail food market.

The Cooperative Societies' central role in people's lives, and the democratic structures within the Cooperatives have made them an important political battleground. All Kuwaiti residents of a particular area above 18 years of age are eligible to be a subscriber of that

---

[35] Ghabra, "Kuwait," p.5.

neighborhood's Cooperative Society. Subscribers are entitled to a share of the Cooperative Society's annual profit, have the right to vote, and to stand as a candidate in the annual election for the board of the Cooperative Society. Women are entitled to vote in the elections for boards of Cooperative Societies.

Islamist groups gained control over many Cooperative Society boards in the early eighties. Serving on a board is a way of developing a base of support in a particular neighborhood which can be used to launch a campaign for election to the National Assembly. The popularity of the Cooperative Societies' activities has meant that individual politicians have built their careers in this manner. At least 19 of the members of the National Assembly elected in October 1992 had built their political careers as members of Cooperative Society boards, or had some substantial involvement in the movement. This compares with 12 members of the National Assembly who had served in leadership positions in professional or cultural associations. Prior to the invasion, the Cooperative Societies had become a center of power for the Islamist groups.

Under the law governing the operation of the Cooperative Societies, the Minister of Social Affairs maintains considerable supervisory powers over their activities. The Minister may for example dissolve the elected Board of a society which he deems to be involved in inappropriate activities, or if mismanagement of funds has taken place. In such cases, the Minister appoints a caretaker board until a new election is held. Despite these governmental powers, the Cooperatives developed into powerful quasi-independent structures, forming the political base for popular Islamist politicians who tended to side with the secular opposition in advocating limitations on the absolute power of the royal family and the ruling elite.

The Iraqi Occupation

The strength of Kuwait's associational and voluntary groups formed the backbone of Kuwaiti resistance to Iraqi occupation. At the center of the network of ad-hoc institutions created during the occupation were the Cooperative Societies. Since the assets of the Cooperative Societies were owned by large numbers of ordinary people it was difficult for the Iraqi authorities to confiscate them. The Iraqi authorities did confiscate government owned enterprises, and most privately-owned companies. The Cooperatives continued to function, although closely watched by the occupation forces. Overtly, Cooperatives continued to sell food and household goods. Covertly, food and goods were distributed free of charge to those in need.

Cooperatives also supplied money to families, and to the resistance. In order to obtain money, cooperatives would sell goods in the usual manner. However, instead of depositing the money in banks, as they are required by Kuwaiti law to do, they would retain the funds for other uses. Cooperatives were able to enter into agreements with suppliers to obtain supplies on credit thus augmenting the funds available to them. An important use of the surplus funds was to pay bribes to the Iraqi authorities to secure the release of detainees.

Abdullateef al-Kharazah, the Director of the Cooperative Societies' Union described how this operation was carried out:

> From the first days of the occupation contacts were made to insure the continuation of food supplies. The Union of Cooperative Societies took the initiative. We had some food, but we met with the following organizations: the Kuwaiti Supplies Company; the Flour and Bakery Company; the Union of Manufacturers and Traders of Foodstuffs; and the National Bank of Kuwait, representing the banks... It was agreed that Cooperative Societies would pay 25% of the cost of supplies received by them, with the rest to be paid later.[36]

By virtue of the physical presence of the premises of cooperative societies in every residential neighborhood, the cooperatives were a focal point for communication. In addition, the inter-connectedness of the cooperative societies meant that cooperative administrators could travel freely from district to district without attracting the suspicions of the Iraqi authorities. This was an invaluable channel of communication during the occupation.

The leadership of the Cooperative Societies changed during the occupation. In many cases, elected members of the Board were outside of Kuwait at the time of the occupation, or left after the invasion to escape from the privations of life under occupation. Vacancies in the leadership were taken by volunteers, who were younger and of a more activist political temperament than the elected administrators they replaced. In fact, many of the leading activists from the professional and cultural associations, whose activities were prohibited under occupation, became active in the Cooperative Societies, recognizing in their unique structures attributes of great utility to the resistance movement.

The more activist approach of the volunteer leadership was evident in the breadth of activities of the voluntary committees which developed

---

[36] For a description of the role of the Cooperative Societies during the occupation see: Salah al-Ghazali, *Sur al-Kuwait al-rabi'a*, Volume 3, (Kuwait 1992).

on the basis of the Cooperative Society networks. These included Popular Committees, and the Islamist-controlled Social Solidarity Committees and other less influential committees. The leadership of the resistance to Iraqi occupation saw themselves as creating a "popular government"[37] to buttress Kuwaiti national identity in the absence of the ruling family and the government. The occupation saw a renaissance in neighborhood solidarity mechanisms which had been weakened by decades of urbanization, and which many Kuwaitis believed to have expired. The Kuwaiti resistance saw itself as "creating a new society equipped with old values," and the assertion of distinctive common values was a natural reaction to the threat to Kuwaiti identity posed by the occupation.

There were also practical aspects about life under occupation which fostered reliance on neighborhood solidarity. There were Iraqi military checkpoints situated around each neighborhood. The behavior of the guards was unpredictable and Kuwaitis were encouraged to stay closer to home, rather than run the unnecessary risk of seeking to pass through a checkpoint. The nighttime curfew imposed throughout the occupation compelled residents to stay close to home after dark.

The voluntary leadership in the occupation took on tasks such as arranging family visits for Kuwaiti prisoners held in Iraq, and providing support to prisoners' families, and to the families of people killed during the occupation. As Kuwaitis sought to boycott government institutions taken over by the Iraqis, so the popular committees took on more governmental functions.

The Restoration of Kuwaiti Sovereignty

While there was some expectation that a new society would emerge out of the experiences of occupation, the reality has been a return to the pre-occupation structures. However, it would be a mistake to assume that nothing was changed by the occupation. The fallibility of the government is now indelibly etched in the consciousness of all Kuwaitis because of the fiasco of the events which led up to the Iraqi occupation. The government's relative weakness was manifested in its abandonment of the National Council, and its agreement to reconvene the National Assembly. When elections were finally held in October 1992, they were marked by vigorous campaigning with much open criticism of the

---

[37] This claim has been made by Abdullateef al-Kharazah in al-Ghazali, *Sur al-Kuwait*.

government, and by the eventual victory of 35 candidates who had run in opposition to government-backed candidates. With 35 out of 50 members of the assembly having beaten government candidates, and six out of the 16 ministers being appointed from elected members of parliament, the government must rule with a legislature in which its supporters are in a minority.

While there has been forthright criticism of the government from parliament, and concrete measures have been taken to enforce account-ability for financial scandals relating to Kuwaiti investments abroad in Britain and Spain in which members of the ruling family are impli-cated,[38] there has been a conscious emphasis on avoiding confrontation between the parliament and the government. Shafiq Ghabra notes, "While the speaker of the parliament elected in 1985 rarely visited the emir, since the 1992 elections the same speaker has visited him con-stantly."[39] In addition, for the first time in Kuwaiti history an official joint committee comprising members of both the National Assembly and the Council of Ministers has been established to facilitate coordination between the two bodies.

The determination to find a modus vivendi comes from both sides. Both the opposition and the government feel chastened by the possibility that their bitter dispute over the reconvening of the National Assembly may have contributed in some way to bringing about the disaster of the Iraqi occupation. The ruling family must be comforted by the realization that even after the occupation Kuwaitis of all backgrounds feel an attachment to their Amir, and to the monarchy as symbols of Kuwaiti national identity. On the side of the opposition, there is the recognition that despite their numerical strength, they are internally divided, be-tween secularists and Islamists, Sunnis and Shiʿis, and indeed even between different trends within the Sunni Islamist movement. The opposition alliance currently united around such issues as ensuring accountability over the government's handling of the public purse, would be unlikely to survive disputes with the government over such issues as expanding the franchise for future elections. The government still holds the whip hand because of its control of patronage, and its ability to exploit primordial divisions within the opposition.

Nevertheless, it is difficult to quarrel with Shafiq Ghabra's conclu-sion that the parliament elected in 1992 has moved Kuwait forward

---

[38] See Ghabra, "Kuwait," p. 21.
[39] Ghabra, "Kuwait," p. 21.

towards a genuine parliamentary system.[40] It would seem that competing political currents in Kuwait are prepared to accept that all their demands cannot be met immediately, and that accommodation with rivals, and respect for the constitutionally established institutions of government, like the National Assembly and the office of the Amir, are in the best interests of the society. Albeit that this mutual acceptance may be based on a competition between the various political factions to be seen to be playing a conciliatory political role in the hope of gaining some political advantage over their rivals from government patronage. In this respect parliamentary politics in Kuwait have moved beyond the zero-sum game of the late eighties.

Changing attitudes within the government should not be discounted as a factor in this generally positive development. Many senior officials in government ministries are Kuwaitis who have been well-educated in western institutions and who firmly believe that a liberal democracy, of the type outlined in the Kuwaiti Constitution, is in the best interests of their country. Thus some opposition demands have their advocates within the government itself.

While there has been a resolution to the dispute over the reconvening of the National Assembly, conflict over the independence of private associations is still raging. This conflict has exposed continuing antagonism between the government and the parliament, and within the opposition coalition.

On August 6, 1993 the Council of Ministers announced that it had issued a decree immediately dissolving all unlicensed public organizations. The ban directly affects a number of organizations that emerged out of the popular committees of the occupation. Some of these organizations had lodged applications with the Ministry of Social Affairs for recognition under the Law of Associations and received no reply, but others, such as the Kuwaiti Association for Human Rights and the Pro-Democracy Committee had not because they wished to avoid the unwanted governmental influence which accompanies registration. The League of Families of Prisoners of War had not sought registration because it regards its purpose as temporary.

The issue which appears to have been most sensitive to the government was the involvement in these groups in international efforts to secure the release of approximately 600 Kuwaitis who are believed to remain in the hands of the Iraqi government having been detained during the occupation.

---

[40] Ghabra, "Kuwait," p. 21..

Early government attempts to draw public attention to the plight of these prisoners of war were widely viewed in Kuwait and abroad as incompetent. The government inflated the numbers of the missing, and published inaccurate information. Meanwhile, non-governmental organizations like the Kuwaiti Association to Defend War Victims, and the League of Families of POWs and the Missing undertook the painstaking task of gathering biographical data on the missing persons, and interviewing former prisoners in Iraq to gather information about places of detention, and the last date when individuals were seen alive. These efforts were effective in bringing pressure to bear on the government's official committee to improve its presentation of the POW issue, and in removing the international embarrassment caused by the Kuwaiti government's inept attempts to make political capital out of the suffering of the POWs and their families.

The non-governmental organizations also began to reach out to the international community, to find channels which may be able to assist in gathering news about the prisoners, and in exerting pressure on the Iraqi government. In their determination to explore all possible channels, the non-governmental groups laid themselves open to criticism from the government. On their humanitarian missions, leaders of these groups traveled to states considered among Kuwait's enemies because of their failure to condemn the Iraqi invasion. In the months prior to the closure announcement, members of these groups were subjected to fierce public criticism because of these contacts. The government claimed that such contacts were undermining Kuwaiti security.

While seeking to undermine the work of these independent groups which were embarrassing the government on a sensitive issue, the government was also seeking to coopt these groups by involving their leaders in the work of a National Committee for Prisoners and Missing Persons Affairs. The non-governmental organizations saw no contradiction in supplementing the government's efforts with their own independent endeavors. Nevertheless, the government did not give leaders from the non-governmental movement influential positions within the official committee, and sought to cloak the activities of the committee in secrecy. Frustrated by the government's attitude, two of the leaders of the non-governmental groups resigned from the official committee in November 1992. The non-governmental groups developed close cooperative links with the Committee of the Detained and Welfare for Martyr's Families established in the National Assembly.

The reactions of both the government and the National Assembly are instructive in seeking to understand the political process in Kuwait, and the limits of toleration for the concept of civil society. It is significant that the first major obstacle on the road towards participatory government along which Kuwait has been progressing steadily since the lifting of Martial Law in June 1991 should arise over an issue so closely associated with the war and the occupation. Four of the unlicensed associations directly affected by the closure order are the non-governmental organizations at the forefront of the popular campaign for the return of Kuwaitis believed to remain in detention in Iraq.[41] In many respects, Kuwait has made a remarkable recovery from the ravages of occupation. The physical damage to public buildings and institutions has been repaired, and the massive environmental damage caused by sabotage to the oil installations impinges little, for the time being at least, on the everyday life of most Kuwaitis. However, the issue of the missing and Prisoners of War remains an open wound which fire-fighters and engineers cannot staunch. More than any other, this issue keeps the memory of the occupation alive, and with it the question of government culpability for the invasion.

The government has not been slow to recognize the importance of the POW issue. For example, a visitor to Kuwait during 1992 would see yellow ribbons, and the slogan "Don't Forget Our POWs" adorning public buildings, and major international hotels. Airliners belonging to the national carrier, Kuwait Air, bore the same motif. This method of raising public awareness, initiated by non-governmental groups in 1991, was quickly adopted by the government as its own. Nevertheless, as long as the POW issue remains unresolved, the government remains vulnerable to the charge that it is not doing enough to bring the plight of the prisoners to an end. The energetic and high-profile activities of the non-governmental groups have constantly placed the government's more faltering efforts in an unfavorable light. Removing this nagging reminder of failed policy, both in terms of the occupation itself, and the POW problem, must be seen as a major motive for the government's decision to close the unlicensed associations.

A second factor lies in the nature of the associations engaged in this campaign. Unlike Kuwait's established professional, cultural and social organizations, the non-governmental groups concerned with the POW issue cut across ideological, class and religious divisions within Kuwaiti

---

[41] They are: The League of the Families of the Prisoners of War and the Missing; the Mutual Assistance Fund for the Families of the Martyrs and POWs; the Kuwaiti Association to Defend War Victims; and the Popular Committee for Solidarity with POWs.

society. Among the missing are people from all backgrounds, Sunni and Shi'i, rich and poor, citizen and *Bidun*.[42] Consequently, the non-governmental organizations are able to mobilize support from all sectors of Kuwaiti society. Their unregistered status has left them independent of government subsidy, and therefore outside one of the mechanisms of control by which Kuwaiti governments have normally contained associational activities. It is these groups which also represent the direct legacy of the nascent popular government of the Kuwaiti resistance to Iraqi occupation.

Many Kuwaitis who played leading roles in organizing the resistance did not cease their activities on the point of the Iraqi withdrawal at the end of February 1991. They continued their work of meeting the needs of the hundreds of thousands of residents and former residents of Kuwait whose lives were disrupted by the war. Having been obliged to organize and operate without government approval or support during the occupation, they were not deterred by the lack of it. In those Kuwaitis who remained in Kuwait during the occupation the revelation dawned that they could organize and achieve without having to rely on the cradle to grave cossetting the Kuwaiti government had provided to its citizens. Some, at least, were mentally liberated from the gilded cage created by the government's conditional distributive largesse. This determination to act regardless of government approbation is subversive of the Kuwaiti system which has traditionally fostered dependency on the government among competing interest groups.

The manner in which the government has responded to this perceived threat is, on the other hand, firmly within the government's divide and rule tradition. The government has sought to exploit differences between Islamists and secularists, and divisions within the Islamist movement, to split support within the National Assembly for the non-governmental organizations. The current Minister of Social Affairs, Jassem Muhammad al-'Aoun, is a leader of the conservative Islamic Heritage Society. The Heritage Society did not form a popular committee of its own to address the POW issue and so lost ground to other Islamist groups which did. Prior to the closure of the organizations, some secular members of the National Assembly, notable among them Ahmed al-Khatib,[43] had called

---

[42] *Bidun* is an Arabic word meaning "without". It refers to tens of thousands of current and former residents of Kuwait who for various reasons have been unable to establish a claim to Kuwaiti citizenship, but who nevertheless acknowledge no national origin other than Kuwait. The fate of this large group of stateless persons is one of the more intractable issues facing the Kuwaiti government.

[43] See, "Kuwait Closes All Human Rights Organizations," *Middle East Watch Newsletter*, Volume 5, Issue 6, p. 8.

attention to the fund-raising activities of unlicensed and unregulated Islamist organizations, such as the *zakat* committees. The sources and the uses to which these funds are put are unknown, although it is supposed that some of it is spent on enhancing the political support for Islamist candidates in elections within associations, and to the National Assembly. The government also came under foreign pressure to control the activities of Islamist funding organizations in Kuwait who are believed to be supporting the work of Islamist groups engaged in violent struggles against the government of Egypt and other states.

Minister al-'Aoun justified the closure order directed at the unregistered associations by referring to the criticism of the *Zakat* committees from secular members of the Assembly:

> In our judgment, charities and volunteer organizations should be treated the same way. Why should charities be closed and not the other private organizations which they would like to see continue despite their illegality because they agree with their objectives and leanings.[44]

Thus has the government sought to characterize support for the threatened organizations as partisan or politically motivated.

While the conflict remains unresolved, it can already be observed that the government's tactics have enjoyed some limited success. The government was able to resist a proposal submitted by a number of members of the National Assembly calling for a general debate on the closure order. In response to the failure of this proposal, the parliamentary Committee for the Missing and Imprisoned and for the Welfare of Martyrs' Families announced its resignation.[45] The Committee is led by the prominent Islamist government critic, Mubarak al-Duwaylah.

Perhaps emboldened by its success in blocking calls for a parliamentary debate, the government reverted to a more authoritarian tone in asserting its prerogatives. For example, Shaykh Sabah al-Ahmad, First Deputy Prime Minister and Foreign Minister, stated:

> In reply to what the Committee of the Detained and Welfare for Martyrs' Families of the National Assembly, particularly those working in the prisoners' sphere, raised about the government not consulting it before issuing the

---

[44] Cited in Middle East Watch, "Kuwait Closes ...", p. 8. It is worth mentioning that other organizations caught up in the closure order are a human rights organization, and the Pro-Democracy Committee whose objectives are shared primarily by Kuwaitis of liberal and leftist inclinations. Minister al-'Aoun's jibe is hardly applicable to the POW's issue, which, as mentioned above, enjoys broad support in all sections of Kuwaiti society.

[45] "Committee for Missing, Imprisoned Kuwaitis Resigns," Kuwaiti News Agency, Aug. 17, 1993, as reported in *Foreign Broadcasts Information Service, Near East and South Asia* (*FBIS-NES*), Aug. 17, 1993, p. 13.

decision to suspend the unlicensed associations, Shaykh Sabah said that *the government "is an executive quarter, and there is nothing to force it to consult on such affairs*," pointing out that the government was implementing the law.[46]

Minister al-'Aoun had earlier called for meetings of unlicensed organizations to be physically broken up by the security forces, although force has not yet been used to enforce the ban.[47]

In this dispute, there are ominous signs of the government and the opposition squaring off for a conflict which may only be overcome by the government resorting to force in imposing the ban, and putting down any parliamentary-based opposition to the order which may emerge. There are however, at least two factors which will lessen the government's desire to press for a show-down. Firstly, the government is vulnerable on the issue of the POWs. Closing organizations perceived as effective on this emotive issue may be simply too damaging. Secondly, the bellicose rhetoric of Shaykh Sabah and Minister al-'Aoun notwithstanding, the government may be too chastened by the experiences of the war and the occupation to risk souring relations with the National Assembly over this issue.

Conclusion

Kuwait offers a rich case study of an Arab society in which citizens have striven over decades to keep the state "within substantive and procedural confinement."[48] To do so, Kuwaitis have sought to create the institutions of a civil society including: a representative parliamentary democracy; a free press; an independent judiciary; and organizations representative of various interest groups independent of government control. In none of these areas have Kuwaitis succeeded in freeing themselves completely of the intrusive attentions of a state bolstered by its control of immense oil-revenues, and the attendant powers of patronage. Nevertheless, the legitimacy of the government was severely shaken by the disaster of the Iraqi occupation, and in the post-war period Kuwaiti civil society has emerged stronger to renew its challenges to government prerogative. It has enjoyed victories over the traditionally narrow-based government dominated by the al-Sabah family, most notably in the October 1992 elections.

---

[46] "Decision to Dissolve Associations 'Irrevocable'," *KUNA*, Aug. 18, 1993, as reported in *FBIS-NES*, Aug. 19, 1993, p. 19, (emphasis added).

[47] Middle East Watch, "Kuwait Closes ...", p. 3.

[48] Shils, "The Virtue of Civil Society."

"Kuwaiti Democracy" by ʿAbd al-Wahhab al-ʿAwdi, *Karikatir*, p. 119, with permission.

The ruling family has rarely wielded absolute authority within Kuwait. The shifting web of alliances that it has struck over the years to secure its grip on power has required that in putting down a challenge from one quarter it has needed to accommodate demands from another. The consultative systems and institutions it has fostered to regulate these competing interests, including the National Assembly, and the various cultural and professional associations have served as focal points for opposition to the government, even as they enabled the government to accommodate and harness factions and groups to its own interest.

Periodically, the consultative systems have broken down and the government has resorted to repression at the expense of the institutions of civil society. However, at these times free association and expression have continued through the *diwaniyyat*, traditional home-based open meetings, within mosques and at other religious or cultural gatherings. The mosque increased in importance as political Islam emerged as a regional force in the late seventies, with a particular impetus being given to the movement by the 1979 revolution in Iran. The traditional *diwaniyyah* became an explicit vehicle of political protest during the campaign for the restoration of the National Assembly in 1989 and 1990. The utility of this traditional gathering in a contemporary political setting was demonstrated by the government's inability to enforce law's inhibiting freedom of association to prevent weekly political protest meetings involving thousands of participants.

During the Iraqi occupation, the strength of Kuwaiti civil society in the form of the Cooperative Societies in particular was demonstrated as non-governmental groups moved into the vacuum left by the collapse of the Kuwaiti government. The ability of non-governmental groups to organize without complete reliance on government subsidy and approbation brought about a shift in the perceptions of some Kuwaitis who remained in Kuwait throughout the occupation. They developed experience in self-help and independent initiatives which they were unwilling to give up with the re-instatement of the al-Sabah family. The challenge to the status-quo represented by the inclination of these groups to act outside the government-orchestrated process of give and take which had characterized associational life in Kuwait until this time led to a conflict which is yet to be resolved as the government moved to dissolve unregistered associations.

The targeted groups were greatly strengthened by the government's vulnerability on an issue which they had made their central concern, the plight of Kuwaiti POWs still believed to be held in Iraqi custody more than two years after the end of the war.

Having been unable to impose their absolute power in the early years of oil production the Kuwaiti ruling family has constantly faced the need to make accommodations which have further eroded their powers and prerogatives. The consultative imperative which has been more pressing on the Kuwaiti ruling family than on their counterparts in the other Gulf monarchies has been augmented by the changing attitudes of a Kuwaiti population that is increasingly better educated and more aware of shifts towards democratization elsewhere in the world.

This argues for further progress toward participatory government in Kuwait. The strongest argument for this optimistic conclusion emerges out of the Iraqi occupation itself. The experience of the occupation demonstrated conclusively that there was more to the concept of Kuwaiti nationhood than an attachment to the ruling family's munificent distribution of oil revenues. Kuwaitis found that they could organize their lives for themselves without government oversight, and without most of the hundreds of thousands of migrant workers and domestic servants who had contributed to a life of ease for most Kuwaitis. The fact that semi-autonomous institutions and organizations had taken root in Kuwait prior to the invasion provided Kuwaitis with the tools for self-organization. The Cooperative Societies, Kuwait's largest participatory organization in particular proved their worth under occupation.

The experience of the occupation has also contributed significantly to an inclination on both the government and opposition sides to avoid breakdowns in the system of rule which marred the pre-occupation period. This professed commitment to constitutional principles will be sorely tested by internal and external challenges which Kuwait must face in the years ahead.

Internally, the most divisive of these is likely to be the rationalization of Kuwait's dysfunctional citizenship laws which will have a direct bearing on the composition of the electorate in future elections for the National Assembly. Broadening the franchise will empower the parliament and ultimately shift the balance of power against the ruling family as the influence of the ruling family's personal access to the electorate diminishes because of a rapid increase in the number of voters and their weak association to traditional power elites. Should the ruling family seek to retain its traditional powers in the face of a growing movement for political representation, then the consequences for civil rights and public organizations would be negative. Others who have prospered and benefited from the current electoral arrangements will also be resistant to change.

Externally, Kuwait faces even stiffer challenges. While Kuwait has moved forward with the institutionalization of greater political participation its neighbors in the Gulf monarchies, and in Saudi Arabia in particular, have remained resistant to such trends. Both Saudi and United States leaders will quickly loose patience with Kuwaiti reforms if they are seen as contributing to instability in Saudi Arabia. On the other hand, Gulf leaders as they contemplate how to remain in power in a turbulent international environment may ponder the Kuwaiti experience of controlled constitutional monarchy and see within it benefits that have accrued to the al-Sabah family in sustaining its throne even through occupation.

The development of the institutions of civil society in Kuwait, as in any country, is inevitably a work in progress. However, we can conclude that Kuwait has benefited from its quasi-autonomous associations, and its controlled participatory political institutions. Attempts by the government to stifle the urge for participation in government have not succeeded for sustained periods of time, and have often resulted in conflict. The government's toleration and even encouragement of representative associations, and the strength of traditional participatory formations such as the *diwaniyyat*, has provided Kuwaitis with remarkably stable government through decades of enormous economic and social change.

ʿAbd al-Wahhab al-ʿAwdi depicts a Kuwaiti voter, left arm encumbered by an array of state provided benefits, while he attempts to vote with the other arm. Taken from ʿAbd al-Wahhab al-ʿAwdi, *Karikatir*, p. 170, with permission.

CHAPTER SEVEN

STATE, CIVIL SOCIETY, AND POLITICAL CHANGE IN SYRIA

Raymond A. Hinnebusch

The widespread collapse of authoritarianism has given new credibility to claims that "modernization" broadens the base of pluralism. According to modernization theory, in eroding primordial isolation and generating a multitude of interests, it creates a mobilized complex society which, beyond a certain threshold, arguably cannot be governed without political liberalization. Eastern Europe has apparently passed the pluralist threshold, while in Latin America and East Asia authoritarian regimes have retreated before more complex societies. The Middle East is not immune and from Jordan to Egypt regimes find the effective governing of a more mobilized citizenry takes pluralist concessions such as multiple parties and a freer press; the aftermath of the Algerian army's nullification of the Islamic electoral victory suggests the alternative is massive repression and instability.

In Syria, however, despite increasing socio-economic modernization, authoritarian rule has appeared remarkably durable. Today, Syria is undergoing a limited liberalization: the private sector is being encouraged, the President is broadening his base beyond the party, government controls over society are being incrementally relaxed. But is the result likely to be political pluralisation or is Syria a true case of "Middle East exceptionalism?"

The links posited by modernization theory between socio-economic development and political liberalization are, in fact, highly problematic and several key intervening variables are likely to either raise the pluralist threshold or possibly shape outcomes closer to authoritarianism or corporatism than the Western pluralist model.

A key intervening variable is the existence of "civil society," a network of voluntary "secondary" associations. To the extent civil society has sufficient autonomy of both state and primordial community to bridge societal cleavages while buffering society from, yet linking it to state power, it can be crucial to advancing stable pluralization. In developing states, "traditional" associations, such as guilds, religious brotherhoods and mosques which arise directly out of pre-modern quarters, villages and families are a legitimate aspect of civil society coexisting with those organizations, such as parties, professional syndicates, unions and business associations generated by modernization and class formation.

Civil society supports an autonomous political milieu in which habits of political association and a political culture hospitable to democratization can develop. If this space is connected with the state, not a counterculture segregated from it, it can integrate elites and mass into this culture. In states without a tradition of a strong autonomous civil society integrated with the state (the Middle East?), modernization need not produce political pluralization but could actually reinforce authoritarian rule with new technologies of control or, conversely, by mobilizing a (Islamic?) counterculture, create the conditions of instability or revolution.

While the addition of civil society to the equation is an advance on simple modernization theory, it leaves crucial issues unanswered which can only be adequately addressed by adding two other variables, namely class and state. These issues include the following.

1) What conditions determine the development of civil society? In fact, it should not be seen as a nearly inevitable outcome of social mobilization (education, a widened middle class) but as advanced or retarded by the inherited social structure; in particular, it is most likely to emerge where a proper balance between dominant classes and state power maximizes political space for it. 2) Is the relation of civil society to democratization, as often is assumed, uniformly positive? Democratization means two changes: limits on and accountability of state power and inclusive participation. Civil society among the dominant classes could effectively limit state power; yet to the very extent these classes are strong, they may retard the development of civil society and political incorporation among the non-dominant classes. Democratization would seem to require not only a strong but also an inclusive civil society. 3) In states where civil society is just developing and unable, by itself, to force a pluralist transformation, what other variables are likely to determine whether pluralization advances? The interests and calculations of state elites are likely to be decisive and this will be most strongly shaped by the relation of the state to the dominant classes.

This essay will therefore explore the relation between social change and political pluralization in Syria through an analysis of the impact of three intervening variables, class, state and civil society.

Syria's Historic Imbalance of State and Class

Historic imbalances obstructed a stable integration of state and civil society in Syria from at least the Ottoman period. The Ottoman state was a military-fiscal apparatus imposed by conquest on a primordially fragmented society composed of kin groups with patriarchal structures compatible with patrimonial rule. There was a thin layer of civil society between them: *awqaf*, sufi orders and guilds organized the urban quarters while in limited rural areas like the Kalamoun mountains and the Damascus Ghouta village associations managed waterworks. Syria had a thriving pluralism of cities and sects, far less amenable to state control than Egypt's hydraulic society. Periodic local revolts and the clientalist connections of communal and tribal leaders to the state deflected arbitrary power. But this discontinuous civil society bridged neither the gaps of a mosaic society or the state-society gulf. Most important, (until the Young Turk revolution) civil society never won power-sharing with the Sultan and his bureaucracy in a parliament.

Imperial rule discouraged the emergence of an independent merchant bourgeoisie which might have united the cities to demand such representation. Local *'ayan* waxed temporarily powerful as a parasitic tax-farming strata between the imperial treasury and the peasants as the state weakened; however, in obstructing the emergence of private property in land until the nineteenth century, the state discouraged the consolidation of a landed aristocracy, an advance beyond tribal fragmentation crucial to state-society linkage.[1] In the absence of powerful independent corporate groups—estates of aristocratic classes and free cities, a separate church—state power was chiefly blunted by the practical limits of pre-modern technology. In the 19th century a private property owning landed class was emerging from Syria's urban notability. But before this agrarian bourgeoisie could consolidate a democratic revolution against the autocracy (incipient in the Young Turk movement with which it was initially associated) the Ottoman empire gave way to an imposed semi-liberal regime under the French.

This state lacked indigenous traditions and it failed to consolidate strong linkages to civil society which did not, itself, uniformly advance in the post-Ottoman environment. The French introduced representative institutions and the nationalist struggle generated indigenous leaders and rudimentary parties with associational links to the urban quarters.

---

[1] Perry Anderson, *Lineages of the Absolutist State* (London: Verso, 1974), p. 372.

Even as new forms of association were developing, however, older ones were being decimated; for example, capitalist penetration destroyed the guilds of Aleppo artisans headed by *shaykhs* who settled disputes and enforced standards[2] A landowning upper class was finally consolidated under the French, giving a social base to the state. This class, however, developing largely through encroachment on peasant small holdings, never attained the legitimacy in the village to give the state stable rural roots. The independence struggle could have been a diluted surrogate for a democratic revolution, but its notable leadership eschewed mass mobilization for fear of its spilling over into social conflict. The high concentration of landed property and commercial wealth in the hands of the notables allowed them to turn the state into their creature after independence; as such they had no incentive to risk a political mobilization of the masses which would only have accelerated demands for agrarian reform. The oligarchy's political parties were fragile parliamentary blocs uninterested in incorporating other classes. Illiteracy and ignorance crippled the masses' "capacity of...political combination".[3]

This narrow-based regime could not survive the accumulating consequences of social change cresting in the late 1950s. Capitalist penetration and social mobilization eroded the self-sufficiency and solidarity of segmental groups as communal land tenures gave way to individual ownership, endogamous marriage declined among educated youth, and modern communications broke down geographic isolation. The patriarchal authority and clientelism on which the traditional elites depended was eroding. Modernization also generated new classes and occupation groups. A small agro-industrial bourgeoisie emerged and generated a working class which formed trade unions, crucial vehicles for drawing the lower strata into secondary association. Expansion of education, the bureaucracy and the army generated a salaried "new middle class"; the new associations and institutions into which it was recruited fostered loyalties to profession, class and nation which competed with those to family, sect, or quarter.[4]

Modernization also stimulated "traditional" civil society. The revival of agriculture was accompanied by new associations, such as the first

---

[2] Jocelyne Cornand, "L'Artisanat du Textile a Alep survie au Dynamisme?" *Bulletin d'Etudes Orientales Institut Français de Damas* Tome XXXVI (1984), pp. 104-105.

[3] Albert Hourani, *Syria and Lebanon* (London: Oxford University Press,1946), p. 91.

[4] Philip Khoury, "Syrian Urban Politics in Transition: The Quarters of Damascus During the French Mandate," *International Journal of Middle East Studies* 16, no. 4 (1984) p. 527.

Syrian cooperative founded in Dair Atiah and merchant-village partner-ships to introduce irrigation pumps in Dair al-Zur. The spread of education, far from uniformly displacing traditional values, spawned new "traditional" associations, such as the religious brotherhood that educated Salamiya youth formed to defend the Isma'ili faith.[5]

This social differentiation resulted in political pluralization as par-ties, press, and interest groups proliferated in the fifties. Ideological parties, such as the Ba'th and the communists, forged political associa-tion beyond personal and parochial loyalties and pushed political activ-ism out from the divans of the notables, and the army barracks to the streets, campuses, even the villages. Thus, a democratic political culture was beginning.

But this broadening of civil society generated class conflict which aborted the consolidation of the liberal state. The middle class was not effectively incorporated into the system. Having only modest property it was, to a great extent, a bureaucratic class dependent on state employ-ment and its shallow commitment to liberalism evaporated when eco-nomic expansion stagnated in the late fifties, ostensibly signalling the failure of Syria's dependent capitalism. Capitalist agriculture unleashed landlord-peasant conflict, while unions challenged employers. It fell to the middle class to initiate the mobilization of peasants and workers into politics but, given the oligarchic domination of society, it could make no democratic breakthrough and turned to the nationalist-socialist move-ments like the Ba'th which were prepared to overthrow the regime. In the late fifties, nationalist crisis resulting from the conflict with Israel and economic stagnation gave credibility to claims that a powerful state able to mobilize the country for development and defense took precedence over democracy. Lacking the rural roots to counterbalance urban radi-calism and strong institutions to absorb middle class activism, the ancien regime could not withstand the military-Ba'thist alliance which toppled it in 1963.

In essence the post-independence regime collapsed because the Ottoman equation had been reversed; an overly dominant state had been replaced by an overly fragile one. Its heritage was ambivalent: civil society had acquired room to develop, particularly among the new middle class, under the liberal state, but the regime's lack of autonomy of the dominant classes obstructed the democratic inclusion of the

---

[5] Norman Lewis,(1952) "The Isma'ilis of Syria Today," *Journal of the Royal Central Asia Society* 39 (January 1952): 69-77.

middle and lower classes. Such regimes are vulnerable to the rise of populist movements which adopt authoritarian vehicles to reach power.

The Ba'th State

The Ba'th created an authoritarian-populist state which has proved highly durable and resistant to political liberalization and societal autonomy. It began with a revolution destructive of bourgeois civil society and intolerant of autonomous association. The Ba'th leadership, dominated by rural minorities, set out to break the power of the urban Sunni establishment. Opposition parties and professional associations— political vehicles of upper and middle class rivals — were repressed or controlled. The mobilization of new pro-regime participants by the Ba'th party apparatus gave the regime roots among those social forces which had been least incorporated into the liberal regime or had paid the costs of capitalist development — rural intellectuals and army officers, workers, peasants, and deprived minorities, notably the 'Alawis.

At the same time, nationalizations destroyed the economic bases of the bourgeoisie, large numbers of whom emigrated. Land reform destroyed the political power of the landed notability and transformed a large part of the landless proletariat into a small holding peasantry dependent on the state. Education and state employment broadened the state-employed middle class. The result was a regime with a social base dominated by elements who, initially possessed of little property and making their careers and fortune through the state, had a stake in statist policies such as a large public sector and subsidized agriculture; conversely, the bourgeoisie, the social force most likely to benefit from liberalization, became a historic rival of the regime.

This fluidization of the class structure, fostering social mobility and broadening social forces dependant on or beholden to the state, created a favorable social terrain on which Hafiz al-Asad constructed an autonomous "Bonapartist" state "above" classes. This regime, in its combination of bureaucratic structures and patrimonial cement is particularly resistant to liberalization. Asad used a combination of kin and sectarian solidarity, Leninist party loyalty, and bureaucratic command to concentrate power in a Presidential-Monarchy while a praetorian guard commanded by 'Alawi clansmen shielded him from challenges. The Ba'th's ideological politicization of the army, and the disproportionate recruitment on political grounds of 'Alawis into senior commands retards the professionalization which might get the army out of politics; the huge military machine absorbs resources from civil society and has extended its tentacles into the economy. The Ba'th party apparatus, with a long history as an authentic ideological movement, a complex organization, and some 500,000 members, is well institutionalized along Leninist lines. It incorporates a statist/populist constituency, overwhelmingly teachers, students, state employees, peasants and workers. With a membership of about 60% lower class composition and only 2% from upper strata,[6] it seems far less vulnerable than Egypt's ASU to transformation into a NDP-like party of the bourgeoisie. The party cannot readily be shunted aside since it remains the regime's main connection to the provinces and villages and crucial to its ability to sustain some support in the Sunni lower and middle classes.

Control of the public sector and of oil rent has given the regime features of a "patronage state" in which societal sectors compete for largesse through clientalism partly organized on sectarian lines. This enabled the state to play off a society fragmented by class, regional and ethnic-sectarian cleavages. The regime sought legitimacy through the struggle with Israel, in which it portrayed Syria as the vanguard of Arab nationalism, the most widely accepted political identity.

This state sharply reduced societal autonomy, destroyed some social forces, created and coopted others. It victimized the most developed parts of "civil society," the traditional suq and the bourgeoisie. In deploying 'Alawi 'asabiyyah in its primitive power accumulation, it stimulated primordial identities and delegitimized itself in the eyes of many Sunnis. Overlapping communal and class cleavages sharply bifurcated regime and opposition, admitting of little compromise or civility between them; opposition took violent forms while the regime was unrestrained by law in its repression. In substituting 'asabiyyah for the investment of political capital in legitimate institutions, Asad set back the potential to liberalize the regime from within.

The Ba'th state was linked more densely to a social base than its liberal predecessor, but the array of corporatist associations through which societal sectors had to articulate their interests under party tutelage lacked autonomy. Ba'thists created and led "popular organizations" (munazzamat sha'biyah) which incorporated peasants, youth, and women and they dominated the leadership of the trade unions. The professional associations (niqabat mihaniyah) of doctors, lawyers, and

---

[6] Hizb al-ba'th al-'arabi al-ishtiraki, *Taqarir al-mu'tamar al-qutri al-thamin wa muqarraratihi* [Reports and Resolutions of the Eighth Regional Congress] (Damascus, 1985), pp. 35-58.

engineers in which the Ba'th was lightly represented retained a certain independence until the Islamic rebellion (1978-82), during which their leaders were replaced by state appointees. The teachers' and agronomists' unions were Ba'th-dominated. Even associations which escaped Ba'th control were, by law, approved and regulated by the Ministry of Labor and Social Affairs.

But the state-society relation was no wholly zero-sum conflict in which the gains of the state meant across the board losses by civil society. Ba'th corporatism had a special "populist" character. While most corporatist regimes play off competing social forces or favor privileged groups such as businessmen's associations, the Ba'th, seeking to mobilize a popular base against the old classes it overthrew, organized previously excluded popular sectors and accorded them privileged access to power denied its bourgeois rivals. Ba'th corporatism was, at least initially, a strategy of inclusion rather than exclusion or demobilization, which worked to the benefit of both the state and its constituency. Groups which hitherto lacked organization acquired new, if still limited, social weight. Thus, the Women's Union mobilized some real activism on behalf of equal employment opportunities and child care, although many women activists thought it too timid to push aggressively for equality in crucial matters of personal status.[7]

The Peasant Union exemplifies populist corporatism. Previous regimes discouraged peasant organization, but the Ba'th, facing intense urban opposition, recruited leaders from the small peasantry and backed their creation of union branches in the villages; by the nineties, much of Syria's peasantry was organized. The union's autonomy is limited. There is no record of dissident challenges to its Ba'thist leadership; constructed from the top down rather than through struggle from below, it lacks the popular muscle to challenge the state. But neither is the union a mere paper organization lacking presence in the corridors of power or the village.

Its relation with the state is based on certain shared interests. The union articulates peasant interests within the limits defined by party strategy: thus it refrains from pressing for further land reform since the state wishes to encourage investment by the agrarian bourgeoisie and it has deferred to the state's interest in the compulsory marketing of "strategic crops." In return, the union enjoys institutionalized channels

---

[7] Bouthaina Shaaban, *Both Right and Left Handed: Arab Women Talk About their Lives* (Bloomington: Indiana University Press, 1988), pp. 28-79.

of access: its leaders sit in party and state committees which make decisions affecting peasants. The union is a player in bureaucratic politics, pushing with some success for higher prices for state-marketed crops in conflict with agencies representing urban (Ministry of Supply) or industrial (Ministry of Industry) consumers of agricultural goods. The union played a role in energizing the land reform process and promoting a system of cooperatives which, as channels of credit, services and inputs, relieved peasants of dependency on landlords and merchants and protected them from renewed land concentration. It has organized small peasants to counter the power of larger proprietors, investors, and middlemen. Thus, union pressure helped implement favorable legislation, such as the agrarian relations law protecting tenants, which might otherwise have remained paper decrees; today it is seen as a major obstacle by investors seeking a more favorable law. The union's access to decision-makers in the long absence of comparable access for landlords and merchants enhanced the weight of peasant against moneyed interests which would, in the normal course of things, have been more potent. [8]

The peasant union and the cooperative system have given the regime a rural base analogous to the large landowners who typically support conservative authoritarianism; the regime has every interest in preserving it since it obstructs the potential for rival political forces to forge rural alliances against the Ba'th. The system also is an obstacle to the large scale commercial agricultural which is an early stage of capitalist development and a potential source of capital accumulation now denied the bourgeoisie. In these respects, the system deters economic and political liberalization. On the other hand, although the union facilitates state control of peasants, it also fosters peasant association which, if regime controls were relaxed, could acquire greater autonomy. The peasant sector is not a wholly state-controlled monolith and retains considerable autonomy because alternatives to the state exist. Although participation in cooperatives giving access to credit and inputs imposes constraints such as state marketing of strategic crops, peasants can opt out and many crops remain in the free market. Peasants pursue investment and accumulation strategies through private kin associations. Families diversify resources: one brother works on the land, a second in

[8] Raymond Hinnebusch, *Authoritarian Power and State Formation in Ba'thist Syria: Army, Party and Peasant* (Boulder, CO: Westview Press, 1990), pp. 197-219.

a petty business and the third a government or party job. Peasants utilize both state and private networks as it suits their interests.[9]

More generally, although the regime at times aspired to "totalitarian"-like control, it never "atomized" civil society, where family, religious and neighbourhood solidarities retain their integrity. Syria is a close-knit society where networks of talk and rumor, informal groups, and personal connections penetrate the state, cut across political cleavages, and often soften the harshness of the regime. While Syria's Ba'thist structures resemble Iraq's, the regime never deployed the systematic terror to pulverize society in a way comparable to Iraq.

Civil Society Under the Ba'th

a) Evasion and Resistance

Major parts of Syrian civil society, the "haves" and the "traditionals," were threatened by Ba'thist redistribution and modernization. Given the limits on the regime's ability to penetrate society, one viable counterstrategy was evasion. As early as 1971 Asad, to win the support of the bourgeoisie in the wake of his overthrow of the radical Jedid regime, started to create the conditions for this strategy. Trade was partially liberalized, a role for the private sector legitimized, and the previous effort to totally control the economy, abandoned. Opportunities for enrichment grew and many Syrians acquired independence of the state through work in the Gulf, Africa or elsewhere and from their ability to smuggle surplus capital out of Syria for investment abroad. In the large informal and black market sectors of the economy state control was blunted by the corruption of officials.

Variations in the regime's ability to control society produced, alongside the more state-penetrated associations such as the peasant union and chambers of commerce, a more autonomous "alternative" civil society. The vitality of small enterprises illustrates how they can grow in the space left by gaps in state control. In certain rural areas, such as Yabroud, independent family-owned light industries developed from a preexisting artisanal tradition. A tradition of emigration fosters the import of technology and the accumulation of capital, closeness to Lebanon permits smuggling to overcome raw material constraints, and product

---

[9] Françoise Metral, "State and Peasants in Syria: A Local View of a Government Irrigation Project," *Peasant Studies* 11, no. 2 (1984).

lines are chosen from those outside of state price controls. Such autonomy is not without limits: the habit of hiding assets from potential nationalization, and the fear of competition from state industries deters the natural expansion of these industries into larger fully legitimate firms.[10]

Table 1. Syrian Labor Force in Trade and Restaurants

	Labor Force in Trade	Total Labor Force	% Labor Force in Trade
1970	139,002	1,524,552	9.1%
1984	253,174	2,246,273	11.3%
1989	338,061	2,882,619	11.7%

Source: Syrian Arab Republic, *Statistical Abstract* 1976, pp. 151-52, 1986, pp. 106-07, 1991, pp. 76-77

Another case is that of small textile manufacturers and artisans in Aleppo. Those who join the officially-approved Syndicate of Artisans or the Chamber of Industries are entitled to buy inputs from state factories or import agencies, to participate in a social security fund, and obtain export licenses from the Ministry of Economy. Alternatively, they may participate in the "parallel" free market controlled by large merchants; artisans are dependent on these merchants for marketing and may pay higher prices for their inputs but they presumably prefer personal relations with a patron to dependence on state officials. In cases of conflict, they rely on traditional arbiters in preference to the state's Labor Tribunals.[11] Despite the pervasiveness of government control, there is an alternative network wherein participants forego certain benefits for greater freedom.

The artisanal and merchant petite bourgeoisie, far from declining under the Ba'th, actually multiplied in the vacuum left by the demise of the *haute bourgeoisie*: it doubled in size during the socialist decade of the sixties—from 110,900 to 216,090 according to one calculation.[12] The number of merchants grew substantially in the more liberal decades from 1971 to 1991. As Table 1 shows, the labor force in trade grew about 7% per year and, despite the austerity of the eighties, had by 1989 increased its proportion of the labor force from 9% to almost 12%. In some respects, the petite bourgeoisie flourished in spite of the regime, but that it sometimes developed in symbiotic relations with public sector suppli-

[10] Anton Escher, "Private Business and Trade in the Region of Yabroud, Syria," unpublished paper presented at the Middle East Studies Association Conference, 1990.

[11] Cornand, "L'Artisant …"

[12] Elizabeth Longuenesse, "The Class Nature of the State in Syria," *MERIP Reports* 9, no. 4 (1979), pp. 4-5.

ers and buyers, suggests it has manipulated the regime to its benefit.[13]

Although these developments suggest the potential for a *modus vivendi* between state and *suq*, the latter produced a second reaction to the Ba'thist state, namely the overt resistance of Syria's Islamic movement. Political Islam was concentrated where religious institutions and the trading economy come together, the traditional urban quarters and markets. It spoke for the more pious segments of society, notably the *'ulama* who resented the secular and minority dominated Ba'th regime. Since they were not organized in a state controlled hierarchy comparable to al-Azhar, the *'ulama* retained considerable autonomy of and capacity to resist the regime. Political Islam also expressed the lingering urban resentment of radical Ba'th policies. Land reform and the substitution of state agrarian credit and marketing networks for the old landlord-merchant ones had deprived merchants and landlords of influence and wealth in the villages. Nationalization of industries, which in a few cases touched artisan workshops, was seen as an attack on business and property as a whole. The partial takeover of foreign and wholesale trade deprived big merchants of opportunities while itinerant peddlers who serviced the villages, were threatened by government retail networks. Government price fixing and market regulation alienated merchants of all sizes. The regime's attempt to win over small retail merchants and artisans failed because state trading bodies could not effectively substitute for the big merchant bourgeoisie. Asad's 1971 partial liberalization of trade reopened opportunities for merchants but they still had to deal with inefficient, corrupt, or unsympathetic government officials.

Political Islam's "counter-ideology" expressed the anti-statist worldview of the *suq*. Along with *'Alawi* and military rule, it rejected state domination of the economy. Islamic manifestos demanded the bloated bureaucracy be cut, state withdrawal from commerce, and an Islamic economy which would legitimate free enterprise and the "natural incentives" of a fair profit. Islam, interpreted to exclude socialism, was a natural vehicle of protest against a rural-based regime's assault on urban interests.

This Islamic political association rose out of traditional civil society. Anti-regime sermons in the mosques stimulated rebellion and the *shari'ah* schools were *Ikhwan* recruitment pools. The *suq* was a consistent centre of anti-socialist merchant strikes. Professional associations frequently mobilized in alliance with the *suq*. Indicative of how the "moderniza-

---

[13] Syrian Arab Republic (SAR), *Statistical Abstract*, Central Bureau of Statistics (Damascus, 1976, 1991).

tion" of this milieu had in some respects empowered rather than diluted it is the fact that many of the participants in the 1980s rebellion were educated children of the traditional middle class able to deploy the modern association needed to confront the regime. The Islamic movement developed a complex organization with offices, chains of command, representative bodies and military branches. The scale and durability of the Islamic rebellion of the early eighties is indicative of this substantial advance in organizational capabilities.

In its mortal conflict with political Islam, the state ratcheted up its control over society, coming briefly as close as it ever has to "totalitarianism." A purge of mosques, religious associations and professional syndicates eliminated these as bases of opposition. The regime resorted to repression, fear and informing to control opposition; the sack of Hamah is a reminder to all of how far it will go to preserve itself. The surviving modicum of press freedom and party pluralism was deadened.

Political Islam lost the battle but it remains deeply rooted in the *suq* and in the pervasive religious sensibility nurtured by the *'ulama*. With a partially autonomous economic base and a counter-ideology, the traditional city remains the milieu most resistant to state penetration, an alternative society with many aspects of civility. But can the *suq* be integrated into the political system in a way that would advance pluralization as long as political Islam remains its dominant political expression? Political Islam is an obstacle to democratization insofar as it fosters communal conflict in a mosaic society and a counterculture not readily incorporated into the secular state, hindering the historic compromise with the regime needed for liberalization.

On the other hand, the Islamic movement is not necessarily anti-democratic: in the pre-Ba'th era, the Syrian *Ikhwan* participated in electoral politics rather than creating secret organizations as in Egypt. In an attempt to broaden its appeal in the eighties, the movement advocated a semi-liberal state. The notion of violent revolution has now been discredited in most Islamic circles. There are signs of a detente between regime and the Islamicists. The government is now attempting to coopt it. It has won the cooperation of such moderate Islamic leaders as Muhammed Said Rahman al-Buti, professor of *shari'ah*, and the Mufti Ahmad al-Kaftaro, who have some followings in Sufi brotherhoods and old quarters like al-Midan. Islamicists are allowed to publish a magazine and have vocal spokesmen in parliament. Ghassan Abazad, a doctor and *Ikhwan* leader from Dera who brokered the return of *Ikhwan* exiles from Jordan, won a seat in parliament as an independent. A big 1992 release of Islamicists from prison to appease Western human rights critics also aimed to mollify Islamic opinion. People are no longer afraid to go to mosques as they were at the height of the anti-Islamic repression. Imams are supposed to deliver sermons approved by the Ministry of *Awqaf* but controls have been relaxed. A peaceful Islamic movement focused on pious personal behavior is spreading and so long as it does not challenge the regime, it will permit this safety valve. Civil society itself, however, limits the movement. Islamics are not strong on campus where, owing to the strong presence of minority groups, secularism is well established. The government can play on fear of the Algerian scenario, especially among Westernized Sunni families and educated working women.

The most favorable scenario for the incorporation of Islamicists into the system would be the participation of a moderate Islamic party in parliamentary elections which resulted in power sharing, rather than absolute victory for the Islamicists and defeat for the Ba'th. The regime has encouraged al-Buti to form a tame Islamic party, although he has feared losing his credibility if he did so. The Ba'th could possibly hold its own in elections: in the only free elections of the Ba'th era, the 1972 provincial council elections, traditional and Islamic forces won in the cities and the Ba'th in rural areas, while in recent parliamentary elections, the party proved effective in mobilizing blocs of votes through the popular organizations and the National Progressive Front. It is hard to imagine political liberalization advancing very far until the detente between regime and Islam deepens enough that the regime can risk Islamic participation in an electoral experiment.

b) The Widened Bases of Civil Society

To the extent that "modern" civil society is most efficacious in transcending primordial and patriarchal political culture, its expansion seems to be crucial to political change. The social mobilization and differentiation unleashed by modernization has potentially generated such a new wing of civil society. Beginning in Syria's liberal period, modernization gave rise to new occupation groups and classes, notably educated middle strata with a broadened propensity for "secondary" association. Under Ba'th rule, political pluralization was reversed but even as the state sought increased control, its development drive, in fostering a proliferation of social forces enjoying more diversified resources, was broadening the formerly circumscribed bases of civil society.

Table 2. Literacy (percent of population over 10 years old)

1960	36.6
1970	46.6
1979	62.0
1989	77.2

Source: Syrian Arab Republic, *Statistical Abstract*, 1976, pp. 90-1;
1991, p. 62

Table 3. Syrian Labor Force with Secondary and University Education

	Total Labour Force	Secondary Education	% of Total	University Education	% of Total
1970	1,524,552	43,222	2.8	25,545	1.7
1984	2,246,273	318,829	14.2	124,177	5.5
1989	2,882,619	582,000	20.2	213,000	7.4

Source: Syrian Arab Republic, *Statistical Abstract*, 1976, p. 144; 1986, pp. 104-05; 1991,
pp. 74-5.

Table 4. Agricultural Work Force as a Proportion of Total Work Force

Year	Agricultural Work Force	As % of Total Work Force
1960	567,600	51.6
1970	748,009	47.6
1976	754.000	37.8
1980	713,000	33.0
1984	570,484	25.4
1989	762,837	26.4

Sources: Syrian Arab Republic, *Statistical Abstract*, 1991, p. 76.

Table 5. Percent Urban Population

1960	36.9
1970	43.5
1981	47.0
1991	50.5

Source: Syrian Arab Republic, *Statistical
Abstract*, 1991, pp. 52, 60.

Table 6. Associational Membership, 1974 and 1990

	1974	1990
Trade Unions	184,918	522,990
Housing Cooperatives	79,415	270,972
Lawyers' Syndicate	1,661	5,291
Engineers' Syndicate	6,573	36,198
Agronomists' Syndicate	1,979	12,442

Source: Syrian Arab Republic, *Statistical Abstract*, 1976: 782-96; 1991: 412-20

The 1960s and 1970s were a period of substantial economic growth which, as Tables 2 through 5 show, accelerated social mobilization, as measured by education, literacy, urbanization and the non-agricultural proportion of the work force. As Table 2 indicates, literacy has doubled since 1960. Table 3 shows that the proportion of the labor force with secondary or university education climbed from about 5% of the population in 1970 to about 28% in 1989. Syria is now a middle income country, with a per capita income quite a bit above that of democratic India. This indicates Syria has developed a significant educated middle class. The differentiated modern work force proliferated as labor in agricultural plummeted from 51% to 26% in thirty years (Table 4). Modernization also eroded the primordial isolation of village and minority sect, incorporating them into a larger-scale society, as the increase in urbanization (Table 5) suggests.

Widened economic development and social-mobilization is not, in itself, enough to bring about pluralization, for the threshold at which mobilized social forces can no longer be contained without it varies greatly. Where, as in Syria, the government employs perhaps 40% of the work force, including a large part of the educated and even professional classes, they lack the independence to challenge the state which more dispersed control of property might provide. Nevertheless, as professionals and workers have proliferated so has membership in syndicates, ostensible networks of civil society (Table 6).

To be sure, these organizations are not autonomous of government and the largest growth is in state-dependent professionals such as agronomists and engineers, while lawyers, often a force for checking state power, have lagged. Presumably more autonomous artistic, cultural, and charity associations have actually declined from 609 in 1975 to 504 in 1990.

On the other hand, the more autonomous housing and transport cooperatives, in which members pool resources, have grown. These figures also exclude associations outside of government control, such as those in which government-employed professionals, to enhance their fixed incomes, pool resources to import goods. Although there is no reliable data on their scale, these informal cooperatives proliferated as, after 1976, inflation radically reduced the purchasing power of professionals on fixed state salaries; the decline of the state's ability to control the economy and provide resources stimulated the formation of autonomous associations outside its control.

The sheer increase in the numbers of educated professionals puts pressure on the state: to contain the brain drain, to meet expectations for jobs the state can no longer provide in sufficient numbers, and to avoid the political threat of the educated unemployed, the regime is moving to incrementally accommodate their expectations for greater economic and personal freedom. Allowing professional syndicates the greater freedom they enjoy in states such as Egypt could satisfy some pent up participation demands. The professional associations had a record of protest on behalf of liberal freedoms until their purge in the early eighties. If these organizations could merely recover their earlier limited autonomy they could give expression to or shelter civil society, as syndicates have in Egypt.

c) Retreat of the State, Bourgeois Resurgence

An independent bourgeoisie is the force most able to carve out some room for civil society and potentially to check state power. By the late seventies, the state, instead of breaking down class barriers, began to reconstruct them. A "new bourgeoisie" took form as the political elite used office to acquire illicit wealth and went into business on the side. The state, flush with revenues after the October war, launched an economic expansion in which private sector elements flourished as middlemen between the state and foreign firms or as contractors for the state. Both upwardly mobile *nouveaux riches* profiting from political connections and old bourgeoisie families coopted by the new opportunities gathered in the shadow of the state. Political, business, and marriage alliances formed between them and the political elite; at the core of this new bourgeoisie was a "military-mercantile complex" of 'Alawi officers and Damascene merchants.[14] Thus, the regime both fostered the reconstruction of a bourgeoisie and yet made it, at least initially, dependent on the state, an ambiguous outcome for civil society. Meanwhile, the gap between bourgeoisie and state had narrowed as the embourgeoisement of the power elite differentiated it from its popular base, muted its conflicts with the old upper class, and gave it an interest in markets and the private sector which eroded its statist ideology. The children of the elite were educated in the West and went into business, merging with and adopting the values of the Westernized bourgeoisie.

The reconstruction of the bourgeoisie, along with the economic

---

[14] Elizabeth Picard, "Ouverture economique et renforcement militaire en Syrie," *Oriente Moderno*, Anno LIX (Luglio-Dicembre 1979); Patrick Seale, *The Struggle for Syria*, (New Haven: Yale University Press, 1979) p. 456.

contraction that afflicted Syria in the eighties, prepared the way for a resurgence of the private sector. Syria's statist economy, hobbled by patronage and populist distribution, failed as an instrument of capital accumulation. The rent-driven expansion of the state during the seventies exceeded Syria's economic base and when rent and growth declined in the eighties, patronage dried up and the state began to shed some of its economic responsibilities. Private business had to be given concessions to fill the economic gap, notably the curbing of state intervention and widening of space for the market. By the nineties, the regime regarded private business as not just as an auxiliary to the public sector, but as a second engine of growth. New laws successfully encouraged investment which possibly exceeded the state investment budget in the early nineties. The private sector's share of foreign trade widened rapidly and new private industries proliferated. The regime is already dependent on the bourgeoisie for much of the country's foreign exchange and exports and its new economic strategy will make it ever more dependent on it for investment and job-creation.

By contrast to the expansionist seventies when the private bourgeoisie flourished on state patronage and contracts, the state now has far less largesse to dispense and a more autonomous bourgeoisie is mobilizing it own capital. Two segments of the bourgeoisie—industrial entrepreneurs and expatriates—have particular potential to widen civil society. In the vanguard of entrepreneurs who have risen from the local petite bourgeoisie are the Seif brothers, the largest private employers in Syria.[15] They started making mass produced shirts, expanded into other garments, and have a reputation for being pious Muslims and hence good employers who value their staff and provide them social benefits. Their apparent combination of private enterprise and a welfare network outside of government control could be a symptom of the potential for the bourgeoisie to reconstruct an autonomous civil society embracing wider strata of the population.

The expatriate internationalized wing of the bourgeoisie is cautiously exploring opportunities inside Syria. The regime's increasing desire to attract and keep expatriate investment—which may be freely exported under the new investment law—puts expatriates in a stronger position to demand greater economic and political liberalization in return. Omran al-Adham, a Paris based expatriate, thinking the time was ripe, published

[15] Volker Perthes,, "The Bourgeoisie and the Ba'th," *Middle East Report* 21, no. 3 (May-June 1991): 31-37.

an open letter to Asad urging him to "show confidence in the people" and give them "the opportunity to demonstrate their innovative power in every sphere," while warning that "economic and political freedom go together".[16]

An independent bourgeoisie poised to launch capitalist development has not, however, been consolidated. The bourgeoisie is not strong enough to force greater liberalization than the state wants. It presents no common front in favor of the market since dominant elements of it are still dependent on monopolies in an over-regulated economy and on state contracts and protection. The bourgeoisie's heterogeneous origins—some fractions fostered by the regime, others once its victims—deters consciousness of common interests. The favor or disfavor of the regime can make or break a business; it can, for example, manipulate currency laws, which most businessmen cannot avoid circumventing and which are generally not enforced, but can always be used to punish opponents. Nor can businessmen yet promote themselves as public figures. Some large merchants who tried to win popularity through press advertisements were broken by the enforcement of currency laws; the regime would tolerate no bourgeois pretensions to political independence.

Business's confidence and investment will remain limited unless it wins greater autonomy in which a bourgeois civil society can be reconstructed. The recent project to create a stock market and the consideration given to demands for private or joint ventures banks are signs of such a reconstruction. Curbs on arbitrary state power and, ultimately, power sharing are also needed.

Societal Pressures and Regime Strategies

Leadership values and strategies, notably their calculation of their interest in democratic initiatives, are the most immediate determinants of political change. The current elite is fundamentally illiberal, having been shaped in a period when liberalism was discredited in Syria; unlike the Soviet apparatchiki, it does not intend to give up power without a fight. But it is pragmatic and prepared to adapt to the new conditions, notably economic constraints and the end of bipolarity, which dictate enhanced reliance on the bourgeoisie and therefore some concession to political liberalization.

The regime is currently pursuing a strategy of calculated political

---

[16] *The Middle East* (May-June 1991), p. 33.

decompression which may widen space for civil society. With the collapse of socialism, the Ba'th party is ideologically exhausted and no longer a threat to private business. The President is broadening his base beyond the party to the business class. A revision of Ba'thist ideology stresses its long neglected liberal component which accepted democracy, freedoms, and a private sector. The draconian controls of the eighties are being relaxed as the Islamic threat recedes. There is greater press freedom; ministers may now be criticized. The security forces are being reined in, religious schools and mosques are recovering their autonomy, and political prisoners released.

Full scale liberalization still holds too many perceived political dangers for the regime. Asad argues that his 1970 rise to power initiated a Syrian perestroika—political relaxation, opening to the private sector—long before Gorbachev and that "the phase through which [Syria] is passing is not suitable for implementing [competitive elections]."[17] The Ba'th could, at the least, lose its parliamentary majority and such an opening could unleash uncontrollable forces. Indicative of the still narrow limits of regime tolerance were the arrests of Syria's human rights activists when they became outspokenly critical of the lack of democracy. Until the social cleavage between state and bourgeoisie is fully bridged, the *'Alawis* would be threatened by any return of power to the Sunni-dominated business establishment. Political liberalization risks Islam would become a vehicle of anti-regime mobilization as long as the ideological gap separating it from the secular minoritarian regime is so wide. The regime is determined to prevent the Algerian and East European scenarios and the security forces have the firepower and personal stake in regime survival to defend it.

There is so far little overt societal pressure for fuller democratization. The bourgeoisie is too weak: its control of the means of production remains limited and fragmented while Ba'th corporatism has obstructed most alliances with other classes. Although events in Eastern Europe, Algeria and Jordan have stimulated some yearning for democracy among the educated classes, the accompanying disorder and Islamic fundamentalism made its natural constituents—businessmen and intellectuals—wary of democracy.

More valued by the bourgeoisie is stability combined with increased personal and economic freedoms giving scope for greater private association. The bourgeoisie is now also accorded growing access to decision

---

[17] *FBIS*, Daily Report, Near East & South Asia (May 17, 1990), p. 27.

makers. Asad has explicitly approved greater political "pluralism" (*ta'addudiyyah*) in which the regime will take account of the views and interests of the bourgeois elements in the more complex social coalition it is putting together. Thus, the populist dominated corporatist system has been opened to the bourgeoisie: the prime minister's Committee for the Rationalization of Imports, Exports and Consumption in which the heads of the Chambers of Commerce and of Industry are included, gives crucial bourgeois access to economic decision-making.[18] Badr ad-Din al-Shallah, head of the Damascus Chamber of Commerce, who earned Asad's gratitude for keeping the Damascene bourgeoisie from joining the Islamic uprising, has been particularly influential in redressing business grievances. Parliamentary elections, though controlled, give some outlet to the politically ambitious. Some ten millionaires in parliament are quite outspoken and a block of independent merchants and industrialists sometimes coordinate for common interests. Some religious and even *Ikhwan*-associated figures have been coopted.

In return for business freedom and security, the bourgeoisie seems prepared to defer demands for political power. This signifies a modus vivendi between a state which needs a wealth generating, conservative social force, and a bourgeoisie which needs the economic opportunities and political protection provided by the state. Since the inegalitarian consequences of capitalism are likely to heighten popular discontent, neither bourgeoisie or regime will want full democratization. The new corporatism, combined with a widened role for parliament and rule of law, may foster new habits of accommodation between them and constrain state power.

Less certain is whether the "popular organizations" in the regime's own base will win the autonomy to defend popular interests even as their privileged access declines. On the one hand, worker and peasant union deputies were outspoken against reductions in social spending and lowered taxes on high incomes proposed in the 1992-93 budget.[19] Yet Asad's instinctive response to rising trade union criticism of pro-capital policies and suggestions the unions relax their ties to the Ba'th, was a warning that freedom had to be pursued in the "framework of responsibility," not "contradiction and fragmentation."[20] As the regime is in-

---

[18] Steven Heydemann, "Liberalization from Above and the Limits of Private Sector Autonomy in Syria: The Role of Business Associations," unpublished paper given at Middle East Studies Association, 1990.

[19] *Middle East Economic Digest*, 8 May 1992.

[20] *Syrie et Monde Arabe*, December 1992.

creasingly committed to capitalist development, business associations will acquire a growing capacity to argue that this requires new pro-business concessions and popular syndicates may find themselves waging a losing battle.

Although Asad's version of "pluralism" allows the state to play off competing "popular" and "bourgeois" interests, and sharply constrains a true pluralist competition of groups and classes, in the longer term economic liberalization could conceivably burst this system asunder. If liberalization leads to a continued flight of skilled labor from the public sector to higher paying private firms, and to better markets for rich peasants, this could break down the regime's incorporation of the popular sectors and align those most able to take advantage of opportunities with the bourgeoisie in a cross-class liberalizing alliance with the potential to advance pluralization.

Until Asad departs, there is little prospect of more than incremental liberalization, but rivals for the succession will need to bid for the support of newly revived societal sectors, and the winner will, like Egypt's Sadat, have an interest in building a base beyond the core 'Alawi-army-party complex, and in stimulating the economic growth needed to consolidate it: this will require concessions of further autonomy to the bourgeoisie and perhaps to the syndicates and unions. The prospects for a peaceful succession without sectarian strife and Lebanonization have been advanced by the Sunni-'Alawi alliances and the modus vivendi between state and bourgeoisie which incremental liberalization is advancing.

While capitalist development is bound to deepen civil society and succession may provide the turning point for greater pluralization, democratization depends on political rights and representation for all social forces. Power-sharing for the bourgeoisie must not mean the exclusion of the popular sectors: if corporatism is not to become the instrument for disciplining popular forces on behalf of capitalist development, the associations representing them must attain the autonomy to defend their interests in a post-populist era. Conversely, the most autonomous part of civil society, the *suq*, must be integrated into the state without destabilizing it. Only through a political incorporation of an autonomous and inclusive civil society can democratization advance.

State, Civil Society and the Peace Process

The rise of Syria's authoritarian state, based on an alliance of the army and a nationalist party, was stimulated by the conflict with Israel, while the construction of a national security state under Asad was a direct response to a perceived Israeli threat. As such, alterations in the international arena and foreign policy may affect prospects for internal liberalization and civil society while the revitalization of civil society could ultimately affect foreign policy.

Asad has enjoyed a very wide scope of discretion in foreign policy making and although economic constraints have narrowed his options over the years, it is the transformation in Syria's international and regional environments which has precipitated the recent changes in Syrian foreign policy. With the decline of Soviet power, Asad realized that the policy of seeking military parity with Israel while obstructing any peace settlement which did not meet Syria's terms, or excluded it, was exhausted. Asad's adherence to the US-led anti-Iraq coalition and his entering the peace process where manifestations of a strategic realignment toward the US in response to this. He hoped the Gulf war would renew the American stake in the peace process and bring the US to again recognize Syria as a responsible and essential partner in it.

So far, the impact of international change on society is limited but real. For example, the West has new leverage to alter internal practices: Syria is already responding to pressure on human rights issues which gives marginally more political breathing space to the opposition. The damage to Syria's trade with the former communist bloc and its consequent need for fuller integration into the world capitalist system has reinforced the regime's dependency on bourgeois civil society. This has particularly increased the leverage of the liberal-minded internationalized wing of the bourgeoisie. The more this is so, the more a return to Hama-like repression would be infinitely more costly than further concessions to civil society.

On the key foreign policy issue, the Arab-Israeli conflict, however, external pressures for accommodation with Israel are not reinforced by domestic ones. Asad has made high strategy in this conflict the reserved sphere of the Presidency and there are no dovish or hawkish constituencies with direct input into the policy process. Indirect domestic constraints exist but are ambiguous in their effect. On the one hand, there are boundaries beyond which the regime still dares not tread for fear of both elite and public opinion. Such legitimacy as the regime enjoys rests squarely on its claim to represent the national interest against Israel. No nationalist regime—especially an 'Alawi-dominated one—can, without grave risk, deviate from mainstream opinion which wants a settlement but insists on an honorable one—along UN Resolution 242 lines; were the regime to so dissipate its legitimacy, it would be poorly situated to pursue even a modest political liberalisation without the risk its enemies would use the issue to mobilize broad opposition. There is no societal pressure on the regime to make further concessions to Israel; and the Islamic opposition is, if anything, less accommodationist than the regime. But there is intense war weariness, a desire to divert resources from the military and, especially among the bourgeoisie, a new perception of opportunities in economic relations with the West.

Even an "honorable" settlement would present the regime with a new challenge. There are public expectations that a settlement would bring major economic and some political liberalization; regime security barons would likely see their power curbed and the military would be downsized. Yet, in the short term, an honorable peace would also be seen as a great foreign policy achievement and win the regime—particularly the president—enormous political capital to invest in a transition from the national security state. The state could also expect considerable economic aid in return for a peace agreement. Over the long run, the regime would have to find an ideological substitute for the Arab nationalism that has cemented its coalition and greater liberalism might be a way of containing the Islamic alternative. The loss of rent derived from Syria's role as confrontation state would reduce its autonomy of the bourgeoisie, while a peace would probably produce an influx of private, Arab and foreign investment, bolstering bourgeois civil society and tying Syria into the pro-business rules of the international political economy enforced by the IMF. Transnational ties would proliferate with the Western world, Syrian business would flourish, and interests could develop in keeping the peace. The accompanying internal pluralization could open the foreign policy process itself to the constraining impact of domestic politics and transnational interests.

Conclusion

Syria's experience shows that the prospects of pluralism, no inevitable outcome of modernization, are shaped, in the first instance, by the historically evolved social structure. Barrington Moore[21] argues that democracy emerged where an independent aristocracy and free cities were organized in class-based estates to extract power sharing from the crown but where the state nevertheless was never captured by the dominant class. Where a balance of the state and the dominant classes exists, it leaves space for a civil society within which independent social forces, above all a bourgeoisie, may develop, and the proposition "no bourgeoisie, no democracy" does not appear to be an exaggeration.

In Syria, by contrast, the historic imbalance of state and class retarded the development of a civil society integrated into the state and hence of a democratic political culture. The pre-modern imperial state tolerated a partly autonomous civil society but it was highly fragmented while the state obstructed the rise of classes integrated into the political structure. A state culture of authoritarianism was congruent with the patriarchal family and civil society did not enjoy sufficient space to generate a strong counter to either Sultan or clan.

Conversely, a weak state, even a formally liberal-representative regime, unable to check the power of the dominant classes on behalf of mass incorporation, is likely to be stuck in an oligarchic rut. Middle and lower class breakthrough comes through military coup or mass revolution, very possibly resulting in authoritarian-populist regimes inhospitable to bourgeois civil society and to democratization. In pre-1963 Syria that was the case; paradoxically, while the burst of new association generated by modernization broadened civil society, it also generated political mobilization amidst sharp class cleavages; civil society developed in opposition to, or at least unintegrated with the state. These pressures could not be contained by a fragile liberal polity unrooted in a indigenous state tradition or in mass society. The authority vacuum was filled by the rise of an authoritarian state and development of a democratic political culture was cut short.

Authoritarian states differ, however, and their particular nature is a second key variable determining the prospects for pluralization and a revival of civil society under them. All authoritarian regimes are threat-

---

[21] Barrington Moore, *The Social Origins of Dictatorship and Democracy: Lord and Peasant in the Making of the Modern World* (Boston: Beacon Press, 1966).

ened by democratization but their origins and class bases shape the extent to which they also have consistencies, above all a bourgeoisie, which would profit from liberalization or rest on those likely to be its victims. Thus, the conservative authoritarianism typical of Latin America originates in the repression of the masses on behalf of the bourgeoisie and liberalizes under pressure from this constituency which prefers a liberal state once the threat from below is mastered.

By contrast populist authoritarianism of the Syrian type which grows out of revolts against the bourgeoisie (but never wholly destroy it) is under no comparable internal pressure and, on the contrary, perceives a threat from this historic rival should it permit liberalization. To the extent political liberalization is typically accompanied by economic liberalization, the bourgeoisie would be the main beneficiaries while the state's own constituents are the likely victims and may be able to manipulate their corporatist and clientalist ties to the regime to deflect this threat. Liberalization depends, therefore, on the regime shifting its social base. But even to the extent the regime makes its peace with the bourgeoisie, investors might prefer the survival of a repressive state since populist authoritarianism, far from disciplining the masses, taught them they had social rights which would have to be curbed under capitalism; this would be especially so if the bourgeoisie acquires privileged political access under the post-populist regime, whether as a class through corporatist mechanisms or as individuals through clientalist connections.

Authoritarian-populist regimes also develop *structures* highly resistant to pluralization. While they exercise their power through the military and bureaucracy, they lack a stable social base in a dominant class (aristocracy or bourgeoisie) and, therefore, substitute the use of primordial (kinship, ethnic, regional) *'asabiyyah* and patronage to assure elite solidarity and the deployment of Leninist party organization and corporatist association to incorporate a popular constituency. The resort to sectarian *'asabiyyah* stimulates an (Islamic) reaction in civil society which retards the modus vivendi with the state needed for liberalization.

The effect of the authoritarian-populist state on civil society is, however, ambivalent. On the one hand, when an authoritarian state represses the rudiments of civil society and political pluralism before they can be consolidated, as is arguably so in Syria, even when the state weakens, civil society may be too underdeveloped to take advantage of this and force a state retreat. This is especially so of populist regimes which, emerging out of class conflict, pulverize the class structure which provides the framework of civil society and attack the countervailing power of the bourgeoisie; the weakness or discrediting of capitalist development which precipitates such regimes also evokes a large public sector through which the state clientalizes society. Where populist nationalism embroils the state in international conflict, as in Syria, a national security state may emerge, which absorbs resources that could otherwise be put to the construction of civil society.

On the other hand, a populist and modernizing state (which stops short of totalitarianism) like Syria dominates but never wholly suffocates civil society, and in some ways actually stimulates its potential components. Petit bourgeois traditional civil society, far from being penetrated and atomized, not only persisted under Ba'th rule but generated a powerful Islamic movement which challenged it. The regime's development drive advanced the requisites of pluralism—literacy, urbanization, modern occupations—while the Ba'th revolution created a more open social structure, with widened opportunity for the deprived strata to acquire such basic requisites of political empowerment as literacy, a sense of equality and dignity, and experience in political organization. Regime dominated or sponsored associations may, like old bottles, be filled with the new wine of civil society to the extent state controls are relaxed; indeed it is crucial that this happen if the transition from authoritarian rule is to be stable.

Authoritarian-populist regimes appear, by nature, to lack durability: they simultaneously suffer from built in constraints on public capital accumulation while, in time, fostering the private accumulation which reconstructs a bourgeoisie in the shadow of the state. This was so of Ba'thist Syria. Once the state was exhausted and a cooperative bourgeoisie had emerged, both acquired an interest in hiving off some state functions to civil society. State control started to contract, liberalizing concessions became unavoidable, and bourgeois civil society began to revive. As yet, the state cannot be forced into more than limited liberalization; patrimonial strategies such as clientalism remain viable since the large public sector and oil "rent" give the state the ability to stand above, play off, and coopt the rival sectors of a fragmented society. Corporatist forms of state-society linkage may be enough to accommodate societal complexity for some time.

But the greater autonomy incremental liberalization accords civil society will invigorate the bourgeoisie, the force with the resources to reconstruct a business-centered civil society; conversely, an invigorated bourgeoisie means a greater class-state balance, widening space for civil society. Having opted to depend on private capitalist investment, the regime will have to be responsive to bourgeois demands for greater rule of law and a general rollback of the boundaries of state power. This by no means implies bourgeois demands for democratization which could only empower potential mass resistance, in the name of populism, to the dominance of capital. But increased societal autonomy is likely, in the longer run, to generate stronger social forces which cannot readily be controlled except through wider power-sharing.

The Syrian case makes clear that a strategic factor in the state-class balance is control of economic assets and that a dispersion of assets is most favorable to civil society and pluralization. The over-concentration of property in a landowning or capitalist class is likely to translate into their capture of the state, especially where, as in Syria, a tradition of a autonomous indigenous state is lacking. Conversely, as in Ottoman and in Ba'thist Syria, if the state controls the main economic assets, it can obstruct the development of an autonomous bourgeoisie. If small property persists, as in the *suq*, it can give the economic independence to resist state penetration, but also integration into the political system. If the state cannot sustain the extraction of a sufficient surplus from its assets, it may have no choice but to foster or tolerate the dispersion of property and economic power among autonomous groups and classes with the potential to check its power. In Syria today, the persisting petit bourgeoisie, part of the expanded new middle class and the reviving bourgeoisie represent forces with the potential to roll back the state. But the public sector continues to give the state autonomy and through it the regime continues to incorporate other social forces with a stake in statism.

Particularly where there is such a stalemate between forces for and against liberalization, as seems to be so in Syria, elites can balance between the two and, as such, their preferences may be the decisive factors in determining whether the regime accommodates civil society and demands for democratization or not. Leaders will initiate democratization experiments if they value democracy or believe it necessary to stability, economic growth or placating international patrons. Rational choice suggests they will share power if they calculate the cost of repression to be too high, if a pact with the opposition on the rules of democratization will protect their interests, or if elite rivalry leads a faction to bid for popular support. If a civil society can bridge the gap between elite and opposition, a modus vivendi favorable to democratization is more likely than if the two are organized in mutually exclusive countercultures. Syrian elites are no democrats and, so far, except for international and economic constraints, only the rudiments of some of these facilitating factors can be identified, (a modus vivendi with the bourgeoisie?) while others appear absent (elite factionalism). As such, elites have opted, so far successfully, to control the revival of civil society through a merely limited political decompression calculated to preserve, not transform the state. Pursued at regime discretion, it can be reversed if it unleashes dangerous opposition. It may take a succession crisis to generate a fuller liberalization scenario.

Although external forces may make themselves felt in the equation through their impact on societal modernization over the long run, their most immediate effect is likely to be on the values and calculations of political elites. But external forces are by no means uniformly on the side of liberalization. If the international arena is perceived as one of conflict and insecurity, elites will put a premium on undiminished state power. On the other hand, international economic leverage over LDCs and the global triumph of liberal over socialist ideology may be coming together in an unprecedented way to pressure elites into liberalization. The full impact of such forces in Syria awaits the outcome of the peace process.

CHAPTER EIGHT

PALESTINIAN CIVIL SOCIETY

Muhammad Muslih

When the Oslo Agreement was signed in Washington, D.C., on September 13, 1993, many Palestinians were angered by the numerous concessions unilaterally accepted by PLO Chairman Yasir Arafat, and the fact that the agreement emerged from secret negotiations between Israel and the PLO, rather than through the on-going bilateral talks initiated in Madrid in 1991. The debate raises important questions concerning the extent to which Palestinian social formations should play a direct role in creating and legitimizing an entity or state. Judging from the ability of Palestinian associational life to endure internal as well as external pressures, it is not difficult to imagine that the infrastructure of political and civic institutions that would support a Palestinian state—whenever that state arrives—may well emerge from the diverse formations of Palestinian civil society. Through a fairly detailed investigation of civil society in the West Bank and Gaza Strip, this paper aims to offer a critical analysis of the nature of associational life in these territories, and the prospects for building a Palestinian democracy.

It may be useful to start with an operational definition of what is meant by 'civil society', and how the term is understood in the West.[1] Civil society refers to an admixture of various forms of associations including unions, clubs, charities, religious associations and other groups that freely interact and communicate with each other in a spirit of civility and tolerance. Such interaction is not only for their own good, but for the sake of the common good as well.[2] Civil society is not the exclusive domain of one country or continent, nor of a particular type of political system. Almost all societies have within them civil formations regardless of the system of government. The distinguishing characteristic of

---

[1] For a general treatment of this subject see John Keane, *Civil Society and the State* (London: Verso, 1988), pp. 35-72; Daniel Bell, "American Exceptionalism Revisited: The Role of Civil Society," *The Public Interest*, no. 95 (1989): 38-56.

[2] See essays in Charles Maier, ed., *Changing Boundaries of the Political* (Cambridge: Cambridge University Press, 1987); Alexis de Tocqueville, *Democracy in America* (New York: Langley Press, 1845), vols. 1&2.

civil society is the nature of its associational life, civility, and tolerance of diversity and pluralism.[3]

Generally speaking, vibrant civil societies have been central to the functioning of Western democracies because they are believed to provide a buffer between the citizen and the state.[4] After the collapse of Communism in East-Central Europe, the idea of civil society gained more attention in the West as an answer to the question of how individuals can pursue their own interests while preserving the common good and, similarly, how society and state can interact and reinforce each other to create and sustain a democratic system.[5] At the heart of this conception is the belief that the state is an indispensable agent responsible for refereeing and regulating the functioning of civil society.[6] Although associational life among Palestinians living in the West Bank and Gaza has long been rich, critics have questioned whether the concept of civil society can be applied to their various associational forms. In this regard, two unique aspects of the Palestinian situation must be considered because they pose difficulties for studying civil society in relation to the state. First, the Palestinians have not had a national government in this century. Since 1967, the Israeli occupation apparatus has functioned as the de facto authority in the West Bank and Gaza. The Palestinians consider the Israeli military regime illegitimate, and their goal is not simply to undermine its control or to temper its arbitrary effects, but to dismantle it altogether.

Second, prior to the signing of the Oslo Agreement in Washington D.C. on September 13, 1993, Palestinians in the West Bank and Gaza accepted an external actor, the Palestine Liberation Organization (PLO), as their "state", clandestinely cooperating with local PLO representatives to sustain a network of institutions through which the PLO sought to exercise political power in competition with the Israeli military regime. With the signing of the Declaration and the exchange of PLO and Israeli letters of mutual recognition on September 9, 1993, the PLO has become an internal actor that aspires to replace the authority of the Israeli occupier in the West Bank and Gaza. The behavior of the PLO toward its constituency in the occupied territories will have an impact on the organs of civil society in these territories.

---

[3] Bell, "*American Exceptionalism Revisited*"; Edward Shils, "The Virtues of Civil Society," *Government and Opposition* 26, no . 2. (Winter 1991): 3-20.

[4] Michael Walzer, "The Idea of Civil Society," *Dissent,* Spring 1991, pp. 293-304.

[5] Adam Seligman, *The Idea of Civil Society* (New York: The Free Press, 1992), pp. 202-203.

[6] Walzer, "The Idea of Civil Society," p. 302.

The characteristics of society in the occupied territories also influence Palestinian associational life. The essence of social organization is a network of *hamulas* (extended families) and smaller families, as well as village, neighborhood and religious solidarities. Palestinian society is mainly rural in character, and even urban centers are closer to the model of a small town than to that of a metropolitan area. As much as 65 percent of the Palestinians in the occupied territories live in villages, whereas the remaining 35 percent live in small towns. The town of Nablus has 130 villages; Hebron 83; Ramallah/al-Bireh 74; Jenin 58; Qalqilya/Tulkarm 43; and Jerusalem/Bethlehem/Jericho 42.[7] Even in Gaza, where close to 85% of the inhabitants reside in Gaza City, the culture is predominantly rural.[8]

This raises interesting questions germane to the study of civil society in a Palestinian context. Can a society with dominant rural characteristics, essentially organized on the basis of lineages, produce enduring civil society organs that transcend local solidarities? Should Palestinian civil society be studied in the context of statelessness or in the context of a national liberation struggle? And, perhaps the central question, civil society in relation to whom?

These questions may be addressed within the framework of the 'state surrogate' paradigm. The concept of 'state surrogate', as used here, is political rather than sociological, and refers to the PLO. As a para-state formation, the PLO has many of the underpinnings of a government, including a bureaucracy, an army, financial resources and, in the West Bank and Gaza, a network of institutions through which it tries to exercise political power. Placing civil society organs in this perspective will help to throw light on the prospects for democratization during the five-year transitional period of Palestinian interim self-government authority and beyond.

The Historical Context

The nature of Palestinian civil society must be considered in terms of the historical context in which Palestinian social organizations have evolved. Palestinian modern history may be roughly divided into three periods.

---

[7] Bernard Sabella, "Al-Diffah al-gharbiyyah wa-qita' ghazzah: as-sukkan wa al-ard" [The West Bank and the Gaza Strip, Population and Land] in *Al-Mujtama' al-filastini fi al-diffah al-gharbiyyah wa qita' ghazzah*, Liza Taraki, ed. (Akka: Dar al-Aswar, 1990), p. 101.

[8] See figures in Salim Tamari, "Al-Takhalluf wa afaq al-tanmiyyah fi al-diffah al-gharbiyyah wa-qita' ghazzah al-muhtallayn" [Underdevelopment and the Areas of Growth in the Occupied West Bank and Gaza Strip], Taraki, ed., *Al-Mujtama'*, p. 206.

In the first period (1917-1948), we find a wide array of associations ranging from religious bodies, clubs, and labor unions, to women's societies, charitable societies, town cafes and village guest houses.

These associations emerged outside the framework of British colonial rule to articulate the interests of their respective societal sectors. Some of these associations were family-based, such as the Dajani Sports Club in Jerusalem, and some were denominational such as the national Muslim Societies (1921-23) and the Orthodox Club in Jerusalem. Others were more open collectivities in terms of their membership, such as women's societies which multiplied after the Wailing Wall riots of 1929, and the Western-style labor organizations which emerged after 1925.

These and a variety of other associations constituted a type of civil society that performed social functions whose benefits transcended the boundaries of the family or the local neighborhood. Women's societies, for example, opened welfare centers, helped poor families, and taught mothers proper sanitation methods. To finance their activities, these organizations held annual flower days, bazaars, lotteries and other such activities. Similarly, social clubs launched programs to combat illiteracy and sponsored lectures on health, education, and other social issues.[9]

By virtue of the national struggle, many of these associations were drawn into the orbit of the political apparatus of the Palestinian national movement. The Arab Executive, a body composed of dominant local politicians who attempted to coordinate the national struggle in the 1920s and early 1930s, was able to bring many associations under its control, using them as instruments with which to mobilize the masses and expand the political base of the dominant political elite.[10] Al-Hajj Amin al-Husayni, a founder of Palestinian nationalism and the leader of the Palestinians during the last two decades of British rule, was also able to draw a large number of associations into his political coalition. Al-Hajj Amin presided over what amounted to a para-state formation, and he used associations not only to mobilize for the national struggle, but

---

[9] Adnan Abu Ghazaleh, "Arab Cultural Nationalism in Palestine during the British Mandate, *Journal of Palestine Studies* 3 (Spring 1972), pp. 37-63; Issa Khalaf, *Politics in Palestine, Arab Factionalism and Social Disintegration* 1939-1948 (New York: State University of New York, 1991), pp. 133-161; Ann Mosely Lesch, *Arab Politics in Palestine, 1917-1939: The Frustration of a Nationalist Movement* (Cornell: Cornell University Press, 1979), pp. 59-67.

[10] Lesch, *Arab Politics*, pp. 102-131; Muhammad Muslih, *The Origins of Palestinian Nationalism* (New York: Columbia University Press and the Institute for Palestine Studies, 1988); Yehoshua Porath, *The Emergence of the Palestinian-Arab National Movement, 1918-1929* (London: Frank Cass, 1974); and the same author's *The Palestinian Arab National Movement, 1929-1939* (London: Frank Cass, 1977).

to expand his scope of power and undermine his political opponents.[11]

In the second period, stretching from 1948 to 1967, we also find a rich variety of Palestinian social formations. With the creation of Israel, Palestinian society was uprooted and the Palestinian national movement collapsed, scattering Palestinians between a number of states. Jordan annexed the West Bank in 1950, granting citizenship to its inhabitants; Egypt occupied and retained the Gaza Strip under an Egyptian military administration. As a result, the Palestinians were unable to play an independent role in shaping their destiny or organizing their associational life. Arab governments, each for its own political purposes, imposed constraints on Palestinian organizing. The Jordanian government, for example, tried to repress the labor movement charging that the movement was under the influence of the Communist Party. Syria and Egypt also restricted the field of Palestinian organizing, with the latter suppressing organizational activities that appeared to stray from the government's line.[12] These restrictions notwithstanding, the Palestinians managed to form social organs in which students, professionals, workers, and women's groups were involved (see Table 1.0).

Some of these organs were heirs to the pre-1948 societies, and all of their organizers benefited from the legacy of the earlier period. As was in the earlier period, the creation of these organs was as much rooted in the tradition of national politics as it was an attempt to forge an agenda specifically related to the concerns of their members. While the groups tried to serve the particular interests of their members, they also worked for the national cause, which in all instances was paramount. This is understandable in view of the dispersion and statelessness of the Palestinians, and the upshot was that these associational formations in the diaspora were engaged with a Palestinian political movement dedicated to a program of national reconstruction and liberation. Some were even co-opted by this movement, *Fatah*, which had an underground army, a bureaucracy, and equally significant a determination to lead Palestinian society in the Diaspora.[13]

For the third period (1967-), this paper will focus on the West Bank and the Gaza Strip, where the richness of associational life endured

---

[11] For details on al-Hajj Amin and the politics of Palestine, see Philip Mattar, *The Mufti of Jerusalem, Al-Hajj Amin Al-Husayni and the Palestinian National Movement* (New York: Columbia University Press, 1988).

[12] Laurie A. Brand, *Palestinians in the Arab World, Institution Building and the Search for State* (New York: Columbia University Press, 1988), pp. 221-237.

[13] For details on the history and organization of Fatah, see Helena Cobban, *The Palestinian Liberation Organization: People, Power and Politics* (New York: Cambridge University Press, 1984).

Table 1.0: Examples of Palestinian Organizing in the Diaspora 1948-1967

Egypt	Jordan	Kuwait
	1953-United Nations Relief and Works Agency teachers form a union	1958-1959-Arab National Movement organizing
1959-Founding of General Union of Palestinian Students		
	1959-Ongoing Ba'th	1959-Fatah begins recruiting and
1962-Founding of League of Palestinian Women		ANM organizing
1963-Founding of General Union of Palestinian Workers		1963-Palestinian Workers Committee
	1965-GUPW founded	Founded
		1966-Palestinian Teachers' Chapter
	1967-1968 Fatah medical services expand to become the Palestinian Red Crescent Society, UNRWA	Founded

Source: Brand, *Palestinians in the Arab World*, pp. 14-15.

despite the revolutionary changes brought about by the Six-Day War. A host of structural features influenced the social and political life of the Palestinians living there. For example, the imposition of Israeli rule introduced a web of administrative and legal arrangements for the purpose of annexing the occupied territories to Israel, and shaped Palestinian society in a fashion that suited Israeli interests.[14] In this setting, two major political forces competed to win the loyalty of the Palestinians.

The first was the Jordanian government, whose instruments of political influence included an administrative infrastructure in the occupied territories, granting Jordanian citizenship to West Bank inhabitants, and extending financial assistance to municipalities, chambers of commerce, public schools, and the Islamic religious establishment. To these should be added the familial, social, and economic ties between the people living on both sides of the Jordan River, as well as the geographic

---

[14] See Amnesty International, Report 1992 "Israel and the Occupied Territories" (London, July 1992); Raja Shehadeh, *Occupier's Law, Israel and the West Bank* (Washington, D.C.: Institute for Palestine Studies, 1985), and his "Negotiating Self-Government Arrangements," *Journal of Palestine Studies*, vol. XXI, no. 84 (Summer 1992): 22-32.

fact that Jordan was the only gateway for West Bank and Gaza Palestinians to the rest of the Arab world.[15]

The second political force was the PLO, whose recognition in 1974 by the Arab states and the United Nations General Assembly reinforced its position as the true representative of the Palestinian people. As a quasi-government with an executive, a parliament, an army, and substantial financial resources, the PLO was able to offer political rewards to enhance its status in the territories. Above all, it used its nationalist credentials for that purpose.

Four types of organizations characterize associational life in the occupied territories during this period: political shops, voluntary cooperatives, voluntary mass organizations, and Islamist groups.

Political Shops

Political shops, or *dakakin siyasiyyah*, practiced what one might call patronage politics and clientelism. Engagement in patronage politics, a practice not unique to Palestinian society, is a strategy often used by dominant political forces either as a tool to muster support, or to undermine the influence of political competitors. The Jordanian government engaged in this practice by employing the political and economic resources at its disposal to support a local West Bank elite loyal to the Jordanian state. A good number of Palestinians occupying senior positions in the chambers of commerce and industry, as well as in other public institutions such as the courts and the school system, remained in the political orbit of Jordan, thanks mainly to the financial incentives that they received.

Over the years, the gradual ascent of the PLO in the occupied territories effectively undermined the authority of the pro-Jordanian elite, but did not eliminate the Jordanian-affiliated patronage system. In many ways, the PLO itself encouraged patronage politics by plowing money into a variety of institutions and political movements operating in the West Bank and Gaza. *Fatah*, which constitutes the backbone of the PLO, was the main architect of this policy.

Fatah's substantial funds, largesse, and its large constituency, have been attractive drawing cards for political climbers with different ideo-

---

[15] Yehuda Litani, "Leadership in the West Bank and Gaza," *Jerusalem Quarterly*, no. 14 (Winter 1980), pp. 90-109; Emile Sahliyeh, *In Search of Leadership, West Bank Politics since 1967* (Washington, D.C.: The Brookings Institution, 1988), pp. 21-42.

logical persuasions. For many years, the occupied territories had no apparatus by which to mobilize popular forces, and local funding for internal organizations and activities was lacking. This enabled *Fatah* to channel its funds into support and propaganda work not only on behalf of its pragmatic politics of compromise with Israel, but also on behalf of Fatah-affiliated local political bosses.[16]

There is no more important or suitable network of organizations in which to examine patronage politics than the trade union movement. In their capacity as representatives of different occupational sectors in various geographic locations, the unions are supposed to promote the economic and employment rights of their members. To do so, they must occupy a space outside the framework of a state apparatus or a dominant political force. The relations of a union with an external actor must be controlled; that is, they should be carried out in a way that promotes the interests of the members and not the political agenda of another entity. In this sense, the autonomy of the unions is central to the existence of viable civil society organs.

Since the first years of the British Mandate, the Arab unions in Palestine were a leftist stronghold, partly as a result of the organizing efforts of the Palestine Communist Party (PCP) which crystallized out of Jewish social groups in 1923. Members of these groups were Russian immigrants.[17] After 1948, the Jordanian government used Communist influence on trade-union activities in the West Bank as a pretext to subdue attempts to revive the labor movement.[18] In the Gaza Strip, the Egyptian authorities imposed a ban on the organizing of labor unions until 1956, after which six labor unions emerged with branches throughout the Gaza Strip. In the West Bank, all organized societal activity was suspended after Israel's occupation of the area, only to be revived by the Communists a couple of years later. In Gaza, however, no labor organizing took place before 1979 due to the Israeli ban. Until the late 1970s, the Communists were in almost full control of the labor movement.

---

[16] For details on the behavior of *Fatah* and other political groups in the occupied territories see 'Ali al-Jarbawi, *Al-Intifadah wal-qiyadat al-siyasiyyah fi al-diffah al-gharbiyyah wa qita' ghazzah, bahth fi al-nukhbah al-siyasiyyah* [The Uprising and Political Leaderships in the West Bank and Gaza, A Study of Political Elites] (Beirut: Dar al-Tali'ah, 1989), pp. 70-130.

[17] Musa Budeiri, *The Palestine Communist Party, 1919-1948: Arab and Jew in the Struggle for Internationalism* (London: Ithaca Press, 1979).

[18] Amnon Cohen, *Political Parties in the West Bank under the Jordanian Regime, 1949-1967* (Ithaca and London: Cornell University Press, 1982).

As a result of political developments in Lebanon and elsewhere in the region in the mid-and late 1970s, the PLO began to re-focus its attention on the occupied territories. The group's growing influence thereafter resulted in sharp rivalries which culminated in major contests to control the labor movement. Two leftist PLO groups, the Democratic Front for the Liberation of Palestine (DFLP) and the Popular Front for the Liberation of Palestine (PFLP), were the first to take charge of labor organizational work benefiting on the one hand from their alliance with the PCP, and on the other from the rivalry between the PCP and *Fatah*.

Determined to break the leftist hegemony over organized labor groups, *Fatah* mobilized all the resources at its disposal, particularly its massive cash reserves, to win what was called the "war of the institutions" in the late 1970s and early 1980s. The competition for control was so intense that grass-roots activists, acting on behalf of PLO groups outside the occupied territories, split off to set up parallel labor organizations of their own. One major split occurred in August 1981 with two separate General Federations of Trade Unions having identical names emerging, one dominated by the left and one controlled by *Fatah*. The *Fatah*-sponsored organization was headquartered in Ramallah, while the leftist-controlled one was seated in Nablus.[19]

In the end, *Fatah* prevailed. Defeated and frustrated in their attempts to maintain their hegemony, Palestinian leftists indignantly watched *Fatah* win over the labor movement they had reared for so long. Today, *Fatah*-supported units, acting under the umbrella of the Workers' Youth Movement, represent about 70 percent of the membership in the executive organs of the Palestinian Federation of Trade Unions.[20] Of course, the Palestinian left has not abandoned its struggle, and continued with its efforts to reestablish its influence over the labor movement and penetrate the mass organizations.

In many respects, the experience of the labor movement is representative of the experience of some other organizations, including the student bodies. These continue to be important focal points of political organization penetrated by local PLO groups and their ideological counterparts in the Diaspora. In this sense, they are mostly used as political proxies

---

[19] Joost R. Hiltermann, *Behind the Intifada, Labor and Women's Movements in the Occupied Territories* (Princeton: Princeton University Press, 1991); Ibrahim al-Fattash, *Tarikh al-harakah al-niqabiyyah min sanat 1917 ila 1992* [The History of the Labor Move ment from 1917 to 1992] (Jerusalem: 1992).

[20] Al-Fattash, *Tarikh*, pp. 67-73; Salim Tamari, "Left in Limbo: Leninist Heritage and Islamist Challenge," *Middle East Report*, no. 179 (November/December 1992), pp. 16-22.

or "*imtidadat fasa'iliyyah*" (commando groups' extensions) and as a means to increase political mobilization on behalf of these PLO groups.[21]

Nevertheless, and despite the fact that a good number of union and student representatives compete for favored access to the state surrogate and its resources, the non-political interests of workers and students have not been totally ignored. Through students' representatives, for example, students are accorded access to decision-making bodies in their respective institutions of learning thus facilitating the redressing of their grievances. Similarly, the unions often try to resolve problems that may arise between employer and employee, particularly problems related to wages, working conditions, social benefits and currency fluctuations.[22]

Voluntary Cooperatives

Voluntary Cooperatives fall into three categories: cooperative institutions, productive projects, and household cooperatives.[23]

These categories emphasize job creation through production. Structurally speaking, the production process of household cooperative takes place inside private homes and gardens; in the other two types, it

Table 2.0: Selected Voluntary Cooperatives circa 1992

Cooperative Institutions	Productive Projects	Household Cooperatives
Food Cooperatives (Tomato Paste)	Food Projects (Biscuits)	Food Cooperatives (Wheat Germ)
Dairy Cooperatives (Milk)	Dairy Projects (Yogurt)	Dairy Cooperatives (Yoghurt Spread)
Chicken Cooperatives	Chicken Projects	Chicken Cooperatives
Agricultural-Industrial (Lamb's Wool Sweaters)	Agricultural-Industrial (Skirts)	Agricultural-Industrial (Scarves)
Consumer Cooperatives	Consumers Projects	

[21] Al-Jarbawi, *Al-Intifadah wal-qiyadat*, p. 21, and his *Waqfah naqdiyyah ma' tajrubat al-tanmiyyah al-filastiniyyah* [A Critical Assessment of the Palestinian Developmental Experience] (West Bank: Bir Zeit University, 1991), pp. 46-48.

[22] See interviews with union representatives in al-Fattash, *Tarikh al-harakah al-niqabiyyah*, p. 51ff.

[23] Unless otherwise indicated, the data used in the analysis of the cooperatives is borrowed and adapted from 'Izzat 'Abd al-Hadi, *Al-Intifadah wa ba'd qadaya al-tanmiyyah al-sha'biyyah* [The Uprising and some Issues of Popular Development] (Ramallah: Bisan Press, 1992). This work is based on field research and is the most comprehensive and up-to-date study on this topic.

involves separate or independent centers run by committees organized on the grassroots level. Membership differs from category to category, but in general there is the producing member (*al-ʿudw al-muntij*), the associate member (*al-ʿudw al-sadiq*), and the supporting member (*al-ʿudw al-muʾazir*). The producers involved in the cooperative institutions are entitled to salaries based on the percentage of profits derived from direct marketing; those involved in the productive project receive monthly salaries regardless of marketing conditions; those engaged in the household cooperative are not guaranteed monthly or annual incomes because the ownership of the project is in the hands of the producers themselves, and because the production process is constrained by the uncertainties of seasonal cycles. As for funding, the bulk of it comes from low interest loans and investments by members, and, in a few instances, from outright grants.

Cooperative units are generally local, in the sense that the vast majority of the members live on the grounds of their respective cooperatives. In the case of the household cooperatives, all members reside on the grounds; in the case of the cooperative institutions, 99.9 percent; and in the case of the productive projects, as much as 86 percent.[24] This is due in part to curfews and other restrictions imposed by the Israeli military authorities, and in part to the nature of the cooperative and the absence of large production centers in Palestinian towns and villages. Nevertheless, crops and other items produced by the cooperatives find their way to the larger Palestinian market whenever local circumstances permit.

The cooperatives embody a practical civil society project backed by a vision. The practical aspect is manifest in the range of the cooperatives' activities (see Table 2.0) which, though limited in scope, contribute to the fulfillment of the daily needs of local Palestinian society, thus alleviating the pain caused by the Israeli military measures. On the other hand, the vision is reflected in the spirit of associationalism that these cooperatives help foster. Two interrelated groups of ideas are those of the neighborhood and those of the small town. The neighborhood idea is specifically that of a compact local community, a family or a network of families, harnessing its resources at its own risk and under its own hierarchy. The purpose is not simply to protect the neighborhood and meet its own needs, but also, whenever possible, to protect and meet the needs of other neighborhoods in the same area. The purest form of this

---

[24] ʿAbd al-Hadi, *Al-Intifadah*, p. 271.

idea is the household cooperative. The neighborhood idea also forms a new strand in Palestinian self-consciousness, namely that of self-reliance and independence from the Israeli economy.

The small town idea, that of a larger cooperative operating in a broader economic framework, has the more universal theme of developing the economic, social, and cultural resources of Palestinian society. A certain economic pluralism is implicit in this idea, for those who comprise the productive projects and the cooperative institutions do not hail from the same socio-economic background, and the cooperation among them cuts across family lines. Both the neighborhood idea and the town idea assumed a distinct shape as a result of the Intifadah. Neither could scarcely have emerged earlier in their present form, because it was only after the Intifadah that the idea of economic independence began to crystallize and receive serious attention.

These ideas form, so to speak, the 'ethical' basis upon which the vision of the cooperatives rests. Cooperatives have maintained a considerable degree of autonomy from the 'state surrogate', but their experience shows that they cannot insulate themselves completely from the political forces that exist in the West Bank and Gaza. In terms of membership, for example, 62 percent joined their cooperative on the basis of family affiliations, economic interests, or both; the remaining 38 percent joined as activists on behalf of local political forces, particularly *Fatah*. While this illustrates that cooperatives have not been fully drawn into the network of the state surrogate, membership in these units is not universal, but rather constrained by the intrusions of the state surrogate.

Voluntary Mass Organizations

Most observers trace voluntary mass organizations to the mid-1970s, when voluntary work committees consisting of boys and girls were formed in Nablus to clean up the older quarters of town. This writer recalls that such voluntary student work was initiated, albeit on a local level, by Bir Zeit College in 1969, before that institution was converted into a four-year college under the name "Bir Zeit University" in 1975-76. The voluntary work movement continued to develop, recruiting students and channeling their energies into voluntary work for farmers who either could not afford or could not find rural workers, owing to their absorption into the Israeli economy.

Although PLO groups were active in mass voluntary organizations as early as 1975, the movement was able to maintain a reasonable degree of autonomy, in the sense that it didn't become a PLO satellite. At the same time, the movement did not strike deep roots due to the utopian vision of its leftist inspirers, who preached a philosophy of agrarian democracy. Practically speaking, this strategy was ill-suited for an agricultural condition that required a real labor force, not a temporary supply of devoted students who would leave, sooner rather than later, to pursue their individual careers. But before turning to their own private lives, advocates of voluntary work left in place the rudiments of an infrastructure that would facilitate the performance of such work in a more realistic fashion and on a much larger scale.

Israel's heavy-handed practices, including measures of economic strangulation and the periodic withholding of basic services , had been felt so much by the defenseless Palestinians that they continued to find in voluntary group action an attractive means to alleviate their suffering. But it was the Intifadah that ensured that such action was a recognizable aspect of organizational life in the occupied territories. One unique feature of the Intifadah was that it led to the creation of relatively autonomous and organized social units with specific functional responsibilities, foremost among which were serving the population and shielding it from t he shattering impact of the Israeli military measures.[25]

Our interest lies less in cataloguing these units than in understanding how they relate to the idea of civil society described above. To reiterate, civil society is a group of units which act both to promote individual and group interests, as well as to inculcate in their members a sense of good citizenship and belonging. With this in mind, it may be useful to begin by constructing a picture of how the work of these units looked like. Of course, innumerable variations of activities can be found, particularly during the tense days and months of the Intifadah. But, speaking very roughly, we may say that we find such activities as those of social work groups and women's groups, which are quite numerous at the town, village, and neighborhood levels. Without attempting to catalogue such groups, an attempt will be made to give due attention to their kind of work and how it has helped to promote associationalism from outside the framework of the state surrogate networks. Unlike the focus of cooperatives on economic development, these groups concentrate on other aspects of social action.

---

[25] Hiltermann, *Behind the Intifada*, pp. 205-217; 'Adil 'Abu 'Amshah, *Al-Awda' al-iqtisadiyyah wa al-ijtima 'iyyah fi al-diffah al-gharbiyyah wa qita' ghazzah qabla wa-athna' al-intifadah* [The Economic and Social Conditions in the West Bank and the Gaza Strip Before and During the Uprising] (Nablus: al-Najah University, 1989), pp. 136-169.

First, voluntary charitable organizations, health organizations, family planning organizations, and organizations for the orphaned, the handicapped, and the elderly all focus on social work. These local private units are independent of similar organizations operating under the direction of the Israeli military governor or of international voluntary agencies, but are commonly affiliated with larger networks such as the General Union of Charitable Societies. The organizations are made up of doctors (including psychiatrists), lawyers, social workers, educators and other professionals. They offer financial assistance to the needy, legal and psychiatric care, and moral support to many of those directly affected by the Israeli occupation.

Apart from these activities, these organizations perform what is known in the West Bank and Gaza as underground social work: helping those injured or wounded by Israeli soldiers, and offering support to the families of the detainees, the deportees, and to those whose houses were demolished by the occupation authorities. In many instances, these organizations launch what are called out-reach activities, especially in cases involving wounded Palestinians who flee to hospitals or local clinics to avoid arrest by the Israeli military. Members of these organizations usually volunteer to offer their professional services free of charge.[26]

Second, voluntary women's groups also operate outside of the control of the state surrogate. The basis of their membership is either the town, village, a quarter or a group of quarters, and their aims are essentially non-political. Like the social work groups, women's groups are sometimes integrated into larger frameworks such as the Union of Women's Committee for Social Work (1982) and United Action Women's Committees Union (1989). Membership is drawn from various professions and different social classes.[27] Women's groups are frequently built around a strong and devoted personality with a tradition of learning and community service. To cite a few examples: Elizabeth Nasir (1909-1988) set up a number of women's and social centers, including *Rawdat*

---

[26] Amin al-Hajj Yahya, *Al-'Amal al-ijtima'i fi dhill al-intifadah* [Social Work during the Intifadah] (Jerusalem, n.p., 1988); Mustafa Barghouthi and Rita Giacaman, "The Emergence of an Infrastructure of Resistance: The Case of Health," in *Intifada: Palestine at the Crossroads*, Jamal R. Nassar and Roger Heacock, eds. (New York: Praeger Publishers, 1990), pp. 207-226.

[27] Hiltermann, *Behind the Intifada*, pp. 126-173; Rita Giacaman & Penny Johnson, "Palestinian Women: Building Barricades and Breaking Barriers," in *Intifada: The Palestinian Uprising against Israeli Occupation*, Zachary Lockman and Joel Beinin, eds. (Boston: South End Press, 1989), pp. 155-169.

al-Zuhur (Rose Garden) school; Hind Tahir al-Husayni (1916—) established numerous schools, including *Dar al-Tifl al-'Arabi* (Arab Child School) and the *Women's College for the Arts*, and participated in founding the *Mustashfa al-Maqasid al-Khayriyyah* (Maqasid Charitable Hospital) in East Jerusalem; Ellen Aql helped found *Dar al-Musinnat* (Nursing Home for Elderly Women), a library for children, and several sewing and textile centers for women in Ramallah; Samah Nusaybeh helped establish *Rabitat al-Fannanin* (Artists Union) in East Jerusalem; Alice Rizq Tarazi participated in founding women's groups in Gaza; and Yusra Shawar played a leading role in creating women's charitable organizations and family planning societies in Hebron and its environs.[28]

Social work and women's groups often operate on the principle of voluntary social action in which individuals and groups work together within a local framework, in many instances free of charge, to promote the welfare of society. They embody a strong element of political pluralism, for the members of these groups are of diverse political persuasions and come from different class origins and religious backgrounds. An expression of this kind of idea can be found in the field of health, where women's groups teamed up with charitable organizations and community volunteers to provide first aid to besieged areas, even setting up day care centers. Other examples include programs to integrate women as full members in the social and economic spheres and diversify the resources available to them.[29]

Thus, these voluntary groups have been instrumental in planting the seeds of an active and engaged citizenship in the West Bank and Gaza. Their work has been supported, and even complemented, by the work of a number of autonomous local bodies such as the Ramallah-based human rights organization, Law in the Service of Man, a West Bank affiliate of the International Commission of Jurists, *al-Hakawati*, or "speakers' forum" in East Jerusalem, as well as newspapers, magazines, and local committees of volunteers who seek to resolve local disputes among Palestinians. In East Jerusalem, for example, the office of Faysal al-Husayni is involved in helping the local Arab population find jobs, solve family problems, and even maintain public order in the face of Israel's lackadaisical performance in this area.

---

[28] The biographical data is taken from 'Izzat Daraghmah, *Al-Harakah al-nisa'iyyah fi filastin, 1903-1990* [The Women's Movement in Palestine, 1903-1990] (Jerusalem: Diya' Center, 1991), pp. 139-175.

[29] Daraghmah, *Al-Harakah*, pp. 74-106; Hiltermann, *Behind the Intifada*, pp. 192-205.

Despite their charitable work and the philosophy behind it, these groups have to cope with four sets of problems: the obstacles and hardships imposed by the Israeli occupation authorities; the prevalence of a small-town, rural culture that encourages religious conservatism and discourages universal participation; the state surrogate, whose constituent groups follow a strategy based on hands-on control; and the political ambitions of what may be called the alternative state surrogate—that is, *Hamas*.

Islamist Groups

Islamist groups offer a social and political vision different from the other groups, while attempting to rival and create parallels for the apparatus of the PLO in the occupied territories. Some wall graffiti of *Hamas* read: "The Qur'an is the sole legitimate representative of the Palestinian people". In 1992, the group founded the Association of Religious Sages in Palestine in Jerusalem. Although *Hamas* claims that the 77 members of this association are senior *waqf* or Supreme Muslim Council clergy, most of them are, in fact, junior clerics in the Muslim Brotherhood or *Hamas* activists.[30]

Islamist groups are not the same thing as *madhahib*, or schools of law, theological schools, or collectivities made up of the followers or devotees of an *'alim* (religious scholar) or inspired teacher and exemplar for his followers. Rather, they are religio-political movements whose aim is to become an institutionalized religion serving as the basis of a state. This applies to *Hamas*, *al-Jihad al-Islami* (Islamic Jihad) and other Islamist groups. To outline the ideological vision of the Islamists and their instruments of action, it is necessary to ask what exactly it is that the Islamists think they are rejecting. In general, Islamist groups in the occupied territories reject not only Israel and the pragmatic policies of the PLO, but the system of ideas and institutions prevalent among the majority of Palestinians and the Arabs in general. These groups maintain that true Islam, as a system of politics and social life, is the only solution to the Palestine problem, as well as for other problems in Arab societies.[31]

---

[30] *Ha'Aretz*, July 6, 1992 in *Foreign Broadcast Information Service*, Daily Report, Near East & South Asia, July 9, 1992.

[31] For details on the history and ideas of these movements see Ziad Abu 'Amr, *Al-Harakah al-islamiyyah fil-diffah al-gharbiyyah wa- qita' ghazzah* [The Islamic Movement in the West Bank and the Gaza Strip] ('Akka: Dar al-Aswar, 1989); Iyyad Barghuthi, *Al-Asl amah wal-siyasah fil-aradi al-filastiniyyah al-muhtallah* [Islamization and Politics in the Occupied Palestinian Territories] (Jerusalem: Al-Zahra' Center, 1990).

With regard to the occupied territories, two examples that provide a brief exposition of the central argument of the Islamists should help illustrate this point. The first concerns the rejection of what one Islamist calls "*namadhij jadidah*" (new models). In a 1990 monograph provocatively titled *Waylun li al-Umara'* [Woe Unto the Princes], Samir Abu 'Asab, a Palestinian from East Jerusalem, provides a general discussion of leadership from an Islamic perspective. With the occupied territories as the explicit subject an d focal point, the author extends the discussion to outline the attributes of the true Islamic leader: "strength and honesty."[32]

A strong leader is conceived of as having not integrity, equanimity, a perceptive mind, and the Qur'an as his inspiring guide, but the *bay'a* of *ahl al-hall wa al-'aqd* (the oath of allegiance given by those who loosen and bind). An honest leader, on the other hand, possesses the qualities of fidelity and uprightness that are consistent with the *shari'ah* and the conduct of the worthy ancestors.[33] According to Abu 'Asab, and many Islamists would agree with him, this is the authentic model of leadership.

The author then argues that many of those who position themselves as local leaders in the occupied territories are not *qada* (leaders), but *zu'ama* (bosses), who rose to positions of prominence with the aid of the "propaganda machine" of Israel and other external powers. A *qa'id* (leader), Abu 'Asab tells us, has a solid popular support base, while a *za'im* (boss) has a support base that tends to evaporate with the *zu'ama* departure from the political scene. There can be no *imara* (authority), and hence no legitimate leadership, we are further told, without freedom, and there can be no freedom in the shadow of occupation. Abu 'Asab suggests that those entitled to lead are either languishing in Israeli jails or fighting in the ranks of the underground Islamic resistance.

Within the framework of these ideas, Abu 'Asab draws sharply critical pictures of three prominent local Palestinians: Faysal al-Husayni, a *Fatah*-affiliated local leader; Sari Nuseibeh, an intellectual with a penchant for provocative political proposals; and Radwan Abu 'Ayyash, a Ramallah-based journalist well-connected to the foreign press. The book offers no extended analysis of the ideas of these three personalities, but denounces that for which they stand in terms of political positions

---

[32] The book, published in Jerusalem in 1990, does not cite the publisher.
[33] Abu 'Asab, *Waylun lil-umara'*, pp. 32-37.

and relations with certain Arab and Western governments. All three are depicted as models of *al-zu'ama al-duma* (puppet bosses), condemned for contacts with Israeli groups; and censured for advocating a compromise settlement and meeting with American officials.[34]

The other example concerns Islamist positions toward a number of social issues: an objection to the dress code of 'westernized' Muslim women; an emphasis on prayer and dignified behavior; attacks on coeducation; incessant calls for the propagation of "moral teachings" in the mass media; and a general emphasis on applying the Islamic tradition to the cultural and social spheres. Behind such positions lies the ideal of the virtuous Muslim life, and the rejection of *taqlid* (blind imitation), which is for Islamists a great danger in the Islam of legal observance.

In the social sphere, the Islamist instruments of action include mosques, schools, charities, clinics, and teaching circles in private homes. Politically, the same instruments of action are used, and to them were added guidance offices, religious committees, and underground cells. In terms of a program of political and social action, what emerges is a vision based on a non-PLO, and in some respects even an anti-PLO ideology of religion intended to give support to the ideology of nationalism. Through such an ideology, the Islamist groups, particularly *Hamas*, seek to exercise and justify control over society. And in terms of organizing, *Hamas* has employed the aforementioned instruments of action to acquire more political space in the occupied territories. The duality of functions that characterizes the political shops of the PLO also characterizes their equivalents in the *Hamas* movement.

It is difficult to say with any accuracy how much popular support the Islamic movement has, because to a great extent the process takes place underground. Until the signing of the Israeli-PLO accord in September 1993, the Islamists seemed to enjoy the support of about 30 to 35 percent of the Palestinians living in the occupied territories. One indication of this was the Bir Zeit University campus elections on 12 November 1992, in which the *Fatah*-dominated PLO list won 67 percent of the vote; *Hamas* 32 percent, and the *al-Jihad al-Islami* 1 percent.[35]

However, the situation has changed since the Oslo agreement. The students' elections held at Bir Zeit University in November 1993 are one important indication of this change. In these elections *Hamas* forged an unprecedented alliance with the Palestinian left to beat *Fatah*. The

---

[34] Abu 'Asad, *Waylun li al-umara*, pp. 46-112.
[35] *The New York Times*, November 14, 1992, p. A2.

victory of the *Hamas*-leftist alliance was both a symptom of Palestinian frustration with the deadlocked Israeli-PLO negotiations and a warning to Arafat and the entrenched PLO bureaucrats in Tunis.

Despite the victory of *Hamas* and the Palestinian left, the balance of forces is not static, and the contest between the secular and Islamist visions of nationalism likely will continue. The clash of political views taking place with respect to the merits and demerits of the Oslo Agreement is a clear expression of the continuation of this contest. Joining the contest is a multiplicity of political forces, secular and non-secular, inside and outside the occupied territories.

The Path of the State Surrogate

The Israeli-PLO agreement has created new challenges for the organs of Palestinian civil society that will test their strength and resilience. To rearrange the power relations among the Palestinians in the West Bank consequent to his entry into Gaza, Arafat will have to interact with the organs of civil society, perhaps opting to strike a balance between security and democracy. Arafat needs such a balance to allow for free political participation, while at the same time neutralizing the destabilizing effect of the opposition.

Israel, for its own reasons, favors security, even at the expense of democracy. From its perspective, security may mean emasculating the Palestinian opposition. On the other hand, Palestinians may not want to give right-wing Jewish settlers the pretext to undermine the implementation of the Oslo Agreement. These settlers are rejectionists through and through, and they will do everything in their power to foil the agreement. Radical elements in the Palestinian community have the same predisposition.

To achieve the balance, therefore, Arafat will have to apply a delicate admixture of persuasion, co-optation, and intermittent political pressure on Palestinian rejectionists in just the right measure. This will require reforming the PLO and organizing its factions into political parties based on more efficient structures of authority, political expression and bargaining. All political forces should be allowed to have full and proportional representation in the Palestine National Council, the Palestine Central Council, and other Palestinian policy-making bodies. This would lay the foundation for a more open Palestinian media and more universal public forms of communication in the occupied territories. It would also allow for a more effective interaction between the Palestinians in the occupied territories and their brethren in the Diaspora. Equally significant, it will provide institutionalized structures through which the radical elements of the opposition may be able to channel their views. This is the road that will facilitate economic prosperity and the emergence of a governable political entity whose members will interact with each other on the basis of civility, trust, and cooperation. It is the road to good government. It is the road that will reinforce Arafat's claim that he is the President of all Palestinians.

These will be Arafat's greatest challenges in his new domain. The PLO Chairman is the keystone of the structure of Palestinian politics, and he must set the stage for the development of a viable political society. But what Arafat should do may differ from what he actually does, not only on account of anti-Arafat opposition and the resistance of entrenched PLO bureaucrats to reform, but also on account of Israel's desiderata, and the personality of Arafat himself.

Classified minutes of meetings between senior Israeli and Palestinian officials reveal a strong Israeli desire to shackle *Hamas* and *Jihad al-Islami* through a proxy, namely the PLO. In this scheme of things, Arafat *the President* (this has been his official title since the PNC declared the establishment of the state of Palestine in November 1988) will become Arafat the *wali* (provincial governor) of Gaza and Jericho.

The president should have his headquarters in Jerusalem; the *wali* cannot. The *wali* has many restrictions on his authority. He can have authority with regard to education, health, social welfare, direct taxation, and tourism, but he cannot have jurisdiction over external security and foreign relations. The president can have an army if he so wished; the *wali* can have only a police force for local security. The president is a sovereign who enjoys the symbols and privileges of power. The *wali* is not a sovereign, but is rather a local governor who must manage the spheres of his authority in coordination with a distant overlord, in this case the government of Israel.

Accepting to be a *wali* rather than a president, at least for the time being, is no easy matter for Arafat. This is the dilemma that he now faces. Arafat, the president of Palestine, has an ego larger than life, and dispensing with his self-image as president is not in the cards. Nor is the idea of acting as president vis-a-vis Israel, if only because the political risks for Arafat would be considerable. Arafat knows that if he were to break out from the framework of his accord with Israel and do things in his own way, Israel would fight with its awesome might. Although Arafat will have to content himself with the role of *wali* vis-a-vis Israel, his behavior toward his constituency in the occupied territories may be different. Here, Arafat will want to be a ruler—a president so to speak—and not just a *wali*. As a ruler, Arafat may choose to reform the institutions of the PLO, or he may act politically in other ways.

On the one hand, he may play the role of a consensus-builder and a coalition-organizer. On the other hand, he may try to seize total power, crushing all forms of opposition, secular and religious in the process. Or, he may assert his dominance by balancing local political groups against each other, extending his support for one group at one time and another group at another time.

In the end, Arafat's choice will be determined by his own personal ambitions, his reading of the situation and of the public mood, and the style of action that the opposition uses. The assassination of prominent Arafat supporters in the occupied territories may be an ominous sign of things to come. Equally significant, Arafat's choice also will be determined by how much pressure the Israeli government will put on him in order to contain or silence Hamas and the rest of the opposition. Whatever his choice, 'Arafat will have important weapons in his hands: vibrant civil society organs; a position of national leadership dating back to the late 1960s; alliances with local political forces; the support of reform-minded Palestinians; and, of course, money and a sizable police force (up to 20,000, or even more, according to some sources). Money will be indispensable for co-optation purposes, and the police force will be necessary to ensure local security in Arafat's domain. Members of the police force are assumed to be Arafat loyalists, and they will be responsible to him.

It remains to be seen whether the Palestinian police force will develop an esprit de corps which a disciplined body of men responsible for security should develop, or whether members of the force will become identified with particular political groups not loyal to Arafat. In theory, this force should be organized and disciplined because it will be mainly drawn from the Palestine Liberation Army, the official armed wing of the PLO, whose members have been sheltered by different Arab governments that gave them training and military discipline. It also remains to be seen whether Arafat will use the force as an organization for public law and order, or as a military body for intimidating or silencing the opposition.

Some Palestinian intellectuals fear that Arafat loyalists will bring their legendary corruption with them to Gaza and Jericho, and continue to pursue their narrow private interests. Should this happen, arbitrary government and cronyism will carry the day. Now more than ever, the Palestinians in the occupied territories will need their associational networks, free press, and vigorous political parties to check whatever authoritarian tendencies the PLO apparatchiks may have.

Likewise, many fear that the PLO bureaucrats may be too inept to make good use of the institutional and administrative skills of Palestinian engineers, doctors, businessmen, educators and other professionals. While one-time commandos may become disciplined cops, it is another thing for them to become creative institution-builders.

Conclusions

By way of conclusion, it may be useful to try to sort out the variety of social formations in the West Bank and Gaza Strip, and to indicate the kinds of questions and answers which emerge from the study as a whole. The issues discussed suggest five questions. What kind of social formations has Palestinian society produced? Do these formations have identifiable boundaries? How much civility have they demonstrated in their interaction with each other? What is the role of Islam in these formations? What role could the formations play if a Palestinian entity or state were to emerge?

First of all, these social formations encompass a wide spectrum, including unions, students bodies, a variety of cooperatives, women's organizations, charitable organizations, social work groups, human rights groups and a host of other voluntary social formations. The nature of these formations can be seen in the context of another question: Were people drawn into these formations by a kind of 'asabiyyah or solidarity oriented solely toward furthering the interest of the formation itself?

On the whole, the answer is negative, and this can be explained as follows. Despite the differences in their political outlooks, all these formations constitute an infrastructure of civil and political institutions that work toward securing the survival of all of Palestinian society in the face of the Israeli government's attempts to stunt the development of that society and atomize it. Equally important, the work of these different formations, whether it is in the area of workers' and students' rights or in the area of providing basic social services to the local Palestinian community, is really a substitution for the occupying power that has chosen not only to neglect, but to disrupt these areas crucial for survival. In this sense, each of these formations represents a distinctive psychological and practical counterweight to the Israeli military regime in the occupied territories. The solidarity of these formations is rooted in an alliance of common interests in the face of an alien power, interests that transcend the local boundaries of the formation or group.

For example, the pooling of the resources of charitable organizations and of women's and medical relief committees to serve the different refugee camps and neighborhoods stand as testament to how these formations look after the interests of all of society. Equally important, they are a shining example of how a small society may deploy its limited resources and produce, almost single-handedly, a rich variety of social organs—despite the awesome power of the Israeli military machine.

Second, do these formations have identifiable boundaries? This question can be answered as follows. The formations discussed are not one solid monolith, but are individual participants or social units whose reality lies in the people who constitute them, and in the activities that emerge from the interaction among those people. We have seen that in the interdependence of the activities of these units and the regulation created by interaction. The cooperatives, for example, were engaged in some trade and commercial exchange with other social units by virtue of marketing their products in Palestinian towns and villages. Similarly, the visible and underground social work of the charitable societies overlapped with the activities of other mass organizations, in that they coordinated their activities in order to offer desperately needed services. Clearly, the boundaries of these units are irregular, the units are special-purpose associations, and each offers whatever specialized services it may have to the larger Palestinian society.

Further, the fact that some of these formations have been co-opted by the state surrogate can be seen in two ways. On the one hand, all politicians seek to expand their power base, regardless of whether they lead a state that exists juridically and politically or whether they lead a liberation movement that has the underpinnings of a state. In the process they may win the support of or draw into their orbit some of the social and political units that exist in their respective societies. This may sound pedantic, but it is relevant to the way in which political forces do the co-opting, and the consequences of that.

The second way the interaction between the state surrogate and civil society may be understood is that the state surrogate has neither consumed civil society nor curtailed its growth. This is true of the cooperatives and the mass organizations, which managed to maintain their own sphere outside the political apparatus of the state surrogate. Equally, political shops were used by the state surrogate partly as instruments in the national struggle, but more importantly as mechanisms for the acquisition of more political space in the occupied territories.

The state surrogate's methods of co-optation are a typical case of patronage politics, but they are also a vivid illustration of the way in which a Diaspora-based political movement was able to mobilize social and political units in the occupied territories, and direct their struggle for political independence and institution-building. This is important in itself, but it must also be seen in the larger context of state-civil society relations. As Michael Walzer has reminded us, civil society requires a political agency to provide the basic rules of associational activity, and the state is an indispensable agent.[36]

By tolerating political pluralism, and making itself accessible to existing social units in the occupied territories, the state surrogate empowered the members of these units. Civil society may exist in the absence of a democratic state, as was the case in Eastern Europe and the former Soviet Union. But it is precisely because the state surrogate has sustained political pluralism that it may be inclined to sustain a pluralistic civil society if and when Palestinian independence is achieved. And it is precisely because Palestinian civil society is pluralistic that it may be able to sustain a state based on pluralism.

Here, then, is the challenge for Palestinian civil society in the occupied territories, and this brings us to our third question, that of civility. As a social virtue, civility is more than just civilized behavior. Civility is above all responsible associational engagement based on the voluntary acceptance of 1) associating and communicating not simply for the sake of a family, or a neighborhood, or a religion, but also for the sake of the common good; and 2) allowing the different political and social formations to inhabit their space uncoerced by fear or repression in order that their members play their dual role of good men and women and good citizens.

Viewed from this perspective, the activities and associational life of the formations discussed in this paper are a clear illustration of civility. The signs of civility manifest themselves not only in tolerance of diversity, but also in the way in which the members of these formations have connected with each other, and reached farther than themselves and their comrades to look after an embattled community. This has fostered and protected the associational networks as well as a sense of camara-

---

[36] Walzer, "The Idea of Civil Society", pp. 301-303.

derie, enabling the formations to sustain their associational life in the face of the overwhelming obstacles of occupation.

However, there are also signs of lack of civility. There is a serious lack of trust between *Fatah* and *Hamas*, and, by extension, between the formations co-opted by these two actors. Another example is patronage politics and the corruption associated with it, and the assassination of Palestinians by Palestinians. These practices may well be a product of their time, in the sense that twenty-five years of occupation have created an atmosphere of despair that made certain Palestinians prone to radicalism and violence. This need not be unique to Palestinian society, however, and would be dangerous to exaggerate because it did not disrupt civil society or check the growth of Palestinian associational life. The threat to this society has been and continues to be the coercive machinery of occupation.

A recent State Department human rights survey of 189 countries notes a 62 percent increase in Israeli killings of Palestinians, despite a decrease in violence in the West Bank and Gaza. It also notes that of the 158 killed by the Israeli security forces in 1992, at least 45 were killed by undercover Israeli commandos disguised as Palestinians, adding that about two-thirds of those killed were unarmed.[37]

When we come to our fourth question, that of the role of Islam in the associational life of the Palestinians in the occupied territories, the question can be recast in three ways. The ideas of religious conservatism among the Palestinians of the West Bank and Gaza are generally deeply rooted, in large part due to the weakening of Palestinian cities and towns caused by political instability, economic decline, and the excessive practices of the Israeli military regime. However, it would be inaccurate to conclude th at the situation will not change. If there were political and economic stability, and if a Palestinian "Law of Return" were allowed to apply to the occupied territories, an atmosphere of confidence may encourage the return of diaspora-based Palestinian intellectuals and professionals, many of whom have secular outlooks. Should this happen, the demographic balance would shift in favor of the cities and towns, giving a boost to the secular and liberal components currently challenged by the forces of religious conservatism.

Another question can be raised in the context of the role of Islam in the creation of the Palestinian national bond. A subtle analysis is necessary to distinguish the religious from other issues. We have seen

---

[37] *The New York Times*, January 20, 1993, p. A8.

how on the scale of the cultural and social spheres, the Islamists have positioned Islam as the embodiment of the virtuous life. How much of a success they had in this regard is difficult to gauge with any accuracy because of the lack of reliable public opinion surveys, partly because of the changing political situation. But at least two examples seem to suggest that the Islamists have seized the initiative in the area of individual and social morality. One is the refusal of Palestinian secular forces to openly challenge the social behavior code promoted by the Islamists, lest they alienate the so-called Palestinian street. The other example is the Islamic political and religious rhetoric that is tolerated, particularly in Gaza and Hebron. On the scale of politics, however, the picture seems to be different. My discussions on this subject last summer in the West Bank and Gaza suggest to me that, at best, the Islamic groups enjoy the support of about 20 percent of the population. On the whole, the significance of this lies in the fact that while Islam has been a central ingredient of the social and cultural life of the Palestinians, it doesn't seem to be the determining factor that provides the impulse to their nationalism. This provides the context for yet another question, namely the relationship between the ideology of religion and the ideology of nationalism. The ideological thrust of Palestinian nationalism has been consistently secular; therefore, in the event the Palestinians are ever granted independence, it may be possible to sustain and promote political pluralism along the lines of a stable balance between the dictates of reason and the dictates of faith.

The final question concerns the role of the social formations in consolidating a Palestinian entity or state. Judging from their associational life and their ability to endure, these diverse formations, when combined, could form what Salim Tamari describes as an infrastructure of political and civic institutions that would support a Palestinian state, whenever this state arrives.[38] Indeed, Palestinian civil society is unique in the sense that its different units do not simply try to help the individual and the rest of society survive in the highly repressive environment of alien military occupation. In addition, they constitute a viable foundation upon which Arafat should build the pillars of a governable Palestinian entity, should he choose the path of reform.

---

[38] Salim Tamari, "What the Uprising Means", *Middle East Report*, no. 52 (May-June 1988), p. 26.

CHAPTER NINE

A CIVIL SOCIETY IN EGYPT?

Mustapha K. Al-Sayyid

During the past three years, intellectual debates over "uses and abuses of civil society" have been echoed in the Arab world.[1] The controversy, which raged in pages of academic journals, was triggered by the wave of democracy that hit the shores of authoritarianism in Southern Europe, South Asia, and Eastern Europe.[2] Some Arab intellectuals believed they also saw signs of the resurgence of civil society in the Arab world. Interest in this development was so strong that the prestigious Center for Arab Unity Studies, an intellectual foundation known for its pan-Arabist tendencies, organized a January 1992 symposium on that topic in Beirut to which almost 100 Arab scholars were invited to assess the extent to which civil society exists in Arab lands.[3] At the same time in Cairo, the Ibn Khaldoun Center for Developmental Studies began publishing a monthly newsletter entitled *Civil Society: Democratic Transformation in the Arab World*.

While Arab intellectuals debated theoretical propositions, a concrete transformation in social processes was taking place in Egypt, Jordan, Kuwait, Lebanon, Mauritania, Morocco, Tunisia, and Yemen (as well as Algeria prior to the military coup in late December 1991)[4] in which many contradictory features were noticeable, particularly in the case of Egypt. On the one hand, divisive social groups were gaining more freedom to express dissenting views in professional associations and in political parties. On the other hand, individuals claiming to act in the name of Islamist organizations were challenging the government effectively, and

---

[1] Ellen Meiksins Wood, "The Uses and Abuses of Civil Society," in Ralph Miliband, ed., *Socialist Register* (Atlantic Highlands, NJ: Humanities Press, 1990), pp. 60-84.

[2] Samuel P. Huntington, "Democracy's Third Wave," *Journal of Democracy* 2, no.2 (1991).

[3] Center for Arab Unity Studies, *Al-Mujtama' al-madani fi al-watan al-'Arabi* [Civil society in the Arab world] (Beirut, 1992).

[4] For an account of democratization experiments in the Arab world, see Louis J. Cantori ed., "Democratization in the Middle East," *American-Arab Affairs* 36 (Spring 1991); Muhammad Muslih and Augustus Richard Norton, "The Need for Arab Democracy," *Foreign Policy* 83 (Summer 1991); Mustapha K. Al-Sayyid "Slow Thaw in the Arab World", *World Policy Journal* 8, no. 4 (Fall 1991).

not only in remote villages in Upper Egypt. In Cairo, Islamists attacks against Copts, foreign tourists and individuals voicing opposition to their mission have reached alarming proportions since the summer of 1992. Victims include Farag Fouda, Egypt's most famous secularist writer, in June 1992; an American and a French law professors during President Husny Mubarak's visit to both the United States and France in October 1993. All were assassinated, besides ministers of information April (1993) and the interior (August 1993), who were wounded, and the prime minister (November 25; 1993) who was unhurt by the attempt on his life.[5] Moreover, many usually-moderate voices of the Islamist movement branded intellectuals critical of their views apostates. The sentence for apostasy, which they believe to be sanctioned by Islamic *sharia'ah*, is death, and the punishment may be inflicted by any Muslim should the government fail to carry out that sentence.

While the state has permitted a degree of autonomy for societal actors, some of them, ironically, have demonstrated intolerance for the exercise of freedom of speech, worship, and action by others. Herein lies the contradiction: If associational autonomy is definitely a measure of the resurgence of a civil society, acts of intolerance cast doubts on its "civil" character. These contradictory tendencies warrant an examination of the extent to which civil society exists in Egypt and the factors likely to affect its evolution.

Operational Criteria for Civil Society

Providing a precise definition of civil society has proven problematic. The concept has been used by many scholars of western political thought, including the natural law school, Hegelian thinkers, and various strands of Marxists. For English philosopher John Locke, civil society was close to what twentieth-century political scientists consider a liberal democracy. Hegel insisted on the crucial position of the "universal class" of enlightened administrators, who, although bound by tradition, do not owe their authority to any type of electorate.[6] Middle Eastern scholars, in contrast, tend to dispute the validity of any definition of civil society inspired by western experiences. Instead, they argue for a

---

[5] *Al-Mussawar*, January 1, 1993, pp. 18, 20-1; Chris Hedges "For Egypt, a New Front in Islamic Crackdown," *International Herald Tribune*, December 10, 1992, p. 2; *Al-Ahram*, April 21, August 19, November 26, 1993, p. 1.

[6] For a discussion of different concepts of civil society, see John Keane, *Civil Society and the State* (London: Verso, 1988).

definition that reflects the specific experiences of Islamic and Arab societies.[7]

Rather than attempt to bridge the gap between different views or to disentangle the concept from the ideological underpinnings of various intellectual schools, this analysis of Egypt seeks a common ground. In addition to the presence of associations catering to the varied interests of citizens in their social activities, civil society also entails state respect for a reasonable measure of societal autonomy, and acceptance of intellectual and political dissension as a legitimate right—so long as it is bound by peaceful methods of individual and collective action.

Under this definition, three minimal conditions are met: the presence of formal organizations of various types among different social groups and classes; and ethic of tolerance and acceptance by the majority of minority legitimate rights, no matter how such minorities are defined; and limitations on arbitrary exercise of state authority. While such criteria are not met entirely in any society; it is inconceivable to find a society in which all three conditions are totally missing. However, these conditions are largely met in liberal democracies.

Formal Private Organizations

Since the early 19th century, increasing social differentiation in Egypt has laid the objective foundation for the formation of a civil society. Modernization efforts initiated by Muhammed ʿAli, particularly the expansion of education, Egypt's integration into the international economy, and the emergence of national bourgeoisie contributed to the development of a working class and a professional middle class.[8] These new classes came to demand the right of association for the professional groups they formed. The first groups to acquire such a right were those formed by the political elite, mostly lawyers and businessmen. While the liberal 1923 constitution provided a legal but shaky framework for political life under the monarchy, the right to establish trade unions was not recognized until the 1940s—three decades after the first Egyptian professional association, the Bar Association, came into being.

---

[7] Brian S. Turner, "Orientalism and the Problem of Civil Society in Islam" in Asaf Hussain, Robert Olson, and Jamil Quereishi, eds., *Orientalism, Islam and Islamicists* (Brattleboro, VT: Amana Books, 1984), pp. 23-42.

[8] See works by ʿAbd al-Basit ʿAbd al-Muʾti and Ibrahim Hasan al-Issawi in the series *Dirasat al-takwin al-ijtimaʿi wa al-tabaqi li Misr: Al-Dirasat al-mahalliyya* [Studies of the social formation and class structure of Egypt: Local studies] (Cairo: National Center for Sociological and Criminological Research, 1988, 1989).

Other groups followed the example of lawyers, doctors, journalists, and engineers in establishing professional organizations to improve their bargaining positions vis-a-vis the state. Authorities encouraged their endeavors because they found such organizations effective instruments for controlling both the middle classes and workers.[9] Thus, the biggest increase in the number and size of membership of voluntary associations took place in the 1950s and 1960s under the tight rule of a military regime that had many features associated with "state-corporatism."[10]

According to the Ministry of Social Affairs, Egypt has a considerable number of associations; there were 12,832 in 1990, and a few hundred more were registered in 1991, for a total of 13,521, or one organization for every 1,824 adult citizen.[11] These are only those associations that come under the supervision of the ministry, all of which are concerned with providing social services, including child and family care, social assistance, care for the elderly, culture, science, literary activities, management and organization, care for prisoners, family planning and community development. According to the 1990 data published by the ministry, 75 percent (9,516) operate only in one field; 25 percent (3,316) operate in two or more fields. Unsurprisingly, Cairo has the largest number of such organizations with 3,266, or 25 percent of the total, followed by Alexandria with 907, or 7 percent of the total. Cairo's share exceeds its demographic weight in the country, reflecting its political centrality in Egypt, although some other governorates, particularly Sharqiyyah and Monoufiyyah have a high number of societies relative to their share of population.[12]

The voluntary associations that do not come under the purview of the Ministry of Social Affairs include 23 trade unions, 26 chambers of commerce, 23 professional associations, and 13 political parties. Although data on membership of these organizations is not available, trade unions, chambers of commerce, and professional associations seem to be

---

[9] Mustapha Kamil Al-Sayyid, *Al-Mujtama' wa al-siyasa fi Misr: Dawr jama'at al-masalih fi al-nizam al-siyasi al-Misri* [Society and politics in Egypt: Role of interest groups in the Egyptian political system] (Cairo: Dar al-Mustaqbal al-'Arabi, 1983).

[10] Robert Bianchi, *Unruly Corporatism: Associational Life in Twentieth-Century Egypt* (New York: Oxford University Press, 1989).

[11] Ministry of Social Affairs, *Al-Mu'ashirat al-ihsa'iyyah fi majalat al-ri'ayah wa al-tanmiyah* [Statistical indicators in fields of social care and development] (Cairo, 1991), pp. 73-80. Information on 1991 was obtained by the author in an interview with ministry officials in Cairo, November 23, 1993.

[12] Ministry of Social Affairs, *Al-Mu'ashirat al-ihsa'iyyah*.

the largest. The trade union federation claimed a membership of 3,363 million in the 1991, while total membership of professional associations is close to 1,5 million.[13]

Although the number of associations expanded considerably in the mid-1970s, when the onset of political and economic liberalization encouraged various social groups to set up their own organizations,[14] the growth seems to have stagnated since the mid-1980s. The largest increase was registered during the period 1976 to 1981, increasing 41%, from 7,593 to 10,731. Since the 1980s, authorities have viewed such expansion as politically risky.

Egypt's voluntary associations may be classified as class-based associations, professional societies, social care and development organizations, traditional institutions, and political parties. The class-based associations are of two types: those that represent businessmen and those that limit membership to workers. The largest representative bodies of this type are undoubtedly chambers of commerce and industry, which are divided into functional and provincial chapters grouped together under a General Federation of Chambers of Commerce in Egypt. This category includes also the Federation of Egyptian Industries, which groups managers of individual firms in both the public and private sectors.

Despite their large memberships, these two older bodies, largely controlled by the government, have lost ground to more energetic business associations that are restricted in membership but are more influential due to their homogeneous character. In recent years, however, they have started to exhibit more autonomy vis-a-vis the state. Both are presently led by influential private businessmen, replacing managers of state-owned enterprises or government officials. Mohammed Farid Khamis, a prominent industrialist and President of the Investors Society

---

[13] Ahmad Faris Abd al-Mun'im, "Jama'at al-masalih wa al-sulta al-siyasiyyah fi Misr: Dirasat ala al-niqabat al-mihaniyyah, al-muhamin, wa al-sahafiyyin wa al-muhandisin fi al-fatrah, 1952-1961" [Interest groups and political authority in Egypt: A study of professional associations of lawyers, journalists, and engineers, 1952-1961] unpublished Ph.D. dissertation, Faculty of Economics, Cairo University, 1984, p. 31; Huwayda A.R. Boutros, "Al-Dawr al-siyasi li al harakahal-ummaliyyah fi Misr, 1952-1982" [Political role of the workers movement in Egypt, 1952-1982] unpublished M.A. dissertation, Faculty of Economics, Cairo University, 1990, p.141. General Federation of Trade unions of Egypt, Al-masicrahe al-tarikhiyya Fi Khamsa wa thalathin 'aman [The historic march in 35 years] (Cairo: GFTUE, 1991).

[14] Center for Political and Strategic Studies, Al-Taqrir al-istratiji al-'Arabi, 1989 [Arab strategic report, 1989] (Cairo: Dar al-Ahram, 1990), pp.458-62; Ministry of Social Affairs, Al-Mu'ashirat al-ihsa'iyyah, p. 254.

of the Tenth of Ramadan industrial town, was appointed to head the Federation of Egyptian Industries; Mahmoud al-ʿArabi, a wealthy entrepreneur with activities in several sectors, is chairman of the Federation of Chambers of Commerce in Egypt. Khamis has been instrumental in mobilizing private business people to put pressures on the government, and al-ʿArabi called publicly in November 1993 for amendment of the constitution to consolidate the expanding role of the private sector and to allow for competitive elections for the presidency.

The newer associations are limited to the largest firms and businessmen with special ties to foreign powers or to a specific industrial town. Many members are former senior officials of the government. These associations include the Society of Egyptian Businessmen in Cairo, the American Chambers of Commerce in Cairo, the Egyptian-American Business Council, the Society of Businessmen of Alexandria, and the investors societies of the three industrial towns of Tenth of Ramadan, Sixth of October, and Sadat City. Organizations for bankers, importers, and exporters exist, but are less active.

Workers are organized into 23 trade unions that belong to the General Federation of Trade Unions of Egypt. Despite its large size, there is no evidence that the federation enjoys much credibility among its rank and file members. Collective protest movements undertaken by workers, sometimes on a massive scale, have not been inspired by the federation's leadership or leaders of such unions, but have been led mostly be dissident trade unionists or workers who had never been officials of trade unions at any level.[15]

Educated members of the middle class usually join one of 23 professional syndicates. The most active are also the oldest, including the Bar Association and the associations of journalists, medical doctors, and engineers, although they are not the largest in terms of membership. The largest two associations are those of teachers and graduates of faculties of commerce. Both are supportive of government policies and rarely undertake independent action, but this docile attitude seems to be disappearing from the teachers syndicate. The differences in how the professional associations relate to the government can be explained by social conditions of members, established traditions in certain syndicates, and the success of radical opposition groups in capturing executive offices.[16]

---

[15] For the details, see Butros, *Al-Dawar al-siyasi*.

[16] Activities of professional associations are well covered in Center for Political and Strategic Studies, *Al-Taqrir al-istratiji al-ʿArabi*, various issues.

A variety of other organizations cater to the different interests of citizens, ranging from benevolent and religious causes to literary and scientific concerns. The most active in this category are university professors clubs, which have become prominent in the country's politics since the early 1980s. Such clubs perform various functions, including those of trade unions and political parties, and serve as forums for debating literary and scientific issues.[17]

Any examination of civil society organizations in Egypt should include neo-traditional institutions, which have continued to be centers of social and political activities, often beyond the control of the government. These mosque and church-based associations use places of worship as centers for social and political activities, a practice in Egypt that dates to the Pharaonic era. In the late 18th century, for example, Cairo's two revolts against Napoleon's armies were launched from al-Azhar. What is unique about the current situation, however, is the use of places of worship by social movements that have modern features, such as their type of education and organization, to recruit and mobilize supporters against other institutions and practices of society. Those who carry out educational, medical, social and political activities in mosques and churches are not traditional clergymen, *shaykhs*, or priests, but young professionals who received their education in the country's Western-type universities and who are alienated for a variety of reasons from the country's social and political system.

Such religion-based institutions have ambivalent relationships with other organizations because their integration in civil society depends very much upon their acceptance of other organizations. Such acceptance, however, does not seem to be a universal rule among these neo-traditional groups, as manifested in their equivocal attitude toward the June 1992 assassination of the secularist writer Farag Fouda by Muslim extremists.

Political parties in Egypt pre-date independence, with the exception of the 23 year period between 1953 and 1976 when legal political activity was confined to a single mass organization. Since the gradual demise of the single party, the number of legally authorized political parties has increased to 13. Apart from five parties—the ruling National Democratic Party, the liberal Neo-*Wafd* Party, the centrist and now Islamist Socialist Labor Party, the leftist Progressive Unionist Patriotic Rally,

---

[17] See comment by M.S. Habib in Center for Arab Unity Studies, *Al-Mujtama' al-madani,* pp. 544-6.

and the newly authorized Arab Democratic Nasirite Party—the other eight parties are not politically significant. The Muslim Brothers and the Communists have not obtained the right to legally establish parties, but they express their views through existing authorized parties.[18] Thus, Communists are present among leaders and activists of the Progressive Unionist Patriotic Rally, and Muslim Brothers have sought electoral alliances first with the Neo-*Wafd* and later with the Socialist Labor Party.

Given the lack of sufficient research on the social background of members of major parties in Egypt, it is difficult to determine which party is most representative of the country at large. Based on the social background of their leaders and party platforms, however, it is possible to draw a rough profile. The National Democratic Party seems to be more of a multi-class party than the others; the Neo-*Wafd* Party seems to receive most of its support from members of the middle and upper middle classes; and the Socialist Labor Party and the Progressive Unionist Patriotic Rally both appeal mainly to the lower and salaried middle class, although they claim to speak for the "workers".

In terms of electoral strength, both the Neo-*Wafd* and the Socialist Labor Party have won hundreds of thousands of votes, reaching nearly 1 million when engaged in an electoral alliance with the Muslim Brotherhood. The electoral strength of the Progressive Unionist Patriotic Rally diminished in the 1980s, falling from some 400,000 to 200,000 votes between 1984 and 1987. The National Democratic Party claims 70% of registered voters, although the low turnout in the 1990 legislative elections and the 1992 local elections suggests that the party has great difficulty in mobilizing supporters in the country at large, particularly in major urban centers.[19]

Spirit of Tolerance

An essential feature of a civil society is a large measure of respect for freedom of conscience and thought, not only by state authorities but more importantly by citizens. In Egypt, various ideologies are present in

---

[18] Leaders of the Muslim Brothers have not even succeeded in getting the Supreme Administrative Court of the Council of State to repeal the 1954 decision by the Revolutionary Command Council dissolving the society. *Al-Ahram*, July 7, 1992, p.7

[19] For an analysis of legislative elections in Egypt, see Center for Political and Strategic Studies, *Intikhabat Majlis al-Sha 'b: Dirasah wa tahlil* [People's Assembly election: Study and analysis] (Cairo, 1986, 1988, 1992).

public debate. Islamist, Nasirite, Marxist, and liberal viewpoints are all reflected in newspaper articles, books, movies, and plays. However, limits on public expression do exist. Any scholarly or literary work that a religious authority deems offensive to religion, particularly Islam, is prohibited. The case of Naguib Mahfouz's *Sons of Gabalawi* is well-known. Books by Tariq al-Bishri, Louis Awad, and Sa'id 'Ashmawi have been censored by al-Azhar, and sometimes even by petty officials of the Islamic Research College. Censorship measures have been supported publicly by some writers who claimed to be advocates of an Islamic solution to all the country's problems.[20]

Lack of tolerance has also been demonstrated by groups of young Islamist militants who disrupt gatherings organized by their fellow students, assault their book fairs, and even attack weddings, believing that these activities are contrary to the true teachings of Islam. Extremists Islamists have carried this fight even further through assassinations and threats of assassination against outspoken secularists. More alarming has been the position taken by some reportedly-moderate religious dignitaries. Although leaders of the Muslim Brotherhood did condemn the assassination of Farag Fouda, they seemed to justify the assassins' actions by claiming that Fouda provoked them by attacking Muslim beliefs. The highly-respected Shaykh Mohammed El-Ghazali, who is close to the Brotherhood, testified during the trial of Fouda's accused assassins that a Muslim who abandoned his religion is punishable by death. The defendants' lawyer, who accepted that Fouda was an apostate, asked Ghazali who should carry out the death sentence in such instances. He replied that it was the duty of the Muslim government to carry out the sentence, but could be carried out by an individual Muslim if the government failed to act.

Ghazali added that no penalty existed in Islam for an individual who acted on such a basis. The statement gave rise to a wide debate in the country. Although some religious dignitaries of the official establishment disagreed with Ghazali's interpretation, most prominent figures of the Islamist movement remained silent, implicitly condoning the statement.[21]

On another occasion, an academic promotion committee at Cairo University, comprised of a majority of conservative Arabic language

---

[20] A list of censored books and movies was published in Helmy Salem. " Hona Mahakam al-Taftish. Hona Quabdat al-Azhar" [Inqustion Tribunals and Al-Azhar's tight Hold in Egypt], *Naqd wa Adab* (Cairo, February 1992), pp. 9-29.

[21] Read Shaykh Ghazali's statement in *Al-Sha'b*. June 23, 1993, and in Al-Ahram. July 18, 20-25, 1993. p. 9.

Cairo, May 17, 1994, Egypte—Egyptian lawyers run for cover into their office building after police fired tear gas at them in Cairo Tuesday May 17, 1994. The lawyers were protesting the death of a colleague in government custody. Ten lawyers were arrested in the clashes over the death of attorney Abdel-Harith Madani, taken from his office April 26, 1994 by government security agents. His family was notified May 6 of his death. (AP Photo/Norbert Schiller, CREDIT: AP by NORBERT SCHILLER)

professors, blocked promotion to full professorship of Dr. Nasr Abu Zeid, an associate professor of Arabic literature known for his critical analysis of Islamist discourse. One of the members of the committee described Abu Zeid as a person of confused belief (Khalal fi al-i'tiqad) who opposes the Qur'an and calls on Muslims to abandon both their holy book and traditions of their prophet. His report to the promotion committee amounted in fact to a trial of the personal convictions of Abu Zeid, rather than an examination of his scientific work. The promotion committee endorsed the view of this professor, Dr. Abdel Sabour Shahin, against recommendations of the two other readers, thus rejecting promotion of Abu Zeid to full professor. Its decision was ratified later by the Council of Cairo University made up of deans of all its faculties. All these reports were published in the daily *Al-Ahram* and in some literary reviews and were commented on by intellectuals of opposed ideological camps in a heated debate throughout the summer of 1993. Some viewed the matter to be a serious assault on freedom of conscience and thought in the country's most respectable university, while others found it a merely an academic dispute to be settled through academic channels.[22]

However, the episode took disturbing proportions when a lawyer claiming to be a zealot of the Islamic cause filed a suit at a personal status and family court, asking the court to order a divorce between Abu Zeid and his wife. In the plaintiff's view, Abu Zeid had demonstrated his apostasy in his scientific work, and was thus disqualified to marry a Muslim woman. While many did not believe such a case to be admissible by any court, a court in Giza opened hearings on the case in November 1993. The agitation surrounding the trial did not enable the court to proceed immediately to the hearing. When the case first came before the court, the lawyer who filed the suit was accompanied by dozens of his supporters, including some prominent *shaykhs*, who made such noise that the court postponed its consideration of the case. Two weeks later, when the court tried to hear the case on November 25, a counter-mobilization of Abu Zeid's supporters disrupted the court again, and the case was again rescheduled. The court ruled in February 1994 to reject the case as inadmissible but the plaintiff appealed this sentence before a higher court, which will not start its proceedings until late summer of 1994. While neither the Muslim Brotherhood nor any of the radical Islamist groups were involved in that trial, many intellectuals in the country found in the Abu Zeid affair a grave reminder of the limits to

---

[22] Documents related to Abu Zeid's case were published in *Al-Qahira*; *Megallat al-Fikr wa al-Fann al-Mu'asir*, April 1993.

tolerance and freedom of thought, conscience and belief in present-day Egypt. Their concern stemmed particularly from the fact that Abu Zeid continued to declare himself a Muslim who limited his scientific work to the analysis of the discourse of some Muslims, not to the Muslim sacred texts, i.e., the Qur'an and the prophets traditions.[23]

Limits on State Powers

Although the Egyptian state does not possess absolute power vis-a-vis its citizens, the real limits to what it can do are based on the perceptions of officials and the political culture of the country, rather than on constitutional or legal restrictions. The permanent constitution of 1971, like similar constitutions of authoritarian regimes, provides for the respect of a long list of civil and political rights, prohibits torture, and stipulates rules for the exercise of state power in different domains. At the same time, it leaves many details to be decided by laws and regulations, and can be interpreted by state authorities in ways that violate the fundamental rights of citizens.

Successive governments in Egypt, particularly that of Anwar al-Sadat, introduced a vast array of laws with myriad restrictions on citizens' exercise of their rights. Not content with such restrictive laws, the government of Mubarak has called for and obtained from a docile People's Assembly renewal of emergency powers initially granted in 1981. Under these powers, the government can take any measures "required by the circumstances," including the suspension of the constitutional rights of citizens. State authorities have, however, accepted certain self-imposed limitations that have expanded the scope of autonomy of civil society organizations in the country, namely respect for the freedom of expression, as its exercise does not entail calls for armed struggle against the government, and enforcement of court rulings, even when such rulings are contrary to preferences of the executive authority. Civil society organizations have not failed to appreciate the opportunities that such self-imposed limitations on the part of the state have opened for the further expansion of their margin of freedom.

It is important to note, however, that state authorities did not accept self-imposed restrictions because they had suddenly become new converts to the cause of democracy. Rather, they found during the 1981

---

[23] On the divorce case, Helmy al-Namnam, "Quadiyyat Talaq Raghm Anf al-Zawjayn" [Divorce case against wishes of the married couple], *Al-Mussawar*. November 19, 1993, no. 3606, pp. 58-61.

"autumn of fury" that the cost of repressing all political and social forces in the country was not only too high, but counterproductive. Sadat was assassinated among "his soldiers" after having ordered the arrest of 1,500 citizens of all political persuasions. Mubarak, his successor and then the vice-president of the republic, was standing next to Sadat when the assassins' bullets put an end to his life. Such a lesson is not easily forgotten.

However, a return to the single mass organization of the 1950s was not practical in 1981 because that formula had been discredited in the eyes of the public and ruling groups since the military defeat of June 1967. The ruling elite appreciated the diplomatic and economic benefits that the regime could achieve through the maintenance of a liberal facade, believing this would induce Western governments and investors to be more sympathetic toward the country. In addition, a liberal political formula offered the additional advantage of isolating the more radical opposition groups intent on continuing the armed struggle against the government because most other opposition groups had aspired to this formula during the last years of Sadat's rule. Thus, Mubarak must have thought that a little dose of political liberalization would not seriously threaten the stability of his government, but rather would ease tensions caused by his predecessor's harsh methods of dealing with the opposition.

An example of a self-imposed limitation was the willingness of Mubarak's government to respect decisions of the judiciary as much as possible. Such willingness, more marked in the early years of Mubarak's rule than during the last years of his second term in office from 1987-1993, opened the way for Egypt's liberal-minded justices to reshape several components of the authoritarian system inherited from Sadat. Consequently, the veto with which the Committee of Political Parties opposed the establishment of the new parties was countered through court decisions, and the number of parties in Egypt increased from four in 1981 to thirteen at present. The deplorable electoral law of the national assembly was amended twice in 1987 and 1990 in anticipation of negative court rulings as to its constitutionality. The national assembly was dissolved on the two occasions before it completed its constitutional term of five years in order to save Mubarak's regime a show-down with the country's prestigious judges. In many other instances, Egyptian justices have equally demonstrated that they became the most effective agent of political change. However, it was Mubarak's regime which had enabled them initially to play such a role, thanks to several laws introduced during Mubarak's first presidential terms which increased their autonomy vis-à-vis the executive authority.[24]

The State and Civil Society

Faithful to its more than five millennia tradition of centralized power, the Egyptian state has been reluctant to permit uncontrolled associational life. Mubarak's government decided to maintain the controls, mostly codified in law, which he had inherited from his predecessors. In dealing with associational activities, the state justified its actions by referring to two important pieces of legislation, namely Law 32 of 1964 on citizens' societies and Law 40 of 1977 on political parties.[25]

The first law requires any society to register with the Ministry of Social Affairs. An important condition for such registration is a commitment by the proposed society not to engage in political activities. The term "political activity" has been interpreted quite loosely, however, and the ministry has denied registration to certain associations, most notably the Arab Organization for Human Rights and its Egyptian chapter, although the first had been given observer status in the UN Economic and Social Council. The ministry also took advantage of the law to intimidate other societies by threatening to suspend their activities if they continued certain actions or if their elected leaders were not approved by security agencies. The ministry even replaced the elected councils of some societies that it suspected of being arenas for activities of Islamist militants as was the case of the Society of Cooperation of the Followers of the Qur'an and the Muhammadan Tradition, as well as another Islamic society in Alexandria in the summer of 1994.[26] Successive electoral victories since the late 1980s by Islamists in professional associations have prompted some leaders of the National Democratic Party to adopt a law that would enable the government to appoint executive councils of professional associations if less than 33 percent of their members participated in elections.[27]

---

[24] CPSS, Al-Taqrir, 1992, pp. 229-307.

[25] For the law on citizens' societies, see Amir Salim al-Muhami, Difa'an an haqq takwin al-jam'iyyat [Defending the right of association] (Cairo, 1992). For the law on political parties Al-Hay'a al'amma li She'oun al-Matabe' al Amiriyyah. Dostour Jomhoriyyat Misr al-'Arabiyyah [Constitution of the Republic of Egypt] (Cairo: HASMA, 1991), pp. 105-122.

[26] Center for Political and Strategic Studies, Al-Taqrir al-istratiji al-'Arabi, 1990 [Arab strategic report, 1990] (Cairo: Dar al-Ahram, 1991), pp. 451-3

[27] Ibrahim Nafi' "Mantiq khati' wa ittijah marfud" [A mistaken logic and an unacceptable attitude], al-Ahram, December 24, 1992, pp. 1,3. Also, Al-Ahram and Al-Wafd, February 17, 1993.

The law on political parties stipulates the many conditions for the establishment of a legally recognized political party. For example, the law bans any party with a religious or confessional platform that appeals to a particular social class or propagates an atheist ideology. It prohibits the formation of any party opposed to the principles of the so-called Corrective Revolution, the term Sadat used to describe his arrest of Nasirite leaders of the former Arab Socialist Union. In addition, it requires approval of a proposed party by a special committee dominated by government representatives. Citizens have the right to appeal decisions of the committee before the Supreme Constitutional Court, and nine parties already won this judicial battle when their disputes with the committee were taken to the court. If the government is intent on preventing the formation of certain parties, however, the judicial battle could continue indefinitely.[28]

Other laws enable the government to arbitrarily curtail the autonomy of specific associations. Recent amendments of the penal code, justified by the government as being indispensable in the fight against terrorism, further strengthen its repressive capacity vis-a-vis associations.[29] In addition, the law on political parties has been amended to ban any activity by people applying for authorization of a new party before approval is granted and to require existing parties to inform the Committee of Political Parties, dominated by the National Democratic Party, of any contacts or joint activities with foreign political parties.[30] Armed with such laws, the government can disqualify people from running as candidates for elected posts in parties or even in general elections. Names of candidates should be approved by the so-called Public Socialist Prosecutor, although this official has not shown much zeal in the exercise of this specific power[31] and the Committe of National Dialogue, which met early in the summer of 1994, recommended stripping the Public Socialist Prosecutor of this power.

Government authorities may limit activities of professional associations, trade unions, and political parties, such as public meetings, for which prior authorization must be obtained.[32] They may also suspend or ban publications of certain societies, a measure taken by Sadat against

---

[28] CPSS, several issues.

[29] See al-Muhami, *Difa'an an haqq,* pp. 105-22.

[30] *Al-Ahram,* July 16, 1992, p. 5

[31] *Al-Ahali,* December 23, 1992, p. 5.

[32] Rahma Rif'at, "Al-Intihakat al-qanuniyyah wa al-idariyyah fi intikhabat 1991" (Legal and administrative violations in the 1991 elections) in *Nadwat al-haraka al-ummaliyya al-Misriyyah fi al-intikhabat al-niqabiyyah am* 1991 [Seminar on the Egyptian workers movement in trade union elections of 1991] (Cairo: Arab Research Center, December 1992).

several opposition parties' newspapers and by Mubarak against *Sawt al-Arab*, the Nasirite weekly, for a critique of the Saudi Arabian government.[33] Moreover, the Public Prosecutor has resorted recently to ban publication of any views or comments on certain issues, most of which relate to cases of corruption among senior government officials.[34] The weight of government intervention is felt most heavily by the trade unions. The law establishing the central organization of trade unions allows the Ministry of Manpower to intervene in their activities, although the International Labor Organization has exerted pressure on the government to draft a new trade union law that conforms to international labor standards, which is being debated in the country at present. Nevertheless, a powerful president of the General Federation of Trade Unions of Egypt, described as "out of line" with respect to the government's open-door economic policy, was removed a few years ago at the instigation of the Minister of Manpower and Training and replaced by the secretary of trade union affairs within the National Democratic Party. The former Minister of Manpower had done his best to dislodge another president of the federation who had allegedly reached the age of retirement, despite a legal opinion opposed to such interpretation of the law on trade unions. The matter was settled only when the minister quit his post in a cabinet reshuffle in October 1993.[35]

However, there is no doubt that Mubarak and his advisers were willing to allow political parties, professional associations, as well as citizens societies a considerable measure of autonomy in running their own affairs and in expressing their members' views on issues ranging from professional concerns to major problems of domestic and foreign policies. In fact, the first decade of Mubarak's regime, spanning his first term in office (1981-1987) plus most of his second term, was marked by this willingness to accommodate opposition groups within a legal framework of political action.

This accommodating approach has been gradually reversed since the summer of 1992. The first sign of reversal was the acceptance by the People's Council of several legislative amendments proposed by the government on various laws, including in particular the penal code and the law of political parties. Amendments of the penal code aimed at stiffening sentences on activities judged by the authorities to constitute

---

[33] Arab Organization for Human Rights, *Huquq al-insan fi al-watan al-'Arabi* [Human rights in the Arab world] (Cairo, 1989), pp. 146-7.

[34] *Al-'Arabi*, Cairo, December 27, 1993. p. 3.

[35] Amin Taha Morsi "Al-inqelab al-akhir fi ittehad al ummal" [The last coup in the workers' federation] *Rose el-Youssef* no. 3410, October 18, 1993, Cairo, pp. 62-63.

encouragement of terrorism, and to allow security forces a freer hand in pursuing people suspected of involvement in such activities. Other amendments further curtailed freedom of political parties in formation and required existing political parties to report to the Committee of Political Parties in advance of any contacts they plan to have with foreign political parties and associations. These early signs of reversal of the accommodative approach coincided with an upsurge in armed opposition actions attributed to people claiming to act in the name of radical Islamist organizations, which led to the murder of tens of people including Copts, foreign tourists, security officials as well as ordinary citizens.

Such legislative amendments in the summer of 1992 did not affect much organizations of the incipient civil society. Those involved in terrorist actions were not known to be active in any so-called civil society organizations. They could be aptly described as marginal groups in every sense of the term. Other measures taken by the government in the last year of Mubarak's second term, as well as immediately after the referendum of October 4, 1993 extended his presidency to a third term, have fallen squarely on different categories of civil society organizations, political parties, professional associations and citizens societies alike.

Alarmed by the success of the Islamist movement in capturing majority of seats in the national council of the Bar Association in September 1992, the government moved cautiously to limit the chances of a repeat victory in other professional associations. Because the Bar Association was considered a stronghold of the liberal and leftist currents in the country's politics, their combined defeat, due partly to infighting, was a clear indications that the Islamists would not be confined to professional associations of the so-called technocratic intelligentsia such as engineers, medical doctors and pharmacists syndicates, and that all other associations of the educated middle class would be targeted in their war of positions against the government. News transpired that the government was preparing a law to make it more difficult for any opposition group to dominate any professional association.

Using blitzkrieg tactics, in February 1993 the government pushed the People's Council to adopt a law on the election of the professional syndicates in less than 48 hours, despite the manifest opposition of 17 of the country's 23 professional associations. Government advisers had reasoned that the Islamists constituted a majority only among the minority of activists in professional associations, and that if the inactive majority in the syndicates were encouraged to participate, a more diversified leadership would emerge. The new law, called the law on Guarantees of Democracy in Elections of Professional Syndicates, required a quorum of half of the registered members of any association in the election of its leading organs. If such a condition was not met the first time the election is organized, another round of elections would take place two weeks later with the quorum reduced to one third of members. If that condition was not fulfilled, the syndicate would be run by an appointed council made up of oldest members of the syndicate and presided over by a judge. Syndicate members who do not take part in elections would have to pay a fine. Voting arrangements should be provided in work sites of the members. One anomaly of this law was its ban of elections on weekends or on official holidays.

Despite vehement opposition of most syndicates that the law stripped them of their right to decide about their internal regulations, subjecting them to uniform standards which do not take into consideration the varied character of their membership, small and concentrated in some syndicates, like those of journalists or musicians, while being large and dispersed in others like those of graduates of faculties of commerce or the lawyers,[36] the law was enacted and several rounds of elections took place already on the basis of this law in some syndicates in December 1993. In most cases, the quorum was met the first time not only in syndicates with limited membership, such as the journalists and social workers, but in many provincial chapters of the lawyers syndicate. Taking advantage of a dispute about the accuracy of voter lists, judicial authorities ordered postponement of elections in the Cairo and Giza chapters of the Bar Association and in all provincial chapters of the Engineers Syndicate. The postponement led to a major confrontation between the government and the E.S. with the engineers declaring a sit - in strike in the national headquarters of their syndicate, and the government complaining to the Public Prosecutor about actions of leaders of the syndicate. The charges addressed against them are unclear.[37] Having realized that the Islamists are capable of winning majorities in syndicate elections under the new law, government representatives invoked several pretexts to postpone election in the syndicates dominated by Islamicists, particularly the Cairo chapters of both laywers

---

[36] See 27 Supra.

[37] On elections of provincial chapters of professional syndicates see al-Sha'b, 21, 28,31 December 1993, Al-'Arabi 13, 20 December 1993, Al-Ahali, 15, 22, 29 December 1993, Al-Wafd, December 1993.

and engineers' syndicate. Although it is too early to judge the impact of the law on distribution of power in the syndicates, it is reasonable to assume the law will probably have little effect on those associations of the technocratic intelligentsia, i.e., scientists, engineers and medical doctors, where the Islamists do not face any serious challenge from other political forces, but it would require, on the other hand, much bigger mobilization on their part in order to maintain their control of other syndicates in which secular political forces used to have a larger following, as was typically the case in the Bar Association, where they might have suffered some losses in recent elections in its provincial chapters.

President Mubarak does not seem to be satisfied that the new law will ensure the dislodging of the Islamists or any opposition groups from their influential positions in organizations of the educated middle class. He has expressed his displeasure with the way some journalists exercise their freedom of speech. In November 1993, the president of the Journalists' Syndicate, a mouth piece of the regime, pushed members to approve a draft law that would have threatened their job security. The attempt was aborted, primarily due to strong opposition by the journalists, who organized public meetings to denounce the measure. On several other occasions, the Minister of Education has warned university professors against involvement in politics, arguing that political parties, not faculty clubs, were the proper place for discussion of political issues. He was referring to debates of public issues by university professors in their clubs. *Al-Sha'b* newspaper, an organ of the Islamist Socialist Labour Party, reported that the Minister proposed changing the universities law to make it legally possible to transfer university professor to administrative posts. In fact, the Universities Law was amended by the People's Assembly on May 30, 1944 to deprive university professors of their right to elect deans of faculties who would be henceforth appointed by rectors of universities, appointed also by the President on recommendation of the Minister of Education.[38]

Mubarak's government has not shown any inhibitions in using "dirty tricks" to confront oppositional voices. Dr. Helmy Murad, the Deputy-Leader of the Socialist Labour Party, together with 'Adel Hussein its Secretary General, were arrested and held briefly following the referendum on a third term for Mubarak on October 4, 1993. Both were interrogated

---

[38] Al-Sha'b, December 2, 1993 p. 1, *Al-Ahram*, 31 May 1994, p.1.

by the public prosecutor, who questioned some of the ideas expressed in their writings that he found to be offensive to President of the Republic and to Egypt's relations with friendly countries. Mubarak was particularly angry over a book they published just before the referendum, in which they explained why people should oppose renewal of Mubarak's presidential term. When the President was unsatisfied with simply censoring the book, the two authors, together with the editor in chief of their party's newspaper and some fellow journalists, were questioned by the public prosecutor for having dared to make their views on such matters known to their readers. During the same period, the President of the Faculty Club of Assiut University and student leaders at several universities—all of whom are activists of the Islamist movement—were briefly arrested following open disagreements with university authorities over faculty and students' problems.[39]

In dealing with the state, civil society organizations have striven to use the political resources at their disposal. Solidarity among such organizations is viewed as the best way to mobilize common resources to expand their autonomy. Very few organizations, however, are willing to engage in confrontations with the state over the question of their autonomy or any other matter. Their leaders view maintaining good relations with the government as the best way to ensure receiving government favors in terms of appointments in legislative or advisory bodies, obtaining facilities and benefits for their members, or simply escaping the wrath of officials, particularly security forces. Thus, solidarity actions have been few and of a temporary nature, such as the formation by major opposition parties and some professional associations of the Committee for the Defense of Democracy to guarantee fairness in the 1984 legislative elections, or joint action by opposition parties in calling for the dissolution of the People's Assembly after the judiciary ruled it unconstitutional in 1990.

The usual practice of civil society organizations is to use their political resources to obtain concessions from the government or to effect societal change in ways consistent with their vision of an ideal social order. Two types of organizations seem to be particularly skillful in using these resources—business and Islamist groups. Business associations use their strategic contacts, knowledge, money, access to the media, and support of foreign powers and international financial insti-

---

[39] *Al-Ahram*, October 10, 1993, *Al-Sha'b*. September 28, October 1, November 12, December 29, 1993.

tutions on which the country is financially, technologically, economically, militarily, and politically dependent in order to pressure the government into accelerating a liberal program of economic restructuring and to consult with them during the decision-making process. Frequent meetings at the highest levels of government between senior government officials and top businessmen, individually as well as in their associational capacities, demonstrate the success of these organizations in attaining some of their goals. Prominent businessmen are often invited to participate in debates about economic policy with senior cabinet members and in the presence of the President. They also have been consulted about major pieces of legislation concerning economic reform.

The Islamist movement has succeeded in using its resources to gain a large space within civil society. Thus, the movement utilizes its members' knowledge and organizational skills, financial resources, and access to mosques, newspapers, publishing houses, professional associations, and political parties, to mobilize opposition to governmental policies or the state. The movement hopes to transform the social order following its gradual takeover of society's institutions. Because of its skills, as well as a history of disappointing performances on the part of its rivals, the Islamist movement in Egypt is the most representative and the powerful actor in a civil society with contradicting features. Islamist militants have succeeded in winning a majority of seats in the professional associations of engineers, medical doctors, pharmacists, scientists, and lawyers. They also run university professors' clubs in Cairo, and Assiut universities and control student governments in most universities whenever students are allowed the opportunity to participate in fair elections.

The strong presence of the Islamist movement—particularly its mainstream organization, the Muslim Brotherhood—in professional associations, publishing, and private business has led several political parties to seek alliance with it. The electoral alliance with the *Wafd* Party in 1984 was short-lived because the *Wafd* was too strong to be taken over by the Muslim Brothers. The relatively weaker position of the Socialist Labor Party and the Liberal Socialist party, however, has contributed to the durability of the agreement they reached with the Muslim Brothers. The Labor-Islamic Alliance made a strong showing in the 1987 legislative elections as well as in local elections in November 1992.

Conclusion

In Egypt, only one of the three criteria for a vibrant, autonomous civil society—the presence of a large number of active formal associations catering to citizens' interests in many areas—is adequately met. Notwithstanding a relatively large measure of freedom of expression, both the state and societal actors routinely penalize dissenters from what are considered correct political positions. Moreover, state authorities have been narrowing the area of autonomy granted to political parties and professional associations in the 1980s.

The first criterion has been met because it reflects a process of social differentiation in society, as well as the myriad interests of citizens, ranging from material preoccupations to social concerns to intellectual pursuits. There is little indication that the Egyptian state, however authoritarian it may become, would ever deny its citizens the right to organize in these fields. Some organizations, especially those active in social welfare, assist the state in attaining its goals. Others do not necessarily constitute a threat to stability because they operate in areas such as sports and friendship that are marginal to any contest for political power. However, the two other criteria for civil society are more problematic.

Some Middle East specialists state that intolerance toward dissenting minorities and the authoritarian state are permanent features of Islamic culture. The mass following of the Islamist movement in Egypt among middle class professionals and university students casts doubts, according to many observers, on whether such attitudes could fade in the future. The record of ruling groups who claim to be defending an Islamic ideal in such societies as Afghanistan, Iran, and Sudan and some of the statements made by spokesmen of the Islamic Salvation Front in Algeria confirm their belief in the incompatibility between Islam and the image of a civil society along the criteria proposed in this study.[40] However, a closer look at the broader setting of the emergence of an embryonic civil society in Egypt suggests another scenario, which, while not ignoring the importance of culture, leaves open the question of the political behavior of people belonging to any specific culture.

According to this interpretation, groups of citizens hold different perceptions of their culture and thus engage in a variety of modes of

[40] See Elie Kedourie, *Democracy and Arab Political Culture* (Washington, DC: Washington Institute for Near Policy).

collective behavior. As such, the presence of one culture in Egypt influenced by Islam would give rise to different attitudes toward dissension as well as authoritarianism. Although secularist positions in Egypt are articulated by only a tiny minority of intellectuals, individuals willing to use force to suppress opposition to an Islamist political order come specific social backgrounds. The assassins of Farag Fouda were frustrated young Egyptians who had not completed their university education and held jobs not requiring any particular skills.[41] Attacks on Copts and foreign tourists, as well as armed clashes with the police, take place primarily in poor districts of Upper Egypt or in squatter settlements located within the "poverty belt" surrounding Cairo. Egyptian newspapers have widely reported the near total lack of public services and the precarious existence led by people in those districts in Assiut and Fayyum governorates and in the Imbaba, 'Ayn Shams and Zawya al-Hamrah quarters of Cairo.[42] Many Islamists do not condone the use of force to settle differences with secularist groups. Ma'mum al-Hudaybi, leader of the Muslim Brotherhood, and several figures among the so-called Independent Islamists have condemned the use of violence, although not always unequivocally. Supporters of nonviolence in the Islamist movement are to be found mostly among professional groups of the middle class and wealthy entrepreneurs.[43]

As for the authoritarianism of state officials, it may stem from a centuries-old traditions of autocratic rule. It also could reflect the realization of state officials that they are incapable of dealing effectively in the short run with the economic and social causes of discontent among the young people of the middle and poor classes. In terms of economic growth, the 1980s could be described as a lost decade for Egypt. Not only did the rate of economic growth drop from 7.4 percent to 5 percent annually, with the per capita rate almost stagnating, but the decade also ended with the significant fall of Egypt from the World Bank's group of lower middle income countries to its group of lower income countries. World Bank statistics also indicated a rise in the inflation rate during the same period, as well as a drop of 10 percent in the real income of industrial workers, their value share of the value added declining from

---

[41] On the social background of the assassins of Fouda, see *al-Ahram*, January 5, 1993, p. 1.

[42] For an account of living conditions in such areas, see *al-Ahram*, December 8, 1992, p. 3.

[43] Several intellectuals expressing various ideologies presented their views on the question of political violence in *al-Ahram*, p.8, throughout the summer 1992.

54 percent in 1970 to 35 percent in 1989. The UNDP *Human Develop-ment Report* put the number of people below the poverty line at 23% of the total population for the 1980's. The economic reform measures that accelerated in the wake of Egypt's agreement with the International Monetary Fund in April 1991 have caused recession, reducing the growth rate to 2.5 recent in 1992, according to official estimates.[44] Under these conditions, the government is concerned that a further democrati-zation would strengthen political opposition, particularly among Islam-ist groups. The tightening of the penal code, the law on political parties, and the law of professional associations indicate a shift by the govern-ment toward harsher methods of dealing with political opposition in general and Islamist groups in particular.

The other method used by the government in its competition with Islamist groups to win the hearts and minds of Egyptian citizens is to outbid them in the claim of conformity to religious, particularly Islamic, values. The Egyptian public has become accustomed to hearing the prime minister read a letter from the Shaykh al-Azhar or other religious dignitaries that states a particular piece of legislation is consistent with Islamic teachings. Prominent religious figures, whose discourse differs very little from that of the Islamist movement, are offered prime time on the government-controlled electronic media to present an official ver-sion of Islamic teachings to the public. The impact of mobilizing the *'ulama* on the government's side does not seem to enhance the govern-ment's legitimacy, but contributes to the credibility of the Islamist discourse.

Several intellectuals advised the government to dispense with such opportunistic use of religion, allowing instead ideological diversity to be reflected in the electronic media. They advocated permitting secularists, more enlightened spokesmen of the Islamist movement, and Coptic figures to address public opinion through the media. The government, however, has responded to this advice partly by allowing some of those intellectuals to address the public through television while maintaining the same dose of religious programs on the electronic media. It adopted some plans to improve access to poor neighborhoods and to deliver public services to their inhabitants.

---

[44] For the economic performance of Egypt in the 1980s, see The World Bank, *World Development Report, 1992: Development and the Environment* (New York: Oxford Univer-sity Press, 1992), pp. 218, 220, 230; United Nations Development Programme, *Human Development Report*, 1992 (New.York: O.U.P.) 1992, pp. 158-159.

The National Democratic Party government realizes that economic reform is imposing sacrifices on the Egyptian people in the short run and that a further democratization of the political system under current conditions would only favor all segments of the opposition, particularly the Islamist movement. It prefers, therefore, to follow a more cautious approach toward the opposition, mobilizing official Islamic institutions to deprive Islamist groups of the claim that they alone are concerned about respect for Islamic values while enhancing its "political control" capacities through various legislative amendments. The cautious approach does not seem to constitute a sufficient deterrence to the acts of armed opposition to the government that have escalated since the summer of 1992, despite execution of 30 Islamist militants and torture of hundreds in Egyptian prisons although acts of armed opposition have recently subsided dramatically following well-organized assults by security forces on hide-out places of radical Islamists and arrest of murder of their leaders.[45] As for an alternative economic policy of "growth with redistribution," neither foreign aid donors with their financial institutions nor influential domestic actors are expected to lend any support to such a policy. All these foreign and domestic constraints have the government wishfully thinking that the implementation of economic reform measures will somehow enable it to get out of its economic predicament, and that economic progress will gradually ease the social tensions that have allowed the Islamist movement to find a large following among the youth of middle and lower middle class origins.

Until the ruling groups in Egypt together with their supporters in the United States and international financial institutions realize that economic liberalism does not offer a magic formula for dealing with diverse economic and social problems of all countries of the South, government-imposed limitations on civil society will increase, and the bloody confrontation between security forces and young impoverished Egyptians who believe that they are fighting for an Islamic cause could flare up again. Under such conditions, the only prospect that one can envisage for Egypt's embryonic civil society is one of a protracted crisis.

---

[45] Egyptian Organization For Human Rights. *Jarimaton bela 'iqab al-ta' thtib fi Misr. Unpunishable Crime, Torture in Egypt* [Comment of the Egyptian Organization of Human Rights on the first supplementary report submitted by the Egyptian Government to the U.N. Committee for Action against Torture, in its session of November 1993] (Cairo, December 1993).

BIBLIOGRAPHY

English

'Abdallah, Ahmad, "Egypt's Islamists and the State," *Middle East Report*, no. 183 (July-August 1993), pp. 28-31.

Abramowitz, Morton, "Dateline Ankara: Turkey After Ozal," *Foreign Policy* 91 (Summer 1993): 164-181.

Abu Ghazaleh, Adnan, "Arab Cultural Nationalism in Palestine during the British Mandate, *Journal of Palestine Studies* 1, no. 3 (Spring 1972): 37 - 63.

AbuKhalil, As'ad, "The Study of Political Parties in the Arab World: The Case of Lebanon," *Journal of Asian and African Affairs* (Fall 1993), pp. 49-64.

—, "Toward the Study of Women and Politics in the Arab World: The Debate and the Reality," *Feminist Issues* 13, no. 1 (Spring 1993): 3-22.

—, "A Viable Partnership: Islam, Democracy, and the Arab World," *Harvard International Review* XV, no. 2 (Winter 1992-1993): 22-23 & 65.

Adams, Charles, *Islam and Modernism in Egypt* (New York: Russell and Russell, 1986).

Addi, Lahouari, "The Islamist Challenge: Religion and Modernity in Algeria," *Journal of Democracy* 3, no. 4 (October 1992): 75-84.

Afshar, Haleh, "Women, State and Ideology in Iran," *Third World Quarterly* 7, no. 2 (April 1985): 256-278.

Ahmad, Feroz, "Politics and Islam in Modern Turkey," *Middle Eastern Studies* 27 (January 1991): 3-21.

—, "The Transition to Democracy in Turkey," *Third World Quarterly* 7, no. 2 (April 1985): 211-226.

Ahmad, Mohammad Sid, "Cybernetic Colonialism and the Moral Search," *New Perspectives Quarterly* 11, no. 2 (Spring 1994): 15-19.

Ahmed, Akbar S., "Media Mongols at the Gates of Baghdad," *New Perspectives Quarterly* 10, no. 3 (Summer 1993): 10-18.

—, *Postmodernism and Islam: Predicament and Promise* (New York: Routledge, 1992).

al-Ahsan, Sayed Aziz, "Economic Policy and Class Structure in Syria: 1958-1980," *International Journal of Middle East Studies* 16 (1984): 301-323.

Ajami, Fouad, "The Summoning," [a response to Huntington's 'Clash of Civilizations'] *Foreign Affairs* 72, no. 4 (September/October 1993): 2-9.

Almond, Gabriel, and Sidney Verba, *The Civic Culture* (Boston: Little Brown & Company, 1965).

Alshayeji, 'Abdullah, "Kuwait at the Crossroads: The Quest for Democratization," *Middle East Insight* 8, no. 5 (May/June 1992): 41-46

Amsden, Alice, *Asia's Next Giant: South Korea and Late Industrialization* (New York: Oxford University Press, 1989).

Anderson, Lisa, "Remaking the Middle East: The Prospects for Democracy and Stability," *Ethics and International Affairs* 6 (1992): 163-178.

Anderson, Lisa, "Absolutism and the Resilience of Monarchy in the Middle East," *Political Science Quarterly* 106, no. 1 (1991): 1-15.

—, "Liberalism in Northern Africa," *Current History* 89, no. 546 (April 1990): 145-148 & 174-175.

Anderson, Lisa, "The State in the Middle East and North Africa," *Comparative Politics* 20, no. 1 (October 1987): 1-18.
—, *The State and Social Transformation in Tunisia and Libya* (Princeton: Princeton University Press, 1986).
Anderson, Perry, *Lineages of the Absolutist State* (London: Verso, 1974).
Arato, Andrew, "Civil Society Against the State: Poland 1980-81," *Telos*, no. 47 (Spring 1981), pp. 23-47.
Arato, Andrew, and Jean Cohen, "Social Movements, Civil Society, and the Problem of Sovereignty," *Praxis International* 4, no. 3 (October 1984): 266-283.
Arian, Asher, and Michal Shamir, *The Elections in Israel, 1988* (Boulder, CO: Westview Press, 1988).
Aruri, Naseer, "Human Rights and the Gulf Crisis: The Verbal Strategy of George Bush," in *Beyond the Storm: A Gulf Crisis Reader*, Phillis Bener and Michel Moushabeck, eds. (New York: Interlink, 1991), pp. 305-323.
—, "The PLO and the Jordan Option," *Third World Quarterly* 7, no. 4 (October 1985): 882-906
Auda, Gehad, "Egypt's Uneasy Party Politics," *Journal of Democracy* 2, no. 2 (Spring 1991).
al-Azmeh, Aziz, *Islams and Modernites* (London: Verso, 1993).
Badr, Gamal, "The Recent Impact of Islamic Religious Doctrine on Constitutional Law in the Middle East," in *The Islamic Impulse*, Barbara F. Stowasser, ed. (London and Sydney: Croom Helm, 1987).
Baker, Raymond, *Sadat and After: Struggles for Egypt's Political Soul* (Cambridge: Harvard University Press, 1990).
al-Banna, Hasan, *Memoirs of Hasan al-Banna Shaheed*, translated by M. N. Shaikh (Karachi: International Islamic Publishers, 1981).
Barghouthi, Mustafa, and Rita Giacaman, "The Emergence of an Infrastructure of Resistance: The Case of Health," in *Intifada: Palestine at the Crossroads*, Jamal R. Nassar and Roger Heacock, eds. (New York: Praeger Publishers, 1990), pp. 207-226.
Barnett, Michael, "Institutions, Roles, and Disorder: The Case of the Arab States System," *International Studies Quarterly* 37 (1993): 371-296.
Bayart, Jean-François, "Civil Society in Africa," in *Political Domination in Africa: Reflections on the Limits of Power*, Patrick Chabal, ed. (London: Cambridge University Press, 1986), pp. 109-125.
Beinen, Joel, and Zachary Lockman, *Workers on the Nile: Nationalism, Communism, Islam and the Egyptian Working Class, 1882-1954* (Princeton: Princeton University Press, 1987).
Bell, Daniel, "American Exceptionalism Revisited: The Role of Civil Society," *The Public Interest*, no. 95 (1989).
Bellin, Eva, "Civil Society Emergent? State and Social Classes in Tunisia" (unpublished PhD dissertation, Princeton University, 1992).
Ben-Eliezer, Uri, "The Meaning of Political Participation in a Nonliberal Democracy: The Israeli Experience," *Comparative Politics* 25, no. 4 (July 1993): 397-412.
Bernhard, Michael, "Civil Society and Democratic Transition in East Central Europe," *Political Science Quarterly* 108, no. 2 (Summer 1993): 307-326.
Bianchi, Robert, *Unruly Corporatism: Associational Life in Twentieth-Century Egypt* (New York: Oxford University Press, 1989).
—, "Interest Group Politics in the Third World," *Third World Quarterly* 8, no. 2 (April 1986): 507-539.

Bilgrami, Akeel, "What is a Muslim? Fundamental Commitment and Cultural Identity," *Critical Inquiry* 18, no. 4 (1992): 821-842.

Binder, Leonard, *Islamic Liberalism* (Chicago: University of Chicago Press, 1988).

Birnbaum, Karl E., "Civil Society and Government Policy in a New Europe," *The World Today* 47, no. 5 (May 1991): 84-85.

Bligh, Alexander, "The Saudi Religious Elite (*Ulama*) as Participant in the Political System of the Kingdom," *International Journal of Middle East Studies* 17, no. 1 (February, 1985): 37-50.

Boulding, Elise, ed., *Building Peace in the Middle East: Challenges for States and Civil Society* (Boulder, CO: Lynne Rienner Publishers, in association with the International Peace Research Association, 1994).

Brand, Laurie A., *Palestinians in the Arab World: Institution Building and the Search for State* (New York: Columbia University Press, 1988).

Bratton, Michael, "Beyond the State: Civil Society and Associational Life in Africa," *World Politics* 41, no. 3 (April 1989): 407-430.

Bromley, Simon, *Rethinking Middle East Politics* (Austin: University of Texas Press, 1994).

Brumberg, Daniel, "The Collapse of the 'Ruling Bargain' and Its Consequences in the Arab World," unpublished paper presented for the "Seminar on Prospects for Democratization in the Arab World," SAIS, Washington, DC, January 30, 1992.

—, "Islam, Elections and Reform in Algeria," *Journal of Democracy* 2, no. 1 (Winter 1992).

Brynen, Rex, "Economic Crisis and Post-Rentier Democratization in the Arab World: The Case of Jordan," *Canadian Journal of Political Science* XXV, no. 1 (March 1992): 69-97.

Budeiri, Musa, *The Palestine Communist Party, 1919-1948: Arab and Jew in the Struggle for Internationalism* (London: Ithaca Press, 1979).

Burgat, Francois and William Dowell, *The Islamist Movement in North Africa* (Austin: University of Texas Press, 1993).

Burrows, Robert D., "The Yemen Arab Republic's Legacy and Yemeni Unification," *Arab Studies Quarterly* 14, no. 4 (Fall 1992): 41-68.

Butterworth, Charles E., ed., *Political Islam, ANNALS, AAPSS*, 524 (November 1992).

—, "State and Authority in Arabic Political Thought," in *The Foundations of the Arab State*, Ghassan Salamé, ed., (London: Croom Helm, 1987), pp 91-111.

Cantori, Louis J., ed., "Democratization in the Middle East," *American-Arab Affairs*, no. 36 (Spring 1991), pp. 1-51.

Carapico, Sheila, "Women and Public Participation in Yemen," *Middle East Report*, no. 173 (November-December 1991), p. 15.

Center for Strategic Studies, Jordan University, "A Public Opinion Survey on 'Democracy in Jordan': Preliminary Findings," unpublished study, Amman: Spring 1993.

Chaudhry, Kiren Aziz, "The Myths of the Market and the Common History of Late Developers," *Politics and Society* 21, no. 3 (September 1993): 245-274.

Chazan, Naomi, "Africa's Democratic Challenge," *World Policy Journal* 9, no. 2 (Spring 1992): 279-307.

Christelow, Allan, "Ritual, Culture and Politics of Islamic Reformism in Algeria," *Middle Eastern Studies* 23, no. 3 (July 1987): 255-273.

Cigar, Norman, "Islam and the State in South Yemen: The Uneasy Coexistence," *Middle Eastern Studies* 26 (April 1990): 185-203.

Cobban, Helena, *The Palestinian Liberation Organization: People, Power and Politics* (New York: Cambridge University Press, 1984).

Cohen, Amnon, *Political Parties in the West Bank Under the Jordanian Regime, 1949-1967* (Ithaca, NY: Cornell University Press, 1982).

Cohen, Jean L., *Class and Civil Society: The Limits of Marxian Critical Theory* (Amherst, MA: The University of Massachusetts Press, 1982).

Cohen, Jean L., and Andrew Arato, *Civil Society and Political Theory* (Cambridge, MA: MIT Press, 1992).

Collings, Deirdre, ed., *Reconstruction, Rehabilitation and Reconciliation in the Middle East: The View From Civil Society* (report from a workshop of the same name held in Ottawa, Canada, June 1993).

Crone, P., and Martin Hinds, *God's Caliph: Religious Authority in the First Century of Islam* (Cambridge: Cambridge University Press, 1980).

Crystal, Jill, "Authoritarianism and Its Adversaries in the Arab World," *World Politics* 46, no. 2 (January 1994): 262-289.

—, *Kuwait, The Transformation of an Oil State* (Boulder, CO: Westview Press, 1992).

—, *Oil and politics in the Gulf: Rulers and Merchants in Kuwait and Qatar* (New York: Cambridge University Press, 1990).

Dahl, Robert, *Democracy and Its Critics* (New Haven, CT: Yale University Press, 1989).

—, "Governments and Political Opposition," in *Political Science, Scope and Theory* (Handbook of Political Science, Volume 3), Fred Greenstein and Nelson Polsby, eds. (Massachusetts: Addison-Wesley, 1975), pp. 115-122.

Dahrendorf, Ralf, *Reflections on the Revolution in Europe in a Letter intended to have been sent to a Gentleman in Warsaw* (New York: Times Books, 1990; London: Chatto and Windus, 1990).

—, *The Modern Social Conflict: An Essay on the Politics of Liberty* (New York: Weidenfeld & Nicholson, 1988).

Dawisha, Adeed, "Power, Participation and Legitimacy in the Arab World," *World Policy Journal* III, no. 3 (Summer 1986): 517-534.

Denoeux, Guilain, *Urban Unrest in the Middle East: A Comparative Study of Informal Networks in Egypt, Iran and Lebanon* (Albany, NY: SUNY Press, 1993).

Dessouki, Ali Hillal, "The Unfinished Revolution: The Postwar Arab World," *Journal of Democracy* 2, no. 3 (Summer 1991).

Diamond, Larry, ed., *Political Culture and Democracy in Developing Countries* (Boulder, CO: Lynne Rienner Publishers, 1993).

—, "Promoting Democracy," *Foreign Policy* 87 (Summer 1992): 25-46.

Diamond, Larry, Juan J. Linz and Seymour Martin Lipset, eds., *Politics in Developing Countries: Comparing Experiences with Democracy* (Boulder: Lynne Rienner Publishers, 1990).

—, *Democracy in Developing Countries* (Boulder, CO: Lynne Rienner Publishers, 1989).

—, "Building and Sustaining Democratic Government in Developing Countries: Some Tentative Findings," *World Affairs* 150, no. 1 (Summer 1987): 5-19.

Diamond, Larry, and Marc Plattner, eds., *The Global Resurgence of Democracy* (Baltimore, MD: The Johns Hopkins University Press, 1993).

Di Palma, Giuseppe, "Legitimation from the Top to Civil Society: Politico-Cultural Change in Eastern Europe," *World Politics* 44, no. 1 (October 1991): 49-80.

—, *To Craft Democracies: An Essay on Democratic Transitions* (Berkeley: University of California Press, 1990).

Dixon, William, "Democracy and the Political Settlement of International Conflict," *American Political Science Review* 88, no. 1 (March 1994): 314-332.

Doan, Rebecca Miles, "Class Differentiation and the Informal Sector in Amman, Jordan," *International Journal of Middle East Studies* 24, no. 1 (February 1992): 27-38.

Doyle, Michael W., "Liberalsim and World Politics," *American Political Science Review* 80 (December 1986).

—, "Kant, Liberal Legacies, and Foreign Affairs, Part 2," *Philosophy & Public Affairs* 12 (Fall 1983): 323-353.

—, "Kant, Liberal Legacies, and Foreign Affairs, Part 1," *Philosophy & Public Affairs* 12 (Summer 1983): 205-235.

Dreze, Jacques, and Amartya Sen, *Hunger and Public Action* (New York: Oxford University Press, 1989).

Drysdale, Alasdair, and Raymond A. Hinnebusch, *Syria and the Middle East Peace Process* (New York: Council on Foreign Relations, 1991).

Eickelman, Dale F., "The Re-Imagination of the Middle East: Political and Academic Frontiers (1991 Presidential Address)," *Middle East Studies Association Bulletin* 26, no. 1 (July 1992): 3-12.

—, "Mass Higher Education and the Religious Imagination in Contemporary Arab Societies," *American Ethnologist* 19, no. 4 (1992): 643-655.

Ekiert, Grzegorz, "Democratization Processes in East Central Europe: A Theoretical Reconsideration," *British Journal of Political Science* 21 (July 1991): 285-313.

Ember, Carol R., Melvin Ember, and Bruce M. Russett, "Peace Between Participatory Polities: A Cross Cultural Test of the 'Democracies Rarely Fight Each Other' Hypothesis," *World Politics* 44, no. 4 (July 1992): 573-99.

Entelis, John, and Phillip Naylor, eds., *State and Society in Algeria* (Boulder, CO: Westview Press, 1992).

Escher, Anton, "Private Business and Trade in the Region of Yabroud, Syria," unpublished paper presented at the Middle East Studies Association annual meeting, 1990.

Esposito, John L., *The Islamic Threat: Myth or Reality?* (New York: Oxford University Press, 1992).

Esposito, John L., and James P. Piscatori, "Democratization and Islam," *Middle East Journal* 45, no. 3 (Summer 1991): 427-440.

Farsoun, Samih K., "Class Structure and Social Change in the Arab World: 1995," in *The Next Arab Decade: Alternative Futures*, Hisham Sharabi, ed. (Boulder, CO: Westview Press, 1988), pp. 221-238.

Fergany, Nader, "A Characterization of the Employment Problem in Egypt," in *Employment and Structural Adjustment: Egypt in the 1990s,* Heba Handoussa and Gillian Potter, eds. (Cairo: American University in Cairo Press for the International Labour Organization, 1991).

Ferguson, Adam, *An Essay on the History of Civil Society* (Edinburgh: Printed for A. Millar & T. Caddel, London, and A. Kincaid & J. Bell, Edinburgh, 1767).

Fernea, Elizabeth Warcock, and Mary Evelyn Hocking, *The Struggle for Peace: Israelis and Palestinians* (Austin, TX: University of Texas Press, 1992).

Ferrarotti, Franco, "Civil Society as a Polyarchic Form: The City," *International Journal of Politics, Culture and Society* 6, no. 1 (1992): 23-37.

Frentzel-Zagorska, Janina, "Civil Society in Poland and Hungary," *Soviet Studies* 42, no. 4 (1990): 759-777.

Gasiorowski, Mark, "The Failure of Reform in Tunisia," *Journal of Democracy* 3, no. 4 (October 1992): 85-97.

Gause, F. Gregory, *Oil Monarchies: Domestic and Security Challenges in the Arab Gulf States* (New York: Council on Foreign Relations, 1994).

—, "Sovereignty, Statecraft and Stability in the Middle East," *Journal of International Affairs* 45, no. 2 (Winter 1992): 441-469.

Gellner, Ernest, "Civil Society in Historical Context," *International Social Science Journal* 43 (August, 1991): 495-510.

—, *Culture, Identity and Politics* (Cambridge, MA: Cambridge University Press, 1988).

Ghabra, Shafeeq, "Kuwait: Elections and Issues of Democratization in a Middle Eastern State," *Digest of Middle East Studies* 2, no. 1 (Winter 1993): 1-17.

—, "Voluntary Associations in Kuwait: The Foundation of a New System," *Middle East Journal* 45, no. 2 (Spring 1991): 199-215.

Giacaman, Rita, and Penny Johnson, "Palestinian Women: Building Barricades and Breaking Barriers," in *Intifada: The Palestinian Uprising Against Israeli Occupation*, Zachary Lockman and Joel Beinin, eds. (Boston: South End Press, 1989), pp. 155-169.

Gillies, David, and G. Schmitz, *The Challenge of Democratic Development: Sustaining Democratization in Developing Countries* (Ottawa: The North-South Institute, 1992).

Goldberg, Ellis, Resat Kasaba, and Joel Migdal, eds., *Rules and Rights in the Middle East: Democracy, Law and Society* (Seattle: University of Washington Press, 1993).

Graham, Douglas F., *Saudi Arabia Unveiled* (Dubuque, IA: Kendall/Hunt Publishing, 1991).

Green, Jerrold D., "Islam, Religiopolitics, and Social Change," *Comparative Studies in Society and History* 27, no. 2 (April 1985): 312-322.

—, *Revolution in Iran* (New York: Praeger, 1980).

Haddad, Mahmoud, "The Rise of Arab Nationalism Reconsidered," *International Journal of Middle East Studies* 26, no. 2 (May 1994): 201-222.

Hagopian, Frances, "After Regime Change: Authoritarian Legacies, Political Representation, and the Democratic Future of South America," *World Politics* 45 (April 1993): 464-500.

Halperin, Manfred, *The Politics of Social Change in the Middle East and the Arab World* (Princeton, NJ: Princeton University Press, 1962).

Halperin, Morton H., and David J. Scheffer with Patricia L. Small, *Self-Determination in the New World Order* (Washington, DC: Carnegie Endowment for International Peace, 1992).

Hanf, Theodor, *Coexistence in Wartime Lebanon: Decline of a State and Rise of a Nation* (London: Centre for Lebanese Studies and I.B. Taurus, 1993).

Harik, Judith P., and Hilal Khashan, "Lebanon's Divisive Democracy: The Parliamentary Elections of 1992," *Arab Studies Quarterly* 15, no. 1 (Winter 1993): 41-59.

Hatem, Mervat, "Egypt's Middle Class in Crisis: The Sexual Division of Labor," *Middle East Journal* 42, no. 3 (Summer 1988): 407-422.

Hermassi, Mohamed Abdelbaki, "Islam, Democracy, and the Challenge of Political Change," in *Democracy in the Middle East: Defining the Challenge*, Yehuda Mirsky and Matt Abrens, eds. (Washington, DC: The Washington Institute, 1993), pp. 41-52.

—, "Notes on Civil Society in Tunisia," a paper presented at an International Peace Academy-sponsored conference in Giza, Egypt, May 28-30, 1992, pp. 7-8.

—, "Political Culture and Democratization in the Middle East," unpublished paper prepared for the November 1991 meeting on democratization in the Middle East, held in Antalya, Turkey.

—, *Society and State in the Arab Maghreb* (Beirut: Center for Arab Unity Studies, 1987).

—, *Leadership and National Development in North Africa: A Comparative Study* (Berkeley: University of California Press, 1970).

Heydemann, Steven, "Liberalization from Above and the Limits of Private Sector Autonomy in Syria: The Role of Business Associations" (unpublished paper presented at the Middle East Studies Association annual meeting, San Antonio, TX, 1990).

Hiltermann, Joost, *Behind the Intifida: Labor and Women's Movements in the Occupied Territories* (Princeton, NJ: Princeton University Press, 1992).

Hinnebusch, Raymond A., "State and Civil Society in Syria," *Middle East Journal* 47, no. 2 (Spring 1993): 241-257.

—, *Authoritarian Power and State Formation in Ba'thist Syria: Army, Party and Peasant* (Boulder, CO: Westview Press, 1990).

Hooglund, Eric, "Iranian Populism and Political Change in the Gulf," *Middle East Report*, no. 194 (January-February 1992), pp. 19-21.

Hourani, Albert, *History of the Arab People* (Cambridge, MA: Harvard University Press, 1990).

—, *Syria and Lebanon* (London: Oxford University Press, 1946).

Hourani, Hani, et al., *The Islamic Action Front Party* (Amman: Al-Urdun al-Jadid, 1993).

Hudson, Michael C., "Democracy and Foreign Policy in the Arab World," *The Beirut Review*, no. 4 (Fall 1992), pp. 3-28.

—, "After the Gulf War: Prospects for Democratization in the Arab World," *Middle East Journal* 45, no. 3 (Summer 1991): 407-427.

—, "Democratization and the Problem of Legitimacy in Middle East Politics," 1987 MESA Presidential Address, *Middle East Studies Association Bulletin* 22, no. 2 (December 1988): 157-171.

—, *Arab Politics: The Search for Legitimacy* (New Haven: Yale University Press, 1980).

Human Rights on the first supplementary report submitted by the Egyptian Government to the UN Committee for Action against Torture, in its session of November 1993 (Cairo: EOHR, December 1993).

Huntington, Samuel P., "Clash of Civilizations?" *Foreign Affairs* 72, no. 3 (Summer 1993): 22-49.

—, "Democracy's Third Wave," *Journal of Democracy* 2, no. 2 (April 1991).

—, *The Third Wave: Democratization in the Late Twentieth Century* (Norman, OK: Oklahoma University Press, 1991).

al-Husseini, Ishaq Musa, *Moslem Brethren* (Beirut: Khayat's College Book, 1956).

Ibn Khaldoun Center, *Grass-roots Participation and Development in Egypt* (Cairo: A study commissioned by UNICEF, UNDP, and UNFPA, 1993).

Ibrahim, Saad Eddin, "Crises, Elites, and Democratization in the Arab World," *Middle East Journal* 47, no. 2 (Spring 1993): 292-305.

Ibrahim, Saad Eddin, et al., *Society and State in the Arab World* (Amman: The Arab Thought Forum, 1988).

Isaac, Jeffrey, "Civil Society and the Spirit of Revolt," *Dissent*, Summer 1993, pp. 356-361.

Johnson, James Turner, "Does Democracy 'Travel'? Some Thoughts on Democracy and Its Cultural Context," *Ethics and International Affairs* 6 (1992): 41 - 55.

Jowitt, Ken, "The New World Disorder," *Journal of Democracy* 2, no. 1 (Winter 1991): 11-20.

Kamali, Mohammad H., "Freedom of Expression in Islam: An Analysis of *Fitnah*," *American Journal of Islamic Social Sciences* 10 (Summer 1993): 178-198.

—, "*Siyasah Shar'iyah* or the Policies of Islamic Government," *The American Journal of Islamic Social Sciences* 6, no. 4 (Fall 1991): 225-237.

—, "The Approved and Disapproved Varieties of Ra'y (Personal Opinion) in Islam," *The American Journal of Islamic Social Sciences* 7, no. 1 (March 1990): 39-65.

Kaufman, Edy, Shukri B. Abed, and Robert L. Rothstein, ed., *Democracy, Peace, and the Israeli-Palestinian Conflict* (Boulder, CO: Lynne Rienner Publishers, 1993).

Keane, John, *Civil Society and the State* (London: Verso Press, 1988).

—, ed., *Democracy and Civil Society: New European Perspectives* (London: Verso Press, 1988).

Kechichian, Joseph A., *Political Dynamics and Security in the Arabian Peninsula Through the 1990s* (Santa Monica, CA: Rand, 1993).

el-Kenz, Ali, *Algerian Reflections on the Arab Crisis* (Austin, TX: Center for Middle Eastern Studies, University of Texas, 1991).

Kerr, Malcolm, "Arab Radical Notions of Democracy," *St. Anthony's Papers* #16 (1966).

Al-Khafaji, Isam, "Beyond the Ultra-Nationalist State," *Middle East Report*, nos. 187-188 (March-April/May-June 1994), pp. 34-39.

Khalaf, Issa, *Politics in Palestine, Arab Factionalism and Social Disintegration 1939-1948* (New York: State University of New York, 1991).

Khalaf, Samir, *Beirut Reclaimed: Reflections on Urban Design and the Restoration of Civility* (Beirut: Editions Dar al-Nahar, 1993).

Khalidi, Walid, "Iraq vs. Kuwait: Claims and Counterclaims," in *The Gulf War Reader*, Cifry and Serf, eds. (New York, 1991).

al-Khalil, Samir, *The Republic of Fear* (Berkeley, CA: University of California Press, 1989).

Khashan, Hilal, "The Quagmire of Arab Democracy," *Arab Studies Quarterly* 14, no. 1 (Winter 1992): 17-33.

el-Kholy, Abdo A., "The Concept of Community in Islam," in *Islamic Perspective: Studies in the Honor of Mawlana Abul A'la Mawdudi*, Khurshid Ahmad and Zafar Ansari, eds. (United Kingdom: Islamic Foundation, 1979), pp. 171-181.

Khoury, Philip, "Syrian Urban Politics in Transition: The Quarters of Damascus During the French Mandate," *International Journal of Middle East Studies* 16, no. 4 (November 1984): 507-540.

Khuri, Fuad, "Invisible Meanings in Conflict Resolution: Some Macro-Ideological Constructs in Arab-Islamic Culture," a paper presented at an American University of Beirut-sponsored meeting in Larnaca, Cyprus, June 24-26, 1993.

Krämer, Gudrun, "Islamist Democracy," *Middle East Report*, no. 183 (July-August 1993), pp. 2-8.

—, "Liberalization and Democracy in the Arab World," *Middle East Report*, no. 174 (January-February 1992), pp. 22-25 & 35.

Krauthammer, Charles, "Iran to become new 'Evil Empire'?" *Democrat and Chronicle*, January 4, 1993 (Rochester, NY).

Lal, Deepak, *The Poverty of "Development Economics"* (London: Institute of Economic Affairs, 1983).

Lawrence, Bruce, *Defenders of God: The Revolt Against the Modern Age* (San Francisco: Harper and Row, 1989).

Lawson, Fred, *Oppositional Movements and U.S. Policy toward the Arab Gulf States*, "Critical Issues" series, no. 9 (New York: Council on Foreign Relations, 1992).

—, "Class and State in Kuwait," *MERIP Reports*, no. 132 (May 1985), pp. 16-21 & 32.

Lawson, Stephanie, "Conceptual Issues in the Comparative Study of Regime Change and Democratization," *Comparative Politics* 25, no. 2 (January 1993): 183-205.

Lawyers Committee for Human Rights, *Laying the Foundations, Human Rights in Kuwait: Obstacles and Opportunities* (New York: LCHR, April 1993).

—, *Kuwait, Building the Rule of Law* (New York: LCHR, January 1992).

—, *Kuwait: Recent Human Rights Developments* (New York: LCHR, March 1990).

Lesch, Ann Mosely, *Arab Politics in Palestine, 1917-1939, The Frustration of a Nationalist Movement* (Cornell: Cornell University Press, 1979)

Lewis, Bernard, "Islam and Liberal Democracy," *The Atlantic Monthly* 271, no. 2 (February 1993): 89-94.

—, "Rethinking the Middle East," *Foreign Affairs* 17, no. 4 (Fall 1992).

Lewis, Norman, "The Isma'ilis of Syria Today," *Journal of the Royal Central Asia Society* 39 (January 1952): 69-77.

Lewis, Peter M., "Political Transition and the Dilemma of Civil Society in Africa," *Journal of International Affairs* 42, no. 1 (Summer 1992): 31-54.

Lindenburg, Marc, and Shantayanan Devarajan, "Revisiting the Myths about Structural Adjustment, Democracy, and Economic Performance in Developing Countries," *Comparative Politics* 25, no. 2 (January 1993): 169-181.

Linz, Juan J., "An Authoritarian Regime: Spain," in *Mass Politics,* Erik Allardt, ed. (New York: Free Press, 1971).

Liphjart, Arend, *Democracies: Patterns of Majoritarian and Consensus Government in Twenty-One Countries* (New Haven, CT: Yale University Press, 1984).

Litani, Yehuda, "Leadership in the West Bank and Gaza," *Jerusalem Quarterly*, no. 14 (Winter 1980), pp. 90-109.

Lockman, Zachary, ed., *Workers and Working Classes in the Middle East: Struggle, Histories, Historiographies* (Albany, NY: SUNY Press, 1994).

Longuenesse, Elizabeth, "The Class Nature of the State in Syria," *MERIP Report,* no. 77 (May 1979), pp. 3-11.

Luciani, Giacomo, ed., *The Arab State* (Berkeley: University of California Press, 1990).

Maghraoui, Abdeslam, "Problems of Transition to Democracy: Algeria's Short-lived Experiment with Electoral Politics," *Middle East Insight* VIII, no. 6 (July-October 1992): 20-26.

Maier, Charles, ed., *Changing Boundaries of the Political* (Cambridge: Cambridge University Press, 1987).

Makram-Ebeid, Mona, "Political Opposition in Egypt: Democratic Myth or Reality?" *Middle East Journal* 43, no. 3 (Summer 1989): 423-436.

Malwal, Bona, "The Agony of the Sudan," *Journal of Democracy* 1, no. 2 (Spring 1990): 75-86.

Mattar, Philip, *The Mufti of Jerusalem, Al-Hajj Amin Al-Husayni and the Palestinian National Movement* (New York: Columbia University Press, 1988).

Mayer, Ann E., *Islam and Human Rights: Tradition and Politics* (Boulder, CO: Westview Press, 1991).

McCormick, Basrett, Su Shaozhi, and Xiao Xiaoming, "The 1989 Democracy Movement: A Review of the Prospects for Civil Society in China," *Pacific Affairs* 65, no. 2 (Summer 1992): 182-202.

Mernissi, Fatima, *Islam and Democracy: Fear of the Modern World* (New York: Addison-Wesley, 1993).

Metral, Françoise, "State and Peasants in Syria: A Local View of a Government Irrigation Project," *Peasant Studies* 11, no. 2 (Winter 1984): 69-90.

Middle East Watch, "Kuwait Closes All Human Rights Organizations," *Middle East Watch Newsletter* 5, issue 6 (New York: Middle East Watch, 1993).

Migdal, Joel S., "Civil Society in Israel," in *Rules and Rights in the Middle East: Democracy, Law and Society*, Ellis Goldberg, Resat Kasaba, and Joel Migdal, eds. (Seattle: University of Washington Press, 1993), pp. 119-138.

Miller, Judith, "The Challenge of Radical Islam," *Foreign Affairs* 72, no. 2 (Spring 1993): 43-56.

Mishal, Shaul, *West Bank/East Bank: The Palestinians in Jordan, 1949-1967* (New Haven, CT: Yale University Press, 1978).

Misztal, Bronislaw, and Barbara A. Misztal, "Democratization Processes as an Objective of New Social Movements," *Research in Social Movements, Conflicts and Change* 10 (1988): 93-106.

Mitchell, Richard, *The Society of Muslim Brothers* (London: Oxford University Press, 1964).

Mitchell, Timothy P., "The Limits of the State: Beyond Statist Approaches and Their Critics," *American Political Science Review* 85, no. 1 (March 1991): 77-96; follow-up comments by John Bendix, Bertell Ollman, Bartholemew H. Sparrow, with a response by Timothy P. Mitchell, "Going Beyond the State?" *American Political Science Review* 86, no. 4 (December 1992): 1007-1021.

Moore, Barrington, *The Social Origins of Dictatorship and Democracy: Lord and Peasant in the Making of the Modern World* (Boston: Beacon Press, 1966).

Moore, Clement Henry, *Tunisia Since Independence: Dynamics of a One Party State* (Berkeley and Los Angeles: University of California Press, 1965).

Moran, Theodore, *Multinational Corporations and the Politics of Dependence: Copper in Chile* (Princeton, NJ: Princeton University Press, 1974).

Mortimer, Robert, "Islam and Multiparty Politics in Algeria," *Middle East Journal* 45, no. 4 (Autumn 1991): 575-593.

Moussalli, Ahmad, "Hasan al-Banna's Islamist Discourse on Constitutional Rule and Islamic State," *Journal of Islamic Studies* 4, no. 2 (1993): 161-174.

—, *Radical Islamic Fundamentalism: The Ideological and Political Discourse of Sayyid Qutb* (Beirut: Amercian University of Beirut, 1992).

Munson, Henry, *Religion and Power in Morocco* (New Haven, CT: Yale University Press, 1993).

Muravchik, Joshua, *Exporting Democracy: Fulfilling America's Destiny* (Washington, DC: American Enterprise Institute, 1991).

Muslih, Muhammad, "The Golan: Israel, Syria, and Strategic Calculations," *Middle East Journal* 47, no. 4 (Autumn 1993): 611-632.

—, "Palestinian Civil Society," *Middle East Journal* 47, no. 2 (Spring 1993): 258-274.

—, *The Origins of Palestinian Nationalism* (New York: Columbia University Press and the Institute for Palestine Studies, 1988)

Muslih, Muhammad, and Augustus Richard Norton, "The Need for Arab Democracy," *Foreign Policy* 83 (Summer 1991): 3-19.

al-Najjar, Ghanim, "Civil Society in Kuwait," a paper presented at an International Peace-Academy sponsored conference in Giza, Egypt, May 28-30, 1992.

Niblock, Tim, and Emma Murphy, *Economic and Political Liberalization in the Middle East* (London: British Academic Press, 1993).

Norton, Augustus Richard, "The Future of Civil Society in the Middle East," *Middle East Journal* 47, no. 2 (Spring 1993): 205 - 216.

—, "Breaking Through the Wall of Fear in the Arab World," *Current History* 91, no. 561 (January 1992): 37-41.

Norton, Augustus Richard, and Jillian Schwedler, "Swiss Soldiers, Ta'if Clocks, and Early Elections," in *Peace for Lebanon? From War to Reconstruction,* Deirdre Collings, ed. (Boulder, CO: Lynne Rienner Publishers, 1994).

Odhibat, 'Atef, "Civil Society in Jordan: A Preliminary Assessment," a paper presented at an International Peace Academy-sponsored conference in Giza, Egypt, May 28-30, 1992, p. 18.

O'Donnell, Guillermo, *Modernization and Bureaucratic-Authoritarianism* (Berkeley: University of California Press, 1973).

O'Donnell, Guillermo, and Philippe C. Schmitter, *Transitions from Authoritarian Rule: Prospects for Democracy* (Baltimore, MD: Johns Hopkins University Press, 1986).

Orum, A. M., *Introduction to Political Sociology* (Englewood Cliffs, NJ: Prentice Hall, 1978).

Pelczynski, Z. A., ed., *The State and Civil Society: Studies in Hegel's Political Philosophy* (Cambridge: Cambridge University Press, 1984).

Peled, Yoav, "Ethnic Democracy and the Legal Construction of Citizenship: Arab Citizens of the Jewish State," *American Political Science Review* 86, no. 2 (1992): 432-443.

Peres, Yochanan, and Ephraim Yuchtman-Yaar, *Trends in Israeli Democracy: The Public's View* (Boulder, CO: Lynne Rienner Publishers, 1992).

Perez-Diaz, Victor M., *The Return of Civil Society: The Emergence of Democratic Spain* (Cambridge, MA: Harvard University Press, 1993).

Perry, Glenn E., "Democracy and Human Rights in the Shadow of the West," *Arab Studies Quarterly* 14, no. 4 (Fall 1992): 1-22.

Perthes, Volker, "A Look at Syria's Upper Class: The Bourgeoisie and the Ba'th," *Middle East Report,* no. 170 (May-June 1991), pp. 31-37.

Porath, Yehoshua, *The Palestinian Arab National Movement, 1929-1939* (London: Frank Cass, 1977).

—, *The Emergence of the Palestinian-Arab National Movement, 1918-1929* (London: Frank Cass, 1974).

Posusney, Marsha Pripstein, "Irrational Workers: The Moral Economy of Labor Protest in Egypt," *World Politics* 46, no. 1 (October 1993): 83-120.

Przeworksi, Adam, *Democracy and the Market: Political and Economic Reforms in Eastern Europe and Latin America* (Cambridge: Cambridge University Press, 1991).

—, "Democracy as a Contingent Outcome of Conflicts," in *Constitutionalism and Democracy,* Jon Elster and Rune Slagstad, eds. (Cambridge: Cambridge University Press, 1988).

Putnam, Robert, *Making Democracy Work: Civic Traditions in Modern Italy* (Princeton: Princeton University Press, 1993).

Rau, Zbigniew, *The Reemergence of Civil Society in Eastern Europe and the Soviet Union* (Boulder, CO: Westview Press, 1991).

Redhead, B., ed., *Plato to Nato: Studies in Political Thought* (London: BBC Books, 1984).

Richards, Alan, "Agricultural Employment, Wages, and Government Policy During and After the Oil Boom," in *Employment and Structural Adjustment: Egypt in the 1990s,* Heba Handoussa and Gillian Potter, eds. (Cairo: American University in Cairo Press for the International Labour Organization, 1991).

Richards, Alan, and John Waterbury, *A Political Economy of the Middle East* (Boulder, CO: Westview Press, 1990).

Roberts, John, "Prospects for Democracy in Jordan," *Arab Studies Quarterly* 13, nos. 3 & 4 (Summer/Fall 1991): 119-138.

Robinson, Glenn E., "The Role of the Professional Middle Class in the Mobilization of Palestinian Society: The Medical and Agricultural Committees," *International Journal of Middle East Studies* 25, no. 2 (May 1993): 301-326.

Rueshemeyer, Dietrick, Evelyne Huber Stephens, and John D. Stephens, *Capitalist Development and Democracy* (Chicago: Univesity of Chicago Press, 1992).

Rustow, Dankwart, "Transitions to Democracy," *Comparative Politics* 2, no. 3 (1970): 337-363.

Sadowski, Yahya, "The New Orientalism and the Democracy Debate," *Middle East Report*, no. 183 (July-August 1993), pp. 14-21 & 40.

Sahliyeh, Emile, *In Search of Leadership, West Bank Politics Since 1967* (Washington, D.C.: The Brookings Institution, 1988).

Salamé, Ghassan, "Islam and the West," *Foreign Policy* 90 (Spring 1993): 22-37.

Sales, Arnaud, "The Private, the Public, and Civil Society: Social Realms and Power Structures," *International Political Science Review* 12, no. 4 (1991): 295-312.

Sayari, Sabri, ed., *Democratization in the Middle East: Trends and Prospects* (Washington, DC: National Academy Press, 1993).

al-Sayyid, Mustapha K., "Slow Thaw in the Arab World," *World Policy Journal* 8, no. 4 (Fall 1991): 711-738.

—, "A Civil Society in Egypt?" *Middle East Journal* 47, no. 2 (Spring 1993): 228-242.

Schwedler, Jillian, "Early Elections in the West Bank and Gaza," *Middle East Insight* VIII, no. 6 (July-October 1992): 5-9.

Seale, Patrick, *The Struggle for Syria*, (New Haven: Yale University Press,1979).

Seligman, Adam, *The Idea of Civil Society* (New York: The Free Press, 1992).

—, "Trust and the Meaning of Civil Society," *International Journal of Politics, Culture and Society* 6, no. 1 (1992): 5-21.

Sfeir, George N., "Source of Law and the Issue of Legitimacy and Rights," *Middle East Journal* 42, no. 3 (Summer 1988): 436-446.

Shaaban, Bouthaina, *Both Right and Left Handed: Arab Women Talk About Their Lives* (Bloomington: Indiana University Press, 1988, 1991).

Sharabi, Hisham, ed., *The Next Arab Decade: Alternative Futures* (Boulder, CO: Westview Press, 1988).

Shehadeh, Raja, "Negotiating Self-Government Arrangements," *Journal of Palestine Studies* XXI, no. 84 (Summer 1992): 22-32.

—, *Occupier's Law, Israel and the West Bank* (Washington, D.C.: Institute for Palestine Studies, 1985).

Shils, Edward. "The Virtue of Civil Society," *Government and Opposition* 26, no. 1 (Winter 1992): 3-20.

Shlaim, Avi, *Collusion Across the Jordan* (New York: Columbia University Press, 1988).

Shubane, Khela, "The Unfinished Revolution: Civil Society in South Africa," *Journal of Democracy* 2, no. 3 (Summer 1991): 53-55.

Sivan, Emmanuel, *Radical Islam* (New Haven, CT: Yale University Press, 1985).

Smith, Pamela Ann, *Palestine and the Palestinians, 1883 - 1983* (New York: St. Martin's, 1984).

Solinger, Dorothy J., "China's Transients and the State: A Form of Civil Society?" *Politics & Society* 21, no. 1 (March 1993): 91-122.

Sprinzak, Ehud, and Larry Diamond, *Israeli Democracy Under Stress* (Boulder, CO: Lynne Rienner Publishers, 1993).

Stephan, Alfred, "The Tasks of a Democratic Opposition," *Journal of Democracy* 1, no. 2 (Spring 1990): 41-49.

Tamari, Salim, "Left in Limbo: Leninist Heritage and Islamist Challenge," *Middle East Report*, no. 179 (November/December 1992), pp. 16-22.

——, "What the Uprising Means," *Middle East Report*, no. 52 (May-June 1988), pp. 24-30.

Tamimi, Azzaz, ed., *Power-Sharing Islam?* (London: Liberty for Muslim World Publications, 1993).

Taylor, Charles, "Modes of Civil Society," *Public Culture* 3, no. 1 (Fall 1990): 95-132.

Tessler, Mark, "Anger and Goverance in the Arab World: Lessons from the Maghrib and Implications for the West," prepared for the American Political Science Association 1991 meeting and forthcoming in the *Jerusalem Journal of International Relations*.

Tétreault, Mary Ann, "Civil Society in Kuwait: Protected Spaces and Women's Rights," *Middle East Journal* 47, no. 2 (Spring 1993): 275-291.

Tibi, Bassam, *The Crisis of Modern Islam: A Preindustrial Culture in the Scientific-Technological Age*, translated by Judith von Sivers (Salt Lake City, UT: University of Utah Press, 1988).

de Tocqueville, Alexis, *Democracy in America* (New York: Langley Press, 1845), vols. 1&2.

al-Turabi, Hasan, "Islam, Democracy, the State and the West: Summary of a Lecture and Roundtable Discussion with Hasan al-Turabi," prepared by Louis Cantouri and Arthur Lowrie, *Middle East Policy* 1, no. 3 (1992): 52-54.

Turner, Brian S., "Orientalism and the Problem of Civil Society in Islam," in *Orientalism, Islam and Islamicists*, Asaf Hussain, Robert Olson, and Jamil Quereishi, eds. (Brattleboro, VT: Amana Books, 1984), pp. 23-42.

Vatikiotis, P.J., *Politics and the Military in Jordan: A Study of the Arab Legion, 1921-1967* (New York: Praeger, 1967).

Vitalis, Robert, "The Democratization Industry and the Limits of the New Interventionism," *Middle East Report*, nos. 187-188 (March-April/May-June 1994), pp. 46-50.

Voll, John O., *Islam: Continuity and Change in the Modern World* (Boulder, CO: 1982).

von Sivers, Peter, "Retreating States and Expanding Societies: The State Autonomy/Informal Civil Society Dialectic in the Middle East and North Africa," unpublished paper of the Joint Committee on the Near and Middle East and North Africa, Research Agenda, Social Science Research Council, 1986-87.

Waltz, Susan E., "Another View of Feminine Networks: Tunisian Women and the Development of Political Efficacy," *International Journal of Middle East Studies* 22, no. 1 (February 1990): 21-36.

Walzer, Michael, "Multiculturalism and Individualism," *Dissent*, Spring 1994, pp. 186-191.

——, "The Idea of Civil Society," *Dissent,* Spring 1991, pp. 293-304.

——, "The Civil Society Argument: the Good Life," *New Statesman & Society* 2, (October 6, 1989): 28-31.

Warnecke, Steven, and Ezra Suleiman, eds., *Industrial Policies in Western Europe* (New York: Praeger, 1975).

Waterbury, John, *Exposed To Innumerable Delusions: Public Enterprise and State Power in Egypt, India, Mexico, and Turkey* (Cambridge: Cambridge University Press, 1993).

—, "Democrats Without Democrats? The Potential for Political Liberalization in the Middle East," in *Democracy Without Democrats?* Ghassan Salamé, ed. (London and New York: I.B. Taurus Publishers, 1994), pp. 23-47.

—, "Corruption, Political Stability, and Development: Comparative Evidence from Egypt and Morocco," *Government and Opposition* 11, no. 4 (Autumn 1976): 426-446.

Weigle, Marcia A., and Jim Butterfield, "Civil Society in Reforming Communist Regimes: The Logic of Emergence," *Comparative Politics* 25, no. 1 (October 1992): 1-24.

Weiner, Richard R., "Retrieving Civil Society in a Postmodern Epoch," *The Social Science Journal* 28, no. 3 (1991): 307 - 323.

White, Jenny B., *Money Makes Us Relatives: Women's Labor in Urban Turkey* (Austin, TX: University of Texas Press, 1994).

Wilson, Mary, *King Abdallah, Britain and the Making of Jordan* (New York: Cambridge University Press, 1987).

Wittfogel, Karl, *Oriental Despotism* (New Haven, CT: Yale University Press, 1957).

Wood, Ellen Meiksins, "The Uses and Abuses of Civil Society," in *Socialist Register,* Ralph Miliband, ed. (Atlantic Highlands, NJ: Humanities Press, 1990), pp. 60-84.

Woods, Dwayne, "Civil Society in Europe and Africa: Limiting State Power through a Public Sphere," *African Studies Review 35*, no. 2 (September 1992): 77 - 100.

The World Bank, *The East Asian Miracle: Economic Growth and Public Policy* (New York: Oxford University Press, 1993).

—, *World Development Report, 1992: Development and the Environment* (New York: Oxford University Press, 1992).

French

Aarts, Paul, "Les limites du "tribalisme politique": le Koweit d'après-guerre et le processus de démocratisation," *Monde Arabe Maghreb - Machrek,* no. 142 (October-December 1993), pp. 61-79.

Burgat, François, *L'Islamisme Au Maghreb: La Voix du Sud* (Paris: Editions Karthala, 1988).

Chidiac, Louise-Marie, 'Abdo Kahi and Antoine N. Messarra, eds., *La Generation de la Réleve: La Pedagogie du Civisme* (Beirut: Bureau Pedagogique des Saints-Coeurs, 1992).

Cornand, Jocelyne, "L'Artisanat du Textile a Alep survie au Dynamisme?" *Bulletin d'Etudes Orientales Institut Français de Damas,* Tome XXXVI (1984).

Göle, Nilüfer, *Musulmanes ets modernes: voile et civilisation en turquie* (Paris: Editions la Découverte, 1993).

Hermassi, Mohamed Abdelbeki, "L'Etat Tunisien et le Mouvement Islamiste," *Annuaire de l'Afrique du Nord* 28 (1989): 297-308

—, "La Societé Tunisienne au Miroir Islamiste," *Maghreb-Machreq,* no. 103 (1984), pp. 39-56.

Marzouk, Mohsen, "Autonomie des Associations Tunisiennes: Les Enjeux Politiques," *L'Observateur,* no. 28, October 8, 1993, pp. 25-27.

Picard, Elizabeth, "Ouverture economique et renforcement militaire en Syrie," *Oriente Moderno*, Anno LIX (Luglio-Dicembre 1979).

Zghal, Abdelkadir, "Le Concept de Societé Civile et la Transition Vers Le Multipartisme," *Annuaire de l'Afrique du Nord* 28 (1989): 207-228.

Zghidi, Salah, "A Question Democratique au Maghreb: Equivoques et Incomprehensions" *Esprit*,1992.

Zubaida, Sami, "Islam, the State & Democracy: Contrasting conceptions of Society in Egypt," *Middle East Report*, no. 179 (November-December 1992), pp. 2-10.

Arabic

'Abd al-Basit''Abd al-Mu'ti and Ibrahim Hasan al-Issawi, in the series *Dirasat al-takwin al-ijtima'i wa al-tabaqi li Misr: al-dirasat al-mahalliyyah* [Studies of the social formation and class structure of Egypt: Local studies] (Cairo: National Center for Sociological and Criminological Research, 1988, 1989).

'Abd al-Hadi, Izzat, *Al-intifadah wa ba'd qadaya al-tanmiyyah al-sha'biyyah* [The Uprising and Some Issues of Popular Development] (Ramallah: Bisan Press, 1992).

'Abd al-Mun'im, Ahmad Faris, "Jama'at al-masalih wa al-sulta al-siyasiyyah fi Misr: Dirasat 'ala al-niqabat al-mihaniyyah, al-muhamin, wa al-sahafiyyin wa al-muhandisin fi al-fatrah, 1952-1961" [Interest groups and political authority in Egypt: A study of professional associations of lawyers, journalists, and engineers, 1952-1961], unpublished PhD dissertation, Faculty of Economics, Cairo University, 1984.

Abid al-Jabiri, Muhammad, "Ishkaliyyah al-dimukratiyyah wa al-mujtama' al-madini fi al-watan al-'arabi," *al-Mustaqbil al-'Arabi* 167, no 1 (January 1993).

Abu 'Amr, Ziad, *Al-harakah al-islamiyyah fi al-diffah al-gharbiyyah wa qita' ghazzah* [The Islamic Movement in the West Bank and the Gaza Strip] (Akka: Dar al-Aswar, 1989).

Abu Amshah, 'Adil, *Al-awdaa al-iqtisadiyyah wa al-ijtima'iyyah fi al-diffah al-gharbiyyah wa qita' ghazzah qabla wa athna' al-intifadah* [The Economic and Social Conditions in the West Bank and the Gaza Strip Before and During the Uprising] (Nablus: al-Najah University, 1989).

Ahmad, Rif'at Sayyid, Second Document in *Al-Nabiyy al-muslah: Al-rafidun* (London: Riad al-Rayyis Books Ltd., 1991).

—, *Al-nabiy al-musallah: Al-tha'irun* (London: Riad al-Rayyid Books Ltd., 1991).

Amarah, Muhammad, *Al-kilafah wa nash'at al-ahzab al-siyasiyyah* (Beirut: Al-Mu'assasah al-'Arabiyyah li al-Dirasat al-Nashr, 1977).

Arab Organization for Human rights, *Huquq al-insan fi al-watan al-'arabi* [Human rights in the Arab nation] (Cairo: AOHR, 1989).

'Ata, 'Abd al-Khabir Mahmud, "Al-harakah al-islamiyyah wa qadiyat al-ta'addudiyyah," *Al-majallat al-'arabiyyah li al-'ulum al-siyasiyyah*, nos. 5 & 6, (April 1992), pp. 115-116

'Awwa, Muhammad S., "Al-ta'addudiyyah min manzur islami," *Minbar al-Hiwar* 6, no. 20 (Winter 1991): 134-136.

— *Fi al-nizam al-siyasi li al-dawlah al-islamiyyah* (Cairo: Dar al-Shuruq, 1989).

al-Banna, Hasan, Majmu'at rasa'il al-shahid Hasan al-Banna (Beirut: Al-Muassasah al-Islamiyyah, 4th ed., 1984).

—, *Rasa'il al-imam al-shahid Hasan al-Banna* (Beirut: Dar al-Qur'an al-Karim, 1984).

—, *Majmu'at rasa'il al-imam al-shahid Hasan al-Banna* (Beirut: Dar al-Qalam, n.d.).

al-Banna, Hasan, *Minbar al-jum'ah* (Alexandria: Dar al-Da'wah,1978).

—, *Al-Imam yatahadath ila shabab al-'alam al-islami* (Beirut: Dar al-Qalam, 1974).

—, *Kalimat khalidah* (Beirut: n.p., 1972).

—, *Al-salam fi al-islam* (Beirut: Manshurat al-'Asr al-Hadith, 1971).

—, *Din wa siyasah* (Beirut: Maktabat Huttin, 1970).

—, *Nazarat fi islah al-nafs wa al-mujtama'* (Cairo: Maktabat al-'I'tisam, 1969).

Barakat, Muhammad T., *Sayyid Qutb: Khulasat hayatuh, minhajuhuh fi al-harakah wa al-naqd al-muwajah ilayh* (Beirut: Dar al-Da'wah, 197?).

Barghouty, Iyad, *Al-aslamah wa al-siyasah fi al-aradi al-filastiniyyah al-muhtallah* [Islamization and Politics in the Occupied Palestinian Territories] (Jerusalem: Al-Zahra' Center, 1990).

—, "Al-Islam bayna al-sultah wa al-mu'aradah," *Qadayah fikriyyah: Al-islam al-siyasi, al-usus al-fikriyyah wa al-'ahdaf al-'amalliyyah* (Cairo: Dar al-Thaqafah al-Jadidah, 1989)

Bedaoui, Abdeljelil, et al., "Al-mu'asasat al-niqabiyyah al-ummaliyyah fi Tunis: Hususatiha, Dawriha, 'Uzmatiha," *Utruhat* 10 (1986).

Boutros, Huwayda A.R., "Al-dawr al-siyasi li al-haraka al-ummaliyyah fi Misr, 1952-1982" [Political role of the workers movement in Egypt, 1952-1982], unpublished MA dissertation, Faculty of Economics, Cairo University, 1990.

al-Bushri, Tariq, "'An mu'assasat al-dawlah fi al-nuzum al-islamiyyah wa al-'arabiyyah," *Minbar al-Hiwar*, no. 19 (Summer 1989), pp. 74-79 & 89.

Center for Arab Unity Studies, *Al-mujtama' al-madani fi al-watan al-'arabi* [Civil society in the Arab nation] (Beirut: CAUS, 1992).

Center for Political and Strategic Studies, *Intikhabat majlis al-sha'b: Dirasah wa tahlil* [People's Assembly election: Study and analysis] (Cairo: CPSS, 1986, 1988, 1992).

—, *Al-taqrir al-istratiji al-'arabi, 1990* [Arab strategic report, 1990] (Cairo: Dar al-Ahram, 1991).

—, *Al-taqrir al-istratiji al-'arabi, 1989* [Arab strategic report, 1989] (Cairo: Dar al-Ahram, 1990).

Center for Social Studies and Research of the Federation of Charitable Societies, *Dalil al-jama'iyyat al-khayriyyah* [Guide to Charitable Societies] (Amman, 1985).

Daraghmah, Izzat, *Al-harakah al-nisa'iyyah fi filastin, 1903-1990* [The Women's Movement in Palestine, 1903-1990] (Jerusalem: Diya' Center, 1991).

al-Din, Rislan Sharaf, "Al-din wa al-ahzab al-siyasiyyah al-diniyyah," *Al-din fi al-mujtama' al-'arabi* (Beirut: Center for the Studies of Arab Unity, 1990).

Egyptian Ministry of Social Affairs, *Al-mu'ashirat al-ihsa'iyya fi majalat al-ri'ayah wa al-tanmiyah* [Statistical indicators in fields of social care and development] (Cairo: EMSA, 1991).

Egyptian Organization For Human Rights, *Jarimaton bila 'iqab al-ta'thtib fi Misr* [Unpunishable Crime, Torture in Egypt; Comment of the Egyptian Organization of Human Rights on the first supplementary report submitted by the Egyptian Government to the U.N. committee for Action against Torture, in its session of November 1993] (Cairo, December 1993).

al-Fattash, Ibrahim, *Tarikh al-harakah al-niqabiyyah min sanat 1917 ila 1992* [The History of the Labor Movement from 1917 to 1992] (Jerusalem: n.p., 1992).

General Federation of Trade Unions of Egypt, *Al-masikrahi al-tarikhiyya fi khamsa wa thalathin 'aman* [The historic march in 35 years] (Cairo: GFTUE, 1991).

al-Ghannushi, Rashid, *Al-hurriyyat al-'amah fi al-islam* (Beirut: Center for the Studies of Arab Unity, 1993).

—, "Mustaqbal al-tayyar al-islami," *Minbar al-Sharq*, no. 1 (March 1992), pp. 3-32.

—, "Hiwar," *Qira'at aiyasiyyah* 1, no. 4 (Fall 1991): 14-15 & 35-37.

—, "Al-islam wa al-gharb," *Al-Ghadir*, nos. 10 & 11 (December 1990): 36-37.

al-Ghannushi, Rashid, and Hasan al-Turabi, *Al-harakah al-islamiyyah wa al-tahdith* (n.d.: n.p., 1981).

al-Ghazali, Salah, *Sur al-kuwait al-rabi'a*, vol. 3 (Kuwait, 1992).

al-Hamidi, Muhammad al-Hashimi, "Awlawiyyat muhimah fi daftar al-harakat al-islamiyyah: Nahwa mithaq islami li al-'adl wa al-shura wa huquq al-insan," *Al-Mustaqbal al-Islami*, no. 2 (November 1991), pp. 19-21

al-Hannachi, Abd al-Latif, "Niqash," *Al-mujtama' al-madani wa al-mashru'a al-salafi.* (Tunis: UGTT Publications, 1991), pp. 54-55.

Hawa, Sa'id, *Al-madkhal ila da'wat al-ikhwan al-muslimin bi-munasabat khamsin 'aman 'ala ta'sisiha* (Amman: Dar al-Arqam, 2nd ed., 1979).

Hawrani, Yusuf, "Al-harakah al-niqabiyyah al-'ummaliyyah ila 'ayna?" [Where is the Labor Union Movement Going?] *Al-Jadid*, 1/2 (1991), pp. 63-64.

al-Hay'a al'amma li Shu'un al-Matabi al Amiriyyah, Dustur jumhuriyyat Misr al-'arabiyyah [Constitution of the Arab Republic of Egypt] (Cairo: HASMA, 1991).

Hizb al-Ba'th al-Arabi al-Ishtiraki, *Taqarir al-mu'tamar al-qutri al-thamin wa muqarraratihi* [Reports and Resolutions of the Eighth Regional Congress] (Damascus, 1985).

al-Huwaidi, Fahmi, *Al-islam wa al-dimuqratiyyah* (Cairo: Markaz al-'Ahram li al-Tarjama wa al-Nahr, 1993).

Ibrahim, Saad Eddin, *Al-mujtama' al-madani wa al-tahawul al-dimuqrati fi al-watan al-'arabi* [Civil Society and Democractic Transformation in the Arab World] (Cairo: Ibn Khaldoun Center, 1992).

—, *Al-khuruj min zuqaq al-tarikh: Durus al-fitnah al-kubrah fi al-khalij* [Exiting Blind-Alley of History: The Arabs and the Great Sedition in the Gulf] (Cairo: Ibn Khaldoun - S. Al Sabah, 1992).

—, *Ta' ammulat fi mas'alat al-aqaliyat fi al-watan al-'arabi* [Reflections on the Questions of Minorities in the Arab World] (Cairo: Ibn Khaldoun - Al Sabah, 1992).

—, *Al-mujtama' al-madani wa al-tahawul al-dimuqrati fi al-watan al-'arabi* [Civil Society and Democractic Transformation in the Arab World] (Cairo: Markaz Ibn Khaldun, October 1991).

Isma'il, Mahmud, *Susiulujia al-fikr al-islami* (Cairo: Maktabat Madbuli, 1988).

al-Janhani, al-Habib, "Al-sahwah al-islamiyyah fi bilad al-sham: Mithal Suriyya," *Al-harakat al-islamiyyah al-mu'asirah fi al-watan al-'arabi* (Beirut: Center for the Studies of Arab Unity, 2nd ed., 1989).

al-Jarbawi, Ali, *Waqfah naqdiyyah ma' tajrubat al-tanmiyyah al-filastiniyyah* [A Critical Assessment of the Palestinian Developmental Experience] (West Bank: Bir Zeit University, 1991), pp. 46-48.

—, *Al-intifaduh wa al qiyadat al-siyasiyyah if al-diffah al-gharbiyyah wa qita' ghazzah, bahth if al-nukhbah al-siyasiyyah* [The Uprising and Political Leaderships in the West Bank and Gaza, A Study of Political Elites] (Beirut: Dar al-Tali'ah, 1989).

Kawtharani, Wajih, *Al-sultah wa al-mujtama'wa al-'amal al-siyasi* (Beirut: Center for the Studies of Arab Unity, 1988).

Kerrou, Mohamed, "Hawla muqawalat al-mujtam'a al-madani," *Utruhat*, no. 15 (1989), pp. 26-29.

Kerrou, Mohamed, "Al-muthakafun wa al-mujtama' al-madani fi Tunis," *Al-Mustaqbal al-'Arabi* 10, no. 104 (1987): 46-60.

Khalidi, Salah A., *Sayyid Qutb, al-shahid al-hayy* ('Amman: Dar al-Firqan, 1983).

Kibi, Zuhayr, ed., *Abu Bakr al-Jassas, dirash fi fikratihi: Bab al-ijtihad* (Beirut: Dar al-Muntakhab, 1993).

al-Kilani, Mohamed, "*Al-mujtama' al-madani*," in Tahir Labib et. al., *Al-mujtama' al-madani* (Tunis: UGTT Publications, 1991), pp. 43-47.

Labib, Tahir, et. al., *Al-mujtama' al-madani* (Tunis: UGTT Publications, 1991).

Mahfuz, Mohammed, "'Usus al-mujtama' al-madani," Al-mujtama' al-madani wa al-mashru'a al-salafi (Tunis: UGTT Publications, 1991), pp. 31-53.

—, *Alladhina zulimu* (London: Riad al-Rayyis Books Ltd., 1988)

Mahmud, Ahmad Shawqi, *Al-tajribah al-dimuqratiyyah fi al-sudan* (Cairo: 'Alam al-Kutub, 1986).

al-Mawardi, *Al-ahkam al-sultaniyyah* (Cairo: 3rd ed, 1973).

Messara, Antoine, "Al-mujtama' al-madani fi mujabaha nitham al-harb: Al-Hala al-Lubnaniyyah [Civil Society against the War System: The Lebanese Case], a paper presented at an International Peace Academy-sponsored conference in Giza, Egypt, May 28-30, 1992.

Morsi, Amin Taha, "Al-inqilab al-akhir fi ittihad al-'ummal" [The last coup in the workers' Federation] *Rose el-Youssef*, no. 3410 (Cairo, October 18, 1993).

al-Mu'assasah al-'arabiyyah li al-dirasat wa al-nashr, suhayr salti al-tall, *muqaddimat hawla qadiyat al-mar'ah wa al-harakah al-nisa'iyyah fi al-Urdunn* [Introductions to the Women's Issue and to the Women's Movement in Jordan] (Beirut, 1985).

al-Muhami, Amir Salim, *Difa'an an haqq takwin al-jam'iyyat* [Defending the right of association] (Cairo, 1992).

Muradh, Da'd, "Tajribat al-ittihad al-nisa", 1974-1981," *Al-Urdunn al-Jadid* 7 (Spring 1986): 61-64.

al-Nabahani, Taqiy al-Din, *Al-takatul al-hizbi* (Jerusalem: n.p. 2nd ed., 1953).

—, *Nizam al-hukm* (Jerusalem: Matba'at al-Thiryan, 1952).

PLO Research Center, *'Isa al-ahu'aybi, al-kiyaniyyah al-filastiniyyah: al-wa'i al-dhati wa al-tatawwur al-mu'assasati*, 1947-1977 [Palestinian Statism: Entity Consciousness and Institutional Development] (Beirut, 1979).

Qutb, Sayyid, *Hadha al-din* (Cairo: Maktabat Wahbah, 4th ed., n.d.).

—, *Al-salam al-'alami wa al-islam* (Beirut: Dar al-Shuruq, 7th ed., 1983).

—, *Al-islam wa mushkilat al-hadarah* (Beirut: Dar al-Shuruq, 8th ed., 1983).

—, *Ma'alim fi al-tariq* (Beirut: Dar al-Shuruq, 7th ed., 1980).

—, *Al-'adalah al-ijtima'iyyah fi al-islam* (Cairo: Dar al-Shuruq, 7th ed., 1980).

—, *Ma'rakat al-islam wa al-ra'simaliyyah* (Beirut: Dar al-Shuruq, 4th ed., 1980).

—, *Fi al-tarikh, fikrah wa minhaj* (Cairo: Dar al-Shuruq, 1974).

—, *Fiqh al-da'wah* (Beirut: Mu'assasat al-Risalah, 1970).

—, "Limadha 'a'damuni?" *Al-Muslimun*, no. 4 (March 1985), pp. 6-9.

Rif'at, Rahma, "Al-Intihakat al-qanuniyyah wa al-idariyyah fi intikhabat 1991", [Legal and administrative violations in the 1991 elections] *Nadwat al-haraka al-ummaliyyah al-Misriyyah fi al-intikhabat al-niqabiyya 'am 1991* [Seminar on the Egyptian workers movement in trade union elections of 1991] (Cairo: Arab Research Center, December 1992).

Rizk, Y. L., *Misr al-madaniyyah* (Cairo: Tiba, 1993).

Sabella, Bernard, "Al-diffah al-gharbiyyah wa qita' ghazzah: as-sukkan wa al-ard" [The West Bank and the Gaza Strip, Population and Land] in *Al-mujtama' al-filastini fi al-diffah al-gharbiyyah wa qita' ghazzah*, Liza Taraki, ed. (Akka: Dar al-Aswar, 1990).

Saghiyyah, Hazim, "Ma'zufat al-mujtama' al-madani," *Al-Hayat*, Tayyarat Section, 18 September 1993, p. 4.

al-Sa'id, Rif'at, *Hasan al-Banna, mu' assis harakat al-ikhwan al-muslimin* (Beirut: Dar al-Tali'ah, 1981).

Salem, Helmy, "Hona mahakam al-taftish; hona quabdat al-azhar" [Inqusition Tribunals and Al-Azhar's tight Hold in Egypt] *Naqd wa Adab* (Cairo: February 1992, Cairo).

Sami', Salih Hasan, *'Azmat al-hurriyyah al-siyasiyyah fi al-watan al-'arabi* (Cairo: Al-Zahra' li al-'I'lam al-'Arabi, 1988).

al-Sayyid, Mustapha Kamil, *Al-mujtama' wa al-siyasah fi Misr: Dawr jama'at al-masalih fi al-nizam al-siyasi al-Misri* [Society and politics in Egypt: Role of interest groups in the Egyptian political system] (Cairo: Dar al-Mustaqbal al-Arabi, 1983).

al-Sayyid, Radwan, *Mafahim al-jama'at fi al-islam* (Beirut: Dar al-Tanwir, 1984).

Munir Shafiq, "Awlawiyyat 'amam al-ijtihad wa al-tajdid," *Al-ijtihad wa tajdid fi al-fir al-islami al-mu'asir* (Malta: Center for the Studies of the Muslim World, 1991).

Tamari, Salim, "Al-takhalluf wa afaq al-tanmiyyah fi al-diffah al-gharbiyyah wa qita' ghazzah al-muhtallayn" [Underdevelopment and the Areas of Growth in the Occupied West Bank and Gaza Strip], in *Al-mujtama' al-filastini fi al-diffah al-gharbiyyah wa qita' ghazzah*, Liza Taraki, ed. (Akka: Dar al-Aswar, 1990).

al-Turabi, Hasan, "Awlawiyyat al-tayyar al-islami," *Minbar al-Sharq*, no. 1 (March 1992), pp. 21-26, 69-72, 81-82, 136-138, 167-169 & 198-199.

—, *Qadayah al-hurriyyah wa al-wahdah, al-shurah wa al-dimoqratiyyah, al-din wa al-fan* (Jiddah: Al-Dar al-Su'udiyyah li al-Nashr wa al-Tawzi', 1987).

—, *Tajdid al-fikr al-islami* (Jiddah: Al-Dar al-Su'udiyyah li al-Nashr wa al-Tawzi', 2nd ed., 1987).

—, *Al-iman wa 'atharuhu fi hayat al-insan* (Jiddah: Al-Dar al-Su'udiyyah li al-Nashr wa al-Tawzi', 1984).

—, *Al-Ittijah al-islami yuqadim al-mar' ah bayna ta'alim al-din wa taqalid al-mujtama'* (Al-Dar al-Su'udiyyah li al-Nashr wa al-Tawzi', 1984).

—, *Tajdid usul al-fiqh* (Jiddah: Al-Dar al-Su'udiyyah li al-Nashr wa al-Tawzi, 1984).

—, *Al-salat 'imad al-din* (Beirut: Dar al-Qalam, 1971).

al-Umari, Akram, *Al-mujtama' al-madani fi ahd al-nubuwah, khasa'isuhu wa tanzimatuhu al-'ula* (Medina: Al-Majlis al-'Ilmi li-'Ihya' al-Turath al-Islami,1983),

Yahya, Amin al-Hajj, *Al-'amal al-ijtima'i fi dhill al-intifadah* [Social Work during the Intifadah] (Jerusalem, n.p., 1988).

INDEX

CONTRIBUTORS

Eva Bellin, assistant professor of Government at Harvard University, is author of articles on comparative politics of the Middle East and North Africa, comparative political economy, and state-society relations in the Middle East.

Laurie Brand, associate professor of international affairs at the University of Southern California, is author of *Palestinians in the Arab World: Institution Building and the Search for State* and *Jordan's Inter-Arab Relations: The Political Economy of Alliance-Making*, and articles on international politics, Palestinian and Jordanian politics and society, and the Arab world.

Neil Hicks, director of Middle East and North Africa at the Lawyers Committee for Human Rights, is author of Lawyers Committee reports on Kuwait, Tunisia, and the Israeli occupied territories.

Raymond A. Hinnebusch, professor and chair of political science and international relations at the College of St. Catherine, is author of *Authoritarian Power and State Formation in Ba'thist Syria: Army, Party and Peasant* and *Syria and the Middle East Peace Process* (with Alasdair Drysdale), and articles on government, politics, and society in Syria, Libya, Egypt, and the Middle East.

Saad Eddin Ibrahim, president of the Ibn Khaldoun Center for Development Studies and professor of political sociology at the American University in Cairo, is author of *Civil Society and Democratic Transformation in the Arab World* (in Arabic) and *Exiting the Blind-Alley of History: The Arabs and the Great Sedition in the Gulf* (in Arabic), and articles on sociology and politics in Egypt, the Arab world, and the Middle East.

Ahmad S. Moussalli, associate professor of political science at the American University of Beirut, is author of *Radical Islamic Fundamentalism: The Ideological and Political Discourse of Sayyid Qutb*, and articles on Hassan al-Banna, Sayyid Qutb, Islam and fundamentalism.

Muhammad Muslih, professor of political science at Long Island University, is author of *The Origins of Palestinian Nationalism* and *Political Tides in the Arab World* (with Augustus Richard Norton), and articles on Syria, Israeli-Syrian relations, the Golan Heights, and Palestinian politics and society.

Ghanim al-Najjar, professor of political science at Kuwait University, is author of articles on human rights and democratization in Kuwait, and politics and society in the Arab world.

Augustus Richard Norton, professor of international relations at Boston University and visiting research professor and director of the Civil Society in the Middle East project at New York University, is author of *Amal and the Shia: Struggle for the Soul of Lebanon*, and articles on the Arab-Israeli conflict, Cyprus, Lebanon, peacekeeping, political violence, the political sociology of Islamist protest movements, as well as political reform in the Middle East.

Alan Richards, professor of economics at the University of California, Santa Cruz, and director of the Democratic Institutions Support Project, is author of *A Political Economy of the Middle East* (with John Waterbury), and articles on development economics in the Middle East.

Mustapha Kamil al-Sayyid, professor of political science at Cairo University, is author of articles on state-society relations in Egypt, international politics of the Middle East, and democratization in the Arab world.

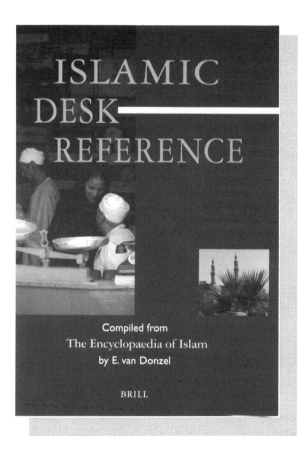